IMAGINING
JUSTICE

JOHN P. CRANK
BOISE STATE UNIVERSITY

Imagining Justice

Crank, John P.
    Imagining justice / John P. Crank
       p. cm.
    Includes bibliographical references and index.
    ISBN 1-58360-533-9 (pbk.)

EDITOR Gail Eccleston
ACQUISITIONS EDITOR Michael C. Braswell

Dedication

To Brother Joe, Mother Mary Anne, Patti Gregor,
Quint Thurman, Sharon Hirzel, Robert Langworthy,
Bruce Colleen, Gretchen Sigler, Mary Stohr, Robert Regoli,
Elder Joe, Steven Lab, Velma and John,

Lives past and present, for vision, doors opened and shut,
frustration, pain, growth.

I am the sum of you, in my own fashion.

Preface

This book concludes a stage in my odyssey through the field of justice. If I have learned anything, it is that the inquiry into justice is frustrating. Any ethical or moral position that one takes immediately marshals contrary forces. Many times I have questioned my work in this field, what I hoped to accomplish, how I always felt as if I were swimming against the social current. I have found my values celebrated by some and blasphemed by others. Justice work, after all, is value-based work. It is freighted with our hopes as well as our fears, and can never be value free. The odyssey has been difficult, and many times I have thought of leaving the field. And I have changed, and my changes have broadened me. And I have watched the field of justice change around me.

The writings enclosed in this book are at once a personal memoir and professional appraisal, surveying the far-flung elements that comprise us and examining the values that motivate us. In it, I attempt to overview our field, to assess where we have been, what we are, and where we are going. This book presents a concept of justice, not as an end, but as a passion that unites the various and sometimes hostile participants in our field.

I owe the development of this book to several reviewers who assisted in the task. My thanks goes to Ronald Farrell, Christian Bierwirth, Michael Braswell, Anthony Walsh, and Timothy Flanagan. Victor Kappeler generously read and commented on the entire work, for which I am indebted. I am delighted that Francis Cullen wrote a foreword for this book. A special thanks is offered to Patti Gregor, who wrote the instructor's guide and endured the tedious never-ending conversations I initiated while developing the ideas presented herein.

Foreword

When I was in graduate school in the 1970s, sociology—my home discipline—entered a time of intense "reflexivity" or self-examination. C. Wright Mills' work on the "sociological imagination," first published in 1959, was read with renewed urgency and, along with other critical writings, prompted us to question the whole nature of the sociological enterprise. As a discipline, sociology had grown too comfortable with its easy embrace of positivism, its consensus background assumptions about the social world, its connection to and service of the state, and its implicit ideological preference for incremental rather than revolutionary reform. Works such as Alvin Gouldner's *The Coming Crisis of Western Sociology* and, from outside the discipline, Thomas Kuhn's provocative *The Structure of Scientific Revolutions* disrupted our "normal" understanding of the practice of social science. Suddenly, new ways of seeing the world seemed possible and new challenges for bettering the world seemed deserving of our hearts and energies.

My purpose, of course, is not to reminisce about my younger days, although this can be a pleasant experience! Rather, my intent is to set a context both for my introductory remarks to *Imagining Justice* and for the journey that readers are about to take through this remarkable book. A privilege of authoring a foreword is that one receives the volume in advance of its publication. As I traveled through *Imagining Justice*, I was reminded vividly of that time in sociology when special books had shaken up that discipline and had caused me to think differently. In a similar way, for those who read this work carefully and fully, their understanding of criminology and criminal justice—or, more broadly, what Professor Crank calls "justice studies"—will never be the same.

Imagining Justice is an important contribution. Few scholars have written a volume of such scholarly depth and breadth. Indeed, in *Imagining Justice*, John Crank is an experienced and creative tour guide who leads us on a fascinating excursion through our discipline. He has mastered the literatures of mainstream criminology and criminal justice, but he is at his best when he weaves into the discussion insights from anthropology, history, philosophy, organization studies, multiculturalism, feminism, and much more. I found myself wondering how he had time to read so diversely and how he could integrate these insights into a coherent vision of the discipline. But he succeeds in this ambitious undertaking. In the end, his project has the potential not simply to inform and educate but also to *transform* and *transcend* our common ways of seeing crime and justice.

Professor Crank's goal, like that of Mills and Gouldner before him, is to shake things up—to make us sufficiently uncomfortable that going about "business as usual" will no longer be possible. He takes special aim at the "normative approach" to the study of justice, a way of thinking he believes dominates the discipline. In this paradigm, state-defined categories of crime are not questioned, and, if only implicitly, existing arrangements in criminal justice are taken as givens. Research tends to be quantitative, focuses on mundane or technical issues, and attempts to produce knowledge that will help criminal justice agencies repress crime more efficiently. Criminal justice education is penetrated fundamentally by this normative approach. Undergraduate courses, for example, mindlessly cover each "component" of the criminal justice "system," conveying descriptive information but little more. Graduate education is more advanced but also similarly formulaic—with the formula being equipping students with the quantitative skills to produce the knowledge that will help control crime and appear in undergraduate textbooks.

Professor Crank does not believe that the normative approach is without merit. The difficulty is that it verges on being hegemonic. It is a way of "doing criminal justice" that is *unnecessarily limiting* and, at its core, unwittingly *intellectually arrogant*. Professor Crank makes a strong case for expanding our scholarly horizons to consider how other ways of thinking and of knowing the world will permit richer insights into crime and justice issues. We must, for example, move beyond "abstracted empiricism" to studies that are theoretically informed and sensitive to the role of context in shaping findings. Our investigations would benefit by being more structural and historical. We should understand that the exalted status of "objective" quantitative social science—of "positivism"—is undeserved and, still worse, potentially self-deceiving. It is not clear that a "real world" is knowable, given that the realities of humans are inevitably social and linguistic constructions that are, as well, tainted by our values. The conclusions produced by positivist methodology almost certainly truncate, if not distort, the true reality that exists "out there."

In this state of affairs, we should welcome the truth claims based on qualitative methodologies, on different voices (such as those coming from multiculturalism and feminism), and on non-scientific fields of inquiry (such as the humanities). In Professor Crank's justice studies, the search for truth is not exclusionary but inclusive; it does not dismiss, *a priori*, insights that fall outside a hegemonic normative approach but listens genuinely to many perspectives; it welcomes a measure of intellectual chaos, if not outright anarchism, in the fundamental belief that multifaceted and intellectually democratic discourse is both a good end and a good means to the end of deeper understanding. The idea that truth and reality can be relative rather than inherent, "objective" qualities is not to be feared but embraced; indeed, it is precisely why many diverse views of reality need to be heard.

Most importantly, Professor Crank insists that much of what we do—in our research and our teaching—is intellectually and morally vacuous if we do not force ourselves, and our students, to ask fundamental questions that allow us to imagine a different, more just, world. It is not enough, for example, to assess, in an antiseptic way, equity in sentencing if we do not consider the meaning of the very concept of "justice." Such an inquiry requires us to enter the world of ethics and philosophy, to learn that there are competing models of justice, and to risk revising our long-held but previously unexamined assumptions about crime and its control. We might even be moved to consider that the study of justice is an empty experience if it is not part of a life committed to the advancement of justice—to a life committed to making the world a better place.

Now, when I write, I prefer that my readers find my logic so compelling that disagreement is inconceivable; in fact, I would enthusiastically welcome my ideas—such as on the worthiness of "reaffirming rehabilitation"—becoming hegemonic in the discipline! Professor Crank, however, manifests more courage and scholarly security than I am able to muster. His intent is not simply to persuade but, where appropriate, to provoke further discourse. His justice studies is not about conformity to a single truth but about participating in an ongoing process in which exchange, even heated exchange, is encouraged. He invites us to take him seriously by questioning his ideas.

In this spirit of intellectual engagement, I will offer three brief reactions to Professor Crank's efforts to have us "imagine justice." These thoughts are not so much criticism as cautionary considerations. Let me hasten to say that I generally embrace his core claims that (1) justice studies needs to be intellectually more diverse and (2) that the legacy of the discipline of criminology and criminal justice will be impoverished if our efforts do not result in a more just world. Nonetheless, I do see justice studies a bit differently.

1. The value of positivism and the dangers of relativism. To have us "imagine justice" in more compelling ways, Professor Crank is correct in suggesting that positivism—especially in the form of "abstracted empiricism"—is a limited means of knowing "what's out there" should be appreciated. His critique is a marvelous corrective to the discipline's tendency to treat science and quantitative methods as sacrosanct. Still, we will never be able as a discipline—nor should we, in my view—escape the firm grasp of positivism. We find ourselves in a situations in which we cannot have any meaningful discussion about most crime and justice issues without appealing to "data and findings" produced through positivist methodology. This holds not only for mainstream scholars committed to a normative approach but also for critical scholars on the left. Take, for example, the claims—all of which would be considered politically progressive—that inequality is linked to violent crime, that capital punishment has no deterrent effect, and that rape and sexual assault are prevalent on college campuses. Each of these assertions is rooted in studies based on positivist methodology. Without such positivist-based data, it would simply be an "opinion" that violence was a cost of inequality, that the death penalty did not save lives, and that sexual victimization of women was not merely a politically inspired feminist social construction of reality.

In the end, positivism offers us some *standards* for assessing what we should believe or not believe. Professor Crank is, again, correct in warning that following such standards is not guarantee against false understandings of "reality." But without some way of arbitrating what is believable, we will be mired in relativism. Relativism worries me because it places us on the slippery slope to the extreme view that all opinions, no matter how derived, are equally valid—much as when creationists recently called evolution "just another theory." To make truth claims to our colleagues, to our students, to the public, and to policymakers, we gain legitimacy by saying that our views are not merely opinions but are backed by data produced by a process in which ideas are scrutinized and subjected to the possibility of falsification.

But perhaps Professor Crank and I are not so far apart on this issue. We are probably at odds in whether positivism should be fully dismissed but in how hegemonic it should be in the discipline. He is more attuned to the ways in which positivism empowers humanistic ideas and counteracts the dangerous "common-sense" opinions about crime and justice that seem ubiquitous these days.

2. Considering other uncomfortable ideas. Professor Crank provides a major service in his chapters on race/ethnicity and feminism in which he shows how writings in these areas bring diversity and perspective to the discipline. He is correct in showing that multicultural and feminist perspectives are often marginalized in criminal justice education and are ignored by many scholars, much to the impoverishment of our knowledge and the pursuit of justice. Even so, if we wish to "imagine justice" more fully, scholars will have to consider—indeed, take seriously—literature that most criminologists might scorn as being "politically incorrect" (indeed, writings that I, too, would disagree with in part if not in whole).

In the current context, it would mean subjecting multicultural and feminist ideas to the same scrutiny that "normative" or positivist justice studies receives. For but one example it might mean hearing the voices of Stephan and Abigail Thernstrom, whose *America in Black and White* presents a mountain of evidence in making the case against multiculturalism and the balkanization it (supposedly) encourages and in favor of an America that is "one nation indivisible" (see also their chapter on "Crime"). Or one might revisit John DiIulio's provocative 1994 essay on

"The Question of Black Crime," published in *The Public Interest*, in which he proposes that the extensive deployment of police in minority neighborhoods and the expanded use of prisons "save black lives" by removing predators from the streets. In fact, DiIulio sees these policies as a form of social justice, as much-needed government investments into neighborhoods in which residents, faced with the dangers of high crime rates, have heretofore been abandoned by the state. These authors' writings annoy, in part because their conservative underpinnings ignore much that should not be ignored. Nonetheless, if we are to "imagine justice" in diverse ways, we cannot simply dismiss either their quest for a nation whose core principles stress our commonality and universal equal treatment or their quest for neighborhoods in which predatory behavior is not excused but attacked and halted.

Other ideas will also have to be entertained. The writings of economists and rational choice theorists—whose theory of human choice I happen to find narrow and incorrect—nonetheless are mapping out new ways to understand crime and justice issues. Similarly, as a sociologist, I have never been fond of research on "individual differences," but now their role in human behavior, including crime, is indisputable. Indeed, such individual differences are sufficiently powerful to question C. Wright Mill's famous admonition that scholars inappropriately attribute structural problems to personal problems (or individual pathology). It may be that structural problems in communities are "compositional," due in substantial part to the "flocking together" of people with personal problems that predispose them to crime.

3. The importance of crime control—saving lives. Professor Crank makes a persuasive case that the fundamental goal of justice studies is to seek justice. In my younger days, I might have immediately agreed. But I now have changed my views—not fully but qualitatively. I certainly am committed to social justice and see considerations of justice as placing important boundaries on what the state might be permitted to do in the area of crime control. Still, I am convinced that criminology—or "justice studies"—has an obligation to produce knowledge that helps the state to reduce crime. In fact, I am not sure how justice is possible when a community is besieged by violence and other predatory behavior. Talk of justice is unsatisfying if people's lives cannot be made more secure.

This is, I suspect, unlikely to be a popular view in the discipline. Admittedly, it is often claimed that criminologists are too cozy with the state and produce knowledge in service of the government's control of crime (a view Professor Crank may share). But I believe that another view on crime control—the "nothing works" view—is more normative in the discipline: that nothing the state does will decrease lawlessness; only social justice will achieve this goal. This professional ideology encourages criminologists to debunk any intervention that, on the surface, seems to be effective. Thus, for many criminologists, the challenge is not to help "the state" control crime—usually they call this "repression"—but to prove that government interventions "widen the net," result in the "displacement of crime," or have the "unanticipated consequence" of making matters worse (e.g., of increasing recidivism). In fact, we earn praise from our colleagues for proving that "nothing works." In contrast, providing knowledge to help "agents of control" reduce crime is to be a "tool of the state." In this context, many criminologists feel that working on behalf of government agencies requires an explanation to prove that they have not "sold out."

As Paul Gendreau and I have recently pointed out (in *The Prison Journal*), this is not the only professional ideology in our discipline but it is a powerful one, especially among the generation of criminologists schooled amidst the tumultuous, politicized context of the late 1960s and 1970s. It is good that we have some trepidation about supplying the state with the technology to control crime, because such control is disproportionately targeted at the poor and the powerless. But in my view, criminologists have become a profession too committed to showing what does not work to control crime and, as a consequence, has few empirically supported theories on what can be done to make communities safer. In our role as critics of the state, we have unwittingly marginalized ourselves in the real-world arena of criminal justice practice and policymaking. Still worse, as we have failed to articulate a coherent crime-control agenda, the "get tough" crowd has stepped into this void and has willingly offered the "state" a host of mean-spirited, "practical" ideas on how to reduce crime. We have felt comfortable preaching about the importance of social justice, and congratulated ourselves for such high-minded views, but we have not *accomplished justice* or showed how crime control could be achieved in a more human way.

But perhaps Professor Crank and I agree once again. In the end, I suspect that we both embrace the view that justice studies cannot simply be about studying crime and publishing articles of minor import but also must be about transforming the world into a better place. In the pursuit of this goal, I happen to place my faith more in positivism, the accumulation of scientific knowledge, and the advancement of humanistic interventions that can be shown, on the basis of data, to "work." Professor Crank believes that this goal will necessitate moving beyond the narrow constraints of positivism to achieve richer insights into crime and justice. He implores us to consider different ways of accessing truth, hearing different voices that heretofore have been silenced or ignored, and asking different and broader questions that scholars (like me) too often place on hold as we go about our business. He believes that imagination is not mere utopian rumination but the first step to creating a discipline that will become engaged in creating a more just world. Indeed, a future in which justice flourishes cannot be chosen if it is not seen as possible. But if enough of us "imagine justice," we may well construct—if only bit by bit—a new social reality in which the pursuit of justice seems not far-fetched but a truly viable.

Let me close by reiterating that *Imagining Justice* is a masterful contribution. It is a work that taught me much, changed my mind on important issues, and at times annoyed me enough that I did a fair share of ranting and raving! The book engaged me and, I must confess, left me envisioning what fun it would be to hold a joint seminar with Professor Crank on *Imagining Justice*. In any event, I hope that this volume affects others as it has affected me. If so, then readers will have enriched their criminological literacy and, more importantly, will have been moved to imagine justice in fresh and exciting ways.

Francis T. Cullen
University of Cincinnati

Contents

Introduction

Overview: Justice in Academe. Over the past 40 years, the academic field of justice studies has expanded at a brisk pace. Scarcely within eyeshot of a university campus in 1960, programs and departments in justice studies—academic units with names such as *criminal justice administration, criminology, social ecology*, and *justice studies* and whose educational focus is the etiology of crime or the study of criminal justice agencies—have been an academic growth engine through the 1980s and 1990s. Today, more than 1,000 colleges have undergraduate programs, and more than 100 have masters degree programs in justice studies. Following Langworthy and Latessa's (1989) call for program expansion at the highest levels of education, many programs are developing Ph.D. programs. In a short time, justice programs are becoming a legitimate organizational form in the academic environment.

The rapid pace of development of justice studies has been associated with a great deal of empirical research and occasional spikes of intellectual expansion. Yet, very little intellectual integration of the field has occurred. This is a consequence both of the academic nature of justice studies and its rapid growth. Its growth has been breakneck, as most of us who have been in a department of criminal justice can testify. The influx of students into justice studies or the addition of a graduate program spurs the hiring of new faculty. This is typically accomplished by a hiring committee made up of department faculty. Growth consequently tends to be a force for decentralization rather than integration. One of the hiring committee's principle considerations is an assessment of instructional needs. With good fortune, the department will hire a talented individual with appropriate strengths. In other words, we tend to try to hire individuals whose specialties are different from existing strengths in the department. Decisions about textbooks and the like fall to individuals with appropriate specializations.

Academic justice departments mimic the normative organization of criminal justice in the United States. The core curriculum is typically divided into the areas of policing, the courts, corrections, juvenile justice, community corrections, and the law. Faculty specialize in these areas, the departments are often compartmentalized into these areas, and the substantive content of texts and other material we use are fashioned after this pattern of organization.

This form of organization informs faculty thinking about justice as well. We tend to think about problems from the normative bases of our specializations, which themselves reflect the normative organization of criminal justice in the United States. Consider the police. When we think about the police, we tend to identify crime problems and then we seek effective police responses to those problems. If we are liberal, we support "velvet glove" style community policing aimed at improving the overall quality of life of minorities, while if we are conservative we may prefer a hard-nosed approach to punishing law-breaking. Both approaches are normative. Each approach begins with the idea that, by identifying the appropriate police practices, we can address the problems at hand. The way we identify problems tends to be defined through the prism of our particular political perspective. Then we look for the best organizational strategy and tactics to solve those problems.

When I am thinking normatively, I am likely trying to assess how a criminal justice organization can solve or reduce some crime problem. For example, I may be concerned with recidivism among drug users in my community. I develop a prison program that targets drug-using prisoners closer to the end of their sentence, so that the effects of the program will endure after they are released. I am trying to find the best organizational strategy within a particular prison to decrease recidivism in a particular population. There is nothing wrong with normative thinking. The systematic examination of organizational behavior is central to efforts to develop organizational policies and link it to identifiable goals. Organizations can have articulable and attainable goals, and systematic procedures can coordinate elements of the organization to achieve those goals. I take as an article of faith that the organization can do something about the problem.

Powerful forces in the local and regional environment of academic justice programs push justice departments toward normative ways of curriculum organization and in how they think about the field of justice studies. Historically, we continue to carry the community college mandate that characterized our rapid growth in the 1960s: we are expected to provide direction and training to agencies in local communities. Students tend to be pre-committed to the field of criminal justice and want classes in practical substantive areas. This, in turn, drives normative specialization in hiring, whereby we seek individuals with specialty strengths in specific criminal justice areas. Part-time faculty are often drawn from the ranks of agency personnel. The successful grants-person has to carefully tend relations with local agencies. For these and for many other reasons, we have hitched our wagon to the practice of criminal justice in the United States, and a substantial part of the justice mission will be normative. One of the pillars of academic justice will always be local community problem-solving.

Yet, in justice studies the place for normative thinking is, in and of itself, limiting. When we think normatively, we are taking fundamental elements of the justice system—and of crime—for granted (see Duffee,

1990:77-97). Normative thinking does not take into account broader considerations of the environment that can affect the outcomes we want organizations to change. When we think normatively, we forget that justice organizations—like the crime they are supposed to do something about—are themselves the product of their municipal and national environments. Put differently, justice organizations cannot be understood simply as causal, independent variables. They themselves are affected by all sorts of influences, from the civil and criminal law to the diversity of their jurisdiction, to the funding carried forth in their operating budget. And by thinking in terms of optimum organizational designs, we sometimes overlook the importance of important values that affect what we do. It might, for example, be effective drug strategy to permit police officers to enter houses without a search warrant, but it violates the powerful values of individual rights set forth in the Bill of Rights.

Finally, by thinking normatively, we tend to confine our thinking to traditional political paths, particularly conservative and liberal ways of thinking about problems and their solutions. Our predispositions are likely to affect the kinds of problems we select. However, our predispositions sometimes affect our findings in ways both innocent and scurrilous. It may be, as Duffee (1990) suggests and as I will discuss at length later, that conventional ways of thinking about justice do not provide for a realistic assessment of either problems or viable solutions.

My purpose in writing this book is to "crack the nut" of normative thinking about justice, particularly in the area of justice education. Our normative tendencies, I think, limit our ability to contribute meaningfully to broader issues of justice. Issues in justice cannot be contained within the normative structure of criminal justice as practiced in the United States. American criminal justice is a part, and a very important one, of the rich potential for justice, yet it is only one part. Normative thinking, by limiting itself to this part, lacks the intellectual juice to transform justice studies into a full-blown Ph.D.-level academic enterprise.

What is needed today is a way to think about the enterprise of justice that will capture its full potential. It is not enough to think normatively: what we must begin to do is recognize the breadth of our field. Our task is to begin with justice as we perceive it to operate in the United States and the world, and from that starting point to imagine the full richness that justice can take. We must study its diverse forms, its nuanced possibilities. Justice studies is an intellectual commitment to comprehend the possible, and it is a moral commitment to personally undertake the quest, to seek a just world, to comprehend in our daily lives what justice means.

What is the breadth of the field of justice studies? If we acknowledge that the field is wider than criminal justice as optimally practiced in the United States—depending on one's goal set—then where do we draw the line? What should we not study? The position taken in this book is that, in deciding what justice studies includes, and by implication what the breadth of our curricula should be, we should err on the side of inclusiveness. Our field, young by academic standards, is in the process of intellectual development. It is not clear that its core ideas have yet been written. Our capacity to think about justice in ways creative and fertile is a necessary and needed dynamic. It is our field's indefiniteness at this juncture that carries promise for what we might provide in the future. We seek a just world, but we are not there yet. Our field is young and carries potential. Our steps, measured in the scholarship of justice, service to the criminal justice community, and in the provision of an ethically meaningful education, will mark our progress.

In this book, I cover many different areas of scholarship that I believe contribute to the idea of justice. I have undoubtedly erred on the side of inclusiveness, thus committing the promised mistake. The purpose of the book is to provide an introduction to the intellectual potential of the field of justice. Some ideas carried herein are probably new to the student, a problem stemming from the typically narrow focus of undergraduate curricula. How many students have, for example, studied feminist criminology, or have knowledge of fundamental issues underlying quantitative and qualitative methods? By assessing the breadth of justice studies, I hope to impart the field's special quality—that there is a richness in the scholarship on justice that is not widely recognized, even among college and university educators.

This book is designed for a seminar. It is meant to be digested, bit by tough bit. I strongly encourage the instructor to provide as auxiliary materials many of the readings herein discussed. Some of the articles, like sections in the book, will be difficult for students, but their purpose is to invoke a sense of the possible in justice studies. Pushing the intellectual and ethical boundaries are always uncomfortable. But this is our most important task. We must begin with ourselves.

Chapter Synopsis. This book is based on the premise that justice cannot be captured by any single morality or standpoint, but emerges from the play among contending perspectives. Each chapter is written with the following purposes in mind: What are the important justice issues and why are they important? For example, one of the chapters deals with race. I do not begin this inquiry at its usual opening question *Is the criminal justice system racist?* I begin with the question *What is race?* This manner of presentation permits me to locate the practice of criminal justice inside broader issues and controversies having to do with the nature of justice itself. It is my belief that our ideas of justice emerge from and are in turn transformed by our efforts to resolve these controversies. A characteristic feature of many controversies is that they shift in content over time. Race is such an example. It has been a compelling issue throughout the history of the United States, though the content of political, social, and economic controversies regarding race have changed. The controversy provides a dynamic that constantly requires intellectual and moral growth.

Chapter 1 reviews the central idea of this book—that the quest for justice is the uniting theme of our field. By linking all justice actors in this shared quest, the justice endeavor itself shifts away from its normative roots. Once we accept the "big tent" notion that different ideas or carriers of justice have a voice, the nature of justice itself becomes an open question, and the purpose of education becomes an open inquiry, not a wrote learning process. Instead of justice being defined in terms of criminal justice rules and practice, justice becomes a problematic whose meaning is unknown and to be determined. Academic education should focus on the diversification of perspectives, and aim at providing students with a broad vision of justice.

In Chapter 2, I write about the academic environment of criminal justice. The chapter, an overview of the social sciences, describes the contributions of different academic fields to justice studies. This discussion is followed by a description of contemporary changes across the social sciences. For example, all social science fields today are attempting to identify hidden Eurocentric biases and are engaged in a debate about whether and how to open their fields to other ways of thinking about the world. By locating and identifying those social science themes, we can see where criminal justice identity must be forged and what issues it must address.

Chapter 3 focuses on the history and development of the various department of justice studies. This chapter addresses a question frequently heard in discussions about the future of the field—what is our purpose? This chapter locates the historical development of the field in its principal environments: academe and practice. These two environments provide different and sometimes conflicting educational mandates—academe in terms of traditional ideas of scholarship and intellectual inquiry, and the professions in terms of a commitment to service, a focus on skills preparation, and normative ideas of ethics. The environments are substantially but imperfectly aligned with the deterministic-free will perspectives, and conflicts between them have adversely affected many criminal justice departments and programs.

Chapter 3 also describes existing models for the organization and educational development of criminal justice. Interdisciplinary, criminological, and public administration models are considered. I conclude that, to address contemporary issues at the level of complexity required to think of justice as a problematic, a field identity should be grounded in ideas of justice generally conceived. Each of the three models provide one pillar of a more general notion of academic justice studies.

Chapter 4 presents a review of contemporary theories in the field of justice studies. The purpose of this chapter is to begin the assessment of perspectives that have been developed to explain the practices and organization of justice organizations. Those of us who have been interested in teaching our students about the developments of theory have typically had two options: either review criminological theory, or develop a list of readings that deal specifically with justice organizations. Neither option is satisfactory for those who are interested in systematic explanations of justice organizations. My intent here is to begin the initial work of assessing what theory is in fact available, and provide an overview of it. The list is inevitably inadequate: the field has developed to a point that a book-length monograph is needed to fully organize and describe contemporary justice perspectives. It is presented as a beginning of an important endeavor in the development of the justice studies field.

In Chapter 5, I examine methodological issues in criminal justice. The central issue in methods is philosophical: How do we know that what we see really exists? This question is relentless, and it will not go away. Yet it is rarely considered. The question has many forms, and whenever we engage in analysis, we encounter one of its forms. For example, the issue of validity—am I measuring what is actually going on—is affected by a broader issue. Is there a way that I can accurately or meaningfully report what I see, unadorned of the social customs that inevitably overlay it? Is there a way I can even interpret to myself what I see in an objective way? The answer to both these questions may be no. Yet, in spite of the illusions we weave about the world around us, we must make important decisions and act on them every day.

Parts II and III of Chapter 5 are overviews of quantitative and qualitative methodologies. They are discussed in terms of the different kinds of information each has to offer. I have tended to approach them, in DiCristina's (1995) terms, anarchically and without preference.

Chapter 6 looks at multicultural identity and its effect on our conceptions of justice. Race is first discussed, and may be the most compelling issue in the field of criminal justice today. A slaver society from its birth, the United States continues to struggle with the overwhelming racial problems that enamate from its history. This chapter begins with what I think is the proper beginning question—what is race? The question has distinct and contrary dimensions. I begin with a discussion of the challenging issue of biological distinctiveness. I discuss its emergence as an administrative tool during British colonialism. These two considerations provide a backdrop against which to consider race in the U.S. criminal justice system.

The next topic is ethnicity. Both race and ethnicity have in common their use as administrative categories that serve political and legal purposes. Some administrative ethnic categories, such as Asian-Americans or Latinos, are so diverse that their categorization contains no meaning other than administrative pigeon-holing. However, in spite of a "common-sense" notion of ethnicity as a sort of "race-lite," ethnicity is a sharply different notion. Ethnicity is about a group's identity, embodied in its self-perceptions of its differences with other groups or with a dominant group. Ethnicity is about social identity, not trait or genome difference, though ethnic groups may create illusions of trait or genome differences to distinguish themselves from other groups. History is a tool in the service of social identity, and may rely on real or mythical ideas of historical unity.

Chapter 7 deals with gender issues. Of all our social pigeon-holing, gender may be the social classification that carries the greatest number of hidden biases. The greater the degree to which we explore its meanings, the more we discover how integral our gender biases are to every aspect of modern society. This chapter provides an overview of contemporary feminist perspectives. In it, I take the position that gender is not inherent to the psychology of particular individuals, but is a "doing" (West & Zimmerman, 1998) that is carried out as a complex set of socially learned expectations. This chapter also examines higher education. Criminal justice and criminology, in educational texts and in research, have sometimes unwittingly sustained gender inequalities. And when taught, gender issues are often ignored or relegated to "minority" status. The chapter closes with a discussion of how male roles are also gendered, and the implications of "masculinities" for the study of crime and criminal justice.

Chapter 8 is on ethics. This chapter begins with a discussion of four ethical traditions, the Aristotelian, Augustinian, the Scottish Enlightenment, and the Liberal traditions. Using MacIntyre's (1990) notion of rationality and ethics, the traditions are assessed for their particular conceptions of a notion of justice. These different notions of justice can be organized into two types, one which ethical decisions are based on preferences among individual interests and wants, and the other in which ethical considerations are weighted against external criteria of the good, such as religion. This allows us to understand how ethics is played out in democratic societies, and to think about ethics in the practice of criminal justice.

Part II of Chapter 8 is about ethics in the practice of criminal justice. The distinction between due process and crime control is presented as a means-ends ethical conflict, in which ends ethics are associated with crime control, and means are expressed by a commitment to due process. Central to Part II is the notion of the noble cause, or the commitments of professionals for good ends, and how this weighs against means-oriented justice practice. Issues related to noble cause are assessed across the fields of justice. The chapter closes with a discussion of the implications of due process and crime control ethics for justice practice.

Chapter 1

The Commitment to Justice

In every bit of honest writing in the world there is a
base theme. Try to understand men, if you understand each other you will be kind to each other.
Knowing a man well never leads to hate and nearly
always leads to love. There are shorter means, many
of them. There is writing promoting social change,
writing punishing injustice, writing in celebration of
heroism, but always that base theme. Try to understand each other (Steinbeck, 1994:1).

Imagining Justice

To understand the dynamism in justice work, it is necessary to encompass all its diverse elements. One must gather together liberals and conservatives, professionals and academicians, federal and local justice organizations, judges, defense counsel, prosecutors, sworn officers, managers,
educators, part-time faculty, and students—the whole contentious gaggle.
They all bring something to the table. What? That *something* is a commitment to justice, a vision of what we should do to bring about justice
in our communities, in the United States, and sometimes in the community of nations. We begin with the world as given and seek a better outcome. We imagine justice, and we initiate the difficult and often contrary
work that is needed to achieve our vision.

It is this lofty goal, imagining justice, that ties our field together. For all
of its contrary and disparate elements, we are united by this shared end—
we seek a world that is less mean, more responsive to the needs of is citizenry. We have hitched our wagon to a special star—a world more just
than the one we entered. We do not know where it will take us, and the
path we follow is surely as important as the end. The inquiry into justice
itself, conducted openly and fairly, promotes the end we seek.

Justice work is difficult. It is in the area of justice and social control
that, as Douglas (1986) has observed, we find the most deeply held values.
It is hard to think against the grain in this moral territory, to act creatively, to seek innovation in the wreckage of failed policy, inflexible belief, and
unconfirmable theory. I have dealt with students of conservative and liberal stripe alike, deeply committed to their values, following paths well-

1

worn yet new to them. I advise them that they can be a slave or a master to their values. They can be mimics, passing on unreflected convictions, using the language of justice to polarize and divide. Or they can reflect on what they learn and can grow, their values providing a spiritual seed for their intellectual growth. To achieve maturity in justice work requires a nuanced vision, breadth of knowledge of the field, a capacity for inquiry outside of ideological straight-jackets, and an ability to cut to the point. It is suited for those who can change and grow.

To use a metaphor, justice work is swimming in a river with powerful and dangerous currents. The river is an allegory for life, and the currents are the values that drench life with meaning. We cannot shed our lives of meaning—to find meaning in the world around us is what it means to be human. After all is said and done, we are cultural creatures, and we are compelled to find meaning in all facets of our existence. But there are many different cultures and they carry distinctive meanings, conflicting values, ways of viewing the world that clash and jar. And in justice work these differences are pronounced, visible, and important. The lives of peoples sometimes depend on the clarity of our vision.

Change and growth, an inevitable outcome of swimming in powerful and contrary currents, is painful. As cultural creatures, the values we carry tie us to specific ethical and moral ways of thinking. Challenges to those ways of thinking are often unpleasant and seem immoral. We might feel that we are not intellectually and morally growing but instead giving in, that we are abandoning the good fight. We are tempted to mobilize our resistance, shore up our misgivings, resist and protect that which we are certain is right. Yet wisdom—and hope—lies in change. The river, after all, is a metaphor for our lives, together, flowing toward an unknown future. Only when we begin to reflect on knowledge and values that we had previously taken as certain and "right" do we begin to change, and can we contribute to our most important enterprise—justice.

The Mills' Legacy

This book is guided by and borrows unashamedly from C. Wright Mills' wonderful work titled *The Sociological Imagination* (1959). The "imagination" depicted by Mills was the ability to transcend the world of everyday troubles, to see the larger social structures and issues behind personal problems. Troubles, he observed, involved private matters and values personally cherished. Personal troubles were often unfocused and were marked by vague worries and fears. Behind a person's troubles were issues, which were directly linked to characteristics of social structure. Mills explained the linkage as follows:

What we experience in various and specific milieux, I have noted, is often caused by structural changes. Accordingly, to understand the changes of many personal milieux we are required to look beyond them. And the number and variety of such structural changes increase as the institutions within which we live become more embracing and more intricately connected with one another. To be aware of the idea of social structure and to use it with sensibility is to be capable of tracing such linkages among a great variety of milieux. To be able to do that is to possess the sociological imagination (Mills, 1959:10-11).

The sociological imagination is the capacity to look beyond the individual problems and see how they are shaped by broad social and economic environment. The imagination is conditioned by particular themes, outlined by Mills in his short book. Themes that inspired the sociological imagination included kinds of knowledge (described in terms of philosophies of science), ways to think about knowledge (the development of theory) and tools used to acquire knowledge (what we call methodology). Through these themes, Mills provided a sense of what the field of sociology was about and a direction for sociological education to take. His work enabled others to understand what the field of sociology was about.

Today, the field of justice studies is in a similar nascent form. Spurred by the Law Enforcement Education Program in 1968, the field of criminal justice education has experienced constant expansion in academic settings throughout the latter twentieth century. At the beginning of the twenty-first century, more than 100 programs nationally offer post-graduate Master's degrees and 10 to 20 (depending on how one counts them) provide Ph.D. degree programs. However, this growth masks an important problem. The academic identity of criminal justice is undefined and unclear, like potter's clay, keening toward form.

Growth in justice studies programs has followed the normative structure of criminal justice agencies, typically separating areas of study into domains of police, courts and the law, corrections, and occasionally juvenile justice. The development of justice knowledge has tended to specialize within these domains, with surprisingly little cross-fertilization of ideas and practices across domains. Research in community corrections, for example, is characterized by substantially different themes and theoretical development than policing, even though the fields have much in common. And topics that are not in themselves normative domains of criminal justice empirical research and practice—feminism, for example—tend to be marginalized in curriculum and poorly understood by both students and faculty alike. The emergence of a unifying identity for justice education is blocked by domain specialization.

In the current era a justice studies growth is concentrated in graduate education. The issue of justice identity is particularly acute in departments or schools launching Ph.D. programs, and can be framed this way: *What is the purpose of a Ph.D. in justice studies?* Many schools have implemented Masters degrees by "muscling up" their four-year degrees, adding either a trim selection of required graduate classes or graduate-level study requirements to selected undergraduate classes. These courses are often aimed at in-service professionals in the middle management ranks of their respective fields. These programs do not require a reconsideration of mission, only its elaboration with the words "graduate" added. Faculty in such programs often find themselves with bleak hopes for the unfulfilled promise of additional faculty members who will enable the development of a full complement of graduate course offerings.

Is a Ph.D. program a further "muscling-up" for criminal justice executives? Or is it something different, focusing not on educational credentialing for criminal justice practice, but instead on academic advancement and intellectual development? And if graduate education takes an academic rather than professional focus, what should that academic focus be? What do we want our Ph.D. graduates to do, and what do we think they should learn? What is to be their larger contribution to society? Now is the time that we need to provide answers to these questions, and this book is intended to contribute to that debate.

The central theme of this book is that the field of justice is about the quest for a better world, however naive or simplistic such an idea might seem. We begin with the real, prosaic, alternatively brutal and inspired world of justice as practiced. We take this world and we try to better it, each in our own way. This vision suggests a purpose for justice education. The purpose of education generally is in providing students with the intellectual skills needed to further justice. The purpose of undergraduate education should be the provision of critical thinking skills to accomplish justice wisely in one's area of study. The purpose of graduate education is to provide skills to expand our knowledge about justice enterprises, and to carry out the inquiry into the nature of justice itself. Undergraduates contribute by learning, wisely and thoroughly, what is known. Graduates contribute by adding to our store of knowledge about justice.

The standpoints of justice professionals and critical academics groups have often been characterized by fundamentally different notions of justice, sometimes described as crime control (associated with justice professionals) and due process (associated with critical academics) (Packer, 1968). One might wonder which conception of justice is right. Indeed, a great deal of empirical research has attempted to assess the relative advantages and disadvantages of these notions of justice. A more appropriate question is *how can we think about these standpoints that permits us to recognize the legitimacy of both?* By acknowledging the legitimacy of both perspectives we can no longer sustain the notion that there is one and only one "right" justice. Justice becomes a problematic, by which I mean that what constitutes just behavior, the good ends that constitute justice, the means that constitute justice treatment, or the morality of the criminal justice system, are open questions. To recognize that justice is a problematic also suggests that the central inquiry concerning justice in an academic setting is an inquiry into the nature of justice, in which each idea of justice, including crime control and due process ideas, are recognized as standpoints.

Once we recognize that justice is a problematic, we enter a realm of intellectual inquiry far broader than a debate between criminal justice professionals and U.S. justice policy critics. We can no longer reject out of hand any notion of justice. Put differently, it means that we are obligated to consider perspectives of the "other"—all those with different views or opinions than ourselves—even if they grate emotionally or seem farfetched and unreasonable. This has far-reaching implications for the field of justice studies. In methodological considerations, the "other" challenges the hegemony of any particular method. In cultural studies, we adopt a multicultural presumption, examining the diversity of meanings justice carries for race, ethnicity, and gender. In ethics, we look at different ethical systems and weigh their contributions to contemporary justice thought.

To say that justice is a problematic is to begin any inquiry into justice with a presumption that the "other" has an equally legitimate claim to be heard. This is a relativistic view of justice, and might be resisted because it is too cacophonic, too given to confusion. One might ask "how can justice have an identity if that identity is whatever someone wants it to be?" However, to state that the relatively youthful justice field already has in place a clear and complete knowledge of justice is an intellectual arrogance witnessed in no other academic field. By characterizing justice as a problematic, we make an admission—we don't know what justice is, and we want to learn more.

As justice studies educators, we cultivate in our students a preparation for the many kinds of people and the diversity of ways they come to terms with the world around them. Students' maturation as justice workers will emerge by recognizing and learning from this diversity. At the level of academic field, we recognize that the voice of the "other" should be listened to. The ability of our field to contribute to justice as it is practiced in the world is strengthened by being prepared to listen to those voices that we have not yet heard.

The Nothing Works Controversy: A Gauntlet Thrown

In 1975, Robert Martinson published his important and highly controversial work on prison reform. Commonly referred to as the "Nothing Works" paper, it was a sharp indictment of rehabilitative prison reform. Clear (1998) captured the impact of Martinson's findings and its impact on then current justice trends:

> A centerpiece of the (Crime) Commission's agenda was rehabilitation—not the old, "failed," medical model based on crime as mental illness, but the newer idea of reintegration based on a view of blocked opportunity for legitimate participation in society. Robert Martinson's paper in 1975 proved a deep challenge, perhaps a fatal one, to this view. Martinson's work has been much debated since its original publication, but at the time it was taken as an astounding indictment of rehabilitation programming: after systematically reviewing more than 200 studies for a New York state Commission on crime, he drew the conclusion that "nothing works." The result sent shock waves through the prison community (Clear, 1998:138-139).

Clear recognized that the Martinson report was a powerful political element in a broad conservative reaction to the Crime Commission's rehabilitative orientation. Whether or not intended as such, the report contributed to the discrediting of policies favorable to rehabilitation.

Trends in justice policy in the United States over subsequent decades increasingly focused on the individual characteristics of the offender and criminal career patterns. As Clear (1998:140-141) observed, research on criminality took a new direction: the documentation of the nature and extent of criminal careers. Why a person offends became unimportant, what counted was "that the person offends." If we were to describe this change of focus using a Millsian language, policy has turned away from the sociological imagination—an examination of underlying issues—and toward the "restricted milieux" of a person's immediate worries—fear of crime and victimization.

Today's crime-control oriented policy-based research is prophetically Millsian. Mills (1959:113) expressed concern that the purpose of policy-informed research might become the "the prediction and control of human behavior." As Clear noted, precisely this happened as justice research tuned its focus in the mid 1970s to the study of criminal careers and selective incapacitation (See, e.g., Greenwood, 1982). The consequence has not been particularly satisfying to either conservatives or liberals. Conservatives are troubled that the bases of funding for policy-oriented justice research are located in centralized, governmentally controlled agencies of crime control. Liberals express concern that research sometimes seems to justify the subordination of individual rights and privacy concerns to information gathering—for example, the Drug Use Forecasting grants solicited by the National Institute of Justice provided funding for local research on prisoners, provided that they agree to blood-tests for alcohol and drugs. Neither side has understood that both of their concerns are intertwined: the sharp centralization and bureaucratization of crime control policy in the United States is interlinked with expansion of governmental authority across the spectrum of crime control. When justice is subordinated to the interests of the state, then the justice imagination—the quest for perspective into the social bases of people's troubles—is abandoned to effectiveness and efficiency in state crime control processes. The "restricted milieux" of personal worries has become a political tool used to justify criminal justice system expansion And in criminal justice departments, normative ways of thinking, organizing, and carrying out research substitute for the broader quest for justice. Mills' prophecy has come home with a vengeance.

The Commitment to Justice

On one level, Martinson's paper can be narrowly viewed as an evaluation of selected prison programs aimed at rehabilitation. At another level, it represented a fundamental challenge to the young field of criminal justice: the practice of criminal justice should be left to the professionals; academics lack the practical knowledge and common sense to contribute meaningfully to justice policy. The question asked is this: Can academia, with its focus on social science and rehabilitation tendencies, provide a meaningful contribution to the practice of criminal justice? Academics have themselves frequently asked this question, though in a different form. What can we do to have our voices heard in the arena of criminal justice decisionmaking and agency policy? Between academia and the professions lies an intellectual barrier with political implications. Academics tend to be focused on the way in which crime is affected by forces that are not wholly controllable by individual rational decisions. Professionals are resolutely focused on the personal responsibilities of individual offenders, regardless of their circumstances.

Martinson's paper was contrarian to the prevailing sentiment in criminology—that rehabilitative programs can accomplish a social good. The paper impugned the notion of a social-science-based conception of justice studies—that social, psychological, historical, or even biosocial elements affecting a person's likelihood of criminality could be addressed in some public policy venue. However, the growth of the field of justice studies has continued, and at the graduate level intensified, embedding itself more deeply in the social sciences and making Martinson's criticisms even more poignant. Are his criticisms more true now than ever?

There are three responses to his criticism. The *first response* is that research has simply established that the claim that rehabilitation does not work is invalid. I will address only briefly this position because it has been thoroughly addressed elsewhere (see, e.g., Cullen & Gilbert, 1982; Cullen, Wright & Chamlin, 1999). In the current age, an increasing body of research demonstrates, not only that rehabilitation is effective when carried out in a rigorous way, but that strategies for the prevention of recidivism based on deterrence and punishment are ineffective. Martinson's criticisms of research, narrowly focused on then-popular rehabilitative treatments, have had a salutary effect on the development of rehabilitative programs because they have forced a greater degree of rigor on the specification and evaluation of rehabilitation programs than had previously occurred. There is an important implication of the first response. It is that research data are never in themselves conclusive. Any meaning associated with data lies in how the data are interpreted and in the values of the interpreter. Consequently, data will always have different meanings when interpreted from different standpoints.

The *second response* is to the implicit criticism that justice studies can be conducted in the social sciences in a way that is useful to the practice of criminal justice. It is this: Martinson's paper is itself a social science product. It was carried out according to empirical principles of social science analysis. Martinson's paper invigorated a perspective that, at that time, had limited academic currency—that rehabilitation might not be a good idea. By acknowledging that Martinson's paper was important even while disagreeing with it, justicians reaffirmed a central principle of the problematic of justice—that what constitutes justice is unknown and a matter of inquiry. When it was written, Martinson's paper was the "other": a perspective that was unpopular and viewed with questionable legitimacy in the field of justice studies. Its grudging acceptance in justice studies has helped open the door to a recognition of the relativity of points of view.

The second response permits us the opportunity to explore the area beyond the opened door. On the other side is a recognition that there is no claim to truth for any particular point of view, but a recognition that perspectives are historically relative. Under different circumstances and issues, different findings and meanings might be equally valid. Findings themselves become relative to one's point of view, as we have witnessed in the interpretations and reinterpretations of Martinson's research across many subsequent research efforts. The other side of the door is a recognition that we do not simply have disputing claims to the truth, one of which is right and the other wrong, but disputing claims in which both can be right (Warnke, 1993).

This is new territory. In this territory, we are no longer looking for some established truth concerning justice practices. We are seeking, instead, knowledge of the many possible forms that such truths can take. The idea that there is no "truth" but only standpoints takes the field of justice studies further into uncharted territory. It means that we do not try to find general, rule-like principles of justice, but try to identify the truth-value of different justice perspectives.

Justice in a pluralistic society, Warnke (1993) advised, may be comprised of different ideas that are not reconcilable to each other (see also MacIntyre, 1988). What is needed is a dialogue, not to establish some sort of synthesis of ideas, but to explore the underlying nature of diversity.

> If we acknowledge the interpretive character of our conceptions of justice, then we also must recognize that they can never reflect an exhaustive account of the meaning of our history and that there will always be

> other equally legitimate interpretations emphasizing different aspects of
> it. Both diversity and dialogue, then, are necessary, not because we could
> be wrong, but because we can never be wholly correct or rather because
> the issue is no longer one of rightness or wrongness as one of continu-
> ing revision or reform (Warnke, 1993:137).

Our different life experiences and cultural settings may bequeath to
us very different notions of what justice is, and different underlying moralities that legitimize justice practices, and the practice of justice itself. In a
pluralistic society, each notion of justice has a claim to legitimacy. The
"door opened" takes us into pluralism in its broadest sense—a respect for
competing claims of justice.

Competing claims for justice presents a dilemma. The problem is that
we must make decisions that are meaningful and we have to act. If everyone has a voice, how can we select a course of action? In terms of the
Martinson inquiry and the interpretive debate left in its wake, we nevertheless must decide and act on that decision, whether we punish or rehabilitate, or whether we do something altogether different.

One way is to try to develop a theory or point of view that allows us
to compare and integrate the two points of view. This new theory, theory 3, might be called meta-theory or synthesis. But how do we know that
this new theory is right? This is what is called a reductionistic problem—
to compare two theories we need a new theory that bridges the two we
compare. But how do we know that the new theory is any good? We need
a fourth theory to explain why the integrative theory is any good. And
how do we know that the theory of the good is any good?—ad infinitum.

A second problem is that, if we can open the door to any old notion
of justice, we run the risk of selecting very undemocratic ideas of justice.
This problem has been described as the "lunatic parent" problem
(Warnke, 1993). Imagine a child learning what is correct behavior. The
child has a lunatic parent. The child must take seriously the demands of
the parent because they are dependent on it. Moreover, given its limited
development as a child, it does not know that the parent's behavior is
lunatical. The child's adaptation to its immediate social environment may
be based on fear and unpredictability, not on sense and reason. In such a
situation, the child does not gain intellectual insight and maturity, but a
damaged life (Warnke, 1993:142). Warnke cites *Plessey v. Ferguson*, sanctioning separate but equal facilities for African-Americans, as an example
of a lunatic parent event. It permitted the enactment of undemocratic
policies that served principles of repression, not democratic pluralism.

The problem is this: if the justice enquiry is open, we do not have criteria to determine whether any perspective is particularly good, and we
don't want to end up sanctioning a perspective, such as the theory of justice embodied in the *Plessey v. Ferguson* decision, that undermines democratic pluralism. How do we pick and choose a "good" idea of justice?

This brings us to the *third response* to Martinson's challenge to reha-bilitation—how can we move from the airy towers of scholarly relativism to the real world? The third response lies in each justice worker's ethical commitment to service and service-related research. In most universities, faculty are contracted with an expectation to teach, conduct research, and provide service. Of these three items, service is typically ill-defined and carries little formal expectation beyond routine committee work. It is in the area of service, particularly in to local communities and regional gov-ernments, that faculty and students can commit to the justice enterprise.

The central theme of this book is that we all carry an idea of justice, and justice work is the work we carry out to test and realize our ideas. To contribute to just ends, we roll up our sleeves and get to work on local problems, time-consuming and frustrating though they might be. Such activities will embed us in local politics, because the practice of justice is part and parcel of local politics. We participate as members of the local family of justice institutions, and sometimes, for political expediency, we supborn our values to those of individuals and groups with whom we dis-agree. This is the nature of politics in a democracy. Relinquishing a strong-ly held position is not a weakness—to the contrary, it is pluralistic democ-racy in action.

The third response, then, is that service and practice, in one form or another, provide a counterbalance against the relativism that can accom-pany an open-ended inquiry into the nature of justice. Moreover, service locates the academic field of justice studies solidly in efforts to build a just society.

If justice faculty and students want to contribute to justice, they must participate in rites of local democracy. They must commit themselves, vig-orously but flexibly. Their commitment to service and their willingness to take the difficult steps needed to enact justice is fundamental to a service obligation. Hard, rough, people-oriented work is needed to enact one's imagined justice.

The breadth of civic responsibility encompasses service to local com-munities, to our professions and to the nation. Civic service, however, is not only a matter of active participation in public or voluntary organiza-tions. Sometimes, one's contribution to the community or country is accomplished through disagreement and opposition to prevailing ways of doing things. Campus life has often provided a forum for the expression of dissent, and higher education has always held as an important value the right to hold unpopular opinions. The formation of the American Associ-ation of University Professors in 1915 was organized, in part, to protect faculty who held unpopular opinions from punishment and removal (Boyer & Hechinger, 1981). And in the 1960s, campuses provided the set-ting for a great deal of the anti-war activity against the Vietnam conflict.

For some justice faculty, the path from their justice ideals to practice is unpopular and controversial. Such faculty, committed to their beliefs in justice, will find few offerings to participate in community boards. For example, many justice workers are strongly opposed to the criminalization of marijuana. Yet, in many communities, an anti-criminalization position is so polarizing that it cannot be expressed without inviting recriminations, and any faculty who articulates a position will almost certainly not be invited to participate in community boards. Service in the justice fields, to capture the full potential of ideas of justice, must recognize the importance of dissent to the development of justice perspective. To locate dissent as an "adjunct" of service would be to miss the point entirely. Dissent and critique are central in any democratic effort to identify just outcomes for difficult situations and circumstances, whether one serves on community boards, voluntary organizations, or academic committees. Indeed, the capacity for dissent defines democracy, a view all too often overlooked in the modern world.

Each of the three responses to Martinson's critique embody important themes of this book. The first response was that Martinson's findings have been challenged in subsequent research. This tells us that, no matter how often we visit and revisit, interpret and reinterpret data, we cannot definitively answer important questions. Data is simply a platform—a convenient condensation of our object of study—for interpretation, and people interpret differently based on their standpoints. This leads to the second response—that justice is a problematic, and growth emerges from considering the claim to legitimacy of the view of the "other." This opens the field to multicultural meaning in its fullest sense. Yet, embodied in the second response is a fundamental problem with no satisfactory resolution—we open the field to the claims of anyone, even when the authenticity of their view is yet to be discovered. The third response is that service ties our ideas to the real world. By focusing on service, we add what I think is a ballast to scholastic research and critique—we become involved in problems as they are encountered in the day-to-day practice of criminal justice.

On Defining Justice

In writing a book on justice, one has to make some effort to define the concept. Justice, however, seems to defy clear definition. Efforts to provide clarity of meaning clash with concerns over its inclusiveness. A review of the literature provides many possible definitions, each with different meanings. Are we talking about governments, criminal justice systems, or individuals? Are we interested in assessing how just a system is based on its own definition of justice, or are we interesting in developing a more just way to ensure our mutual well-being?

One way to think about justice is in terms of criminal justice practice. The *Dictionary of Criminal Justice* (Rush, 2000:186) defines justice as "the purpose of a legal system." However, it also notes that legal systems are themselves diverse, and thus justice practices may also differ. The ethics and morality of a society, the dictionary continues, determine the values that undergird its system of justice. However, justice practices are embodied in the criminal justice system. The criminal justice system can be defined as the "distribution of penal sanctions and the administration of agencies in law enforcement, prosecution, and punishment (Duffee, 1990:1). Actors in this system tend to view their work as "doing justice" (Manning, 1999:31). Doing justice means that justice is carried out by carrying out the laws, policies, and procedures of the criminal justice system efficiently and effectively. This is a normative notion of justice, in which justice is achieved by carrying out the legal standards of right and wrong in a society. The normative notion of justice also carries a powerful moral component—justice actors tend to believe strongly in their work.

A different notion of justice is sometimes called social justice. Lynch and Stretesky (1999:17) define social justice as:

> First, a society exhibits social justice when it (1) provides for the needs of the members of society, and (2) when it treats its peoples in an equal manner. In turn, equal treatment implies that people are provided with more than quantitatively similar outcomes; they must be provided with similar opportunities and chances . . . each of which is respected and valued.
>
> Second, when we examine societies that do not exhibit social justice, we cannot be satisfied simply to critique the injustice we see. We must seek solutions or find mechanisms that promote and generate social justice.

The concept of criminal justice, the authors continue, is embedded in the concept of social justice. This definition of social justice represents a fundamentally different notion from the normative notion presented above. Sometimes called a "critical" definition, it is premised on the idea that social justice must be achieved before criminal justice issues can be dealt with. It is a kind of justice that we do not have, but that we might seek. If we accept that the field of justice studies should also include social justice as an object of study, we are talking about a sharply different kind of justice studies field than one focused on normative issues. We open the discussion to exploration of the diverse forms that justice might take, rather than simply study the forms it has taken.

A third way also begins, not with the criminal justice system, but with the system of relations among people and how that system is maintained. This is called distributive justice, and like social justice, other kinds of justice tend to flow from it (Walzer, 1983). Distributive justice can be defined as the "component of justice concerned with the allocation of the goods and burdens of society to its members" (Pollock, 1998:348). Distributive justice tends to determine the way in which criminal justice is practiced by a society. The constitutionally protected goods of "right to life" and "property," for example, are protected by laws against murder, assault, burglary, arson, and robbery, to name a few.

Distributive justice in the United States occurs under conditions of "complex equality," which means that "the principles of justice are themselves pluralistic in form; that different social goods ought to be distributed in for different reasons; in accordance with different procedures, by different agents; and that all these differences derive from different understandings of . . . social goods."[1]

The idea of complex equality is different from the notion of equality described in terms of social justice. In social justice as defined above, equality was an "ought" to which we should ascribe. In distributive justice under complex equality, equality is different for different groups. Consequently, justice is itself a variable, something that can be different under different circumstances. Democracy, in Walzer's vision, is capable of diverse forms of justice, according to the desires of its membership. Walzer takes democracy as given, and provides for the possibility of diverse forms of justice within it.

Walzer's characterization raises problems of subjectivism and relativity (Warnke, 1993). If a pluralistic society is just because it is willing to accept different ways to distribute primary goods, then what is to prevent it from selecting a most undemocratic manner of justice? Second, it may continually face internal conflict among different groups with differing ideas of justice. Third, we have no way to assess the adequacy of any given notion of justice. Once we accept the principle that the distribution of goods in a society is a question to be democratically decided, we have no external criterion by which to say that one system is better than another. This issue is discussed extensively in Chapter 8.

In the comparison of the three ideas of justice above, we witness one of the central quandaries facing any effort to identify what is just. On the one hand, we have current practice, acted out in justice systems that are already in place in many democracies. These are often not very satisfactory, often tend to reflect at least in part existing status or class relations, and are frequently inequitable, particularly against the poor and unemployed. Second, we have a proposed way to do justice to improve our system of justice with another that we don't know, but which addresses some of the more intransigent problems in current justice practice. Third, we have a way to propose diverse forms of justice within the existing boundaries of democratic society, although we face the relativistic position that all systems are equally just if enough people support them. We trade one standard—a normative idea that justice is enacted by the efficient activity of criminal justice system personnel—with a standard that we don't know in a practical way, or with no standard at all, in which the largest group in the society or a powerful polity in the society is the winner, and justice is whatever that group wants it to be.

This abstract issue is central to this book, and is a critically important issue in the justice studies fields today. What is to be the purpose of criminal justice education? Are we a normative educational organization, our primary purpose to prepare individuals for practice in criminal justice organizations? That is, is our purpose to act as an agent of the criminal justice system? Should we advocate a way to carry out justice? Or should we set our focus on obtaining as broad notion of justice that we can, that locates criminal justice as practices as only one of a number of alternatives, each of which might be equally or more meaningful than criminal justice as practiced in the United States today?

Central to this book is that justice is a term whose full meaning is unknowable. The field of justice studies matures by more fully exploring the diverse ideas that justice can take, both in theory and in practice. This is a non-empirical notion of justice that locates the field in the humanities as well as in the social sciences. It also suggests that the name of the field of endeavor is justice studies, which suggests a broader, more open-ended investigation into the nature of justice itself. Throughout this book, I will consequently refer to those programs, departments, and academic emphases that are diversely called criminal justice, law and society, and the like as "justice studies." Criminology is described herein as a distinct branch of justice studies with sociological roots. Similarly, the topics discussed in each of the chapters in this book are concerned with providing a sensibility about the topic at hand. Just as the inquiry into justice is open-ended, the other topics begin with a consideration of the underlying nature of the subject discussed.

Distinguishing Between Justice and Crime

The distinction between criminal justice and criminology is well-known. Criminology is the study of the etiology of crime. Criminal justice focuses on the institutions, organizations, and individuals responsible for crime control.

In its most simplistic form, crime and criminal justice are associated in a one-way causal chain: crime occurs, and criminal justice organizations respond to crime. This simple causal perspective of crime and criminal justice, characteristic of the normative approach to criminal justice, is sharply inadequate for understanding the behavior of the criminal justice system. In the most general sense, crime exists because we have laws identifying particular behaviors as crime; consequently, crime definitions cannot exist independently of our concept of justice or crime control. In a literal sense, the state creates "crime" by making laws that identify particular behaviors as illegal. Changes in what is considered a crime may reflect the extent to which the state's leadership views particular behaviors as a potential threat (Homer-Dixon, 1994).

Second, sometimes justice organizations are themselves part of the etiology of crime. Consider prison: the prison experience may brutalize some prisoners and increase the likelihood that on release they will engage in further crime. Prison also provides an environment where an individual's peers are criminal, thus creating an opportunity for youthful offenders to be socialized into criminal behavior. Prisoners may make post-prison contacts for criminal activity. The prison experience has removed an individual from normal life cycles and employment experiences, sharply restricting his or her legal options to gain a living. And children of prisoners may lionize their parents, developing antagonistic attitudes towards the justice system.

Third, the structure of society—particularly the inequalities among social groups—has been associated with the production of crime as well as with criminal justice (see Barak & Henry, 1999). The relationship between crime and criminal justice is not causal but spurious—each is a consequence of broad-based social inequalities and efforts by some legislators to keep those inequalities in place. It has been suggested that the criminal justice system focuses on the poor in order to deflect attention away from the harms committed by the rich and big business (Reiman, 1998).

Finally, some members of the justice system are directly involved in the production of crime, both in terms of violations of substantive and procedural law. Corrections officers may use excessive force on a perceived wrongdoer, or police may violate due process in order to "get" a "bad guy." For all of these reasons, the distinction between crime and criminal justice is muddy. It is unreasonable to view justice organizations and crime as independent social phenomena related in a simple causal chain.

In this book, I make the following distinction. The study of criminology, as widely carried out by justice faculty and research institutions, is the study of the etiology of crime—its causes, whether they include justice organizations, social groupings, patterns of class or status inequality, or individuals randomly reacting to external stimuli. Such a study is beyond the purpose of this book. I will focus on developments in the justice field itself. I am interested on our efforts to seek justice, not in causes of crime.

However, as the previous discussion indicated, justice and crime are integrated notions. I will consequently also explore issues having to do with crime when they interpenetrate justice issues. For example, research in areas such as social inequality has a place in such a perspective, for those that study inequality are seeking to make justice equitable or fair across the social spectrum. This means that I will not focus primarily on predictors of crime. My interest herein is instead how etiology of crime perspectives inform the field of justice, who the proponents are, and how it is located within the field of justice studies. By keeping this perspective bounded in terms of justice, not crime, explanations, I can maintain the central focus of this book—an analysis of the means by which participants in justice studies seek justice from the world given.

Note

[1]   For example, I have the advantage of title "Dr. This or That" in a classroom, and that provides me with standing. My education is a social "good" that provides me with rewards in an academic setting. That title and classroom standing, however, provides me with no other benefit in another circumstance—I am equal to a construction worker in a Bank, for example. And I am less than a construction worker on a new construction site, where the social "good" is the experience he or she has attained through years of work. Walzer (1983:8) argues that all goods are social, because we have to assign meaning to them. "A single necessary good, and one that is always necessary—food, for example—carries different meanings in different places. Bread is the staff of life, the body of Christ, the symbol of the Sabbath, the means of hospitality, and so on. If the religious uses of bread were to conflict with its nutritional uses, it is by no means clear that which use would be primary."

Chapter 2

Fields of Inquiry: The Intellectual Environment of Justice Studies

The field of academic justice studies is characterized by a pervasive ambiguity: What is the appropriate way to carry out the inquiry into justice? This ambiguity stems from the timing of our involvement in academics. Justice studies has begun its academic ascent in an era in which traditional scholarly boundaries among the social sciences are weakening. The sheer variety of fields available for the study of human problems is astonishing—the simple cataloguing of theoretical and conceptual perspectives available across the social sciences would itself be a worthy and immense undertaking.

I have argued that the core of the justice enterprise is an inquiry—a commitment to identify and explore the meanings of justice. This inquiry is not served by adopting a particular model as hegemonic, but through the process of "borrowing" models that exist in other disciplines as well as developing our own perspectives. Accordingly, this chapter will look at other fields and the models they have developed that contribute to the explanation of justice processes. I make no claim that the list of models discussed below is exhaustive, or that I adequately cover all of the fields in the social sciences. This chapter seeks three accomplishments—(1) a review of the fields that have contributed the core ideas of justice studies, (2) a look at closely allied fields to consider what they have contributed and how their ideas might further the development of knowledge in justice studies, and (3) an examination of the interrelationships between the fields and what these interrelationships suggest about the academic field of justice studies.

When we ask which field provides the most appropriate way to think about justice, we are entering into an inquiry into the nature of justice itself. Is criminal justice best approached as a multidisciplinary science, adopting models from many fields? Relatedly, are we as an academic field best served adopting models from other fields that have already explored profound and important questions? Do we have an area of knowledge or focus of inquiry that constitutes a domain of study and scholarship? If we do, what kind of approach do we bring to it?

In this chapter, I will review fields of inquiry that are commonly used in the justice fields, such as sociology, political science, and law, as well as others such as anthropology whose ideas hold potential to contribute to justice efforts. I use the term *field* because it captures the general academic domain covered by an area of study. It is at once an academic designation and a general area of inquiry. Only the law is called a perspective, as a matter of convenience. I also substitute the term "field" for the term "discipline." They are interchangeable, but the use of a single term aids clarity. I also prefer "field" to "paradigm," a word whose overuse has rendered it effectively meaningless. *Models* refer to systematic and structured ways of thinking within particular fields. A field may contain many models. Finally, *perspectives* represent broad ways of thinking about particular problems. For example, in the field of criminal justice, perspectives include normative, institutional, and conflict. Figure 4.3 in Chapter 4, for example, is a model of the relationship between institutional and technical ideas of organizational structure.

Field Review

My point of departure will be sociology, which has been the parent discipline for justice studies. I will focus on the development of criminology as a branch of sociology and as a field highly interrelated with justice studies. Political science, like sociology, has served as a parent discipline in some universities. Yet, in spite of its tremendous capacity to contribute to the field of justice, a recognition of the contributions of political science to model development in justice studies are scant. I will accordingly devote a large section in this chapter to a consideration of the contributions of political science to international perspectives in justice. A companion field, public administration, is discussed next.

The law, considered next, represents a field grounded in a belief in free will, and is foundational for the practice of criminal justice. The study of the law has been almost exclusively contained within schools of law, and its contribution to the academic study of criminology and criminal justice is often under-appreciated and unrespected in many criminal justice departments. The role of the humanities in the development of justice knowledge will be discussed. This is followed by considerations of history and anthropology, both of which provide important sources of perspective and model development for justice studies programs.

Sociology

The field of sociology has, more than any other field, provided the academic setting and organizational environment for the emergence of the fields of justice studies. The influence of sociology on the emergence and development of justice has been influential and pervasive. The core ideas of the fields overlap, and their university departments and programs are frequently linked administratively. Many justice programs have a criminology focus, and emerged as administrative subunits of sociology programs.

Sociological Origins. The field of sociology has always been pulled by twin influences—a tendency toward conservatism rooted in explanations of society in terms of structure, and an advocacy for the plight of the underdog. Nisbet's (1966) review of the foundations of sociology reveals these powerful themes. He identified two events in the nineteenth century whose consequences provided the core identity of early sociology.

1. *The Industrial Revolution*. The Industrial Revolution had a powerful impact on the field of sociology. Concerns over the impact of the industrial revolution on the poor and the working class affected nineteenth century thought along several dimensions:

   a. Shattering of traditions. The industrial revolution shattered traditional patterns of social life. For radical and conservative alike, it was the undoubted degradation of labor, the wrenching of work from the protective contexts of guild, village, and family, that was the most fundamental, the most shocking characteristic of the new order.

   b. Urbanism. A revulsion for the city and the kinds of changes it foretold for society became the subject of social passions. Concerns over the city led to a nostalgia for the rural past.

   c. The factory and mechanical division of labor. These were seen by conservatives as calculated to "destroy the peasant, the artisan, as well as family and local community" (Nisbet, 1966:30).

2. *The French Revolution*. The French Revolution, Nisbet argued, had a profound effect on European traditions. It was, he noted, the first ideological war in history:

   . . . by its very nature the French Revolution was possessed of a suddenness and dramatic intensity that nothing in the Industria Revolution could match. The stirring declaration of the Rights of Man, the unprecedented nature of the laws that were passed between 1789 and 1795, laws touching nearly every aspect of the social structure of France—not to mention the sanguinary aspects of the Revolution, especially those embodied in the terror—were sufficient to guarantee to the revolution a kind of millennial character that was to leave it for a whole century the most preoccupying event in French political and intellectual history (Nisbet, 1966:31).

Comte is widely credited as the "patriarch of sociology." Blending the fields of history and philosophy, Comte developed his ideas of a "positive philosophy," which he later called "sociology" (Martindale, 1960). The purpose of the field of sociology was to establish scientific laws that described regularities of social events. Events could be provided by historical analysis.

Comte asserted that the methods of sociology were observation, experimentation, and comparison. Yet he distrusted both observation, which sometimes amounted to little more than the collection of facts without meaning, and experimentation which was a dangerous venture at the social level. He viewed society as an organic whole, and because all parts of organic wholes were related, experimentation carried immense power to undo the good that society had to offer. Hence, Comte's social philosophy is sometimes described as a rejection of the excesses of the French Revolution (Martindale, 1960). We can see in Comte's ideas a belief in the importance of scientific methods and in the progress of societies, central enlightenment themes. These are themes of the enlightenment, and have been central themes throughout the history of sociology. In the current era, these themes are increasingly challenged across the social sciences. This is an issue to which we will return at the end of this chapter.

Concerns with the French Revolution and tendency toward conservatism is also evident in the writings of early and mid nineteenth-century sociologists such as Le Play, Saint-Simon, Compte, and de Tocqueville. Martindale describes this as follows:

> The ideological properties of early sociology are undeniable. Only a conservative ideology was able to distinguish the discipline. The linkage between science and reformist social attitudes (e.g., scientific socialism) was severed. In renouncing political activism, sociology became respectable enough to be received into the ivy-colored halls of the universities. It was received as a scientific justification of the existing social order (Martindale, 1960:530).

We derive from the conservatives of this era the distinctive elements that characterized sociology—and emphasis on society over the individual, a focus on social institutions, a distrust of the dislocating effects of individualism, a recognition of the importance of traditions, and a recognition that religion and the sacred are inescapable elements of modern life (Nisbet, 1978).

The conservative image of social life is present in many aspects of the justice system today. Contemporary justice movements such as community-based policing and reintegrative shaming, though appearing twenty-first century cutting edge, actually are rooted in conservative and early sociological thought, emphasizing anti-Enlightenment fears over uncontrolled individualism and the importance of community over the individual. Community corrections, grounded in the notion that a person's best chance for rehabilitation is in maintaining community and family ties, is a notion with a strong tradition in conservative thought. Every time a judge sets aside a prison sentence, believing that a juvenile will be better served by maintaining work relations and family bonds, the conservative spirit of sociology is invigorated.

In diverse ways, sociology continues to nourish the field of criminal justice. Institutional, normative, critical and conflict perspectives that are central to a great deal of justice theory and research emerged from sociological theory. These perspectives are discussed at length in Chapter 4. It is likely that these perspectives will continue to occupy an important place in the conceptualization of criminal justice practices.

American Origins of Criminology—The Chicago School. One of the most important contributions of sociology has been in the study of crime, or criminology. Both American sociology and incipient criminology are typically traced to the Chicago School. The Chicago School dominated sociology from the First World War until the 1930s (Coser, 1978). The Chicago School's link to conservative thought and early sociology is clear in many of its early products. *The Polish Peasant in Europe and America*, by Thomas and Znaniecki (1920), examined modes of social organization, the values that were associated with them, and how changes in social organization affected the morality among Polish migrants. This kind of writing carried the perspective of the moral preeminence of society over the individual.

Early criminology is associated with the works of Robert Park (1926; Park & Burgess, 1920), one of the developers and chair of the Chicago School. Park developed the model of the city as an organism made up of particular ecological elements, a model that continues to be taught today. He viewed urban life in terms of ethnic and racial groups, who created niches for themselves. The relations among these groups were determined by processes of invasion, dominance, and succession. Burgess, another member of the Chicago school, also focused on the relationships between juveniles and urban neighborhoods (1925).

Shaw and McKay (1931, 1942) continued Park's focus on the ecology of urban areas. Their work, oriented toward both reform and scholarship, was on the relationship between urban zones and delinquency. The work carried out by these researchers carried a common theme—destabilization of neighborhoods from change and economic dislocation. When neighborhoods are disrupted, delinquency emerges as an urban problem. This body of work is solidly grounded in the conservative traditions of sociology—a distrust for the disruptive effects of uncontrolled capitalism and a belief that a person's values and morality are based in social life.

The body of work produced by the Chicago School is sometimes called social ecology theory, referring to the idea that crime occurs in particular social contexts. Social ecology has proven to be fruitful—several contemporary crime control perspectives can be traced to it. One of these perspectives is *design ecology*, according to which the physical design of places facilitates or mitigates against crime (Lanier & Henry, 1998). This perspective emerged from the early work of Newman (1972), who developed the idea of "defensible space." To prevent crimes, it is necessary, Newman argued, to build areas that contribute to feelings of territoriality among urban residents.

Routine Activities Theory (Felson, 1998) is considered by many to be the heir to design ecology. Both perspectives look at how normal human mobility patterns create conditions in which some kinds of crime prosper. Routine activities theory stems from the logic that crime activity is predictable and routine, and flows from routine patterns of human activity. Routine activities theory is fruitful for criminal justice professionals: it intersects in practical ways with the body of contemporary police procedures called problem-oriented policing.

The social ecological model of crime developed by Sampson (1995) also has its roots in the Chicago tradition. As Binder and Binder (2001) note, Sampson's research has extended the research tradition to the relationship between violent behavior, residential instability, and poverty. Because of the fruitful work of Sampson and others, the study of community-based contextual effects in the genesis of crime is now a well-established tradition in criminology. Today, it is useful not only for furthering our knowledge of crime and place, but for understanding the limitations of contemporary governmental policies that foster concentration of racial and ethnic minorities (Binder & Binder, 2001).

Sociology has provided the academic foundation and intellectual stimulus for the development of the field of criminology. Criminology focuses on the etiology of crime, and typically discusses justice institutions when they are perceived to contribute in some way to crime. However, it has expanded its etiology substantially beyond sociological contexts. Sociological criminology focuses on the social contexts of crime, particularly as they apply to sociocultural, structural, and organizational contexts (Lanier & Henry, 1998). Yet, some criminological perspectives today are not deterministic, but recognize the role of free will in the production of crime. Free-will perspectives are particularly evident in rational choice theories of crime. And the field of criminology today includes perspectives as diverse as biosocial theory and psychological theory. These perspectives recognize the contribution of free will, but only to a point. They also locate deterministic factors in nonsocial arenas—in a person's psychology, or in their inborn traits. In sum, the field of criminology is much broader than one might think if one looked only at social factors in crime causation. Figure 2.1 summarizes the principal criminology theories, their basic ideas, and the associated practices of the criminal justice system.

Figure 2.1
Theories of Crime

CLASSICAL, RATIONAL CHOICE, AND ROUTINE ACTIVITIES THEORY

Idea. Assumes that humans are rational, free-thinking individuals. People are free to choose crime as one of a range of behavioral alternatives. Choosing pleasure over pain, people seek to maximize their own self-interests. Choices people make are based on ideas of economic utility. Rationality may be limited or conditional on other factors.

Criminal justice practice. Fines, because they can be equalized and staged in progressive severity; prison, because time served can be adjusted and staged at different levels for different offenses; death penalty only as the ultimate sanction for serious offenders; and environmental manipulation and adjustments of routine activities of potential victims to avoid crimes (Lanier & Henry, 1998:90).

BIOLOGICAL THEORY

Idea. Some people are born criminals, with a predisposition to commit crime. Human behavior is a mix of the environment and of biology. Biological traits are randomly distributed, and extremes may be either bad or good.

Criminal justice practice. Treat the defect, protect society from the untreatable. Surgery, drugs, incapacitation, eugenics for the untreatable, genetic counseling, manipulation of the environment.

PSYCHOLOGICAL THEORY

Idea. Personalities are shaped by early childhood development experiences in the family. Some are inadequately socialized or suffer traumatic experiences. A variety of perspectives are subsumed under this perspective. An individual's personality is seen by some theorists as a blank slate, by others as trait-based. Phenomenological approaches look at the importance of socially constructed meanings. Criminals have learned incorrect ways to think.

Criminal justice practice. Evaluation and treatment to help individuals uncover childhood root causes. Training to control problems. The role of discipline in the home and school is important. According to cognitive theorists, individuals may have to learn new ways to think, redesigning destructive thought processes. Environmental approaches focus on manipulating community resources to prevent problems.

DIFFERENTIAL ASSOCIATION THEORY

Idea. People learn to commit crime as a result of exposure to other's criminal behavior, ideas, and rationalizations that are favorable to violating the law. People are rule followers, and the rules they follow depend on which groups socialize them.

Criminal justice practice. Restitution, reparation, and social rehabilitation. Group therapy and counseling for children of immigrants to provide them with appropriate skills. Law flexibility in dealing with lower-class cultural contexts. Parental skills training.

Figure 2.1, *continued*

DRIFT AND NEUTRALIZATION THEORY

Idea. Crime becomes an option for people when their commitment to conventional values and norms is neutralized by excuses and justifications.

Criminal justice practice. Public exposure and declaration of excuses and justifications. Education for ethics and self-deception.

CONTROL THEORY

Idea. Humans are rational and self-interested. Behavior is controlled by the bonds they have to significant reference groups.

Criminal justice practice. Prevention and rehabilitation through increased bonding. Work training that strengthens families and increase commitment to conventional occupations. Participation in conventional school activities.

LABELING THEORY

Idea. Humans are vulnerable to how other people see them. They are affected by their social status and are vulnerable to informal social controls. If peoples are labeled as criminal or "bad" by the people around them, they will eventually internalize the label and become criminal.

Criminal justice practice. Radical non-intervention. Tolerance rather than moral indignation, restitution, reparation, rehabilitation. Victimless crime is decriminalized. Diversion programs to avoid stigmatization. Decarcerate the prison population. Imprison only the most serious offenders.

SOCIAL ECOLOGY THEORY

Idea. Actions are determined by the social environment. Choices people make occur in environmentally structured contexts. Crime is a consequence of the particular characteristics of the physical environment. Population movement, physical space, and density all affect the environment and are important in understanding the causes of crime.

Criminal justice practice. Change the physical environment. Community mobilization, develop programs to assimilate immigrants and provide order for disorganized communities.

CULTURE CONFLICT THEORY

Idea. Society can be described in terms of a dominant culture and a diversity of subordinate or ethnic cultures. The law represents the rules by which the dominant group controls subordinate groups. By following their own cultural values and norms some people are in conflict with dominant culture, and their behaviors are seen as criminal.

Criminal justice practice. Education and cultural socialization in schools. Increased opportunities for assimilation and changing values of diverse ethnic groups. Greater flexibility of the law in dealing with immigrant groups. Decreased policing of the streets.

Figure 2.1, *continued*

ANOMIE/STRAIN THEORY

Idea. The opportunities available for people to achieve occupational goals are differentially available to people according to their social status. The lower one's status, the less likely one will have the opportunity or means to achieve the ends society perceives as "good." The means-ends strain creates problems of frustration and anger. Some people will choose illegal means to achieve the ends they are taught are good.

Criminal justice practice. Provide economic opportunities to lower classes. Programs should aim at increasing the legitimate opportunities for youth, and at providing the skills needed to participate in legitimate society. Create jobs, education, welfare and child care programs. Organize local communities to have an investment in conventional society. Community and youth participation programs prepare youth for participation in conventional society.

CONFLICT AND RADICAL (MARXIST) THEORY

Idea. Capitalism, coupled with private ownership and vast inequities in wealth create conflict and provide the conditions for crime. For conflict theorists, different groups have differing interests. For radical theorists, the source of conflict is in the class structure of capitalism's exploitative system of economic production.

Criminal justice practice. Restructure wealth and ownership. Move ownership to employees. Enforce laws equally against rich and poor. Decriminalize consensual crimes, minor property theft, and drug offenses. Changes may include movement to a socialist economic policy.

Source: Adapted from M. Lanier and S. Henry (1998). *Essential Criminology*. Boulder, CO: Westview Press.

Figure 2.1 allows us to juxtapose theories with the practice of criminal justice. We can see that justice system practices are associated with particular theories. Theories on the etiology of crime are also implicitly theories of justice system behavior.

The Future of Academic Criminology. What does the future hold for criminology? In the 1998 presidential address to the American Society of Criminology, Margaret Zahn (1999) discussed criminology's future and the challenges it will face. Her address was cast in the spirit that motivates this book. She identified three major areas of concern.

1. *Theoretical development:* The fields of environmental crime and electronic crime are important new areas that are underdeveloped. The impact of environmental crime is far-reaching—particulate pollution alone kills four times as many annually as homicide (Situ & Emmons, 1996). As a field of study, environmental crime will require that we recast our conceptions of victimization. Criminology also should expand its boundaries to incorporate perspectives from biol-

ogy, biochemistry, and make better use of historical studies. Research on community structures, Zahn suggested, needs to be related to practitioners' concerns.

2. *Public Policy Involvement.* Zahn argued that the American Society of Criminology should take policy positions on topics central to criminological study. The ASC, she noted, should formulate alternative conceptions of crime and justice problems. The National Policy Committee, ASC's policy board, could develop position papers on alternative ways to handle issues such as juvenile delinquency and drugs, and relay those alternatives to federal, state, and private agencies.

3. *Building just communities.* Echoing the central theme of this book, Zahn contends that criminologists can begin the work of building just communities. Citing evidence provided by the Amnesty International, she noted fundamental areas on injustice in contemporary criminal justice practices, particularly against women. She warned participants that:

> "As individuals we have discussed failed drug policy and the privatization of prisons, and have worked on juvenile justice issues. But as a professional organization we have remained silent. But silence is not neutral and providing substantiated evidence of violations of international standards does not make us politically partisan. Justice Brandeis said once 'The greatest danger to liberty lies in . . . a silent self-absorbed citizenry that doesn't care enough to join the argument.' I don't believe that we are uncaring, but as a professional society we have remained silent" (Zahn, 1999:13).

Zahn concluded with a call for knowledge that would further the work of building just communities. Criminology will be judged, she cautioned, not by the knowledge we produce but how we use it. In her clarion call we can see the future of justice studies as well. For their striking similarities of vision, criminology and justice studies will always carry intertwined destinies.

Political Science

Political science has deep historical traditions in the academic environment. Well before justice studies burst onto the academic setting, political science had established a distinguished history in American universities. As early as 1914, there were 38 distinct political science departments, and 89 political science components existed in history, economics, or sociology departments (Morn, 1995). Political science has been an important part of the academic history of justice studies, though to a lesser degree than sociology. In many colleges and universities, justice studies programs are tied to political science rather than to sociology.

Academic justice studies has shared many of the problems faced by political scientists. Concerns over social, criminal, and political dimensions of justice issues characterize both fields. One of the principal subfields of political science, public administration, bears a close resemblance and overlapping domain of content to criminal justice. It is simply astonishing that the field of criminal justice has been so uninformed by political science.

The academic history of political science in some ways parallels sociology. In the United States, Lester Ward is often described as a foundational figure for both political science and sociology (Seidelman, 1985), and introductory books in both fields commonly include discussions of Max Weber, Karl Marx, and Alexis de Tocqueville. Many of the issues that have affected sociology have also typified political science. Both experienced a "behavioral" period in the 1960s, an efflorescence of the belief that empirical analysis would provide a unifying glue to their respective fields, that they could create accurate and meaningful images of the world through the collection of everyday "objective" knowledge. And both witnessed a fragmentation of the behavioral approach in the 1970s. An explosion of methods literature challenged core ideas of independence and objectivity in quantitative research. A recognition that "objective" research was not really objective but carried hidden assumptions, reinforced the status quo, and sometimes masked the biases of political sciences upset the hegemony of the behavioral perspective. And the social and political problems that behaviorism addressed, from race to delinquency to poverty, proved to be more intransigent and less amenable to policy-based solutions than anticipated. An "end to ideological" view, in which beliefs were to be replaced by accurate and objective knowledge about political decision-making through an informed electorate, proved to be premature.

From the 1970s forward, political science and sociology both underwent fragmentation of their "core" identities. The emergence of justice studies has occurred in this post-behavioral disarray, and has important implications for justice identity. Justice studies, unlike other social sciences, has never enjoyed a core academic identity, but by the same token, has not had to undergo the painful process of shedding one either.

Differences between justice studies and political science are often a matter of emphasis. The field of justice studies generally takes its starting point as the study of the institutions that carry out justice activities. Political science is the study of government and politics. The overlap is substantial: When justicians begin discussing the relationship between citizens and the government, they explore an area already visited by political scientists. Similarly, due process issues mobilize the activities, professional commitments, and moral sentiments of many justicians and political scientists alike. Many of the "big picture" questions associated with criminal justice—where do justice institutions come from, what is their relationship with government, what is the legal, moral and philosophical basis for court activity—are also political science topics.

In view of the similarity of their background, and particularly of the mutual affinity of political science and criminal justice for justice policy at regional and national levels, it is surprising that political science has had so little impact on the field of criminal justice. It is beyond this book to review the whole of the field of political science, or to trace its breadth for potential and actual contributions to justice studies. In this chapter, I will focus on two issues: (1) the implications of the history of political science for criminal justice, and (2) how criminal justice theory might be informed by an important subfield of political science, international relations.

Political Science Origins. Like other social sciences, political science emerged in a period in which principles of empirical sciences and progress were central to notions of field identity and research development. For early political scientists, empirical research into government could provide a way to inform policy and establish the importance of the field. Seidelman's (1985) history traces the early history of the field. The story he tells can be seen as a cautionary tale for those who believe that criminal justice can forge an identity around empirically based justice system policy.

> Political advocacy has always taken place through the profession, by combining advocacy with aspirations of scholarly objectivity. But the very continuity of this shared perspective suggests that there has been a gap between political and professional ambitions and claims on the one hand, and their extremely minimal impact on the course and direction of American political life on the other (Seidelman, 1985:14).

Political identity in the United States has historically organized around what Seidelman called the first and the second traditions. The first tradition refers to institutionalists, who were distrustful of government and believed that complex institutional arrangements might provide democratic stability unattainable by popular vote alone. This tradition was symbolized by a "political vocabulary of system, mechanism, control, realism, skepticism, and facts" [5]. By institutionalism is meant a belief in the ability of institutional devices for solving social and political problems. Political institutions, rather than common passions, social diversity, and progressive individualism, provided the basis for social order. The Constitution is the most significant product of the first traditionalists. It is a document with an impressive array of checks and balances that divided powers and procedures so that a popular will could never gain the upper hand on government.

The second tradition referred to radical democrats, for whom governance occurred through popular virtue and sentiment, and was enacted through political groups close to the electorate. The best government was visible and controllable by the people. Power was shifted away from central government and toward state legislators. The Articles of Confederation was a document produced by the second tradition radical democrats.

Political science represented a third tradition, intentionally organized by the founders of political science as an alternative to first and second traditionalists. Setting itself as a scientific and progressive alternative to the ideologies of institutionalists and radical democrats, third traditionalists sought the cultivation of a reasoned electorate grounded in an empirical science of politics. Democracy would be enlightened, its practices informed by a science of governance. Citing Lippman (1961:61), Seidelman noted that "The scientific spirit is the spirit of democracy, the escape from drift, the outlook of free men. Its direction is to distinguish fact from fancy, its enthusiasm is for the possible, its promise is the shaping of fact to a chastened and honest dream." The Third Tradition was characterized by the following themes:

1. An unambivalent philosophy of triumphant modernism.

2. The state can be a conscious reflection of and actor for an interdependent society.

3. Citizens and their energies and support are essential to the survival of modern democracy.

4. A spirit of sciences was essential to a free democracy. This was to be carried out in schools, and would create a national culture committed to innovation and experimentation.

The early third traditioners were committed to the spirit of progress and the contribution of political science to reform. Political scientists were caught up in the progressive movement and viewed themselves as the voices of political reform. The founding of the American Political Science Association in 1903 occurred in an era of reform that Lowi (1985) described as the first peacetime nationalization of politics since the founding of the United States itself. Hence, modern mass government and modern social science, based in professional associations, emerged at the same time. The social science disciplines, and particularly political science, were irrevocably related by the idea of liberal governance. Lowi describes this relationship as follows:

> National government in the United States, emerging late and slowly, built nevertheless on liberal lines. So did the social sciences, especially political science . . . Liberal government could be justified by concerning itself with conduct deemed harmful only in its consequences. Social science could analyze such a system and also serve such a system by concerning itself with hypotheses about conduct about and its consequences" (Lowi, 1985:ix).

By "liberalism" is not meant the contemporary distinction between political liberalism and conservatism which are little more than hodgepodges of similar ideas differentially applied (Shively, 1997). In its historical form, liberalism was the political philosophy embodied in ideas of enlightenment utilitarianism. The most important purpose of liberal government was to enhance the ability of citizens to develop their capacities to the maximum extent possible. A strong government served the public by enabling all participants to better develop their own personal ambitions and energies.

In the 1920s, third tradition reformers adopted a scientific approach to administration. This progressive view was aimed at what was viewed as amateurish government, and reformers advocated more informed, professional forms of governance. Inevitably, it was thought, revelations about bad government would stir public outrage and lead to change. Under the leadership of the age, political science became committed to the "pure science of democracy." The goal among this generation of third traditionalists was to "create a public respectful of science and democracy" (Seidelman, 1985:16).

In the 1960s political science transformed itself into a behavioral enterprise. Ethical and critical perspectives were replaced with an objective orientation to the production of knowledge. Underscoring the behavioral perspective was a belief in the rightness of quantitative analysis for the study of political phenomena. This belief was coupled with a faith that the pluralist system of politics was fundamentally fair and the conviction that social science could play a redeeming role in politics.

The behavioral image of politics, Seidelman argued, worked so long as political institutions were stable and fundamentally just. Behavioral analyses didn't work if politicians were fundamentally deceptive, or if institutions and public sentiment were too unstable to be reliably measured. The image of trust and stability both were shattered by the late 1960s, precipitated by the partisanship and cynicism that accompanied Nixon's presidency and the transience of "good works" political practices when scaled against the intransigence of social problems. Political science faced a crisis of "authority, of morality, and of fundamental purposes—a crisis that questioned cherished procedural definitions of democracy and the constitution of political authority" (Seidelman, 1985:189).

Pluralistic politics, a positivist system in the behavioral regime of third traditioners, was seen by many citizens and academics as a justification for an inequitable status quo and source of restriction of access to political constituencies with moral claims, such as women and African-Americans. The principle goal of the third tradition—to tie its views about pluralistic political science to the practice of state power—collapsed in the post-behavioral era. The field of political science, like the polity, had become highly pluralistic.

In the current era, the identity of political science has lost its "professional coherence" (Seidelman, 1985:18). Today's scholars, Seidelman laments, tend to trace the dimensions of their unsolvable disputes rather than reconcile their differences. The unity provided by the third tradition—the idea that a central theme of good government, scientifically developed, aimed at the training and preparation of politicians and an informed electorate—has passed.

How will the lack of a "core" identity affect political science? Without a central unifying theme such as that provided by third traditionalists, academic pluralism has the capacity to be deeply divisive. This is not necessarily bad. As Lowi (1985:xvi) ryely observed, "collisions will be organizationally destabilizing as well as intellectually productive."

Conflicts within political science are mirrored in the polity. Neo-conservatism has emerged as a powerful strain of political thought that sought a minimalist role of government. Gaining strength both in academic circles and among the public, it is exerting a powerful impact on political theory and citizen voting behavior, breathing new life into first traditionalism. It is also closely tied to a high level of partisanship at the congressional level. Certainly, the impeachment and attempted conviction of President Clinton in 1999 was what some have called the greatest degree of political partisanship witnessed by the electorate since the civil war—a will to choose sides rather than to seek middle ground.

In the history of political science, we in justice studies witness a cautionary tale of our own efforts to seek relevancy. In professional meetings and in executive councils, I have participated in discussions about making the field "relevant." We travel similar idealistic ground, both through the hegemonic focus on empirical methods, a concern for policy relevance, and a sort of normative belief in the ability of government to carry out good works. Several lessons can be learned from the experience of political science.

The first lesson is that the field of justice studies is unlikely to cohere around behaviorism, or perhaps around any central domain of content or method. Some of our graduate programs are oriented behaviorally, and behaviorism has been heralded as the organizing principle that should guide Ph.D. program development. If political science, and sociology for that matter, are guides, what we observe is that the heady days of behaviorism are passed. The world has moved on and we must move with it.

The second lesson is this: Some of the problems faced by our government are intransigent to the peculiar kind of democratic heritage we have in the United States. The resurgence of first traditionalism in the United States reminds us that there is a profound distrust of government, and that it will be categorically resisted even when it seeks unquestionably good ends. Efforts to mobilize the justice field around a common view of scientific crime control are likely to be disappointing—the political will is fragmented both inside the field and among the electorate, and the greater our efforts to develop a unity of vision, the greater will we mobilize opposing views. The idea of an overarching criminal justice system, run by technical criminal justice professionals, is snake-oil to many people both among the citizenry and in the halls of academe. Academic criminal justice is, for many people, just another governmental institution to be distrusted.

A third lesson is this. Seidelman chided political science for its inability to develop new prescriptions, for its historically recurring tendency to reinvent old and unsuccessful prescriptions as if they were new solutions. As our field once again initiates an exploration of the viability of private corrections, or "rediscovers" the political concept of "community," as if for the first time, one cannot help but be concerned that it is a lesson that many justicians have failed to learn as well.

Fourth, the justice studies field, for all its social science pretensions, is not science—it is at its core about values. Our claims to "objective knowledge" are seen by some as a throwback to the behaviorism of the 1960s, and more darkly by others as a behavioral mask for the expansion of crime control into the free-thinking academic setting. Can we succeed where political science has not—can we develop a body of scientific information around a central set of values celebrating scientific rationality and the objectivity of the state? More importantly—do we want to? The answers may be "no" and "no."

As an academic enterprise, justice studies emerged in a historical time when other disciplines were fragmenting. Perhaps we as justicians are better served by progressing, not as a unity, but as a congeries of issue-committed professionals, linked only by the common theme of "doing justice," for all the ambiguity the term carries. Such a focus may be consistent with the way in which the social sciences are reorganizing around significant worldwide problem and issue areas today, a trend discussed in the final section of this chapter. Perhaps only by acknowledging the sheer diversity of justice can we avoid repeating the wrong lessons of the past.

International Relations. This section echoes Russell's (1997) observation that criminal justice scholars routinely ignore the literature from international relations. In this section, I will follow Russell's (1997) recommendations and briefly consider models, developed within the spectrum of international relations, that might be useful for the study of state security systems within particular countries. By state security I refer to the systems of internal justice systems and external security systems concerned with terrorism and other threats external to the country.

Russell identified two perspectives that might be fruitful for the conceptualization of justice system processes in an international context. One, called *realpolitik* or neorealist theory, (Legro 1996) holds that the world is basically anarchistic and nations make rational choices aimed at achieving security. Nation-states are concerned with increasing their power relative to other states (see also Krasner, 1983).

The principle competing perspective was the *neoliberal* (also called the neoliberal institutionalist) perspective. According to this perspective, complex interdependencies exist between nations. These interdependencies are often institutionalized, and govern the behavior of nations to each other. It is the institutionalization of expectations and patterns of conduct, not the actual presence of power, that determines the relationship among nations.

The neoliberal perspective, Russell suggested, was particularly useful for criminal justice scholars because it focused on shared or mutual understandings of crime problems. Such problems include terrorism, the drug trade, internet-based crime, smuggling, and international organized crime. Some of these problems are on the rise, and have contributed to an increase in the number of foreign policy initiatives between nations. The expansion of international (and sometimes internal) justice system activities may occur as the result of these shared understandings.

Russell suggested that "regime analysis" provided a way to study these shared understandings. He defined the term "regime" as "implicit or explicit arrangements." Arrangements included norms and principles in an area of international relations, implicit rules that guide the behavior of important actors, and multinational agreements among nations that seek to regulate conduct in issue areas (Kratochwil & Ruggie, 1986; Haggard & Simmons, 1987). Regimes emerged under two circumstances. First, policy windows—events involving destabilization or change—represent opportune times for regime formation. Terrorist attacks, for example, represented policy windows in which regime formation occurred. Second, international increases in kinds of criminal activity initiated regime formation. Geographic changes in the illicit drug trade, for instance, might spark the formation of a multi-national alliance providing intelligence about particular individuals and groups.

Hence, regime analysis provides a way to study the expansion of international justice system activity. Regime analysis represents an extension over realpolitik ideas because it recognizes how informal understandings affect regime formation. It is also a normative theory, because it links the growth of regimes to the presence of actual criminal, illegal, or otherwise harmful activity.

A third way to look at the comparative development of state justice and security systems is *cultural analysis* (Duffield, 1999). It has emerged in response to the perception that neorealist theory fails to capture important dynamics in nation-state security behavior. In particular, many nations have failed to adapt their security in accordance with changes in their international position, hence failing to conform to neorealist expectations. Of particular interest to Duffield was the behavior of Germany, who failed to revamp their security after the fall of the Soviet Union. According to neorealism, Germany should have beefed up its security in response to its growing power and worldwide status. However, it did not. Why?

Duffield (1999) suggested that an explanation lay in the most "venerable" of cultural ideas for understanding state security behavior, a state's political culture. He suggested that a study of political culture provided the key to Germany's behavior. He suggested that German political elites "shared a set of beliefs and values—a political culture—of great relevance to national security policy and that this political culture appears to have shaped several central aspects of German security policy after unification" (Duffield, 1999:791). Political culture accounted for the failure of Germany to adapt its security apparatus to its increased strength and power.

A fourth model for looking at a state's security apparatus is the *environmental scarcities* model developed by Homer-Dixon (1994). Homer-Dixon contended that the most compelling issue in the twenty-first century was environmental scarcity, and argued that scarcity initiated a chain of events that resulted in persistent, sub-national violence. Scarcity had several effects:

1. The income of elites was reduced, and they turned to the state for income support. Elite rivalries emerge.

2. Expansion of the numbers of marginal group members who need help from government.

3. Increasing numbers of peoples are displaced from rural areas to cities. This in turn lead to the development of ethnic identity and conflict.

4. Revenues to local and national government is reduced, making it more difficult for governments to respond to scarcity-induced problems.

Because of these various problems, scarcity resulted in sub-national and persistent conflict. As a result of conflict, security would develop in one of two patterns. Either it would harden in its efforts to control increases in violence. In this condition, internal security—the justice system— would "beef up," expanding its capacities to deal with economic problems as crime problems. However, when scarcity problems became too great, they overwhelm internal security, and governments might collapse.

Public Administration

Public administration is a traditional subfield of political science. It is practically oriented and aimed at preparing individuals for a career in local and regional policy-related positions. Derived from the term "policy sciences" first used in the 1950s (Lasswell, 1951), public administration has undergone increasing academic development. The relationship of public administration to political science is much like the traditional relationship of criminal justice to sociology—it is sometimes viewed as a gloss for executive training and policy development, lacking in enduring intellectual themes and caught up in the "sound byte" issues of the day.

In the current era, the field of public administration is increasingly taking on the theoretical and epistemological concerns of its parent discipline. Simply put, it is maturing as a social science. Below, I will briefly identify perspectives on public policy development. Sabatier (1999) identifies and provides discussions of six perspectives central to the analysis of public policy.

1. *The Stages heuristic* is a positivistic account of the stages that comprise public policy decisionmaking. Popular in the 1970s, it has been criticized as being more of a typology than theory. The stages that provide the analytic framework for the study of policy are initiation, estimation, selection, implementation, evaluation, and termination (Brewer, 1974).

2. *Institutional rational choice.* This perspective assesses how institutions affect the behavior of rationally minded individuals. This framework assumes that individuals are motivated by self-interest. By institutions is meant both organizations and collectives of rules and procedures in and across organization sets. It may be the most utilized framework for the study of public policy in the United States.[1] This perspective looks at how rational actors are affected by their institutional arrangements, and also how they try to affect their arrangements (see Ostrom, 1999).

3. *Multiple streams.* This perspective perceives the policy process as in terms of (1) a problem stream consisting of data about various problems, (2) a policy stream that involves the proponents of solutions to the problems, and (3) a political stream involving both elections and the people elected. According to this perspective, the streams are usually independent, but windows of opportunity sometime open that allow for the streams to interact.

4. *Punctuated equilibrium.* This perspective argues that the United States is typified by lengthy periods of incremental change punctuated by brief, dramatic policy changes. This perspective is useful for both the study of legislation and federal budgetary practices (see Baumgardner & Jones, 1993).

5. *The advocacy coalition network.* Sabatier (1999:9) describes this as the "interaction of advocacy coalitions—each consisting of actors from a variety of institutions who share a set of policy beliefs—within a policy subsystem." This perspective analyzes both the system in which the coalitions interact and the broader contexts in which they participate. Values emerge as a central consideration in this model, particularly the values held by policy elites. This perspectives, like the ones above, presumes individuals act from a position of bounded rationality. However, the inner core for the valuation of self-interest is alternative values and beliefs not personal gain (Schlager, 1999). This model, then, represents a sharp break from the economically driven model presented by institutional rational choice.

6. *The policy diffusion network.* This is a perspective for analyzing policy changes across political systems. This framework looks at the mathematical properties of adoptive practices of innovations and is mathematically driven by models of diffusion processes. It does not explain the innovation per se but assesses how it comes to be accepted across different systems after its emergence.

These sketches of policy perspective are almost so brief as to discredit the rich scholarship that has been constructed to develop and assess them. Considered together, they show how the field of public administration is incorporating a diversity of perspectives into the analysis of policy. These perspectives recognize the role of taken-for-granted assumptions, economic systems, rational decisionmaking, and sometimes, simple blind chance in comprehending the development and proliferation of public policy nationally and internationally.

The relative newness of the field of public policy in the social sciences may place it at an intellectual advantage in the development of social science knowledge, an advantage from which the justice field might learn. Members of the public policy field are not beholding to a core perspective. Instead, in its relative newness it can explore and seek bridges across different fields, free to select according to the relative efficacy and success of particular perspectives for the kinds of problems that define it as a policy field (Ostrom, 1999; Kiser & Ostrom 1982), for example, developed the *Institutional Analysis and Development* framework (IAD) in order to integrate the work of political scientists, lawyers economists, anthropologists, social psychologists, and others who have studied how institutions affect individuals and vice versa. The IDA framework evolved from the work of participants in the "Workshop in Political Theory and Policy Analysis" at Indiana University.

Public administration has provided an important contribution to the development of the justice field. Justice studies departments are often organized in functional areas such as the police, the courts, and juvenile issues. This model is based on the notion that each area has different administrative concerns in the implementation and calculation of justice. This model provided the foundational structure for curricular instruction for the SUNY-Albany school of criminal justice. Remington (1990) describes the founding of SUNY-Albany as follows:

> In the early 1960s Lloyd Ohlin and I were asked to consult on the advisability of creating a School of Criminal Justice in New York State. We both recommended the creation of the school, though we differed somewhat in our judgment of what the school should emphasize. Ohlin believed that there was a need to create a new discipline of criminal justice, which would bring to the field the same kind of research and teaching interests that had been devoted, for example, to the study of the economy. He was inclined to stress criminology as a conceptual basis for the new school. My view in 1962 was that New York State would benefit from a university commitment built on the best features of the public administration model. Such features still survive in our present schools of public policy, such as the Kennedy School at Harvard. I saw the need for individuals trained and sophisticated in handling important community problems that called for a response from government, such as deciding whether the criminal justice system or some other means of social control would be more effective (Remington, 1990:15-16).

The public administration model, Remington emphasized, was the best to provide knowledge and preparation for practice in the justice field:

> Stressing public administration also is a way of emphasizing the fact that both the development of knowledge and the application of that knowledge in day-to-day practice is important. This is particularly true in the field of criminal justice, where emotional and political considerations often take priority over careful, systematic efforts to assess the actual effectiveness of programs (Remington, 1990:16).

Many of Remington's ideas are characteristic of Master's degree development in criminal justice, discussed in Chapter 3.

Law and Legal Perspective

The legal perspective and the social sciences operate under sharply different presumptions about human nature. Consider first the social sciences. The social sciences construct knowledge based on causal theoretical models. Social sciences consequently expand their knowledge base through greater understanding of the factors that affect human behavior. Analysis in the social sciences occurs by testing whether these causal relationships hold in real-life circumstances. Models are called "deterministic," which means that some factors are thought to determine others. In this sense, a person's behavior might be determined by their psychological state, by their social circumstances, by their family environment, or by their genetic make-up.

The practice of law in the United States, on the other hand, carries in it a theory of the individual, one who is permitted to seek his or her well-being substantially unobstructed by the government. It is a free-will notion of law, powerfully enlightenment in notion, that individuals have natural rights which supercede government restrictions. What individuals can expect from government is security and protection. The authority we cede to the government is authority to protect its citizenry through the provision of security. The law is the tool society uses to protect the natural rights we individually are endowed with. The purpose of the law is the protection of natural rights. The law, consequently, is the rational product of individuals acting on behalf of their self-interest in accordance with principles of natural rights.

The Law and Natural Rights. By natural rights is meant that people have a right to certain freedoms and protections, and the purpose of the law is to provide those freedoms and protections. Thomas Paine describes the "rights of man" in the following quote.

Natural rights are those rights which pertain to man by right of his existence. Of this kind are all the intellectual rights, rights of the mind, and also the rights of acting as an individual for his own comfort and happiness, which are not injurious to the rights of others. Civil rights are those which appertain to man in view of his being a member of society. Every civil right has for its foundation some natural right pre-existing in the individual, but to the enjoyment of which his individual power is not, in all cases, sufficiently competent. Of this kind are all those which relate to security and protection . . .

The natural rights which [man] retains in [society] are all those in which the power to execute it is as perfect in the individual as the right itself. Among this class, as is before mentioned, are all the intellectual rights, or rights of the mind; consequently, religion is one of those rights. The natural rights which are not retained, are all those in which, though the right is perfect in the individual, the power to execute them is defective . . . He therefore deposits this right in the common stock of society, and takes the arm of society, of which he is a part, in preference and in addition to his own . . .

From these premises two or three certain promises will follow:

First, That every civil right grows out of a natural right; or, in other words, it is a natural right exchanged.

Secondly, That civil law properly considered as such is made up of the aggregate of that class of the natural rights of man, which becomes defective in the individual in point of power, and answers not his purpose but when collected to a focus becomes competent to the purpose of everyone.

Thirdly, That the power produced from the aggregate of natural rights, imperfect in the power of the individual, cannot be applied to invade the natural rights which are retained in the individual, and in which the power to execute is as perfect as the right itself . . . Paine, The Rights of Man, in M. Curtis (ed.), *The Great Political Theories* V. 2 (1981):64.

Though written prior to the American Revolution, the democratic fervor in Paine's words continues to excite today. The spirit and energy of natural rights are carried in a utilitarian logic that no government has a right to revoke. Society is a compact, an aggregate created by individuals. Society exists only and explicitly for the purpose of insuring that individuals can sustain their natural rights. Indeed, there is no other reason for society. Society exists as an instrument whose purpose is to further the rational ends of its citizenry. Democratic processes rationally cede authority to the government, and the government in turn provides its citizenry with life, liberty, and the pursuit of happiness. Natural rights include sovereignty, the right of revolution against tyranny, democracy, liberty, the pursuit of happiness, and property rights.

Natural rights are closely tied to free-will political philosophy. Law is independent of economic or social circumstance. It is rational, and all individuals stand before the law as equals. The notion that the law should be relative to a person's social and economic circumstances has histori-cally been distasteful to the United States legal tradition. As Wallace observed,

> Even when antecedent conditions are acknowledged as cause of criminal behavior, the study of these conditions is deemed largely irrelevant . . . Demographic characteristics, such as sex and age, are offered as ultimate causes that cannot be changed. Consequently etiological research is con-sidered unimportant for policy development because it searches for unchangeable causes (Gottfredson, 1982; Wallace, 1991:223).

Nor do statistical models of causation inform legal decision-making. The law is grounded in the concept of the case at hand. Statistics reflect what happens to others and its bearing on the current case is indirect. The question typically faced in a court of law is "Did the person charged commit the act with which he or she is charged and what was their state of mind?" Statistical averages across many cases do not tend to illuminate that question.

Tonry (1998) captures the disdain many lawyers have for statistical analysis in the following quote:

> The NAS [National Academy of Science] panel concluded that "lawyers . . . have little sympathy for the complexities of social science research and an often inadequate grasp of the potential and limitations of research in the criminal justice field (White & Krislov, 1977:30). Lawyers are notori-ously skeptical of research and statistics . . . Lawyer's advocacy roles may create a tendency toward cynicism about research; in litigation and in administrative agency proceedings, technical information and expert witnesses are things to be deployed in the effort to obtain the result a client wants rather than resources to be drawn upon to obtain the right answer. Lawyers are professionally predisposed to believe that there are "lies, damn lies, and statistics" (Tonry, 1998:105).

The legal tradition of personal responsibility is grounded in the Enlightenment. It carries with it the enlightenment tradition that an indi-vidual, shed of the historical constraints of church and state, can act on their own will to better their economic and social circumstances. Indi-viduals themselves, not the church and state, become the agents of their destiny. Yet, to the same degree, individuals are accountable for their behavior. Free will moves both directions—a person may act to improve their lives, but they may destroy their lives as well. The law, a product of the enlightenment, intends that free will should not be used to commit criminal acts. Only in cases of immediate compulsion does the law over-look the compelling responsibilities of free will. Free will, then, is a nec-essary fiction of the law, a philosophical basis on which the criminal law is grounded, and which it requires to work.

The characteristics of contemporary jurisprudence, although reinforced by Enlightenment philosophy, predates it and can be found in the
late medieval period (1300-1600) in England (Bellamy, 1998). As Jenkins
(1999:108) observed, the issues confronted in the practice of the courts
have a "remarkably modern feel to them." This view fell out of favor in
Europe and England at a later date as Roman Law took hold, but it survived in the United States where its forms of jurisprudence and court
behavior continue to carry surprisingly contemporary elements. Reading
the following discussion of court behavior, the reader might think she or
he is reading a description of the courts today:

> Already noted was the role of the judge in adversarial procedure, which
> was to serve as an impartial referee between two contending parties.
> Adversarial systems we originally based on the private accuser, later
> replaced by the public prosecutor; consequently, the proof available for
> the judge's decision was essentially what the contending parties pre-
> sented at their "battle" or trial (Johnson & Wolfe, 1996:48).

The effects of pre-enlightenment jurisprudence on contemporary
courts is witnessed in other ways. The 12-person jury system is a British
product that can be dated to the twelfth century. The formation of both
petit and grand juries in England created the opportunity for nullification
of harsh laws. Early English juries, Johnson and Wolfe noted, may have
manipulated facts presented to them in order to pardon accused individuals
on grounds of self-defense or justifiable homicide. The trial jury ensured that
the outcomes of criminal prosecutions were weighted by local conditions.

The legal construction of behavior in free will is so different from the
ideas of social determinism carried by the social sciences—Wallace correctly referred to them as paradigmatically different—that it is unclear
that they belong in the same field. And in the history of justice studies
education they often have not fit well together. Justice studies departments have infrequently hired lawyers as tenure-stream faculty, and a J.D.
is not considered in most departments to satisfy the requirements for promotion and tenure. (In some departments, an LL.D. does, but rarely will a
justice studies department specifically advertise for an LL.D.) Similarly,
one does not routinely encounter social scientists teaching required classes in law schools.

The differences between legal and social construction of behavior
present a paradox: Are we agents of our own behavior, or are our moti-
vating values carried in broader social institutions? The paradox is a true
conundrum—both answers collapse into further paradoxes. If we are
agents of our own behavior, then how is society even possible? How can
a selfish creature produce a caring society? Isn't the inevitable outcome
of a selfish individual a similarly self-protective, constraining social system—a leviathan? In the act of ceding to a government of our choosing
the authority to act in order to protect citizens from the threat of harm,

don't we end up choosing not to choose?[2] On the other hand, if our values are carried in the traditions of broad social institutions, how can personal (selfish) motivation even arise? That is, if we are determined by the forces around us, how can the notion of free will even emerge. Is free will no more than a legal fiction?

Law and Society: Toward a Social Science of the Law. Academic departments have bridged the conflicts between social sciences and law in various ways. One such way is by using social science techniques to study the law, a way of analysis sometimes called the sociology or social science of law. Often organized under the umbrella term "law and society," this is a blended perspective that places analytic primacy on tools of social science investigation. As Wallace (1991:227) observed, "law and society scholars study the legal system as they would study any other social institution; thus the law and the legal process are merely new laboratories for testing psychological and sociological theories." However, the law and society perspective is at its roots a social science perspective: it examines the social determinants of law and the courts.

Black's writing on the behavior of the law (1976) is an exemplar of quantitative approaches to the law. It locates the sociology of the law squarely within the deterministic models characteristic of the social sciences. Black pronounces the law to be a quantitative variable with the following behavior:

> It increases and decreases, and one setting has more than another. It is possible to measure the quantity of law in many ways. A complaint to a legal official, for example, is more law than no complaint, whether it is a call to the police, a visit to a regulatory agency, or a lawsuit . . . More generally, the quantity of law is known by the number and scope of prohibitions, obligations, and other standards to which people are subject, and by the rate of legislation, litigation, and adjudication (Black, 1976:3).

The quantity of law changes across time and space. It is consequently possible to look at the changes in law and other aspects of social life. One can construct a sociology of law, according to which law varies by the sociological features of societies. Black considered the relationship between the law and several aspects of social life: stratification, the vertical aspect; morphology, the horizontal aspect; culture, the symbolic aspect; organization, the corporate aspect; and social control, which is the normative aspect. Each of these aspects in turn was also described in multidimensional and quantitative terms. All aspects of social life, and the law, related to each other in predictable ways that were quantitatively measurable and predictable.

Black's theory is evolutionary in scope. He observed, for example, that "Over history, across the world, law has been increasing." [131] By looking at patterns of evolution, he concluded that a new society would come into being. It would be the culmination of two historical trends—one toward order and the other toward differentiation. It would be a society of equals, people who were specialized and yet who were interchangeable, "at once close and distant, homogenous and diverse, organized and autonomous, where reputations and other statuses fluctuate from one day to the next." [137] In sum, the sociology of law developed by Black is in sharp distinction to free will constructions of the law. The behavior of the law within societies is a quantitative, predictable phenomenon determined by broad social forces. This is oppositional to viewing the law as a natural consequence of freely willing individuals applying principles of self interest.

Not all sociologies of law are grounded in broad, deterministic theory. For example, a social constructionist approach may be used as an analytic framework for studying the law. By social constructionist, I mean the way in which meanings (in this case, legal meanings) emerge in the context of concrete human interactions. A social constructionist would look at how the courtroom players create meaning within the legal environments and how their legal tools acquire their meaning in courtroom interactions. The meanings of the law, hence, doesn't exist as an "objective reality," independently of the players, but emerges from their ongoing interpretations of the situations in which they find themselves (Berger & Luckmann, 1966).

Mertz (1994) provided a framework for thinking about social construction of sociolegal studies. This perspective recognized the way in which particular, local dynamics affected the behavior of the law. She identified five themes that characterized a social construction perspective.

1. *The law is underdetermined and has unintended consequences.* The law and its applications, when applied in a highly structured legal setting, is refracted and reshaped. This is not simply indeterminancy, which can be described as the "slippage" between rule and application (see Singer, 1984). The "inherently social character" of legal processes introduces a fundamental underterminancy, beyond the control of formal prescriptions.

2. *Coherence is a legal fiction.* The law is grounded on clear coherences that don't work very well in application. The law constructs a "fictional" image of coherent individuals and communities. Legal discourse, for example, seems profoundly unable to accommodate any image of gender beyond traditional ideas of male and female. For example, sodomy often is the defining feature of homosexual identity, even though such relationships, like male-female, are complex and many faceted.

3. *The locus of authorship.* This asks—where does the idea of "local community" come from? The EPA, for example, in part legitimates its policies by claiming that they promote local values. U.S. courts claim to represent Native American interests while actually disempower-

ing them. In one case described by the author, the Havasupai conceptions of themselves as a community changed as the result of their reply to a Bureau of Reclamation study.

4. *Social-cultural construction and contest.* Concepts of local custom and customary law become redesigned or reinvented (in the current political vernacular) in their interactions with Western law (Cohn, 1989). Decisions about who is the "authentic" voice of a peoples may mask colonial efforts to shift power away from the peoples so represented.

5. *Legal discourses and the power of the frame.* There is power in legal categorization. One has only to imagine being place on a list of communists during the McCarthy era to comprehend this. The social constructionist position asks "how the assumptions underlying the very system of classification itself matter—how they fit with or do violence to social systems and expectations . . ." One of the compelling identities of the current era is that of "victim." In man courts, being officially recognized as a victim places an individual in a legally advantageous position with regard to a felon—for example, speaking during trial, or at a parole request.

The sociology of law approach hence is one that opens the door for an understanding of the law and its behavior through social-science methodologies. The sociology of law is rich in deterministic perspective. However, like other areas of contemporary sociology, it increasingly recognizes the unique and unpredictable in human interaction. And it brings to bear on the analysis of the law the same tools that social sciences being to bear on other areas of discourse.

Many social scientists have resisted the cold logic of free will and its responsibility-based ideology. It seems to lack humanity—it rejects the idea that the difficult world circumstances we confront have a profound effect on us, and can shape our likelihood to commit crime and violence. Yet we must recognize that the stony justice of personal responsibility is bound to the same history that produced the idea that the individual can have a personal destiny, that we can seek our own fate unfettered by the institutions of the past. Free-will ideology, like the belief that our behavior is determined by broad forces around us, are hopelessly and forever linked. Our search for justice requires that, in spite all their conflicts, we recognize that they each define and mobilize a commitment to justice, and that each contributes to our efforts to seek a world more just than the one we encounter.

Humanities

As a form of knowledge, the humanities are fundamentally different from the social sciences. Comprised of the fine arts, literature, philosophy and ethics, languages, and history, the humanities study the unique and particular. Consider Beethoven's Fifth Symphony. It captures the imagination because of its powerful vigor, not because it enhances our ability to predict what other pieces of classical music sound like. We like it for what sets it apart from other music, not for what makes it similar.

The field of justice studies, Halstead (1985) suggested, would benefit from a wider exposure to the humanities. He argued that justice studies were over focused on the statistical analysis of data, and that important considerations of human values were excluded.

> A criminal justice pedagogical perspective which is limited to the statistics analysis of data leaves little room for human values. An exclusively empirical approach at any subject gives us knowledge only on what a subject is, and that only as structured or limited by preconceived categorization. Statistics, surveys, and data analysis fail to inform us about its values or what direction the study of the subject should take and why (Halstead, 1985:151).

Justice research, Halstead contended, was overwhelmingly empirical. This is evidenced in several ways. First, justice studies faculty take an empirical approach for the presentation of information about their field. Second, most were educated to take a statistical view of their field. Third, scholarship produced by criminal justice faculty was overwhelmingly empirical. The problem with such an empirical approach was in its pretensions to be value-free. This was simply inaccurate. To the contrary, it represented a value hegemony: the focus of the study of the justice field is on observable, recordable behavior.

Fourth, values, not rationality, may be the correct way to think about the practice of criminal justice. The professional field of criminal justice embodies value-based decisionmaking in every aspect of its activity (see Crank & Caldero, 2000). Judges do not dispassionately deliver sentences, but frequently deliver stern lectures on the immorality of defendant's behavior.

Fifth, a value commitment may account for the early decisions of criminal justice workers to become involved in the field—they are committed to "doing something for society." Justice education should explicitly recognize the value-basis of the field. Sixth, justice work is embedded in a complex and value-laden environment. Education should prepare future professionals for the kinds of moral and ethical decisions they will routinely make in the practice of their work.

What does a humanistic perspective have to offer the justice enterprise? Halstead argues that a study of the humanities provides breadth of perspective:

> Unlike the perspectives of the social sciences, the point of view of a humanistic historical consciousness develops the capacity for intense self-consciousness; that is, the ability of a man (sic) to see himself as subject and object at the same time. By developing a new humanistic historical perspective of criminal jurisprudence, the criminal justice educator may discern a way to initiate a *dynamic* approach toward the subject (Halstead, 1985:161).

A humanistic perspective can be incorporated into existing curricula by expanding the scope of readings required for classes. Also, classes that represent the application of the humanities to the field might be developed. These include classes on ethics, languages, history, religion, ethnology, literature, and philology. By expanding the field of justice studies in such a direction, Halstead suggested, the study of justice would mature as an academic field.

Over the 15 years since Halstead's paper was published, one can see various ways in which humanities has been integrated into the justice curricula. The instruction of ethics has become important in many curricula at both the graduate and undergraduate level. The role of women as justice practitioners and as recipients of crime control practices is increasingly recognized as an informed area of justice pedagogy. The importance of historical perspective is increasingly recognized. Many scholars are interested in ethnographic methods, endeavoring to ascertain the underlying values of the situations they study. And post-modern researchers are trying to comprehend the underlying emotional and symbolic dynamics of justice practices and research alike.

Yet, in spite of the expansion of humanities interests, it is unclear that any humanities are being mainstreamed into core curricula at any level. Consider history and criminal justice. It is increasingly common for introductory textbooks in criminal justice to include elements of criminal justice history, both nationally and internationally. Yet, classes devoted specifically to historical perspective are infrequently encountered in justice curricula, a phenomena Conley (1993) refers to as the "benign neglect of history." In gender studies, Renzetti (1993) argues forcefully that feminist analyses are not achieving mainstream recognition in spite of theoretical and pedagogical advances. Language instruction continues to be viewed as a general educational requirement but is not emphasized in many departments, in spite of the significant and growing needs of many justice agencies for foreign language speakers. The trend toward ethics training in the justice field is reflected in justice curricula, and many departments offer ethics classes. But these classes are not part of the core, and typically are taught by instructors who have a special interest in ethics.

In sum, broad institutional pressures to expand justice studies into the humanities have resulted in the expansion of curricula devoted to these topics, but individual classes are marginalized rather than systematically integrated into core requirements beyond textbooks at the introductory level. The core curricula continues to be defined by the central values associated with social science. As Halstead observed in the mid 1980s, criminal justice continues to be interdisciplinary, but only limitedly so: it is interdisciplinary within the fields of the social and applied sciences, with their emphasis on empirical method.

A recognition that the humanities are important to the further maturity of the justice fields does not mean that we will find clear answers to compelling justice dilemmas therein. An assessment of issues facing the humanities today are remarkably similar to those discussed previously regarding the social sciences. MacIntyre (1990:7-8) noted four problems facing the humanities:

1.   There is a remarkably high level of skill in handling narrow questions of limited detail.

2.   A large number of incompatible doctrines comprise the major standpoints of the discipline. Each has its professional area of skill and each has bases that are often communicated by "indirection and implication."

3.   All debate is inconclusive.

4.   In spite of these divisions, we act as if the university acted as a single, "tolerably unified intellectual community."

MacIntyre's observations are revealing, both for their similarity to problems in intellectual development in the social sciences, and for their cautionary implications for the field of justice studies. We can acquire much from the humanities that will add to our breadth of knowledge. We will not, however, find answers to the intellectual dilemmas that divide us—field fragmentation, value disagreements, and proliferation of standpoints. MacIntyre's consideration of the humanities suggests that similar dissensus over core issues exists in that realm of scholarship. Yet it is these frictions, these fundamental disagreements, that encourage the continued development of thought. That justice studies might encounter conflicts through the study of history, political and moral philosophy, or linguistic theory, deepens our penetration into the diverse forms that justice can take. In this regard, conflict among competing standpoints is a necessary precondition to field growth and breadth.

History

Among the departments commonly labeled as a social science, history alone claims kinship to the humanities. In this section, I argue that it has much to contribute to the study of justice.

When justicians think about history, they tend to think of introductory, opening statements in articles or books. Students, and many faculty for that matter, are only interested in current issues and want to know what works and what doesn't. History only indirectly addresses these questions, and so is often relegated to a support role. As recently as 1991, only 50 of the 1000 or more academic programs in the United States offered a course in History (Nemeth, 1991).

According to Conley, history differs from the social sciences in two key dimensions, substantive and methodological (Conley, 1993:350-351). Substantively, history focuses on the finite and the particular. Unlike social sciences, its identity is not based on the identification of regularities in human behavior. It is a celebration of the unique and the search for detail. For many historians, their field is not about a search for underlying principles of truth, but focuses on that which is contingent and interpretive in the human past.

What Is History? When students think of history, they tend to imagine a sterile retelling of some period in the past. If it only were so simple, history would be a straightforward storytelling endeavor, a photograph of the past in words. Yet, when the field of history is considered, one encounters all the issues that affect the social sciences throughout its history.

Consider the issue of objectivity. One imagines that history is simply a retelling of succinct elements of the past. Yet the history of history tells a different story. The development of the field prior to the 1960s carried values of scientific neutrality, progress, and objectivity similar to the other social and physical sciences. It carried all the ideological baggage associated with the Enlightenment. This baggage can be described as:

1. The Enlightenment faith in the heroic model of science, in which historians imagined themselves to be neutral investigators of the past.

2. The belief in progress, according to which historians framed historical periods in terms of development and sequential stages.

3. Behind events was an orderly process of change. Improvement was steady and progressive (Appleby, Hunt & Jacob, 1994:241).

As long as these notions existed in harmony, history could be imagined to be a phenomenon independent of individuals, a slate upon which humankind wrote their legacy. This changed in the 1960s. Increasingly, when confronted with history, researchers asked "Whose history?" This transition mirrors issues faced by all the social sciences since World War II. The objective idea of history is under full assault by postmodern skeptics of historical analysis:

> Dorothy's dog Toto exposes the Wizard of Oz as an ordinary middle-aged man; similarly, the skeptics believe, they have revealed historians to be no more than specialized storytellers whose claims to recover the past as it actually happened belong to the smoke screen of scientific pretensions. Historians, as Hayden White has maintained, 'do not build up knowledge that others might use, they generate a discourse about the past' (Appleby, Hunt & Jacob, 1994:244-245).

Nor can the argument concerning subjectivity easily be discounted. Histories begin with the curiosity of an individual, and they are written under the influence of that person's particular cultural or personal predispositions. All knowledge, as Appleby et al. (1994:255) observe, is "subject centered and artificial." What this means is that "knowledge seeking involves a lively, contentious struggle among diverse groups of truth seekers." In other words, the study of history can be described with the same intensity and dynamics that this book describes as central to the field of justice studies.

This is not to say that history is wholly relative, that there is no "there there." The study of history parallels the study of culture. One begins with a body of information and decides to what detail one wants to focus. Readers of Morn's (1995) history of the Academy of Criminal Justice Sciences will note that trends are extracted from masses of records, and the subjective interest and training of the historian provide the critical glue to give those records narrative meaning. One must recognize that at some point history is simply a selective extraction of the stories of all humankind. Qualified objectivity might be resurrected by historians, but as Applegate et al. note, it must take into account the inescapable elements of subjectivity, artificiality, and language dependence.

History and Justice Studies. Criminal justicians often find historical scholarship to be of little use in addressing policy needs (Conley, 1993). With its focus on the unique, it is difficult for policymakers to comprehend how history can assist in the formulation of policy. Justice studies, emerging in the 1960s as a policy-oriented science, has sought the general principles and rules underlying behavior on which policy can be constructed.

Current Ph.D. training, Conley argues, does not teach students how to "find the intersection between history, biography, and social structure" (Conley, 1993:351). Consequently, the opportunity to develop broader perspective on the historical context and behavior of American criminal justice is impeded. The diverse methodology available for students of history provide many skills that can inform the justice enterprise.

A re-thinking and expansion of historical perspective into justice studies is needed. Conley suggested that current policy and practices are linked to the past through a process of dynamic evolution, and justicians could benefit by studying that process. He described the process as follows:

> In a broader sense, history provides a baseline from which to compare and contrast reform initiatives with reforms attempted in the past. Historians have documented what happened, how reforms materialized, what social forces shaped those reforms, which political and social values were expressed, and what choices resulted in the process of change. In their study of the impact of reforms, historians analyze the results and explain the reasons for success or failure. History, as a field of intellectual inquiry, depends on its ability to make connections between similar topics across time and place; to compare, contrast, and determine relationships (Conley, 1993:353).

And, as Conley noted elsewhere,

> Although historians may not wish to claim a policy-oriented focus for their research, social scientists and policy-makers can use historical research to inform their policy recommendations . . . As Michael Hindus reminds us, "When the major policy alternatives in the criminal justice arena are distilled down to the essentials, almost everything has been tried before (Hindus, 1979:220, in Conley, 1993:352).

Historical research can provide a larger contribution than as an adjunct to policy and technical research. Historical study contextualizes justice processes, embedding them in social, institutional, and cultural contexts, and locating them in conjunction with singular events and great women and men. Justice institutions, processes, and policies are dependent variables, explained by their various contexts. Historical perspective is thus fundamentally different from policy-based studies, which treat policy as independent of and causally prior to crime. The study of history can be thought of as a counterweight to our tendency to treat current problems as unique and special simply because they are compelling. Historical perspective resists the cramped vision that often accompanies a narrow policy orientation. By studying the historical evolution of social structures and policies, human history in all its breadth and creativity becomes the tableau on which we search for justice.

Justice and the Sanitization of History. The field of criminal justice is in part normative: its assessment of crime and criminality mirrors society's image of wrongdoers. The practice of justice is profoundly moral, and research measures that morality for purposes of expanding it or contracting it, whether or not researchers believe in the objectivity of their work. That is, researchers assess the effects of punishments (or rehabilitations) that have predictable effects on offenders, and hence can provide the stuff of policy.

Researchers are no less moral than the justice system they study, though they may not be moral in the same way. Some researchers are interested in the field of justice studies because of their commitments to the practice of justice in the United States today, just as others are resolutely focused on what they perceive to be the shortcomings, weaknesses, or unfairness of the U.S. criminal justice system. Too often, researchers end up looking for policies that justify their particular morality. And they tend to self-select those aspects of history that justify their moral outlook and that discounts other interpretations. That is, they tend to sanitize history.

What does *sanitize* history mean? It means that we tend to over-emphasize historical elements that justify our view about how things work and ignore or under-emphasize historical data with which we disagree. The tendency to sanitize is a corollary of the power of our morality—the stronger our views, the easier it is for us to accept evidence in favor of our views and discount the remainder. History, however, is seldom reducible to simple morality plays, and the issue of historical "sanitization" is complex.

The exchange between Kelling and Moore (1988) and Williams and Murphy (1990) provides a case in point (Conley, 1993:353). Kelling and Moore (1988) presented an evolutionary model of the history of policing in the United States, according to which three historical stages (the political, reform, and community problem-solving eras) were compared in terms of seven characteristics (legitimacy, function, organizational design, police role, relationship to environment, demand management, tactics and technology, and outcome). Using this model, they provided a conceptual model of changes that have occurred to the police in different historical epochs. Their historical analysis was informative and contextual, allowing the reader to think about how the environments of police departments have changed over time and how those changes affected the work carried out by the police.

Williams and Murphy (1990) responded with a different view of United States police history. Referring to their perspective as a minority viewpoint, Williams and Murphy described the important role that minority groups, particularly African-Americans, have played in the development of police history. They discuss how police in the United States evolved from slave patrols in the South. They also observe that the "reform" era had virtually no impact on minority citizens. And they note that a central tenet of community policing, that there are such a thing as cohesive communities, overlooks the central problem of economic and social disintegration in many urban minority communities.

Williams and Murphy's (1990) paper brings into the foreground several important issues. First, a reader might ask "Which one is the right interpretation of history?" The answer is that both expand our knowledge about the genesis of United States policing. Neither is more right than the other. Both papers further the justice imagination, each in their own way.

The second and more complicated issue is moral. If policing is a good thing, and it evolved from slavery—a bad thing—we are left with the uncomfortable conclusion that a good is produced by a bad. This conclusion is troubling for those who want human history to be wrapped in tidy ribbons of morality. Herein lies one of the strengths of historical perspective—it will challenge a researcher's most valued beliefs.

Third, the exchange in these two papers provides an important counterpart to the idea that we tend to sanitize history. The counterpart is that history is an inexact, interpretive field of study. As a field of investigation, history does not hold many iron-clad truths, and one person's sanitization may be another's astuteness. History is a field that yields abundant meaning and a great deal of insight into what it means to be human. But any historical interpretation selectively highlights and shades, silhouetting particular events or individuals and leaving the remainder in the background. The insight that can be gained from history is as broad as the sum of human experience—if one has patience and knows where to look.

In this section I have assessed only a small part of the humanities. Literature, philosophy, and language are other disciplines within the humanities with potential to contribute to the justice field. That these areas contribute to higher education is recognized by their common inclusion into university core requirements.

Anthropology

The field of anthropology is surprisingly central to justice studies, though its contributions are generally unrecognized. I will highlight some of those contributions here.

Qualitative methods, discussed in Chapter 5, are central to anthropological research. Many of the skills that constitute qualitative methods have a long history in anthropological investigation. Qualitative methods are fundamentally different from the more commonly used quantitative skills typically required for advanced education in justice studies. Of more recent vintage, though related to anthropological methods, are the ethnomethodological methods derived from sociology in the 1960s. I am saving a chapter to discuss the differences between quantitative and qualitative methods, and so will not belabor them here. It is important here only to give anthropology its due.

Some of the symbolic currency widely used in justice studies research also derives from anthropology. The concept "culture" is one such term. The term culture carries a great deal of intellectual freight. Culture, broadly conceived, contains the symbolic and behavioral content of a society. It is a grand concept, capturing the spirit and substance of entire societies.

In criminal justice, the use of the term "culture" tends to be limited and incorrect. It is common to read about the culture of the police, for example, as is it were some dark force that can be corrected with adequate oversight. Some empirical researchers attempt to assess the presence of culture with narrow attitudinal surveys that contrast gender or ethnicity. Compare these narrow notions of culture above to the following quote from Swidler (1986):

> Since the seminal work of Clifford Geertz (1973a) the older notion of culture as the entire life of a people, including their technology and material artifacts, or that . . .as everything that one would need to know to become a functioning member of society, have been displaced in favor of defining culture as the publicly available symbolic forms through which people experience and express meaning . . . culture consists of such symbolic vehicles of meaning, including beliefs, ritual practices, art forms, and ceremonies, as well as informal cultural practices such as language, gossip, stories, and rituals of daily life (Swidler, 1986:273).

The breadth of this concept of culture is breath-taking. Culture represents the integral way in which we organize our thoughts, how we think about how other people think about us, the way in which we interpret and assign value to the clutter that presents itself as the outside world. Consider another definition of culture:

> . . . every experience takes place within a vast background of cultural presuppositions. It can be misleading, therefore, to speak of direct physical experience as though there were some sort of immediate experience which we then "interpret' in terms of our conceptual system. Cultural assumptions, values, and attitudes are not a cultural overlay which we may or may not place upon experience as we choose. It would be more correct so say that all experience is cultural through and through, that we experience our "world" in such a way that our culture is already present in the very experience itself (Lakoff & Johnson, 1980:57).

Let us think about the implications of this definition of culture for the relationship between a person's values and their behavior. We in justice studies often bring a very common-sensical idea to the value-behavior linkage.[3] We tend to believe that if we can change a person's values, they will act appropriately. This places value causally ahead of behavior, and is a way of thinking about organizational change that undergirds much criminal justice reform. Yet, the definitions of culture presented above would immediately dispose of that idea. First, it would suggest that acts as well as beliefs are learned behavior, a part of our repertoire of cultural experience. Moreover, their beliefs may have arisen from acting correctly, a notion that reverses the value-behavior causal direction.

Secondly, challenging someone's attitudes will invoke a culturally rich response, a response that marshals the fundamental way they comprehend and interact with the world. Attitudinal change is different from getting someone to "recognize the truth." Attitudes and behavior may be related in a feedback loop, according to which a persons behavior creates circumstances that reaffirm their values (Crank, 1998). Hence, a person's values already mirror social "reality," though it is a reality of that person's own creation, and are not amenable to attitudinal reformation.

Third, the idea that beliefs cause acts may itself be a cultural predisposition—and one quite difficult to break, as of course cultural predispositions are. The idea of free will is that our actions flow from our decisions, freely made. However, if our actions are free will, then they shouldn't be affected by values, only by cold logic. How can we change someone's values if they are selfishly motivated by free will?

Another term often used in justice studies research is "ritual." Rituals are similarly an area of long and colorful investigation in anthropology. It is a term that we in justice studies tend to use in a superficial way, looking at formal ceremonies carried out by organizations in the conduct of their activities. What we have not explored are the implication of rituals and ceremonies for organizational heath and well being, nor do we look at how we use rituals to reinforce our sense of social or organizational identity. Two exceptions to this are Manning's (1997) study of police funerals, and VanMaanen's (1978) assessment of police training.

What can we obtain with a study of rituals? Trice and Beyer (1984) argue that rituals carry both manifest and latent consequences.[4] Consider the ceremony of a trial. The manifest consequences are as follows; In an adversarial contest, the state attempts to demonstrate the guilt of a citizen accused of a crime. Representatives of the state exchange information in a structured proceeding with representatives for the citizen, and the outcome will produce a fair evaluation of the suspect's guilt or innocence.

The latent consequences are central to understanding its dynamics. In the ceremony of a trial, the state affirms to the public that it is determined to punish the person brought before it. The state's commitment to its citizenry is reaffirmed by the state's effort to punish the presumed wrongdoer. If the state is successful, the defendant's status is publicly degraded. We bear witness to the spectacle of the judge upbraiding the defendant at the time of sentencing. One can watch the defendant, wearing an orange jumpsuit, led off with head bowed to an unknown, dark destiny. As citizens, our moral rightness for going along with the rules of the state is affirmed. In a supreme act of ceremonial power, the physical body of the defendant is relinquished to the state.

Bell (1992) recognizes the importance of power to the enactment of ritual activity. Rituals invest symbols with meaning, and they act out patterns of subordination and superordination. They thus reinforce patterns of social solidarity. Once we recognize this aspect of the ritual process, we recognize that judges can never be dispassionate. Central to their role is the investment of the symbols of state power with emotion. A good judge will emotionally saturate the courthouse with the righteousness of the state, and the body of the defendant will be formally seized. The trial is, using Bells kind of analysis, a ritual with clear protocols that acts out and asserts the power of the superordinate in a charged, emotional context. It is not much different in principle from many rituals in so-called primitive societies, only more familiar to us.

The potential contributions of anthropology to justice studies are many. It informs our methodology, providing a way of thinking about the practice of justice in an everyday context. It enriches our conceptual language. It provides theoretical interpretation for some of the symbolic language used in justice studies and practice. In sum, it is a much needed corrective for a tendency to overestimate the rationality and "rightness" of the U.S. criminal justice system. Anthropology, by illuminating the diversity of the human experience, informs us of the breadth justice can achieve. Anthropology can add breadth of perspective to a great deal of contemporary curricular offerings in justice studies.

The Interplay of the Fields: Wallerstein and the Development of the Social Sciences

In this section I develop and expand on ideas of the social sciences described by the Gulbenkian Commission (Wallerstein et al., 1996). Most of the models described above are grounded in social science traditions. Their roots "lie in the attempt, full-blown since the sixteenth century, and part and parcel of our modern world, to develop systematic, secular knowledge about reality that is somehow validated empirically" (Wallerstein et al., 1996:2).[5] In this section, we will look at the relationship of the social science models to each other and to the humanities, keeping an eye to what they tell us about the justice enterprise.

The question addressed in this section is: How can we think systematically about these fields that helps us locate the identity of justice studies? I will use the Gulbenkian Commission's distinction between idiographic and nomothetic sciences to distinguish among the various social sciences, and consider their recommendations in an effort to look at the "fit" of justice studies into their schemata.

A Model of the Fields. The different academic fields can be described according to where they are located on an idiographic-nomothetic continuum. Idiographic sciences yield propositions about knowledge that are limited to a contiguous space-time region, for example, a particular episode (time) is located in a nation-state's bounded geography (space) (Galtung, 1967). These sciences do not construct broad rules or seek regularities that apply across space and time. They are singularizing sciences, interested in the specific case, not the general principle. They look at the unique characteristics that describe times and places. If one considers the French Revolution in terms of the unique historical dynamics that propelled it, he or she would be thinking idiographically. Similarly, in the field of justice studies, if one views the practices of the courts as if they were the product of a particular kind of government and its legal system at a particular (historical) time, one is approaching the study of justice studies idiographically. This is idiographic because it develops perspectives for particular episodes and events bounded to each other graphically that explain what happened at some (historical) time. The humanities are idiographic. Among the social sciences, history alone is considered an idiographic science. The qualitative methods widely used in anthropology are also idiographic, and will be discussed at length in Chapter 3.

Nomothetic sciences are generalizing sciences. The propositions developed in generalizing sciences are abstract and theoretical, and the phenomena studied can (hypothetically) be found over a wide range of space-time regions. Put differently, nomothetic propositions are not limited in space or time. For example, a theory is nomothetic if it explains the way economic relations affect the distribution of power in different countries and in different historical epochs. To extend the "courts" example, if one studies the courts in order to find patterns that existed cross-culturally, one is studying them nomothetically. To the extent that the social sciences study regularities of social phenomenon, they are nomothetic.

The distinction between nomothetic and idiographic sciences is not sharp. Instead:

> they represent two different foci: the detailed, realistic, concrete description and explanation of something meaningfully interrelated [idiographic]; and the testing of general, less realistic, more abstract propositions about something scattered and not in the same sense interrelated by the unity of time, space, and action, like classical drama (Galtung, 1967:23).

The difference between nomothetic and idiographic sciences is freighted with historical significance. The emergence of nomothetic sciences is one of the more revolutionary outcomes of the Enlightenment. The idea that a physical or social science can search for "true" principles or broad regularities of human behavior is an outcome of historical conflict in which an area of study was wrested from the domain of church and state and subjected to secular study.

The physical sciences are the most nomothetic of the sciences, and carry in their heritage often-told stories of Enlightenment conflicts—for example, the ex-communication of Galileo from the Catholic church for suggesting that the Earth revolved around the Sun. The sciences represented the "disenchantment" of the world, defined as the search for an objective knowledge unconstrained by revealed and/or accepted wisdom or religious tradition (Wallerstein et al., 1996). This included religious knowledge.

The social sciences were heirs to the same secular "truth-seeking" vision of knowledge as the physical sciences. They were married to a belief that underlying rules of human behavior could be identified through empirical methods. Hence, from its Enlightenment beginnings, the social science endeavor has been committed to a nomothetic vision: the identification of rule-like behavioral regularities from observable phenomena.

> The creation of the multiple disciplines of the social sciences was part of the general nineteenth-century attempt to secure and advance "objective" knowledge about "reality" on the basis of empirical findings (as opposed to "speculation"). The intent was to "learn" the truth, not invent or intuit it (Wallerstein et al., 1996:13).

The idiographic humanities, represented by philosophy and literature, are at the other end of the spectrum. They represent an older tradition in which the universities, were responsible for the transmission of religious knowledge and the arts. The law, also idiographic, is similarly traced to an older, common-law tradition. All three fields trace their roots to the middle ages.

Each of the fields of knowledge presented in this chapter can be characterized according to its location on the nomothetic-idiographic continuum. The continuum is presented in Figure 2.2. I have followed Wallerstein et al.'s (1996) recommendations regarding the nomothetic-idiographic orientations of the disciplines to locate them on this continuum. Figure 2.2 locates the fields on a continuum.

Type I: Nomothetic Fields. Two social science fields that are substantially nomothetic, economics and demography, are presented as type I fields. Economics was not discussed in this chapter, though an economic calculus is increasingly used in criminal justice. Risk analysis, a form of economic analysis widely used by insurance companies, has been used to describe the likelihood of criminal behavior, though this brand of research is highly controversial. Demographic factors are often incorporated into aggregate explanations of criminal behavior, and are frequently used to describe area-level inequalities. Both of these fields bring principles of generalizing theory to bear on the study of crime and justice.

Figure 2.2
Continuum of Fields of Knowledge

Nomothetic fields of knowledge inquiry
(Physical sciences: Mathematics, Biology)
   Social Sciences

         Type I: Nomothetic
                 Economics
                 Demography

         Type II: Nomothetic with idiographic components.
                 Sociology
                 Anthropology
                 Political Science
                 Criminology

         Type III: Idiographic with nomothetic components
                 Public Administration
                 Criminal Justice

         Type IV: Idiographic
                 Law
                 History
                 Anthropological methods

Idiographic fields of knowledge inquiry
(Humanities: Art, Languages)

Type II: Nomothetic Fields with Idiographic Elements. Most of
the social science fields are located here. These models are historically
nomothetic. However, the nomothetic hegemony in the field has been
replaced in recent years by several trends: the encroachment of qualitative methods, a recognition that traditional fields were ethnocentric and
biased by race and gender, and the growing realization that many real
world processes are not time reversible—their causality simply cannot be
reproduced by the application of causal models.

    Criminology carries a mix of elements, some of which seem to fall
solidly into a purely nomothetic field of inquiry, and others which are
more like idiographic research. It has a strong sociological tradition. It is
a field that has emerged after the 1960s, and incorporates many ideo-
graphic elements into a study that tends toward the nomothetic end of
the spectrum

Type III: Idiographic Fields with Nomothetic Elements. Two
fields are presented—public administration and criminal justice. Both
fields are historically normative—they have approached the existing
structure of government as a given rather than as a problematic to be
explained. This stems from the practical orientation of both fields. They

tend to be oriented toward the preparation of students for entry-level career-work or for mid-career educational enhancement, and so provide instruction on topics that will assist in practical endeavors. Curricula tend to be organized around functional divisions of government or of criminal justice. They take the current structure of government and the values that justify it for granted and where possible they provide training in organizational, criminological, and policy theory to make students more effective.

Recent trends in criminal justice reveal idiographic elements. They are not summarized here because they form much of the substance of this book. The field has expanded beyond its normative basis, and today witnesses a diversity of theoretical foci and research modes.

Type IV: Idiographic Fields. These are the humanities and the law. The law is presented as an idiographic field because, in practice and instruction, the law applies very specifically to the United States in the current era. Within the United States it undergoes substantial regional and local variation. It undergoes constant change under the common-law principle of precedent, and the law in 10 years may be sharply different than the law today.

The humanities represent a second field of inquiry for studying the potential for the justice enterprise. The behavioral ardor that characterizes the justice field has sometimes blinded it to the singularizing and interpretive humanities. Yet, the justice enterprise is about a sense of commitment and fulfillment, and profoundly tied to our sense of inspiration and value. An old tin-type of a lynching, for example, can convey information about racism that can never be obtained by an attitudinal survey.

Anthropological methods are not a "field" per se, but represent an orientation to research methodology. It is distinguished from, yet closely tied to, anthropological theory. This might seem to be an odd distinction, yet it reveals important dimensions in the maturation of the field of anthropology. Anthropological theory has contributed the notion of culture and has developed such theoretical ideas such as ceremony and ritual. Anthropological methods, on the other hand, have provided a methodology for studying the behavior of groups—ethnography—and learning about the particular structures, dynamics, and meanings that uniquely identify those groups.

The nomothetic-idiographic location of different fields is imperfect. If any field is examined closely, exceptions can be identified. For example, I have located history as an idiographic field. Yet, the works of such great historians as Toynbee's *A Study of History* (1934-1954) and Spengler's *Decline of the West* (1926) represent efforts to unite historical periods under a common theoretical umbrella. The Anthropologist Harris's *Cannibals and Kings* (1991) is clearly nomothetic, setting forth a general theory of culture based on the relationship between population pressure and resource availability. And the psychologist Shweder's *Thinking Through Cultures* (1991) is sharply idiographic, barely retaining the modern notion of "individual."

The previous discussion is a work in broad brush strokes, permitting the development of perspective rather than a critical examination of individual fields. It masks much hidden complexity within each field. To understand the social sciences today and the issues that affect them, a more nuanced assessment of this "hidden complexity" is needed, In the following section, I will explore the hidden complexity in the social sciences in the current era.

Toward Diversification. After 1945, the social science fields began a process of dramatic and long-term diversification. This trend was toward the adoption of perspectives and methods that disrupted the traditional identities of social science fields. History, which among the social sciences was traditionally committed to a idiographic orientation, began to accommodate perspectives that assessed patterns across the broad sweep of history. The other social sciences incorporated idiographic elements. These trends toward idiography were initiated by developments after World War II, particularly the increasing recognition that non-Western societies could not be adequately understood using general theories of development or western ideas of "progress" (Wallerstein et al., 1996:45).

The trend toward diversification accelerated in the 1960s. Wallerstein identified three organizing concepts—scientific uncertainty, cultural relativism, and distrust of technology—that marked the expansion of perspectives in the social sciences.

1. *Scientific uncertainty*. The Newtonian assumptions of the natural sciences began to break down. A recognition in the natural sciences that nature was "active and creative," and that scientific observers themselves affected the behavior of natural events, made it easier for social scientists to examine their own nomothetic assumptions. Complex systems analysis demonstrated that many systems were not time-reversible, which meant that it was insufficient to "know the 'law' and the initial conditions in order to predict future states" (Wallerstein et al., 1996:62).

2. *Cultural relativism*. The study of culture exploded across the social sciences. Cultural awareness was characterized by three elements: the development of non-Eurocentric studies such as Womens Studies, a recognition of the explanatory importance of highly situated historically analysis, and an appraisal of the values of technological achievement in comparison to other values.

3. *Technological distrust*. The values of technological development increasingly were received with skepticism. Hermeneutic and postmodern approaches to inquiry sharply challenged the values associated with technology. Though sometimes accused as anti-theoretical, these challenges represented a powerful backlash against the oversold idea that social sciences could or should mimic the search for regularity that characterized the physical sciences.

The social sciences began to shed their image as purely behavioral sciences. Giddens' (1994) resolution of the problem of agency, by contextualizing human agency in time and place, is an example of this transition. In political science, idiographic trends were encapsulated under the organizing term 'interpretivism,' meaning that "researchers should interpret each political event and idea more or less in itself, seeking to retain the richness of its detail while making a general patterned interpretation of what process unfolded through the events" (Shively, 1997:14). Shweder's (1991) explorations of the cultural limits of psychological theory and methods show a concern that seeming regularities are methods artifacts, and that psychological traits are bounded by their cultural settings. In anthropology, Geertz (1973b:41) offered that "generalizations (about the nature of peoples) are not to be uncovered through a Baconian search for cultural universals, a kind of public-opinion polling of the world's peoples . . ." In the field of criminology, DiCristina, in a short methods treatise (1995), argued for an end to the hegemony of "scientific" criminology in favor of an expansion across the diversity of available methods. These are but a few of many examples. Their common thread is the increasing contribution of idiographic ideas to the traditional social sciences.

The Re-Enchantment of the Social Sciences. The nomothetic/idiographic mix of perspectives is changing the social sciences. The term "re-enchantment" captures the breadth of this change (see, e.g., Shweder, 1991). Wallerstein and his colleagues (1996:81) describe re-enchantment as a "call to break down the artificial boundaries between humans and nature, to recognize that they both form part of the same universe framed by the arrow of time."

Re-enchantment is a sweeping term, carrying in it a fundamental rethinking of the what has been called the disenchantment of the universe, the principle goal of Enlightenment philosophes. The ideal of the "neutral scientist" freed science from the orthodoxies of church and state in the Enlightenment. Yet in the social sciences it promised the impossible: that a researcher could assess the world around him or her without value commitments, objectively, and detached from the objects of study.

By re-enchantment is not meant an abandonment of the notion of empirical analysis, but a recognition that humans are not neutral actors in the process of scientific discovery and analysis. Re-enchantment carries with it a rejection of the idea that we can acquire objective knowledge and conduct value-free research. As Abu-Lughod (1989:vii) observed, knowledge in the social sciences is "produced through collective definition, that is, it represents a transient human 'consensus about the world' . . ." Re-enchantment means that we, as social scientists, are discovering that we don't know and cannot identify objective, "hard scientific" rules that govern human conduct. The rules are whatever we want them to be.

Re-enchantment is closely tied to uncertainty. Uncertainty takes many forms. For one, social scientists are encountering more uncertainty and unpredictability in human behavior than has been traditionally recognized. The best of the empirical models in the social sciences explain a proportionally low percent of observed variability of events they seek to explain. Proponents of data analysis often argue that we have simply failed to account for all the variables that affect system outcomes. Yet, it may be that systems are to a certain extent non-determinative. Simply put, humans may not be very predictable.

A second aspect of uncertainty, and a fundamental challenge to ideas of predictability, is the idea that systems of human interaction are not time reversible. This means that, as Gould (1989) noted with regard to the evolution of species and Abu-Lughod (1989) observed with regard to the emergence of the European-centered world system in the late 1300s, if we were to rewind the historical clock and replay it, things would probably work out in a completely different way. For the field of justice studies, this means that even if we developed a perfectly predictable model for explaining the behavior of criminal justice systems at some point in time, we might acquire no useful knowledge of future or of different criminal justice systems.

Third, social scientists are only beginning to recognize the full implications of the European hegemony of our ideas. For example, in anthropology, the idea of culturally bounded "tribes" in Africa, a core idea in the evolution of its disciplinary knowledge and integral to the notion of "culture" itself, is now recognized as a flawed notion stemming from the way in which colonialists viewed the landscape of African social geography. This view failed to account for complex and sophisticated relationships between different groups that transcended the political geography imposed by Britain. The idea of peoples confined to geographies may be an illusion of the observer (Appadurai, 1988). Clifford (1992) argues that the appearance of villages created an image "culture," and the one was taken for the other: anthropologists saw villages and created cultures; the static image of enduring, stable "cultures" is a metaphor for villages. This metaphor overlooks critical aspects of inter-village life such as trade, transport and communication. Hence, what Geertz referred to as the "root metaphor of anthropology"—culture—may be founded on a false idea of stability and identity more descriptive of a Western systems of classification than a realistic assessment of actual group and intergroup behavior.[6]

Today, anthropologists are turning the tables on traditional "European" ideas. Rabinow (1996:36) suggested a reversal of traditional anthropological research strategy:

> We need to anthropologise the West: show how exotic its constitution of reality has been; emphasize those domains most taken for granted as universal . . . and show how their claims to truth are linked to social practices and have hence become effective forces in the social world.

We are beginning to find that our most fundamental ideas of process- es carry hidden European biases, biases that can only be identified through the deeper or "thicker" study of more diverse settings. For exam- ple, Abu-Lunghod's research into the development of world-systems described how European ideas of the inevitability and rightness of the Western world system and has obscured our perspectives to instability and transience in international economic and social processes. Today, as we increase our breadth of perspective, we are creating the conditions for Kuhnian revolutions in knowledge (See Kuhn, 1962). In the social sci- ences, we are at such a threshold. Old theories can no longer simply be expanded by adding more variables. And historically taken-for-granted ideas of rationality and objectivity are today controversial. We are under- going "re-enchantment:" a re-thinking, not of our theories, but of the assumptions and root metaphors that are hidden within them.

All of these "change dimensions" contribute to the re-enchantment of the social sciences. They swirl around a core idea—that nomothetic ideas are inherently flawed, and that what regularities may instead be located in the transience of historical time and place (Giddens, 1976, 1994). Re- enchantment conveys the idea that behavior is a creative process, not one regulated by rule-like prescriptions. The future is an unknown, unpre- dictable, and beyond the reach of social science prophecy.

The re-enchantment of the social world challenges traditional ideas of distinctive boundaries between individual social science disciplines. It is no longer accurate to speak of a single way to think about a social science discipline, but instead how disciplines are interpenetrated by many con- flicting perspectives. The theoretical landscape of the modern social sci- ences is increasingly multidisciplinary, a bringing together of individuals from different disciplines to address particular problems. Fragmentation is occurring within disciplines, as their complexity mirrors intricacy in the world they study.

We social scientists are learning that a world of six billion people is an astonishingly complicated place. Simple ways of looking at the world simply don't work. Fragmentation is not haphazard, but is organized around issues in local, regional, and global environments. Multidiscipli- nary groups form to study such diverse and intractable problems as vic- timization, resource decline, terrorism, population growth, and aging. Each field brings a high degree of specialization to the problem, and in concert a broader knowledge about the problem is learned.

Fragmentation is accompanied by intra-disciplinary conflict. The con- flict is disturbing, in the way that a thunderstorm disturbs. Its potential for damage is immense, and it is noisy and blusterous. In its passing the air is freshened, and its rains invigorate the landscape. So, in the social sciences today, brash and surprisingly brutish ideological and ethical conflicts cre- ate a great deal of mischief in many departments and professional soci- eties. But conflict nurtures the social sciences, creating opportunities to think about seemingly unresolvable problems in new ways.

Opening the Social Sciences. The Gulbenkian Commission called for an opening of the social sciences, by which they meant an abandonment of what they viewed as increasingly arbitrary divisions among the diverse disciplines that constitute the social sciences. The disciplines of the social sciences, they recommended, could be integrated through the compulsory hiring of multi-disciplinary faculty, the development of integrated research programs, and the development of university-allied institutions to work on important problems. However, there are several problems with this advocacy.

First, what is meant by the notion that social sciences have arbitrary divisions? If, in fact, the social sciences are increasingly incorporating idiographic elements into their various fields, then opening the social sciences makes no more sense than suggesting that we open the humanities—which makes no sense at all. How does one open a "Beethoven's Fifth Symphony?" The argument that the social sciences are increasingly idiographic, in other words that they are about the study of unique phenomena and the special characteristics of time, space and scope, is better understood as a persuasive argument for encouraging their continued intra-disciplinary development.

Second, the idea of opening the social sciences is a notion similar to the idea that there are a few core concepts common to the social sciences that are obscured by a complex terminology across the fields, and that through mutual understanding we can bridge the social sciences, hack through the maze of terminology, and grasp this "core" set of concepts. However, we have to ask—whose concepts, what "bridge," which core ideas? The centralization of ideas around a few key concepts suggests a common nomothetic development around key terms. Again, one must ask—which way is it? Are the social sciences becoming more idiographic or can they be "opened up" around a simplified set of core ideas? The themes contradict each other.

Third, the idea that the social sciences can be bridged by a few key ideas is an argument against pluralism. Pluralism is more than a determination of what the important concepts in the social sciences are. At the core of pluralism is the idea that the way in which we evaluate the relative importance of concepts is itself up for grabs. As MacIntyre (1988) observed, at the core of the democratic process is the ability to tally and weigh expressions of preferences, and behind this notion is the debate over the rules we use to tally and weigh. How can we select a core set of social science concepts if there is no agreement on even the principles—the weights and balances—we use to determine those concepts? The study of the human "kinds" is enriched through the complex pluralism of the social sciences. Efforts to reduce it to cornerstone terms will only reflect existing power relationships or administrative preferences regarding the structure and behavior of the social sciences.

Fourth, the Gulbenkian Commission's recommendations face countervailing institutional forces within disciplines. Disciplinary professionalization is characteristic of the current age. Participation in prominent professional societies and publication in appropriate and highly esteemed journals are indispensable for faculty who seek national recognition and promotion in most universities. Appropriate scholarship and professional organizational participation are highly institutionalized forms of academic life and will not easily be abandoned. Faculty who seek the security of tenure dare not overlook involvement in the professional and scholarly life of their disciplines.

All these problems with opening the social sciences bear on the field of justice studies. Institutional pressures for identity formation are particularly intense in the current era. The discipline is young in academic terms and seeks academic legitimacy. It is in a period of intense growth in many universities and colleges. To acquire academic legitimacy and reap the spectrum of academic rewards, justice programs and departments must look and act academic. In the current era, processes of identity formation are occurring in the justice fields at precisely the moment that identity fragmentation is occurring across the social sciences. Academically, this means that justice studies programs and departments need not—and probably should not—try to fit itself only into a nomothetic "straightjacket" wholly focused on the identification of broad, rule-like regularities. It should not view itself as only a uniquely defined "behavioral" field, focused exclusively on the identification of uniformities and underlying order.

The justice identity, sheltered for many years under the umbrella of other fields and today emerging as a field of inquiry in its own right, is a fusion, adapted from other fields, just as in the current era other models are increasingly invested in each other around substantive issues. Individually, the disciplines considered in this chapter contribute to the identity of the academic justice enterprise. The core umbrella term that drives our field, justice, is sufficiently complex and multivocal to provide for a pluralism of ideas around which to construct an academic enterprise. In short, the field of justice studies, like other social sciences, is in the current era enriched by both nomothetic and idiographic development.

Garland's (1990) development of penology in two contexts—the sociological context of institutional theory, and the historical context of cumulative detail and historical contingency—is an exemplar of the melding of nomothetic and idiographic components. His research shows how justice studies can prosper by looking at regularities across justice and political systems, by examining the unique characteristics of particular circumstances, and by revising and remaining available to the diversity of ideas and people that contribute to the identification of just (or unjust) processes.

Metaphorically, justice will never be a single voice of "truth" but formed from many, an inheritor of the vitality, methods, and disciplinary knowledge available across the social sciences. That justice has no "true voice" permits us to abandon an expectation—that justice is not simply "out there" in rule like form, as if it were a truth, a "thing" that can be discovered independently of those of us who study and care about it. We act out justice by virtue of our efforts to identify and understand it. We are inseparable from it—its identity is our behavior. Together, the many academic voices provide a broad base for "model borrowing," for an inquiry into justice, so that we can assess how our endeavors fit into the broader justice inquiry, so we can observe, comprehend, and respect the perspectives carried by other justice workers.

Justice studies is emerging as a full-blown area of academic inquiry in the current era of re-enchantment. For those of us who are engaged in the quest for justice, this is a recognition that rule-like principles are a partial and insufficient prescription for justice, and that humans are in a constant process of adaptation and self-creation. The many voices enable us to recognize that justice is an idea always bounded by the vision of the observer and contextualized within time and space.

Notes

[1]   It should be emphasized that this perspective on institutional theory is sharply different than the one I discussed in the previous chapter, which looks at the way in which broad institutionalized values and taken-for-granted assumptions constrain and enable behavior.

[2]   Dawe (1978) provides a lucid discussion of this paradox and its panoply of implications.

[3]   One of the few exceptions to this is the fine body of work on police culture written by Peter Manning, who brings contemporary ideas of symbolic analysis to the study of police behavior (see Manning, 1989; 1987).

[4]   Trice and Beyer focus on rites and ceremonials, which they suggest are more intentional and broader of scope than ceremonies. I think that we are in a grey semantical area. Their typology of cultural characteristics has much to offer, but the elements overlap in a variety of literature sufficiently that what they call rites and ceremonies are what others would consider rituals.

[5]   The humanities, history, and the law extend their roots to pre-enlightenment traditions.

[6]   See Featherstone, 1995:139-145 for a discussion of issues surrounding traditional ideas of culture.

Chapter 3

Justice Identity in Academia

Criminal justice education has sometimes been accused of being little more than a rag-tag of vocational offerings splintered together to create the semblance of academic enterprise. Central to this accusation is the perception that criminal justice education has no identity and lacks college-level rigor. In the past, this accusation has sometimes been accurate. Criminal justice departments expanded dramatically in the 1970s, their spectacular growth masking internal conflicts and undercutting efforts to ensure the academic quality of educational offerings. As Ward and Webb (1984) observed, many university administrators were more interested in the largesse of federal dollars than in the real work needed to establish a university discipline. Even today, many justice studies departments find themselves locked in perpetual combat with administrators for adequate staffing, for whom criminal justice is a cash cow that provides large numbers of student-to-faculty ratios.

In this chapter, I explore the curious history of justice studies and the various and contradictory influences in the development of academic justice identity. Part I focuses on the history of criminal justice education. An institutional perspective is used to identify the broad forces that influence the curriculum and structure of criminal justice programs. Central to this perspective is the idea that criminal justice education has faced two audiences, a local audience of community professionals and a collegial audience comprised of academicians and college administrators. Its academic audience exerts its influence in formal and informal pressures on departments to satisfy formal criteria of educational competence for both faculty and students, and to provide college-level academic rigor for criminal justice classes. Its community audience has historically pushed programs in the direction of agency training, embodied in the Wiltbergerian model of education. The Wiltbergerian model, expedited by the junior college movement in the 1960s, has predominated through much of the history of criminal justice education. With the demise of the LEAA in 1981 and the expansion of post-graduate education, criminal justice departments have had to turn to their academic audiences for legitimacy, forcing a re-thinking of Wiltbergerian ideas of criminal justice education.

In Part II, I attempt to identify the "identity" of criminal justice education. By identity, I mean the focus and breadth of the field in terms of scholarship, service, and curriculum offerings. In it, I argue that etiology of crime (criminology orientation) and policy-based justice (public administration orientation) are inadequate bases for the academic enterprise of criminal justice. This also applies to interdisciplinary ideas of justice, which superficially appear to be consistent with contemporary trends in the social sciences, but which undercut efforts to develop a justice identity and can administratively fragment the field. I conclude that a justice identity, grounded in ideas of service, grounded in liberal arts education, and committed to a broad vision of justice, provides the identity needed to guide the academic development of the field into the twenty-first century.

Part I: A Brief History of Criminal Justice Academics

Historical information is rich and cluttered. The quantity and diversity of influences over any particular event bedevils efforts to organize our history thematically. Particular players are important movers in some periods, and broad uncontrollable changes in the institutional environment of education in others. The historical record of justice practices brims with evidence of unintended consequences, latent effects, and common sense gone awry.

Historical analysis always involves a trade-off. The more textured and "thick" the review of history, the less well it organizes into periods or epochs. Indeed, at some point, history is simply the individual stories of everyone who has lived. On the other hand, the organization of history into stages or epochs is a selective highlighting of particular factors that gives a sensibility and meaning to the past.

Halstead (1985) suggested that the justice enterprise in academia has passed through three stages. The first, technical/vocational, characterized its incipient growth and its junior college setting. Education during this period was strongly vocational. Instructors and students alike were almost exclusively police officers, who were the only ones interested in the class content. The second stage, professional/managerial, also focused on job concerns. However, criminal justice instructors were focused on organizational change rather than a perpetuation of the status quo (see also Sherman et al., 1986). Educators sought to professionalize justice by emphasizing human relations and knowledge about human behavior (see Betz & Marsh, 1974). The third stage was the empirical/behavioral stage. This stage represented the final transition of justice to an academic enterprise legitimated in terms of values of independent scientific inquiry. Typically housed in academic institutions in the disciplines of sociology or political science, the discipline emphasized the social context of crime and the institutions that dealt with crime. The third stage is the dominant perspective of justice curricula today.

Halstead's ideas are consistent with the way most people view the history of justice studies. It is an evolutionary view, describing the movement of justice studies programs through academic stages and arriving at a modern "behavioral" form. It recognizes important historical periods in the development of justice studies.

The social sciences, however, have been moving sharply away from the "behavioral" model and have been doing so since the 1960s. Moreover, the influence of government funding on the development of justice studies should be recognized. A more complex picture of justice history provides insight into its sometimes chaotic development. Of particular interest is the intersection of the junior college movement in the 1960s, its intersection with the Wiltbergerian, vocational model of justice education, and the continued expansion of the community college function into comprehensive four- and six-year (Masters) programs in the current era.

Below, a discussion of Morn's (1995) history provides insight into the development of the Wiltbergerian model. This is followed by a discussion of the great transformation in higher education, which locates the emerging field of justice in broad trends in undergraduate education in the United States. Finally, an institutional perspective is presented to systematically think about the conflicts that have characterized the development of the field of academic criminal justice, and about what is needed to resolve these conflicts.

Morn and the Early History of Criminal Justice Education

Morn (1995) provides a history of justice studies as witnessed through the eyes and written records of its participants. According to Morn, at the beginnings of the twentieth century the term "criminal justice" normally referred to criminal law and court processes. Criminology was an embryonic field that studied the etiology of crime and was eventually housed in sociology departments.

The early development of criminal justice education was closely tied to the progressive movement in the United States at the beginnings of the twentieth century. In many major cities, police agencies prior to the professionalism movement were affiliated with local political machinery, and positions in police departments provided a ready source of job for deserving party members. Police work offered little job security, and employees were likely to be replaced if the political party in power was turned out in the next election. Police officers often supported their political leadership by stuffing ballots, controlling electioneering processes, and generally ensuring the election of their preferred candidate. Among the police, graft and corruption were endemic problems. Graft was widely tolerated as a way to supplement police officer incomes. Indeed, one area in New York City was known as the Gold Coast because it offered the police particularly lucrative sources of graft (Fogelson, 1977).

The progressive movement emerged in the late 1800s as the focal point of resistance to political corruption. Articulating an ethic of efficiency and honesty in governmental activities, progressives sought to reconstruct police organizations to reduce political influence. By separating politics from police organizations, progressives recognized that they could undermine the power of political machinery where it counted the most—by taking away jobs from party locals. The International Association of Chiefs of Police (IACP), founded in 1893, carried the progressive influence into police management. Calling itself the voice of police professionalism, the IACP undertook broad reform of police organizations (Brown, 1981). Among the concerns of its membership was the establishment of police standards and training. By establishing standards, agencies could control personnel practices that had been previously controlled by party faithful. Police training was consistent with the progressive efforts to "clean up" urban politics and provide leadership under the guidance of an expert staff.

The following quote describes the linkage between progressivism and education in Philadelphia in 1911.

> In 1911 a reform mayor, Rudolf Blankenburg, came to power. He appointed George D. Porter director of public safety and James Robinson superintendent of police. This triumvirate set out to remodel the police department along military lines. A patrolman's manual was published and made required reading in the recently established School of Instruction. Four week-long courses were set up for all recruits, and both written and oral examinations were required at the end of the session. In addition, weekly quizzes on the patrolman's manual were conducted at the precinct station houses (Morn, 1995:28).

Though perhaps not much by contemporary Peace Officer Standards and Training, the in-house training regimen was a prototypical model for future efforts to educate the police. Also typical of the era, the training reforms described in the quote above were undone by Chief Smedley Butler in the 1920s, who abolished the School of Instruction in favor of on-the-job learning.

Police education and training were the principle means for the professionalization of the police. The link between education and training can be seen in the history of criminal justice education at San Jose State University. A criminal justice degree was initially provided in an associate of arts program at San Jose Teachers College in 1930, which later changed its name to San Jose State University (Kuykendall, 1977). This program was founded as a two-year program by George Brereton, who was one of August Vollmer's students. Another of Vollmer's students, William Wiltberger, took the leadership of the program in 1934. The model he established placed its long-term imprint on criminal justice education:

> As he (Wiltberger) saw it there were only two paths to follow. An educational institution could graduate people who knew the tasks and techniques of a job so that they could go out immediately and do it; or it could graduate people who were inadequately trained but had an academic background in general education. Wiltberger chose the former over the latter, thereby establishing a model that I call the "Wiltbergerian" model, replete with far-reaching ramifications for police education for decades to come (Morn, 1995:45).

By *ramifications*, Morn stated that the model was designed to assist the police rather than satisfy the expectations of academics. Wiltberger established the criminal justice program with three goals in mind. It should train people to do police work. It should be a placement service of its graduates. And it should be a center of service for the police departments in his area. Curriculum was organized in terms of functional specializations in the police department, and police experience was the central criteria for selecting instructors. The first two years of education focused on technical details of police work. The second two years were creatively developed, with a focus on skills that would enhance particular aspects of police work. Instructors were drawn from those with practical experience rather than from the educational elite.

The Wiltbergerian model was a service model, emphasizing the role of academic justice departments for entry-level preparation of students for employment in the community The Wiltbergerian model focused on service to the criminal justice community, but failed to address issues of legitimation in its academic environment. The School of Criminology at the University of California at Berkeley, founded on the Wiltbergerian model, became a site of long-term institutional conflict. This conflict, commonly called "town and gown" conflict, represented the differing interests and values of the local criminal justice community and the academic community. Berkeley first attempted to resolve the conflict by focusing on its local community constituency, ignoring constituencies in its academic environment. In its later years it reversed its position, alienating the local community.

The School of Criminology program at the University of California at Berkeley represented the origins of the police educational movement in California. Under the founding leadership of August Vollmer, the program focused on police "professionalism" training and education, and provided police officer education at the Berkeley campus. Vollmer's goal was not to simply provide technical training, but also to provide students with education in related topics. These topics included sociology, psychology,

psychology, abnormal psychology, and statistics (Ward & Webb, 1984:98). In 1939, the program was established as the "Department of Criminology." By the 1940s, the school was well established. However, from the 1940s to the 1960s a disagreement about academic and practitioner images of criminal justice revealed fundamental legitimacy problems affecting the school. It had to deal with its two legitimating audiences, the local criminal justice community and the academic community. Its inability to resolve conflicts in the two audiences resulted in a sustained legitimacy crisis over the appropriate focus on criminal justice education and ultimately resulted in the demise of the program.

The mechanics of the development and downfall of the Berkeley program is a widely told story. Under the Wiltbergerian model, the School of Criminology defined its mission in terms of "town" rather than "gown," developed its curricula for service to the criminal justice community, and hired its faculty from that community. This created problems within its academic environment. In 1947, a "Committee on Educational Policy upon Criminology" challenged the school's academic legitimacy, stating that it lacked academic character and that it supplied no need not already met by other majors in other departments in the social and natural sciences. The committee argued that the curricula was not criminology at all, but was narrowly limited to police administration and crime detection.

The academic audience, however, was not single-minded about the school. Many advocates of police training held influential positions in the university and resisted efforts to broaden the curriculum. As Morn observed, the organization and development of the School of Criminology was stymied over an issue that perplexed criminology and police educators. What was the nature of criminology? Should it emphasize crime causation or on police administration? The conflict was carried into the selection of the dean of the school, and was resolved in terms of police education, narrowly defined. On February 24, 1950, O.W. Wilson was named Dean of the School of Criminology, and the emphasis was to be police administration. The program offered two options: criminalistics and law enforcement. At this historical point in its town-gown conflict, town carried the day.

Conflicts involving the Berkeley school were unresolved and continued into the 1960s. A report issued in 1959 by the "Cline Committee," an Academic Advisory Committee set up to investigate the School of Criminology, issued a scathing report. The School of Criminology, it stated, was too applied and lacked any central focus. After a great deal of internal debate, the school was reformed and criminal justice education dramatically changed. The California State University system was encouraged to take over applied elements of criminal justice education, and criminological education would be organized around the core discipline of crime causation. By 1964, a doctorate in Criminology was established. Police education, which had been Vollmer's educational priority, became a "casualty of academic politics" [70]. The school of criminology henceforth took on the trappings of academic rigor and scholarly research. However, it continued to be involved in the education of practitioners. In 1968, a survey showed that 72 percent of the individuals receiving degrees were employed in criminal justice agencies. Seventy percent of the faculty were part-time, and graduates were used as instructors.

In the 1960s and early 1970s the School of Criminology revamped its curriculum and instruction practices to a *Law and Society* model. This model, more critical of prevailing justice policy than the supportive Wiltbergerian model, used sociological perspectives to study justice processes. In the early 1970s the increasingly "critical" orientation of the school alienated elements of the community that had traditionally supported them. This conflict between "town and gown" was particularly evident in the involvement of some faculty in demonstrations and political activism:

> This dispute came to a head with the Anthony Platt case. Platt, a Marxist scholar and outspoken critic of the Berkeley police, had received a doctorate in 1966. He was believed to be one of the best students to graduate from the school . . . However, his political activism and subsequent arrests by the police were embarrassing to administrative officials and he was denied tenure (Morn, 1995:111).

In 1973 an academic review committee recommended the school's disestablishment. No new majors were accepted after June, 1973, and the school was closed. The School of Criminology, at one time in the center of the educational movement in criminal justice, was thus relegated to historical status in justice education. It had failed to negotiate the delicate political boundaries of its twin legitimating audiences, the academic environment and the local criminal justice community, for which it was deprived of its existence.

In spite of the collapse of the Berkeley program, criminal justice education spread rapidly across the United States in the 1960s. The Wiltbergerian model was its predominant form, and its curricula was based on police administration and criminalistics. The junior college movement aided the rapid dissemination of the model and provided a regional emphasis. However, the central question of identity continued to affect academic education in justice studies. What kind of education should the police have? The answer, Morn observed, depended on what one thought the police actually did.

> Clearly, the turbulent 1960s highlighted two police problems. On the one hand there was crime: its prevention and its detection . . . The solution was technical training, something the community colleges and state colleges had been doing for 30 years. University criminologists might help a bit with theories on criminal behavior. Vollmerites might help too by providing better administered and controlled police departments.

On the other hand, the 1960s exposed deeper problems of order maintenance, dealing with an ethnically diverse society in which public hostility was closely connected to police insensitivity and brutality. One does not easily learn empathy and sensitivity in a crime lab or through organizational flow charts. Part of learning that was the concept "criminal justice" itself, in other words, seeing oneself as a police officer in something much larger than policing (Morn, 1995:88-89).

One might add to this the increasing recognition that, if criminal justice was to survive in an academic environment, it would have to develop an intellectual and curricular base broader than normative, "law and order" considerations of law and justice education and training. Both Berkeley solutions, the first as justice service organizations and the second openly critical of the police, proved to be unsatisfactory.

In the 1960s, criminal justice education experienced sharp expansion. The Law Enforcement Assistance Administration (LEAA) provided a powerful spur for education, and its effects are well-known. Less well understood is the impact of the community college movement on criminal justice education. It contributed to a dramatic growth in community college enrollment, facilitated the entrenchment of service-based education in local communities, and shifted the role of community colleges from liberal arts preparatory institutions to centers of vocational training.

The LEAA. The LEAA spurred the development of criminal justice education in the United States in the late 1960s and through the 1970s. Emerging at the height of the junior college movement, the LEAA provided funds for in-service personnel to go to college. It had two important effects on criminal justice education. The expansion of justice education across the United States, with which it is historically associated, continues to be felt today. Second, the LEAA contributed to the advancement of the Wiltbergerian vision of education as service to the local criminal justice community.

The LEAA was created in 1968, when the Omnibus Safe Streets and Crime Control act was passed into law. Title I of the act created the LEAA, which was charged with dispensing block grants to states for disbursement. These funds were typically provided without strings; as Feeley and Sarat (1980) noted, the federal government deliberately avoided earmarking the use to which these funds were to be put. Innovation was encouraged. Within each state, a state planning agency determined how the funds would be spent and disbursed funds to regional planning units. These planning units were often managed or controlled by police personnel, and a large proportion of the funds consequently flowed to police departments and served police purposes such as crime fighting technology and hardware.

A component of the LEAA was the Law Enforcement Education Program (LEEP). The LEEP was a funding mechanism for the in-service education of police officers, and many officers took advantage of the opportunities it provided. In 1969, its first year, LEEP provided 6.5 million dollars for the education of police officers. By 1972, there were 177,472 people studying police science in colleges and universities. The LEEP educational boom was underway. Through the 1970s, the program provided more than $400 million per year for education. Loans were provided for individuals working in or preparing for employment in the criminal justice system, and loans were forgiven at the rate of 25 percent each year the person was so employed (Rush, 1994). These loans were more likely to be used by in-service students than by college students anticipating a career in policing. Fifty-five percent of the students using these loans were in-service and received 84 percent of the LEEP moneys, while pre-service students, accounting for 45 percent, received 16 percent of the funds (Morn, 1995).

The impact of LEEP on criminal justice education is in part revealed in the growth of justice programs in colleges and universities in the United States in the years when LEEP was active. In 1960, only 40 associate and 15 baccalaureate degrees were offered in the United States. By the late 1970s, more than 600 institutions were offering degrees, ranging from an associate's degree to a Ph.D. (Durham, 1992).

In 1973, more than 80 percent of the participants of LEEP were in-service students, that is, students who were currently employed in full time jobs in local criminal justice agencies.[1] Most of these were employed in police departments (Goldstein, 1986). As Goldstein noted, the emphasis was on educating the hired rather than hiring the educated. The emphasis on in-service education enabled police chiefs to use officers who had achieved the ceremonial distinction of educational attainment while resisting the potentially threatening effects of education on police department routines and activities. Education reinforced the status quo, and many programs were no more than adjuncts of local police departments.

> By recruiting non-college personnel and training them in police work, and only then encouraging them to take college studies, the administrator can successfully sidestep any challenge to existing practices and policies. In many cities the local college program is a captive of the agency, servicing it in much the same manner as an in-house training program: the agency dictates the choice of subject matter, and the orientation and operating policy of the agencies administrators are mirrored in the orientation and philosophy of the teaching staff (Goldstein, 1986:248-249).

The LEEP funds bolstered the two-year college base of criminal justice education; In-service students could enroll in one of the rapidly growing numbers of two-year local community colleges and remain in their jobs. Their affiliations and loyalties could uncomplicatedly remain to their agencies, largely unaffected by the broadening experiences and diversity of ideas associated with four-year educational attainment.

LEEP emerged during an era in which the junior college movement was undergoing transformation away from baccalaureate preparation and toward a vocational orientation toward education. Even though police reformers since the 1930s had been arguing for a four-year police educational program, the LEEP program and the community service mission of two-year programs stamped police education with a technical and vocational patina. And, in spite of growth in the number of four-year state colleges around the United States, the nature and purposes of police education was unclear. Incertitude over what justice educators should impart to students—a liberal arts education or vocational preparation—was captured by administrators of two-year programs who were interested in vocationalization, not preparation for four-year programs.

To understand the vocational turn of criminal justice, one should give equal or greater weight to the community college movement and the advocacy of its administrators than to LEEP, which was captured by the community college movement. It is to this odd twist in 1960s educational history that I now turn.

Justice Education and Institutional Legitimacy: From Agency to Academia

LEEP, by emphasizing the vocationalization of criminal justice education, contributed to the institutional conflict between "town" and "gown" without providing a mechanism for resolving it. LEEP enabled the sustained growth of criminal justice education by providing the good that universities thrive on—students. Growth in student population translated into academic revenue. The expansion of academic criminal justice programs was in this way seduced by the presence of federal funding. The seduction of organizational structure has been described as follows:

> The use of the term "seduction" is selected to suggest that organizational innovations initiated by grants or similar sponsorship are not changes that otherwise would be unattractive. To the contrary, such changes may have a great deal of appeal to agency executives (Crank & Langworthy, 1996:216-217).

Crank and Langworthy observed that many police departments had expanded their operations and activities as a result of federal funding, and wondered what would happen after funding ended (see Scott, 1992). The LEEP was a source of federal funding that provided monies for colleges and universities, and the "seduction of structure" described by Crank and Langworthy occurred in this case with regard to the implementation and growth of criminal justice programs, departments, and curricula. What would happen to programs and departments of criminal justice education once LEEP disappeared?

The end of LEEP support in the early 1980s created a legitimation crisis among programs—either develop a departmental or program mission consistent with academic (rather than agency) expectations or vanish. Many smaller programs, particularly programs in community colleges, feared declining enrollments. Programs in four-year colleges were not as hard-hit, and many increased enrollment through this period (Durham, 1992). Durham attributed this to the diversity of the student populations and the ability of the institutions to attract students other than in-service agency personnel.

The institutional crisis can be stated as follows: LEEP-based educational programs had justified their existence in terms of their mission to local agencies. The values that undergirded these programs were values consistent with justice agencies rather than academic departments and reflected their funding from LEEP. They tended to be local and crime control-oriented. Their students held careers in justice agencies and reflected the normative crime control values characteristic of criminal justice agencies.

With the end of LEEP funding criminal justice departments had to develop a new legitimating mandate. To justify their continued existence, they had to cloak themselves in the ceremonies and rites of academia. Faculty could not be justified only in terms of their rank or experience in local agencies, but rather in terms of academic issues of scholarship, service, and teaching, with service relegated to the least important. Departments were expected to participate in the more critical life of the university rather than the crime-control work of local agencies. The Wiltbergerian model of criminal justice education, integral to the historical development of academic justice studies, had received a hard blow.

Many social science academics viewed criminal justice programs with hostility. Criminal justice education was perceived to be little more than technical and administrative training, which indeed it was in many places. The academic rigor of technically based criminal justice programs was suspect; many observers expressed concern that the typically narrow curriculum offerings did not satisfy college level educational expectations (Durham, 1992:8).[2] Yet, at the end of LEEP funding, the growth of justice studies programs continued unabated. In spite of critics, it remained a highly viable academic enterprise. To understand justice studies' sustaining growth, LEEP should be considered in the context of the broader community college movement in the Untied States.

LEEP and the Community College Movement. One of the most surprising outcomes of the discontinuation of LEEP was a non-event. In spite of the discontinuation of LEEP funding in 1981 and legitimation crises in many departments, program growth continued at what was, for academia, a breakneck pace. Instead of heralding the end of criminal justice education, the end of LEEP scarcely amounted to a blip on the radar screen of criminal justice growth in college programs and enrollments.

Consider the following statistics. In 1960 there were 40 associate degrees and 15 baccalaureate and graduate degrees in criminal justice. When LEEP was initiated in 1967, there were 152 associate programs, 39 baccalaureate programs, 14 masters programs, and 4 doctorate programs. In 1972 these numbers had increased to 505 associate, 211 baccalaureate and 50 graduate degree programs (Foster, 1974; in Langworthy & Latessa, 1989). In 1978, shortly before the end of LEEP, about 1,200 programs in criminology or criminal justice existed (Pelfrey, 1978). In 1984, three years after the end of LEEP, this number is estimated at 1,500 (Ward & Webb, 1984). In 1986-1987, Langworthy and Latessa (1989) estimate that there were 911 degree-offering criminal justice programs.[3] Of these, 518 offered an Associates degree, 256 offered a Baccalaureate, 12 offered a Masters of Arts or Science, and 23 offered a Ph.D.

By any count, these are heady numbers, and much of the growth occurred during the years of LEEP funding. Yet when we review these numbers we observe that dynamic growth occurred both before and after the LEEP program. From 1960 to 1967, for example, in the seven years prior to LEEP, degree offering programs expanded by 300 percent. And after the end of LEEP degree offering programs continued to expand. In 1994, the ACJS Guide to Graduate Programs reported 108 graduate programs in Criminal Justice (Academy of Criminal Justice Sciences, 1995). The numbers of masters programs has increased by more than 300 percent since Latessa and Langworthy's 1989 report, a scant five years, and all post-LEEP!

The research conducted by Langworthy and Latessa (1989), together with subsequent findings from various Academy of Criminal Justice Science (ACJS) reports, is evidence that the implementation and growth of criminal justice programs cannot be understood only as a consequence of LEEP funding.

An alternative explanation for the growth of criminal justice education is that LEEP represented a part of the broad array of forces that heralded the community college movement that began in the United states in the early 1960s. The community college movement—the development of local, service-based two-year colleges in community settings and fulfilling local needs—spread through processes of institutional diffusion throughout the United States. Moreover, the community college movement, emerging in the early 1960s, was already well under way by the time LEEP was funded. LEEP was an important stimulus to criminal justice education, but the community college movement provided the context within which LEEP prospered, and justified LEEP's vocational orientation in local two-year colleges.

The community college movement, LEEP, and criminal justice education were natural partners. Academic interest in criminal justice education was growing, providing student revenues for colleges and universities beset by state budgetary problems in the 1970s. Moreover, crime and criminal justice was on the public mind. National interest in criminal justice was steadily promoted in the 1960s and 1970s both in response to conservative perceptions that crime was "out of control" and to liberal concerns about the unfairness of justice processes. And two-year colleges provided a mechanism for the delivery of educational services to criminal justice agencies in local communities. The public service emphasis of the community college movement was consistent with the Wiltbergerian model of criminal justice education—provide training, services, and personnel for community agencies.

If this is the case, how should we think about the role of LEEP for academic development? The LEEP program can be understood as a product of the general two-year college movement in the United States, that part of the movement geared toward local criminal justice agencies. The funding of LEEP occurred from 1968 to 1981, within the period in which the junior college movement was having its broadest influence. Junior colleges were the principal source of academic growth associated with LEEP (Sherman et al., 1986). The early form of education was local and sometimes disparagingly called "cop-shops" (Goldstein, 1986). However, the "cop-shop" idea was simply an expansion of professional programs across the social and applied science curriculum of two-year colleges. It was a characteristic of the junior college movement.

That the junior college movement in the United States was the prime mover for the dramatic proliferation of criminal justice college programs is suggested by overall two-year college enrollments from 1960 to 1980. Kerr (1991) observed that, from 1960 to 1980, junior college enrollment in the United States grew from 400,000 to 3,600,000—a 900 percent increase. Additionally, the sharp growth in two-year colleges was only one aspect of the dramatic change in education across the United States. Kerr referred to the period of 1960 to 1980 as the "great transformation," and described it with the following statistics:

1. College enrollments grew from 3.5 million students in 1960 to 12 million in 1980.

2. The system of higher education changed from being nearly half private in terms of enrollment to 80 percent public.

3. The great growth of community colleges were marked by enrollments that were less than 400,000 in 960 to more than four million in 1980. As a result, most states could be said by 1980 to provide universal access to higher education to all high school students who wished to attend.

4. The great transition of teachers' colleges to comprehensive colleges and universities specializing in many professional fields . . . carried their enrollments from roughly 500,000 to almost three million (Kerr, 1991:xii).

In sum, the process of criminal justice growth occurred against a backdrop of dramatic growth across the academic board. The foundation of LEEP itself occurred in a broader political environment in which pressures for police education were already strong (Sherman et al., 1986). LEEP may consequently be itself an outcome to the same broad forces that characterized the "great transformation"in higher education—a national transition to universal public education at the college level, the development of comprehensive universities, and growth in the professional fields. These dynamics shaped the form of education provided by LEEP and influenced the way criminal justice education is organized and taught today. Further, LEEP provided a substantial investment in criminal justice education, spending $274.75 million from 1969 to 1976 (Sherman, 1986). Yet the federal government was providing funding for a wide variety of programs during this period. From 1960 to 1980 the federal government provided university and college programs with 10 billion dollars in student aid. In other words, LEEP accounted for 2.75 percent of the total federal student aid budget.

The Junior College Movement and the Vocationalization of Education. Advocates of higher education for the police have sometimes argued that the resistance to baccalaureate education lies with the police and other justice agencies. Yet, the history of the junior college movement suggests that the opposite has occurred, and that the vocationalization mission, morphed in the current era into the "community college mission" of liberal arts and comprehensive (four- and six-year) colleges and universities, continues to dominate criminal justice education. Against the common-sense argument that colleges are struggling to bring up the education of practitioners, a counter-argument can be made that educators are primarily responsible for the failure of a liberal arts-based four-year education to take hold in the 1960s and 1970s. The problem of limited practitioner education may lie, not with the police, but with college and university educators who found their organizational interests— enrollments—best served by vocational training. Consider the history of the vocational training in college settings in the United States.

The period from 1960 to 1980 is associated not only with the growth in the two-year college educational model. It also is associated with a broad transformation in the purposes of two-year education, from liberal arts preparatory institutions to vocational training. In 1960, about three-fourths of community college students were enrolled in liberal arts transfer programs. Transfer programs refer to two-year programs who are designed to prepare students for upper-division work at four-year colleges. By 1980 this pattern had reversed, and nearly three of four were enrolled in technical, administrative, or semi-professional programs (Brint & Karabel, 1991).

A variety forces pushed junior colleges toward vocationalization. The downturn of the economy in 1970-1971, for example, encouraged the expansion of vocational training programs. However, the most powerful of these was the advocacy of junior college administrators, who sought a particular market niche for their programs in an academic environment dominated by four-year programs. Junior college administrators, dissatisfied with their "junior" role in the advancement of four-year education, developed programs that redirected students toward middle-level occupations not requiring four-year degrees. Two-year colleges thus developed a marketing niche—preparing students for employment. Administrators aggressively pursued this niche, even though students wanted preparation for four-year degrees. Marketing was, in this sense, *against* student demand. In other words, vocational development happened precisely at a time when demand at the junior college level was for preparation for four-year programs. Administrators viewed their task as overcoming the "degree-fixation" of their students (Brint & Karabel, 1991).

The vocational focus of two-year programs, Brint and Karabel suggested, underwent institutional processes of development and diffusion. The vocational model advocated by junior college administrators originated in California and rapidly spread across the United States. The model was complete with ceremonial criteria of credentialing, providing students with certificates and awards for two-year program completion. By loosely coupling the two-year college mission (focused on vocational training for second-tier jobs) to the actual needs and desires of students (preparation for four-year programs) the junior colleges established their niche in college life. Vocationalization directed junior college students toward the most readily available market niche—local community positions in the trades and service occupations.

It is against the backdrop of two-year vocational program development that the dramatic growth and Wiltbergerian focus of criminal justice programs and curricula in the period 1960-1980 should be highlighted. The growth of criminal justice education carried an emphasis on contribution to the local community, a program that worked well for vocationally oriented two-year programs. The Wiltbergerian model, which sometimes fared poorly in more advanced academic settings, provided an appropriate practice-oriented model for two-year programs.

Many of the issues of criminal justice education are holdovers from this vocational birthright. Though many programs are today housed in four-year and graduate programs, the vocational stamp continues to typify criminal justice education. In the current era, the advocacy of a four-year degree for police officers continues to be controversial. Many programs are invested in an administrative philosophy that encourages the vocationalization of criminal justice education, and by consequence keeps the status and employment of police, as well as other justice professionals, on a lower educational level.

If proponents of educational reform want to change the powerful hold vocational training has on criminal justice education, they must begin, not with the justice system, but with their own academic administrators. They might be surprised by the ferocity of administrative efforts to retain two-year degrees, technical-vocational programs, and minimalist certificate credentialing that their own institutions provide, even if they are four- or six-year (Master's degree) level institutions that pride themselves on the rigor of their educational standards.

Post-LEEP Trends in Graduate Education. The evolution of justice programs is currently marked by increasing numbers of graduate programs. Graduate program development and growth, particularly in Ph.D. programs, provides the environment for scholarship and for the education of students with field-wide perspective. In this section, I discuss two trends in graduate education. The first is the sheer growth in the numbers of graduate programs. The second is the particular form or model of graduate curricula that is emerging.

Growth in Graduate Programs. The post-LEEP period has witnessed a spectacular expansion of Master's degree programs in justice studies. From 1989 to 1994, the number of Master's degree programs increased by approximately 300 percent (ACJS, 1995; Langworthy & Latessa, 1989). Justice studies graduate education is increasingly integrated in the life of universities.[4]

Langworthy and Latessa (1989) argued that growth at the Ph.D. level was central to the development of field identity. Academic criminal justice programs, they observed, were inadequately staffed by individuals trained within the field of criminal justice. Echoing the concerns of the Joint Commission of Criminal Justice and Criminology (Ward & Webb, 1984), they recognized the need to hire and prepare faculty who are capable of contributing to the scholarly needs of the field. The growth that was occurring in the field could not be met by Ph.D., preparation in justice programs, but instead was being carried by part-time faculty. The numbers of individuals receiving Ph.D.'s in justice and related programs were sharply outpaced by efforts to hire such faculty. The demand for Ph.D. faculty could not be met by existing Ph.D. granting institutions. Growth was outstripping efforts to hire qualified instructors. The problem confronting programs at the beginning of the 1990s, they observed, was that insufficient Ph.D. granting institutions were available to provide the pool of talent needed to grow the field.

The lack of a "brain trust" of students also adversely affected the development of knowledge central to academic identity.

> It is obvious that criminal justice higher education has grown to a sizeable mass. It is not as evident, however, that this mass is being served by an infrastructure capable of providing it new knowledge. The discipline must develop the capacity to generate new knowledge and pass along this growing body of knowledge to the next generation of scholars if the discipline is to survive (Langworthy & Latessa, 1989:185).

Langworthy and Latessa (1989) concluded that the continuing development of the academic field of criminal justice field required an increase in the numbers of doctoral institutions.

The university audience of Ph.D. granting institutions is likely to favor a research orientation. Students are expected to learn broad research skills to conduct behavioral research and develop the intellectual skills to understand the fundamental issues underlying justice in a democratic setting. Students do not simply develop skills to become better administrators, but learn how to critically examine the role of justice organizations and activities in a variety of contexts. As Langworthy and Latessa noted, they should possess the skills to contribute to the body of basic knowledge about justice. The Ph.D. mission contains within it a commitment to the development of basic knowledge and the application of that knowledge to a variety of settings. This reflects the commitment to basic research that characterizes Ph.D. granting institutions.

A "basic research" mission does not fit easily with the more regional mission of many comprehensive universities, who are concerned with the provision of service to their regions vis-à-vis the professional training of undergraduate and master's level students. The expansion of Ph.D. education, with its focus on basic knowledge, carries a fundamentally different mission than Master's-level education, often aimed at applied technique for middle-level managers.

Graduate Education in Criminal Justice. Undergraduate development developed around a particular model of education, described previously as the Wiltbergerian model. At the graduate level, the Albany Model has been recommended as a guide for curriculum development (Travis, 1989). Remington (1990) advocated for a public administration model for the Ph.D. program in Albany, New York in 1962. He believed that a public policy approach, with individuals trained and sophisticated in handling important community problems that called for a response from government, was the appropriate model for graduate education. This vision was at once committed to service to the community and assessing the efficacy of criminal justice responses to community problems. The Albany "public administration"model is similar to the Wiltbergerian model in that it is committed to community service, though at a higher level—it locates its service responsibility as administrative training, not in introductory career preparation. However, the Albany model is more than a vocational model for middle-management workers. Criminal justice solutions are viewed as only one of many possible venues available in a policy context. By studying alternative policy frameworks such as advocacy coalition (Sabatier & Jenkins-Smith, 1999) and institutional analysis and development (Ostrom, 1999) public policy education incorporated political, social, and environmental contexts in the formulation of just outcomes for social problems. In this framework, Remington's policy-oriented ideas enable a broader conception of justice practice than provided within the normative confines of the Wiltbergerian model.

Travis (1989) suggested that the Albany model provided a basis for the development of post-graduate education. Travis described the Albany model as follows:

> . . . the Albany model was designed to provide graduate training in justice as a separate discipline. To this end, a core of knowledge was identified including substantive areas in Law, Justice Administration, Criminology, and Planned Change. To this core of substantive knowledge was added a requirement of research and data analytic expertise. The goal of the Albany model was to produce graduates broadly knowledgeable about criminal justice who would be capable of producing and consuming research on crime and crime control.
>
> As was typical of the discipline at the time the school was founded, the curriculum was schizophrenic. Two levels of training were expected. The Master's degree was designed to produce generalists who would, it was hoped, assume positions as planners and administrators of criminal justice agencies. Doctoral graduates were expected to become researchers and scholars. Thus, the Albany model attempted to meet the professional educational goal of criminal justice education at the Masters level, and the academic goal through the production of Doctoral graduates (Travis, 1989:5).

Albany, in other words, adapted to its town and gown audiences the way in which successful institutionalized organizations do: it provided both audiences with a role in its organizational structure and practice. The Master's curricula aimed at the provision of leadership and managerial training for the criminal justice community, and at the Ph.D. level, education emphasized scholarly rigor, satisfying the academic audience.

Travis suggested that the Albany model provided a basis for the development of post-graduate education nationally. In a national survey of graduate programs in criminal justice, he found that the content of the Albany program was widely replicated. He concluded that "the Albany model, either directly or indirectly has been used as the basis for the development of graduate curricula at other institutions" (Travis, 1989:5).

In an opposing article, Albanese (1989) argued that no particular model characterized Ph.D. education in criminal justice. Examining seven Ph.D. granting programs in criminal justice, he identified three whose curricula paralleled the Albany model and four whose curricula were different in significant ways. He found that both requirements and electives varied widely in the Ph.D. programs, and concluded that the development of higher education was haphazard.

Travis and Albanese may have been talking past each other. Travis conducted his research on Master's granting programs and collected information from graduate program directors. Albanese assessed the curricula of Ph.D. programs. It may be that Master's programs are undergoing processes of institutional diffusion, and the Albany model—as Travis found—is emerging as the predominant model. However, Ph.D. programs have not yet reached sufficient numbers for processes of diffusion to occur, and the form of Ph.D. education—as Albanese found—is still up for grabs. As Albanese noted, three of his quite small (7) sample matched the Albany model, and all three programs—Rutgers, Albany, and Cincinnati—are highly successful programs. At the Ph.D. level, there is as of yet no curricular formula that commands institutional isomorphism.

The 1990s: Patterns of Convergence and Divergence in Justice Education. Within academic departments, the decade of the LEAA was often marked by conflicts between faculty that identified themselves as criminal justicians and those that viewed themselves as criminologists (Ward & Webb, 1984). These conflicts revolved around what Sorensen, Widmayer and Scarpitti (1994) called paradigmatic differences. By *paradigmatically different* was meant that the central ideas underlying the fields are fundamentally different. In the 1970s and into the 1980s, criminal justice and criminology were divergent in profound ways: criminology programs stressed the etiology of crime and encouraged basic research into root causes, and criminal justice programs emphasized the application of criminal justice policy to concrete justice settings (Sorensen, Widmayer & Scarpitti, 1994). The difference was not simply philosophical or pedagogical; conflicts between the two fields were emotionally charged. Indeed, the founding of the International Association of Police Professors in 1963, who changed their name to the ACJS in 1970, was a response to the perceived underrepresentation of practitioners in the American society of Criminology (ASC), and embodied the rift between the two fields. The differences described by Sorensen, Widmayer and Scarpitti (1994) are clarified by the recognition that they tend to correspond to differences in institutional audiences. Criminologists tended to attend to the academic audience and criminal justicians have been more concerned with the needs of their local criminal justice community.

Differences between criminologists and criminal justicians are revealed in various ways. In surveys conducted in the late 1970s and early 1980s, members of the ASC rated sociological journals as the most important, and ACJS members selected journals that focused on criminal justice or on criminology (Regoli, Poole & Miracle, 1982). Differences in a faculty member's preference for criminology or criminal justice was associated with the type of institution in which they worked (Ward & Webb, 1984). Graduate-level faculty tended to focus on basic research, while faculty at undergraduate institutions often viewed their role in terms of teaching and applied research. The distinction between applied and basic research extended to institutional type as well. Ward and Webb (1984) observed that

> Those who ranked (the graduate programs in) State University of New York (SUNY) and Florida State as the top program named the *American Sociological Review* as the journal in which they would like to publish;

> the others most often chose the *Journal of Criminal Justice.*[5] With
> regard to attitudes, those who ranked SUNY and Florida State the high-
> est were most likely to agree on the importance of theory and develop-
> ment in research; the others were more likely to agree that research
> should focus on agency problems. (Sorensen, Widmayer & Scarpitti,
> 1994:152).

Sorensen, Widmayer, and Scarpitti (1994) suggested that a trend
toward convergence of criminal justice and criminology occurred in the
1990s. They noted that faculty estimated similarly the relative importance
of journals in criminal justice and criminology (Williams, McShane & Wagoner, 1992). And methodologies used by researchers in criminal justice
and criminology were converging, though the subject matter itself continued to be a source of divergence (Holmes & Taggart, 1990). Figure 3.1
below reproduces Sorensen, Widmayer, and Scarpitti's analysis of institutional characteristics, academic workload, work style attitudes, and
achievements (1994:158).

Figure 3.1 provides statistical profiles of justice faculty according to
whether they belong to ASC, ACJS, or both. First, consider overall patterns of faculty affiliation with the American Society of Criminology
(ASC) or Academy of Criminal Justice Sciences (ACJS). The ASC is the
leading professional association for criminologists. Founded in 1941 as
the Society for the Advancement of Criminology, the ASC today is associated with the study of the etiology of crime. The ACJS is the major national association associated with the field of criminal justice today. Membership in the two associations substantially overlaps, though the mission of
the two organizations differs and efforts to participate in joint projects
between the two associations has been politically hazardous for elected
leadership of the respective organizations.

An inspection of data in Figure 3.1 suggests that membership status
in the ASC and ACJS is associated with substantial differences in virtually
all important aspects of the academic enterprise. Membership in the ACJS
is associated with consistently higher levels of undergraduate teaching,
administrative duties, and public service. The research workload, on the
other hand, is significantly lower than for ASC members. ACJS members
are also significantly less likely to work in Ph.D. granting institutions, and
are more likely to have teaching as their primary orientation. Using a set
of predictors that included a wide range of variables associated traditionally with criminal justice and criminology respectively, Sorensen, Widmayer, and Scarpitti (1994) were able to classify ACJS and ASC members
correctly 90.6 and 85.7 percent of the time, evidence that two competing paradigms continued to operate in the field of justice studies.

Figure 3.1

Institutional Characteristics, Academic Workload, Workstyle Attitudes, and Achievements

	ACJS	ASC	Dual	Significance
Institutional Characteristics				
Highest Degree Offered				$X^2 = 55.49$***
Associate	7.1%	0.0%	2.3%	1-2,2-3
Bachelor's	24.4	24.2	19.6	
Master's	49.2	18.5	54.0	
Doctorate	19.3	57.3	24.1	
Area of Highest Degree Offered[a]				
Criminal Justice	61.3%	18.8%	54.3%	$X^2 = 46.44$***
				1-2,2-3
Criminology	10.7%	12.4%	14.6%	$X^2 = 0.64$
Sociology	14.9%	67.3%	23.6%	$X^2 = 74.34$***
				1-2,2-3
Other	24.5%	19.1%	17.8%	$X^2 = 1.59$
Primary Orientation				$X^2 = 34.90$***
Research	12.6%	35.9%	21.5%	1-2,2-3
Teaching	67.2	30.7	39.1	
Equal	20.2	33.4	39.4	
Academic Workload (Weekly Hours)				
Undergraduate contact teaching	8.6	6.5	7.5	$F = 4.83$***
				1-2
Student advisement	6.2	3.4	3.8	$F = 14.86$***
				1-2,1-3
Administrative duties	11.8	6.6	8.8	$F = 9.46$**
				1-2,1-3
Public service	4.5	2.3	3.0	$F = 10.33$**
				1-2,1-3
Research	5.0	19.7	14.7	$F = 70.75$***
				1-2,1-3,2-3
Workstyle Attitudes (10-Point Scale)				
Teaching undergraduate courses	8.8	7.1	7.8	$F = 15.20$***
				1-2,1-3,2-3
Private counseling for agencies	4.5	2.5	3.5	$F = 18.56$***
				1-2,1-3,2-3
Conducting research	6.4	9.2	8.4	$F = 54.11$***
				1-2,1-3,2-3
Theory testing and development	4.7	7.3	6.2	$F = 19.66$***
				1-2,1-3,2-3
Writing research articles	6.3	8.9	8.3	$F = 37.63$***
				1-2,1-3,2-3
Professional Achievements (Total Number)				
Total publications	14.4	27.4	25.6	$F = 6.09$**
				1-2,1-3
Scholarly books	0.4	1.7	1.3	$F = 13.57$**
				1-2,1-3
Refereed journal articles	7.4	16.5	13.7	$F = 9.26$***
				1-2,1-3
Journal review manuscripts	0.9	5.7	3.2	$F = 9.00$***
				1-2,1-03,2-3

*$p < .05$; ** $p < .01$.; *** $p < .001$
[a]Because some respondents listed more than one area (e.g., sociology and criminology), the categories should be interpreted as dichotomous variables indicating the presence of response. If the respondent indicated only an area other than those listed, we categorized it as "other."

Source: Jonathan Sorensen, Alan Widmayer and Frank Scarpitti (1994) "Examining The Criminal Justice and Criminological Paradigms: An Analysis of ACJS and ASC Members." *Journal of Criminal Justice Education* 5-2 (1994): 158.

In spite of the evidence of significant differences between ASC and ACJS members on key measures, Sorensen, Widmayer, and Scarpitti concluded that a pattern of convergence is occurring. This is suggested by their analysis of dual members who are recent graduates and who appear not to be exclusive in their preference for the ASC or the ACJS. The authors considered that the rift between the fields was less intense, and newer members for both the ASC and ACJS were equally committed to research. A third paradigm might be emerging, representing a convergence of criminology and criminal justice:

> Persons representing this paradigm are concerned with criminal justice agencies and are committed to the discipline, as evidenced by their areas of training and the departments in which they currently teach, but they are more strongly committed to knowledge creation than the previous generation of criminal justice educators. Perhaps the crime-related educators and researchers in this new generation are members of a discipline that is finally carving out its own niche, separate from the criminal justice education of the past, less concerned with criminal justice agencies, and including the etiology of crime (Sorensen, Widmayer & Scarpitti, 1994:164-165).

The convergence has other forms. There are also students trained in sociology, political science, and criminal justice Ph.D. programs. They are committed to basic research, yet they are also interested in the life and practices of justice agencies, from the regional to the national level. They are skilled in the craft of basic research, but place a great deal of importance on recognizing the contribution of basic research to local agency policies and practices.

The issue of convergence seems to involve a search for a "something" that those who participate in the field can all agree on. This something, according to Sorensen and his colleagues, is two-fold: the development of new knowledge and a focus away from the community audiences. Convergence will come from young faculty who share a commonality of interest in both ASC and ACJS issues. It will reflect an increasing reliance on the academic environment as the source of legitimacy, and view its responsibility in terms of knowledge acquisition.

The academic audience appears to be asserting itself as the primary source of legitimation for the field of justice studies.[6] Academic legitimation is occurring through research and publication, and in the current era is consequently witnessing proliferation of scholarship across the justice spectrum. Scholarship encompasses crime, which is an important part of justice, but which is only one characteristic of justice system processes and outcomes. Scholarship also includes studies of the theory and practice of law, inquiry into the understanding of organizational environments and dynamics, essays into the ethics of individual and organizational behavior, history (and theory of history) of jurisprudence and justice practice, political philosophy, moral and hermeneutic interpretation of justice practices, and considerations of the nature of communication and meaning.

Four aspects of the academic environment, however, mitigate against convergence, and may in fact promote conflict within the field of justice studies. First, the social science environment is not one that promotes harmony. As previously discussed, the Gulbenkian commission found that the social sciences are becoming more diverse. Conflict and disagreement among academicians, not harmony, accompany this diversity. Fragmentation is occurring in all of the parent disciplines of criminal justice. If justicians model field development on other social sciences, it is reasonable to conclude that they will also encounter the problems faced by the other social sciences.

Secondly, Sorensen and his colleagues suggested that the search for new knowledge is a uniting theme for the field of criminal justice. Characteristic of social science development since the 1960s is the recognition that knowledge is more than the collection of raw data. Integral to knowledge development is perspective, or in the current vernacular, "standpoint." Indeed, in the social sciences, it is unclear that there is any knowledge that is not somehow dependent on our standpoint. Standpoint is more than what we observe, or the data that we think about, it is the rules, tropes, "common sense," and values that we use to understand data and to give it meaning. The research and curricular hegemony offered by normative practices under a Wiltbergerian model vanishes.

Characteristic of the social sciences in the current era are two related notions: a recognition of the depth to which traditionally accepted ideas are in fact "standpoints" and a diversification of standpoints from the view of politics, gender, ethnicity, world-view, culture, and race. Efforts to reconcile standpoints will not be unifying, and are likely to push the field of justice studies deeper into fundamental issues of political philosophy and method. Precisely those issues that will be the most contentive are also likely to increase the vibrancy and depth of the academic maturity of the justice field.

Third is an increasing focus in the social sciences on substantive problems. Such problems have led to the formation of interdisciplinary coalitions, conferences, and workshops in which faculty share a common interest and scholarship in the substantive problem. This sort of interdisciplinary thrust will increase specialization around problem areas, not academic identity.

Fourth, the missions of justice departments will inevitably be closely tied to the mission of the university or college of which they are a member, and this will encourage diversity, not focus of purpose. University and college missions diverge considerably. Ph.D. programs in research I or II institutions, for example, have strong research and grants-ship foci, and will be concerned with preparing students for academic careers. Univer-

sity administrators are increasingly asserting that masters and baccalaureate programs in comprehensive institutions should adopt a "community
college" mission across the social sciences. And two-year programs continue to tie faculty to a five-class teaching load aimed at vocational preparation. To the extent that faculty are dispersed across these different institutional types, they will of necessity carry different notions of the
purposes and audiences of criminal justice. Put simply, diversity of college type and mission is reflected in diversity in departmental mission.

Part II: Higher Education and Justice Identity

In a field marked by patterns of academic divergence and ongoing
conflicts regarding purpose, is it possible for justice studies to claim an
articulable identity? This section focuses on the issue of identity in a complex institutional and intellectual setting. The problem of justice identity
in an academic environment is summarized by Albanese (1989):

> Graduate education in criminal justice wanders around the disciplines of
> law, sociology, public administration, political science, psychology,
> among others, with little standard content or format. In fact, it can be
> argued that some programs offering graduate degrees in criminal justice
> falsely promote their product with a constellation of course offerings
> having no clear substantive direction (Albanese, 1989:4).

In this section, I discuss issues regarding the identity of justice programs in broad-based liberal arts academic environments. It extends and
elaborates the institutional perspective described above, where I suggested that the field is moving away from the Wiltbergerian model of justice. The university environment provides the primary source of legitimation for criminal justice education today. The local community
continues to play an important role regarding placement of students and
opportunities for research. If the criminal justice audience is the academic environment, then what should be its focus of inquiry? *What is the
appropriate scope and focus of inquiry that constitutes the field of justice?* Its companion question is *What direction should graduate education take into the twenty-first century?* These are the most compelling
questions confronting criminal justice education today.

Defining an identity for justice education is a daunting task. The central issues were described by Flanagan in 1990:

> As the academic study of crime and justice matures, however, the notion
> of "defining the field" becomes controversial. Commentators decry the
> lack of "identity" or universally accepted definitions in the content of the
> field of the field of inquiry. Others argue that the pluralism inherent in a

multidisciplinary field that focuses on a *problem* stifles the maturation of the presumed discipline . . . One person's "pluralism" is another's "fragmentation," and some have argued that more "social control" of criminal justice education is needed (Shernock, 1990). The accreditation process is viewed as the vehicle through which greater integration and standardization of curricula can be secured. Conrad observed more than a decade ago that "from the time when Abraham Flexner reformed medical education, accreditation has been the preferred method for maintaining the standards of professional education" (Conrad & Myren, 1979:17). However, Conrad argued that "It is natural for a new field of instruction to function in a swamp of ambiguity," and warned that standard-setting with regard to curricular *content* could thwart the intellectual advancement of the nascent field. In a related argument, Myren argued for broadening the intellectual scope of these academic programs around the concept of "justice" rather than narrowing the problem or the range of disciplines that might contribute to our thinking (Conrad & Myren, 1979).

To assess the diversity of criminal justice education, Flanagan conducted a national survey of Ph.D. programs. Like Albanese (1989), he found that there was a high degree of diversity in curricular content across Ph.D. programs in the United States. He noted that the courses most likely to be required were statistical analysis and research methods, required in 9 and 10 of the 13 programs he surveyed. Notably, these courses are not about the transmission of the knowledge of the field, but rather about the tools needed to acquire knowledge. Seven programs, he observed, required a criminology or criminological theory course. No other specific course was required in more than three of the programs, suggesting a lack of standardization in curriculum content.

Diversity in curricular content, Flanagan suggested, reflected the developing nature of Ph.D. justice programs in the United States. The most frequently required courses—the development of analytic skills—suggests that our field is behavioral and tool-oriented—we are interested in statistical and methodological skills. Chapter 5 will discuss the role of quantitative and qualitative analysis, and what our methodologies tell us about justice. Flanagan, also like Albanese (1989), suggested that no particular model of criminal justice education predominated at the Ph.D. level. However, it should be noted that his analysis was limited to Ph.D. programs, and may not reflect the extent to which the content of baccalaureate and masters degree programs have become comparable (Travis, 1989).

What, then, is an appropriate identity for criminal justice education? A variety of academic models have been advanced. Below are considered three models that have been historically important in the development of criminal justice curricula: policy studies, etiology of crime, and interdisciplinary. Each provides important elements of a broad-based justice curricula. However, none are adequate as a conceptual or organizational focus for justice education. This part concludes with a discussion of a proposed model of justice education, one that locates the justice imagination at the center of the academic enterprise.

The Policy Studies Perspective. Policy represents a set of practical skills and body of information that, used effectively, can transform our ideas of justice into political practice. For many justicians, it is not enough that their contributions only extend to what they individually are able to accomplish. They also want to contribute to the wider social body, to see ideas carried out in the law, in municipal procedure and policy, in agency protocols, or in the development of new programs regionally and nationally. To achieve this wider venue, justicians want to be part of a policy apparatus, to effect changes in concert with others, who have influence, and who share a like-minded perspective or similar concerns.

The Relation of Policy to Justice. Public policy has been sparsely defined as "whatever the government chooses to do or not to do" (Dye, 1981:1). Governance in a pluralistic society, however, is highly fragmented. And at each horizontal and vertical level of government, many actors affect policy. At the legislative level, state and national legislators enact new law. In the municipal arena, mayors and city councils carry out legislative activities, often on the counsel of area stakeholders and community groups. Courts interpret. Regulatory agencies, because they have wide discretion in carrying out congressional mandates, are also involved in the policy-making process. Local police, prosecuting attorneys, and probation officers carry wide discretion in their daily activities, and in the practice of their craft both interpret and create street-level justice policies (Hojnacki, 1997).

The history of criminal justice is marked by a concern for policy relevance (Gilsinan, 1997). In a widely cited example, Cloward and Ohlin's (1960) work on delinquent gangs was incorporated into the model cities program in the early 1960s. After the assassination of president John Kennedy, the model was used by President Johnson in his *War on Poverty* programs in the 1960s. More recently, Wilson and Kelling's (1982) "Broken Windows" paper has become an article of faith in many police departments.

During the 1990s, policy research facilitated by federal grants was an important dynamic for many justice programs. Research on a wide variety of justice topics both provided justice studies departments with additional revenue and allowed the field to conduct practical research on crime problems. Grants-based, policy-oriented research helped the field of justice studies develop a core knowledge about the efficacy of many theories of crime control and prevention (see, e.g., Sherman et al., 1997). As a result, the field today has an empirical knowledge base absent in the 1970s and 1980s. Policy studies also gives the field relevance. The field of justice studies has a vitality and energy that flows from the poignancy of the issues it deals with and from the concreteness of the problems it addresses.

The fusion of policy and science is central to a policy studies perspective. The terms "policy" and "science," however, form an uneasy means-ends alliance. Science is a means for the collection of information. It is also a claim on the objectivity of the information so collected. The ends represent ideas of justice, of right and wrong. They are grounded in moral and ethical concerns about the purposes justice should serve. In other words, scientific means are used to justify value-based ends.

The problem is this: how can claims of objectivity be squared with advocacy positions that support particular policies? And if justicians advocate particular ends that they hold valuable, how can they claim objectivity?

Paris and Reynolds (1983) suggest that justicians need to be more open about the value bases of our research. By acknowledging the values that direct research interest, justicians are more likely to be trusted in political environments, where all activity is informed by political values. A perspective that links valued ends and scientific means is called "rational ideology" (Paris & Reynolds, 1983). By rational ideology is meant that a system of knowledge is open and subject to scientific verification, but its bases conform to broad values held by the investigator. However, for an ideology to be rational, value bases must be made explicit.

Justice advocates tend to disguise their values in scientific language (Gilsinan, 1997). Arguments between criminologists, for example, are often couched in terms of data and theory, yet they carry values that are clearly obvious to any observer. Observers find themselves wondering "What are they really trying to accomplish?"and being distrustful of "hidden agendas." As Gilsinan (1997:28) put it, proponents of particular value-based positions do not admit to the values and ideological commitments that underlay their perspectives, and become involved in irrational and unresolvable debates. Arguments over the death penalty, for example, are often grounded in technical research, yet represent strong values about the importance of human life whether or not openly acknowledged. Gilsinan's concern is that justice policy analysts abandon issues of substance and become bogged down in technical issues, when legislators are in fact primarily interested in the substantive issues.

In the legislative marketplace, substance is more important than research. By substance, I mean a clear notion of what is to be accomplished, and how it will be achieved. Social scientists, Gilsinian contends, hide their values instead of making them explicit. Hence, while social scientists provide "scientific means" for analysis of processes and goals, they abandon the more important issues of the substance of criminal justice policy and goals to legislators and advocates with clearly stated values.

What is needed is a specification of the values that underlay justice perspectives, what values justicians want to transform into practice, and what policies will enact those values. This is the notion of a rational ideology—the identification of values, and implementation of policies that can be assessed to see if they achieve the ends justicians want them to achieve.

How does a criminal justician become involved in the legislative process? They become advocates for a particular perspective, and participate in local, regional, and national activities that enable their voice to be heard. At the local level, faculty participate in community action committees and civic boards, participate in Peace Officer Standards and Training boards, and provide presentations for various community groups. Nationally, faculty are invited to evaluate grants by federal agencies such as the National Institute of Justice, and they may sit on national commissions or blue-ribbon panels. They also conduct grants work, often in conjunction with local agencies, on diverse topics with broad policy applications. The theoretical writings of criminologists has at times been incorporated into broad policy. And some criminologists write with the clear intent of contributing to the policy debate (Currie, 1985).

The Limitations of Policy. As a central organizing principal, policy studies is an insufficient, though important base for the field of justice studies. It pulls the field in a normative direction, and does not provide a way to think about broader—and important—philosophical, moral, theoretical, and contextual issues. It tends to take crime as a measurable problem, the justice system as a given, and proceeds from that premise. In short, it carries many of the problems associated with normative theories, discussed previously. This is not to say that policy studies necessarily embed the justice enterprise into crime-control advocacy. The diversity of "frameworks" for the analysis of policy are more developed than much of the comparable research in the field of justice studies (see, e.g., Gilsinan, 1997).

Policy is inadequate as a basis for legitimizing the academic enterprise of criminal justice. The inquiry into justice emerges in the moral tension between the current state of justice and the justice we seek with our scientific and humanitarian inquiry. There are visions of justice that involve systemic change. Rather than take the existing policy or justice apparatus as a given, it plays the outsider role of "critic" and argues for broad, sweeping change. There are many far-reaching perspectives contribute to the breadth of the field; they inflame our imaginations, and excite us with a sense of what we as a just people might be. The justice inquiry makes room for the rebellious, creative mind. Policy studies may inadvertently discourage open dissent. Consequently, though policy studies should be an important part of criminal justice education, it is in itself insufficient as a basis for justice identity.

The Etiology of Crime Perspective. Studies of the etiology of crime represent a fundamentally different kind of perspective than policy studies. Policy studies tend to focus on justice efficiency and effectiveness within prevailing conservative and liberal values. Etiology of crime focuses on the crime act or actor and attempts to explain it. Because the government itself is sometimes seen as an agent or cause of criminal conduct, etiology can be sharply critical of existing crime control practices.

***The Relation of Crime Causation and Justice*.** Crime causation, like policy studies, is integral to criminal justice scholarship and education. Its contributions to the field of justice studies is manifold. It is through the identification of types and causes of crime—and by implication, ways to prevent crime—that criminal justice holds out the greatest hope for doing something about crime. This can take the form of policy studies mentioned above, which can be thought of as a specific kind of crime causation perspective—one in which criminal justice outcomes can be addressed within the existing legislative framework. These work "within the system." Causation, however, also may take a broader notion of injury than state defined crime. Peacemaking and critical perspectives that examine harm, for example, are clear efforts to break out of normative thinking about crime.

Criminology perspectives have contributed to the justice enterprise by constantly challenging justice practices. Many perspectives resist the idea that the existing "normative" system is either inevitable or particularly just. Perspectives of crime causation sometimes are openly critical to crime control practice, challenging the crime-control values and reliance on effectiveness measures that undergird contemporary crime policy and agency practices. These perspectives work "outside the system," in that they sometimes provide recommendations not available within the political landscape of liberal and conservative ideas. There are theories of crime that do not believe that criminal justice policy can contribute to crime control. Some theories question the assumption that justice systems and crime are related in cause and effect fashion. Labeling theorists may contend, for example, that justice systems are implicated in the production of crime. Proponents of critical theory may argue that criminal justice education is ideologically based in a crime control perspective, and rather than extending justice knowledge departments of criminal justice expand crime control into a free-thinking academic environment.

In its more rebellious forms, criminology presents itself as an alternative to "professional" or Wiltbergerian ideas of criminal justice education. This is evident in sociological traditions of crime causation. It has focused on the relationship between the individual and the community, and sought prevention of crime with intervention strategies aimed at individual offenders. Sociological research has focused on community-based institutions associated with criminal behavior, such as the family, school, and workplace (Feeley & Simon, 1992). This perspective has sometimes leveled stinging criticism at crime control policy for its failure to recognize how crime is rooted in the social environment, the social biases of crime control practice, or for the failure of crime control advocates to comprehend its sometimes harsh impact on community life (Shelden, 2001).

Crime causation has provided academic legitimation for the development of criminal justice education. The sheer variety and richness of criminology perspectives contribute much to knowledge about justice (see

Figure 2.1). The diverse perspectives that represent etiology of crime perspectives provide an intellectual tension that has been fruitful, and etiology of crime is central to many criminal justice theories. It is and continues to be a fruitful way of thinking about social relations (or the collapse thereof) among people and between individuals and the state.

Limitations of Crime Causation. A limitation with etiology of crime perspectives is that crime and justice are not equivalent concepts. Understanding crime does not always inform efforts to contribute to a more just world. There are many ways to look at justice that are not about criminal activity, yet are important to inform our thinking about crime. There are, for example, theories of justice and democracy that inform our ideas about crime but are not written with crime per se in mind. For example, some ideas of political philosophy are not based on notions of individual responsibility. (See MacIntyre, 1988). Similarly, Tocqueville's ideas about democracy are widely used (and frequently misused) in criminal justice literature, yet he did not write about crime. Burke's conservative philosophy, a reaction to the Enlightenment, seems to characterize contemporary trends in the conservative movement. By informing ourselves of the important literature of political philosophy, we learn about the context in which ideas of crime and criminality emerge.

Three divergences between crime causation and justice studies are important for this discussion. First, much of the research in the field of justice studies focuses on the nature of justice perspective, and is unrelated to crime causation. Some of these perspectives are discussed in chapter four. Further, many individuals in the justice field view their work primarily in terms of the protection of democratic traditions. Skolnick's classic (1966) work titled *Justice Without Trial* was an essay into the behavior of the police. It did not focus on crime per se, but rather on the relationship between police and democratic institutions. Yet it is now in its third edition, and it continues to be a central reading in many courses.

Second, by focusing on official crime measures, justicians are always working with a governmentally created term. A problem repeatedly confronted in the field of justice studies, and for which many scholars have talked past each other, lies in the tension between the concepts of crime and justice. Crime, literally, cannot exist without the presence of a law identifying some behavior as a crime. In this practical sense crime is always tied to the concept of a state that creates laws, the breaking of which causes crime. Yet, in many places in the world, states act with cruel impunity with regard to their citizens in ways that violate democratic sense of justice, but which are not crimes per se. The term "crime" is a limiting concept that does not fully capture the breadth of justice endeavors. Amnesty International, for example, frequently publishes research on state-level injustice (see, for example, the 1999 report "not part of my sentence" on the treatment of female prisoners in the United States). The injustices they report are more closely tied to the idea that humans should be treated fairly than to the idea that justice is about some arbitrary state standard. By holding up the term "crime" as the focus of the field, justicians implicitly acknowledge the supremacy of the state, and relegate to secondary status concerns over justice that are not clearly "crimes."

Third and finally, criminology is historically a sub-field of sociology and the actual study of crime is only a art of the student's overall education. Issues of public policy and the implementation of justice policy have been frequently ignored (Ward & Webb, 1984). More troubling, criminology programs have had difficulty acknowledging their role in the training of students for careers in criminal justice, particularly in the sub-fields such as policing and corrections involving sworn officers. The academic field of justice studies has achieved much of its viability by operating across both its academic and community audience. History has taught us that failure to acknowledge the importance of the criminal justice community can be perilous. The historical failure of criminologists to recognize their important role in teaching and preparation of students for career positions in the justice fields suggests that it is inadequate as a model for justice education.

The Interdisciplinary Perspective. An interdisciplinary perspective to justice is one in which a variety of ideas and experts from different fields are brought to bear on crime and justice issues. It is embodied in problem-solving groups that bring together sociologists, lawyers, psychologists, anthropologists and professionals who have distinguished agency experience. Central to an interdisciplinary perspective is the idea that crime is a complicated human behavior with causes and consequences that overlap many different fields of inquiry. Only through an interdisciplinary approach can a full understanding of the causes, correlates, and consequences of crime emerge.

The Relationship Between an Interdisciplinary Perspective and Justice. Many observers of justice programs argue that an interdisciplinary approach is the most suitable. Recognizing that the field as of yet lacks a core identity, it is suggested that knowledge about crime and justice will emerge by bringing together many different perspectives. Hale, in her 1997 presidential address for the Academy of Criminal Justice Sciences, presented such perspective:

> I believe it is time to accept that the study of crime and justice is an eclectic field, and that its diversity makes it vital to both higher education and society. Rather than focusing on how our programs are different—the trite debate of professionalism versus academic discipline—we should use our diversity to our advantage. By acknowledging that criminal justice programs in higher education are heterogenous, and are as varied as the crime problem and the criminal justice system's response to crime, we can use our diversity in discussions with administrators to

obtain more resources to enhance and strengthen our programs. "What's in a name?" or, to quote Gertrude Stein, "A rose is a rose is a rose is a rose" (Hale, 1998:390).

The interdisciplinary perspective described by Hale above has a strong appeal. It carries the notion that knowledge about crime benefits from an infusion of ideas from many sources. Those of us who teach justice in its diverse forms readily acknowledge that we don't have "all the answers." The promise of the interdisciplinary perspective is that, with sufficient breadth of vision, we can eventually understand crime and do something about it. It is also consistent with one of the trends in the social sciences: that many problems in the world today have been intransigent to solution, and interdisciplinarity can increase the body of ideas and provide professional breadth in fundamental problems affecting human populations. The IAD policy framework discussed in the previous chapter was an example of an interdisciplinary coalition brought together to consider the relationship between rational decisionmaking and institutional analysis. Clearly, interdisciplinarity is a powerful tool in the social science armamentum.

The Limitations of an Interdisciplinary Perspective. Interdisciplinarity suffers from two problems. First, to suggest that justice studies is interdisciplinary conveys the academic message justicians don't have a core idea of what they are about. How can justicians construct an academic identity when there is no core around which to build?

Second, interdisciplinary programs in higher education have often fared poorly. They are sometimes organized only for a fixed period and end at some specified time, when a formal report is issued. Truly interdisciplinary programs—programs and departments that are designed as permanent organizational units—often receive the final meager budget crumbs after core departments have been allocated their budgetary share.

Faculty in interdisciplinary programs often confront problems of loyalty. They are frequently expected to participate and teach classes in both their core discipline and in the interdisciplinary program. And interdisciplinary programs have a limited academic viability—when funding is short and programs and faculty are cut, interdisciplinary programs face the leading edge of funding cuts. Consequently, the interdisciplinary approach does not fully satisfy the academic identity issue, and faces problems of academic legitimacy.

Toward a Justice Perspective

We imagine justice—this is the central theme of this book. In our commitment to justice we carry out the difficult and frequently controversial work that transforms our imagination into a reality. The noble goal ties all elements of our field together. For all of its contrary and disparate elements, we are united by this shared end. We seek a world that is less mean, more responsive to the needs of its citizenry. The justice commitment is not only an end we seek: it is an inquiry. The inquiry into justice itself, conducted openly and fairly, promotes the end we seek. The breadth of the inquiry, serving interests as different as crime control advocates and critical thinkers, is a source of conflict and fragmentation in the field. Yet it is this breadth that insures that ideas won't be excluded, that we continue to reach beyond the available stock of ideas and seek new ways to formulate and enact justice.

The core theme that unites the diverse elements of the justice field is "justice sought." This is an inquiry, a vision of growth and development that guides the field of justice studies as well as the inspiration that inspires us individually. At the personal level, it is found in a commitment to service in all its forms, including service through scholarship, education, and practice. Academically, it is found in breadth of vision. Concerns of justice are the common, consolidating identity, fusing such disparate passions as the treatment of victims, fairness in police behavior, social relations among intimates, child-rearing practices, state-sponsored violence, legal precedent, the culture of corrections officers, and the training of administrative executives in justice organizations. By identifying with an idea of justice, we move away from the idea that some particular conception of justice is "right." Justice concerns become what they should be in an academic endeavor—questions to be addressed through the application of scholarship, whether the scholarship is expressed in pedagogy, science, or humanities.

The inquiry into justice is inclusive. As stated at the outset of this book, the search for justice is best served academically by erring on the side of inclusiveness of ideas and perspectives. The idea of inclusiveness is described by breadth of vision. Flanagan (2000) identifies four areas of studies that characterize the justice perspective, and that considered together capture the breadth of the justice inquiry.

1. *Social control in organized societies.* This focus point allows students to "examine and evaluate the contribution of law as an instrument of social control across cultures and over time" [7]. Law is not accepted as is, but locates legal systems in time and place.

2. *Moral questions involving fundamental concepts such as integrity, justice, fairness and equity.* Central to education is the idea that an educated person recognize and consider the breadth of moral and ethical problems in their field of interest. This is particularly important in the field of justice, where normative ideas of right and wrong have frequently been unquestioned.

3. *How societies construct organizations and institutions to achieve desired social goals.* In the field of justice studies, these are public safety, justice, and the legitimate and measured sanctions of social

deviants. Criminal justice agencies should be understood as part of a "larger, loosely coupled, community-based interorganizational networks . . ." [8]. This area looks at local dynamics, and also asks about the dynamics that constrain or enable those networks at the local and national level.

4. *Provide a frame for analyzing the change process—at the individual, organizational, institutional, and community levels.* By frame, Flanagan cites Freedman (1996:2):

> . . . to explore the ordeal of being human—the drama of discovering the darker side of the self, the responsibility of imposing meaning on one's life and one's society . . ."

This idea of frame is clearly hermeneutic: it sometimes involves introspection in order to discover the meanings of that which one studies. The "frame" also includes methodological considerations, including a recognition of the limitations and properties of scientific method.

Flanagan's recommendations are heady in their breadth, providing the field of justice studies with a set of contexts—international, national, methodological, and theoretical—for studying issues involving justice. None of the four areas focus specifically on crime, nor do any rely directly on policy. Instead, each is about contextualizing crime and justice practice and policy in ways that require that we reflect on the nature of the justice enterprise. They are prescriptions for diversity of vision—they push us toward the pluralistic complexity, discussed in the previous chapter, that characterize the social sciences today. Importantly, each area also allows for us to inquire into the rules we use to study, think about, and conduct research on issues of crime and justice. They locate scientific studies within a hermeneutic sensitivity—a need to continually reflect on who we are, what we do, and ask ourselves why we are doing it.

The four areas of study proposed by Flanagan are enabling: they locate the field of justice studies squarely within contemporary trends in the social sciences, as described by the Gulbenkian Commission (Wallerstein et al., 1996). They contextualize justice studies within time and space. This important idea provides a counter-balance to the powerful normative hold U.S. practices have held on the field of criminal justice. It allows us to recognize that all our core ideas—of crime, of justice, and even of democracy—occur in a particular time and space. They are not universal. This is a tremendously liberating vision, permitting up to sustain the hope that we can develop ideas more just than those we see practiced, that the future is unbound by the limitations of the past.

Closely related to the location of justice in time and space is the idea that historical systems may not be time-reversible (Abu-Lughod, 1989). This notion is a fundamental challenge to model development in justice scholarship. Time irreversibility has several implications. First, it means that, even if we develop a model of justice system activity that worked in the past, it might not be replicable. For example, if we were to look at the relationship between crime and poverty in inner cities in the 1960s, we might reasonably conclude that poverty and crime were spuriously related by migration patterns and historical patterns of racial prejudice that structured opportunities for employment and property ownership. The relationship between poverty and crime, and even the fundamental meanings of the terms, may change so much that the 1960s model cannot be replicated, even if it were valid then. Time irreversibility is not mystical, it simply recognizes the incredible complexity and transience of relationships among things.

Second, time-irreversibility tells us that the appearance of seemingly equivalent conditions in the present era would not necessarily lead to the same outcome that occurred in the past. Third, it tells us that if we try to undo the causes, we cannot assume that the outcomes will also be undone. How, then, can we learn from our past mistakes? The answer to this question, in the form in which the social sciences are emerging and in which the justice enterprise will participate, is that we carefully consider the panoply of current characteristics of the problem, and that we reach across the disciplines to develop solutions to substantive problems. The past is an important ingredient in any solution to problems, but it is only a part.

Fourth, time-irreversibility suggests that our habitual ways of thinking may limit our vision more than it may inform it. "Common sense" solutions, based on cultural habit, are likely to be fundamentally misleading. Fifth, time-irreversibility tells us that we must be open to new ideas of justice. We cannot assume that what worked in the past will work in the future. We must be flexible to the changes that time brings, and keep our focus on the here-and-now, in all its cacophonic splendor.

Across the liberal arts and humanities, a diversity of vision has emerged to replace the hegemony of European-dominated thought since the 1940s. In the field of justice studies, we witness an expanding focus on gender, a stirrings of explorations into ethnicity, and a continued focus on race and the inequalities associated with it. Each of the topics of gender, ethnicity and race is covered in a separate chapter later in this book. Research and scholarship on these topics has undergone a dramatic transformation in the 1990s, from inquiry that focused on how these topics related to mainstream patterns of justice practices, to an examination of the topics as unique justice enterprises in themselves. The idea that a view can be hegemonic is replaced by the recognition that all points of view, theories, and perspectives are standpoints. This is a clear turn away from the idea that a general determinative model can map all patterns of justice behavior. It is a nomothetic turn in the field of justice studies, and parallels similar developments in other social sciences discussed in Chapter 3.

By including ethics as one of the four areas of study, Flanagan recognizes the contribution of the humanities to justice studies. It may be a turn, as Flanagan noted above, toward an exploration of the darker side of the social contract. Clearly, many aspects of the justice inquiry are not a celebration of the human spirit. Ethics requires that justicians consider how human behavior is mobilized by the darkest human fears and meanest justice cruelties, but that we also recognize how ordinary people sometimes practice extraordinary kindnesses

What constitutes an ethic suitable for the field of justice studies? An ethical vision is described by Pepinsky (1993:393-394) in his essay on justice literacy. His vision parallels the ideas of justice in this book.

> I am sustained by the diversifying community of interest I discover among those who want to know what I seek to discover. That is my core, and it is expanding. The beauty of this core is that I do not have to reduce the priority I give to any of the areas discussed in this (special) issue (of the Journal of Criminal Justice Education). However we accomplish it, I would observe only that becoming less peripheral is a two-way street; if you're going to garner my core attention, you'll have to learn and respond to my core concerns. I think that giving a damn about what we mean by crime, criminal, and justice is a natural starting point. Every area advocated in this issue begs the question: Why should your crime and justice be mine? All of us are qualified already to join this discussion.

Pepinsky's vision is a demanding one. It places at the center of the field of justice studies not a core curriculum, nor a methodology, nor a datum, concept or paradigm. At the center is an inquiry, and justice flows from the inquiry. The inquiry begins in the classroom with a question and response (Question—What is justice? Response: I don't know, because I don't know you). The question directs the field, and the response provides an ethic—justice can only emerge from learning about people, what Pepinsky called a diversifying community of interest.

Pepinsky's vision seems relativistic—justice can be whatever one wants it to be. Indeed, one might fairly argue that his vision celebrates relativity. Relativity in this sense forces us to acknowledge that, in the moral and ethical work of justice, no perspective can hold hegemony. Diversity of perspective may be our field's strength—it denies satisfaction with any one standpoint; it demands that the inquiry continue. It locates us academically and links together the disparate elements of the field—social worker, police officer, social critic, theoretician, quantitative methodologist. It identifies us as justicians through our commitment, through our willingness, as Pepinsky noted, to give a damn.

As Pepinsky (1993) observed, our search for justice is a point of departure—a question, not an answer. We should not take the criminal justice system as a given, only as one enacted fragment of justice's potential. The question is accompanied by an ethic: our responsibility is to recognize our commitment to fairness. Individually, our answer is carried out in the career decisions and voluntary activities through which we seek justice. For those of us who are faculty, if we are effective in our academic quest, our students will follow the same inquiry.

Preparing for Change. The ideas provided by Flanagan and Pepinsky above can be understood as organizing principles for the field of justice studies. They capture the breadth of the justice enterprise. They locate the justice enterprise squarely within the traditions and contemporary concerns of the social sciences. They recognize the important contribution of the humanities to justice. In a word, they are enabling—they invite scholarship and service at the highest levels, while insuring breadth and rigor in justice education at all levels.

How can we relate their ideas to contemporary curricula and practice in higher education? For programs in two-year colleges, the Wiltbergerian, vocational studies model continues to be the standard. This model performs a critically needed function for education—it is relevant for students and it is consistent with the vocational mission. In itself, it is inadequate and needs to be expanded to include the transfer function. Two-year programs must re-institute efforts to prepare justice students for four-year programs, a task for which students are all too often unprepared. Criminal justice students often seek two-year degrees for two reasons both related to expense: they tend to be less expensive per credit hour and they often are more accessible, so students can stay close to home. Yet many students carry hopes of transferring to four-year programs after they graduate.

Unfortunately, transfer to four-year programs is complicated by the vocational orientations of two-year programs. Some students graduate only to find that many of their classes will not transfer to four-year programs. Others have classes that are protected by articulation agreements which require four-year programs to accept the equivalency of two-year classes. Often, they find that the course content of the "equivalent" classes left them unprepared for the critical thinking and knowledge base needed for upper division work.

Two-year programs need to recognize and accommodate the needs of their students, which often involve a four-year or higher education. The vocationalization movement in criminal justice has not provided students with what many want—preparation for upper division work in a four-year college or university. It will be recalled that the two-year vocationalization movement was a product of two-year college administrators, who sought a unique identity for two-year programs *in spite* of student desires for transfer to a four-year program after graduation. If two-year programs seek state-wide articulation equity with state colleges and universities, they must also take on the responsibility, often lacking, of preparing students for the hard intellectual work of critical thinking in four-year institutions.

Comprehensive universities today provide diverse baccalaureate and Masters programs, and are the primary carriers of the justice identity.

These institutions often carry local, "community college" missions and are increasingly steered in the direction of vocationalization. Boyer (1990) noted the contradictory expectations faculty face in these institutions, anticipating careers balanced with scholarship and education, and pushed instead into large classes and heavy service commitments.

Flanagan's (2000) prescription for the current vocational and "community college" tendencies in comprehensive is to fortify justice students with a strong liberal arts education. He suggested that the American College Model described by Berberet and Wong (1995:48) provides the needs of education for criminal justice students today. The model works at the "intersection of liberal education and professional education."[7] Flanagan observed that a central feature of the employment marketplace is change and rapidity of obsolescence, and technical training will not provide adequate preparation for their long-term career needs. Students consequently need both intellectual curiosity and the kinds of academic skills that will enable them to adapt to change. By linking the criminal justice curriculum to the liberal arts core curriculum ad the careful selection of electives, a process Flanagan calls *skillful joinery*, students can become adequately prepared for their work in the justice fields.[8]

At the level of the Ph.D. the academic landscape presents a variety of program types. It is likely that these programs will provide the identity for the future of criminal justice education. Some programs and departments in universities have a narrow research orientation that focuses on immediate crime and policy problems. The normative orientation of these programs fails to capture the needs of justice inquiry (Sullivan, 1994):

> Existing doctoral programs in the U.S. differ in details but are depressingly similar in demanding a great deal of methodology and then teaching the substantive elements of criminal justice on a piecemeal basis. Practically nowhere is a larger, more holistic view of the field, in its moral and political settings, developed and considered (Sullivan, 1994:449).

The normative orientation resulted in inadequately prepared students who lacked of field-wide perspective and knowledge.

> Students have no vision of the whole in its context. Rather, they strongly tend to see the police, the courts, corrections, types of crime, or problems of criminal law. Within these pigeonholes, they then look for problems that can be quantified, or at least handled in terms of the behavioristic methodologies they have been taught. The result is an unspoken acceptance of the system as a whole and of its context (Sullivan, 1994:550).

Sullivan calls for a wider vision of the justice field. What is needed, is a perspective that recognizes the limitations of the normative policy-oriented thinking. Where is the broader vision, the concern for the ethics of the state as well as the individual? What vision, he challenges, can provide Ph.D. level direction for the field of justice studies? He calls for a renaissance in justice education, that educators impart the holistic elements of the justice field. Broad questions of values and ethics, as well as more rebellious views of the justice of the state and of agencies that represent the state are central elements of the inquiry into justice. Once we acknowledge that justice as practiced and taught in the United States is value-based and specified in time and space, we locate normative practices as only one variety of many possible justices. The relevant question "what works" is preceded by the moral question "why do we want it to work?" We return to Pepinsky's question—*What is justice? I don't know, because I don't know you.* This simple recognition demands that we acknowledge that our field is first and foremost a humanities, and is irreconcilably connected with fundamental questions of ethics and morality.

The idea that justice is an inquiry bounded by human contexts legitimates the study of justice as an academic endeavor spanning the social sciences and engaging the humanities. The focus is broad, not narrow. It provides for the growth of basic knowledge. It allows for independence of inquiry, central to the academic enterprise. And a full spectrum of ideological positions can operate within it comfortably. It presumes neither that crime control is good or bad, but rather promotes study of crime control in the spirit of academic inquiry and openness. Finally it is involved in the life of its community and region—its members actively participate in local agency assessment and policy formation, justice research institutes, and in major university settings.

There are those who might argue that an open-ended inquiry into justice will only fracture the field and lead to atomization of interests. Yet, in practice, the theme can be unifying, allowing justicians to look at problems through new "eyes," expanding one's vision. Consider community policing. If we are to think about community policing as a justice inquiry, we need to consider the nature of the relationship between the individual and the state, the role of mediating institutions, and the nature of social control. We should consider macro-micro problems in social theory. We might look at some of the recent IAD applications to community analysis. We consider the implications of ethical problems at the practical levels, to help deal with concrete problems, and at the theoretical levels, so that a "way of thinking" provides guidance through ambiguous and unanticipated situations. We challenge taken-for-granted ideas of common sense in police practices. We look for demographic changes and assess their impact on service populations and areas of high mobility. We consider the cultural impact of linguistic differences.

Practice in community policing requires police officers who can deal with diverse ethnic problems. That the police should train for ethnic and minority sensitivity is a far cry from early, Wiltbergerian concerns over "nuts and bolts" technical training. It is consistent with Vollmer's recognition that practitioners should be trained in all the social sciences related to their work, recognizing that the complexity of that work has expanded dramatically since Vollmer's days at Berkeley.

Today, the enterprise of police work has expanded to encompass issues and needs such as public order in a multi-ethnic environment, justice activity in complex municipal environments, community organizing, language skills, and multi-media communication. Contemporary education involves a broadening of the police task in dimensions both technical and humanitarian and reflects the needs of police work in a multi-ethnic, internationalizing environment. The vision recognizes the importance of Wiltberger's ideas of service to the criminal justice community, and locates service within wider concerns over the nature of justice in a complex democracy.

The United States is undergoing permanent and long-term change, becoming what some have called the first truly international civilization (Kaplan, 1998). Even as service oriented programs try to make justice education more practical, our notions of practicality are changing, swiftly adapting to an enormously complicated world of coexisting ethnic groups and complex technologies. If academics are to provide the kinds of vision, focus, and direction needed by our changing society, we will take on a wide vision that recognizes the role of all of our society's participants. Our core has to be an inquiry, for we surely don't have the answers now. In our efforts to prepare students for a career in justice we as educators, like our citizenry, will have to become international in breadth. Perhaps, if our inquiry is broad enough, we can provide a vision sufficient to meet the needs of a truly international citizenry.

Notes

[1]   Rush's (1994) and Goldstein's (1986) figures on the percentage of in-service officers in LEEP substantially differ. I can offer no explanation for this difference.

[2]   Durham (1992: 39) observed that ". . . the competitive conditions of resource distribution within the university environment do involve hierarchies, and resources are often distributed in accord with such hierarchies. Disciplines perceived as providing services incidental to the university mission may be at a severe disadvantage when the time comes to allocate resources."

[3]   These numbers are not strictly comparable. The figures offered by Ward and Webb, for example, refer to courses of study, not actual degrees. The numbers are intended to provide a sense of both growth and academic institutionalization.

[4]   The numbers of Ph.D. granting institutions listed in the ACJS report, 22, is stable. The ACJS report listed 22, 1 less than the 23 reported by Langworthy and Latessa. This does not mean that institutional processes of infrastructural development are not occurring. Many departments may be gathering strength and developing plans for the next push toward full academic legitimacy—the expansion of Masters (and some

Doctoral) degrees in comprehensive schools and Ph.D. programs in doctoral and research schools.

[5]   The *Journal of Criminal Justice* was the flagship journal of the Academy of Criminal Justice Sciences from 1976 to 1983. In 1984 the *Justice Quarterly* became the ACJS flagship journal.

[6]   Speaking theoretically, the legitimation crisis is being resolved in the ways long-term institutional crises are—through the creation of structures and formal policies that absorb the crises formally into the organizational chart and formal organizational practices (Meyer & Rowan, 1992). For criminal justice education, this means that programs are increasingly focusing on what has become, since the decline of the LEAA, their primary legitimating audience.

[7]   Quoted in Flanagan, 2000:10.

[8]   A central strength of the American college Model is that it consistent with many trends in higher education today—it recognizes that colleges have to attend to their community college function, it addresses the need for academic rigor, and provides for the assessment of educational outcomes increasingly integral to institutions during periodic external reviews.

Chapter 4

Toward Justice Perspective: The Development of Theory in Criminal Justice

One of the primary purposes of this book is to provide a view of the contexts in which justice issues emerge, and how those issues are linked to central problems in its environment. This chapter is an overview of the theoretical contexts of justice thought, to provide the reader with an overview of what I think are central perspectives in the field of justice studies.

In this chapter, I attempt to sketch the central theoretical perspectives used to explain the practice of justice. Theoretically, our field has developed a variety of perspectives. In this chapter I discuss normative, functional, institutional, and conflict perspectives. In constructing this typology, I am creating theoretical meta-structure in the justice field where none currently exists. I recognize that my pigeon-holing of perspectives is arbitrary, and that other equally valid ways of organizing a meta-theory of justice is possible (see, e.g., Garland, 1990; MacIntyre, 1990; Walzer, 1983). My purpose is to develop, in broad strokes, a systematic picture of the kinds of theories that are being used in the field of criminal justice today, why they are important to the justice endeavor, and what they are trying to explain. Many examples of each type of perspective are presented, with no claim on my part that the review of the literature is complete.

This chapter reviews contemporary theoretical developments. This review is not inclusive. It provides an overview of material that has been recently written, and assesses how it can be systematically organized into a presentational form for justice studies. Clearly, there is broad literature on criminal justice and punishment that can illuminate any review of the field of justice studies. The sparkling review and systematic assessment of the social theory of punishment by Garland (1990), for example, provides a reader with insight into the works of Durkheim, Weber, Foucault, and Marx among others, and their important historical contributions to how we think about punishment today.

I take a different approach. Recognizing that major historical works have already been clearly and thoroughly examined, I am concerned with recent scholarly efforts to develop theory in justice studies. This is a relatively unbroached topic, and one that will provide a sense of where the field is today. Five general categories are used to describe contemporary developments in criminal justice thought. These, each considered below, are normative/rational, structural/functional, institutional, conflict, and contemporary critical perspectives.

Normative/Rational Perspective

The earliest models that we used to explain criminal justice organizations can be called normative or rational models of organizational behavior. These perspectives correspond to the free-will ideas of criminal justice practice. They carry the idea that organizations control what they do, and that organizational behavior is internally directed. If free will is the idea that individuals control their own destiny, normative theory of justice organizations is the idea that an organization controls its behavior and sets its goals independent or fully cognizant of external influences.

Normative/rational models of justice organizations represent the earliest models of organizational behavior. The central idea of these models is straightforward: the behavior of organizations can be understood by what the organization states that it does. Consequently, to understand organizations, we should look at its formal goals, policies, organizational chart, and the like.

Central to these ideas of organization is the notion of rationality. Indeed, the importance of rationality to this concept of organizational purpose cannot be overstated. By rationality, I mean the ability of the organization to freely select among known alternative courses of action in order to achieve its formal organizational goals (Feeley, 1997). Rationality presupposes that the organization knows what its full array of possible courses of actions are, and that it can freely pick and choose among various actions in order to achieve important goals.

Theories of rational organization can be traced to the writings of Weber (1954). Weber described bureaucratization as a phenomenon that marked the increasing rationality and complexity of Western societies. Bureaucracies are a form of organizational design that match modern, differentiated society. Bureaucracies are also differentiated, capable of multiple objectives and goals. They are rationalized, in that formal organizational purposes lie in explicit written roles, which individuals are expected to fulfill. Rational organizations have emerged in Western society because they "work." They are effective at achieving desired outputs. The coordination and control of activity are the critical dimensions by which formal organizations have succeeded in the modern world (Meyer & Rowan, 1992).

Justice, Norms, and Values

Normative/rational models of organizational behavior are closely tied to normative models of citizen behavior. A theory of the behavior of justice organizations consequently requires a complementary theory of citizen behavior. A matching theory of citizen behavior is one in which citizens act according to broad norms, which represent consensus about right behavior, right behavior being behavior that preserves the state. This perspective is briefly reviewed below.

If justice organizations have goals, how do they know what their goals should be? How do we know what behavior is wrong, what sorts of behavior deserve to be criminally sanctioned, and how justice organizations should go about it in a way that is fair for society? The answer, from a normative/rational perspective, is that society is characterized by a set of norms, the most egregious violations of those norms deserves to be criminally sanctioned, and that justice organizations can operate rationally to do something about crime.

In a normative model, the relationship between crime and criminal justice agencies is plain. Agencies exist to do something about crime, and their policies and practices are organized to achieve that goal. To be sure, chiefs must account for the whims of mayors and city council-members, and judges and prosecutors can be removed if they act against the grain of public opinion. However, these elements represent the way in which political life is carried out in our fractious democracy, and their influence is perceived, within this model, to be subtle and indirect. The bottom line of criminal justice organizations is dispensing justice.

Justice systems operate on a set of beliefs that are consistent with a normative perspective of social behavior. Simply put, the normative perspective is the idea that individual behavior is in line with acceptable "norms." Individual behavior reasonably close to the "norm" is tolerated. Some behaviors are so inconsistent with acceptable "norms" of behavior that they must be punished with a sanction, and with criminal sanctions in extreme cases. Norms are associated with values. Behavior consistent with norms is considered good, and the more it deviates from the norm the more it is seen as "bad." For example, in the language of the criminal law, minor transgressions are described as mala in se, or bad in their own right, and major violations are mala prohibita—morally offensive. The greater moral offensiveness is provided to those behaviors most distant from acceptable (normative) standards of behavior. The further from the norm our behavior is, the more deviant we are. As we deviate, we encounter social sanctions. Sanctions may range from a raised eyebrow to the death penalty, depending on the magnitude of our deviations and the importance of the norm.

Justice organizations represent the government and are responsible for enforcing behavior that is perceived by lawmakers to threaten the social order. The written law codifies the threshold of behavior perceived to be threatening to society or influential groups in society.

Norms are value invested, which means that those who do the work of norm enforcement—justice professionals—perceive their work as "good." When the membership of justice organizations are polled, membership they state that their work was about doing something good for society, about getting bad people off the streets, about making society safe for ordinary people (Crank & Caldero, 2000). They do not critically examine these values, to the contrary. They take the criminal code as a given and put into place objectives and goals that achieve crime control objectives. Norms enforcers, such as police officers, probation and parole officers, and prosecutors, tend to view their work as doing what is best for society. Norms enforcement, in a word, is an uncritical acceptance of the status quo, and its preservation occurs through the execution of the criminal law.

Academic educators in justice studies have tended to think about their teaching style and the organization of curricula in normative terms. Departmental curricula is frequently arranged in terms of the functional divisions of the justice system—we tend to specialize in police, juvenile delinquency, corrections, intermediate sanctions, and the law. Each is organized primarily around their contribution to anti-crime activity. To be sure, most university-level textbooks also include a broad array of issues involving these different segments of the criminal justice process. The normative perspective is important, but not all-inclusive. When we teach classes, we frequently adopt a policy-oriented or "what works" perspective. Our curricula tend to begin with what Travis (p.c.) referred to as a "catechism" of justice (though at the time he was referring to the police). This means that we tend to take justice organizations as a given, and then examine how do they relate to broader crime control.

Limitations of the Normative Perspective. Langworthy's (1986; 1992) criticisms of research on police organizations are aptly applied to the normative traditions of criminal justice education. He noted that research on police organizations has generally been normative. It began with the premise that doing something about crime was the most important police goal, that different kinds of crimes required different ways to organize units or plan strategy and tactics. Consequently, research on police organizations has attempted to identify the best kinds of structures that would enhance the crime suppression mission. Researchers have tended to ask questions, for example, such as *what is the best kind of police patrol to increase arrests and lower crime in some geographic* *area?* Yet hidden within the question, and with the normative perspective generally, are a limiting set of assumptions that in and of themselves reflect a level of thinking inadequately broad for academic recognition. Let us think critically about the above question on police patrol and arrests:

1. The question assumes that particular types of police organizational structures or tactics produce particular kinds of crime control outcomes, a presumption that Langworthy was unwilling to accept. The relationship between structures and outcomes was, he contended, contextualized by the environment in which structures were practiced. In some communities, for example, aggressive police practices might intimidate criminals and lead to lower levels of criminal activity, while in other areas it might alienate the citizenry and embolden criminals.

2. The question fails to consider the possibility that both the structure and the outcome are spuriously related. Put broadly, it may be that sometimes both crime and justice dynamics are outcomes, produced by broader environmental conditions. It might be that, by looking at both justice systems and their characteristics as dependent variables (outcomes), we can develop a richer perspective on justice system dynamics. Kohfeld and Sprague (1990), for example, have shown how both crime and police response are consequences of demographic factors.

3. The relationship between crime and arrests is complicated and, at this state of our knowledge, unknown. There is scant compelling evidence that arrest practices deter crime either at the specific or general deterrent level.

4. The question puts us at a particular relation with crime control efforts, a relation that many academics are unwilling to accept for both reasons of ideology and academic independence. The question carries in it the presumption that the solution to crime is based in a crime control perspective, and the only question *is how do we develop the best crime control solution?* Ways of dealing with crime may lie in other directions as well, for example, in prevention techniques.

5. The question assumes that the valued end is arrests, and at that point we can cease to address the question. Such an assumption should not be made casually. Arrests may be an undesirable end—juveniles are exposed to the criminogenic effects of jails and prisons, for example, or ex-offenders face lowered job prospects, pushing them towards a renewal of criminal activity.

6. The question makes fundamental assumptions about the role of government in the lives of citizens. It resumes that the intervention of the government can have some kind of effect on citizen behavior. At a more profound level, it presumes that government should intervene in the affairs of citizenry, and that its intervention is "good."

7. The question puts us in a value-based relationship with justice agencies. It presumes that their basic purposes are morally right, and that only their particular tactics need to be considered. It thereby limits the moral breadth of the justice field, suggesting that those who question the inquiry are in some way morally inferior.

In the end, the normative theoretical perspective comes up short, for two important reasons. First, as items 1 to 3 above noted, the perspective makes too many assumptions about the independence of justice organization decisionmaking. Too often, research has found that programs don't act as we expected them to, or what worked in one setting doesn't work in another, or that programs or policies carried hidden assumptions that were unexpectedly revealed, or that programs were contaminated by individuals or groups, both outside and inside the organization, who were uncomfortable with what the organization was doing. Justice systems operate in a variety of contexts, and failure to account for those contexts is a significant shortcoming of this literature.

The normative perspective comes up short in a second way as well, as suggested by items 4 through 6. In an important sense, all justice questions are ultimately moral questions. The quest for justice demands that we seek that which we believe is just: this is the central theme of the book. Every time we implement a program to curb law-breaking, we are making assumptions about the nature of justice. The normative approach presumes the morality of the status quo in both criminal justice and in governance. For many justicians this morality is an open question, not a value to be taken for granted. Many justicians are morally troubled by current justice practices, and do not accept the presumption that justice is achieved when government agencies efficiently carry out crime control efforts.

The issue that moves our field forward and us individually through our careers, the quest for justice, carries an unknown end. Within that vision, a normative perspective carries an important part, but in both a theoretical and ethical sense it is only one part. The other perspectives, presented below, provide additional parts of the theoretical framework of criminal justice and enable a deeper exploration into the values that undergird the justice system.

Structural/Functional Perspective

Functional theory refers to theoretical perspective in which the parts of a whole are considered for their contribution to the welfare of the whole. Structural theory refers to the social structures that make up a society. The ideas of structure and function are closely tied to each other. Giddens describes structural/functional theory straightforwardly as follows:

> To study the structure of society is like studying the anatomy of an organism; to study its functions is like studying the physiology of an organism. It is to show how the structure 'works.' .. Structure is understood as referring to a 'pattern' of social relationships; function, to how such patterns actually operate as systems . . . (Giddens, 1994:60).

Structural/functional theories differ from free-will perspectives in that they recognize that an actor's motivations may not be fully known to the actor, and that an actor's behavior may have consequences that are unintended or of which we are only incidentally aware. The history of the police professionalism movement, for example, is a case study of the unintended consequences of well-intentioned acts and changes by thoughtful, purposive police reformers (Walker, 1977). For example, by focusing on organizational changes consistent with administrative control, reformers under the banner of police professionalism initiated a series of changes that profoundly limited the professional decision-making authority of individual officers (Roberg, Crank & Kuykendall, 2000). Free-will theories of organizational reform have for the most part simply ignored unintended consequences of reforms (see Giddens, 1994:7).

Feeley: A Functional Systems Model

The development of functional theory has a rich heritage in sociological and anthropological literature. The term "function" has been used to include (1) a mathematical function, (2) "useful activity" as in activity that is instrumental in achieving a purpose, (3) "appropriate activity" which includes useful activity but may also include outcomes that are unintended, and (4) "system-determined and system-maintaining activity," which is the idea that social life is organized in systems (Martindale, 1960:444-445). The latter definition is the most interesting and the most complicated, because it recognizes that social systems are teleological—they organize themselves to guarantee their survival, and their parts exist primarily to contribute to their continued survival.[1]

The teleology of criminal justice systems has been widely noted, though not expressly recognized. Bayley's famous dictum—the police are to the government as the edge is to the knife—is a teleological statement.

It locates the police in a particular relationship with nation-states—they exist to protect the state from internal threat. From the perspective of state leaders, the survival of the state depends, at least in part, on the ability of the police to do their work. A functional analysis at the nation-state level, recognizing the teleology of nation-states, consequently requires that we look at how the criminal justice system contributes to the state's survivability.

Within individual justice organizations, functional theory examines how the behavior actors contributes to the well-being of the organization. The formal development of functional theory in the criminal justice field can be dated to 1973 (Feeley, 1997). Feeley identified two criminal justice system models, the rational goal model and the functional systems model. The rational model, Feeley observed, was of limited explanatory value for understanding the behavior of justice organizations. In practice, organizational goals and policies are frequently ignored, displaced, or simply ignored. Individual justice actors sometimes violated organizational directives in order to increase their effectiveness, or to achieve their personally desired ends. A rational model of organization simply could not account for the diversity of behavior seen in most organizations. A functional systems model, Feeley suggested, could account for a broader range of behavior displayed by justice organizations.

Feeley employed Etzioni's (1960) definition of functionalism to define and discuss functional systems in criminal justice. According to Etzioni, the starting point for organizational analysis should not be the formal goals and policies of the organization. Analysis should assess the actual behavior of the social unit itself, what the organization actually did and how its behavior contributed to effectiveness. In this sense, functional and rational arguments diverged in the way in which they approached the analysis of organizations: Rational models focused on official organizational pronouncements—goals and policies—while functional arguments turn their attention to what the organizational actually does. Extending the functional perspective to the field of criminal justice, Feeley developed the following conception: Criminal justice is a . . .

> system of action based primarily on cooperation, exchange, and adaptation, and emphasize these considerations over adherence to formal rules and defined roles in searching for and developing explanations of behavior and discussing organizational effectiveness (Feeley, 1997:123).

The "rules" followed by organizational members were not formal or official statements; rather, they were informal "folkways." Feeley described systems in which the informal relations, not formal roles, predominate in relations among system actors. The system might be comprised of rational individuals, however they often pursued individual or collective goals quite different from official organizational goals, policies, or other formal pronouncements.

The functional perspective put forth by Feeley also recognized that justice organizations sometimes contain competing or conflicting goals. Actors within the organization may support some goals and not others, and organizational goals may receive different emphases. Consequently, the analysis of functional systems required the assessment of the actual behavior of the organization. Feeley's ideas of functional systems differed from many functional perspectives, in that he did not develop the idea that the functional parts of justice systems contributed to the overall whole. Rather, the use of the functional perspective provided a basis for analyzing the behavior of an organization apart from its official pronouncements. The strength and essential contribution of Feeley's paper was twofold—(1) the identification of models of organizational behavior in a field where theoretical models were essentially absent, and (2) the recognition that assessments of organizational behavior should look at unintended consequences and the occulted motivations of organizational actors.

Hagan: Loosely Coupled Systems. Hagan (1989) noted that criminal justice theory was broadly framed in consensus and conflict models. Consensus theories, Hagan observed, predicted a central role for legal variables in justice outcomes. Conflict theories, on the other hand, looked for the influence of extralegal variables in justice effects. Hagan argued that neither perspective adequately predicted many kinds of justice outcomes, yet no other perspectives had emerged to provide direction for criminal justice research. The sheer variety and unpredictability of findings, Hagan suggests, has contributed to a sense of bewilderment on the part of researchers. Needed was perspective that accounted for the complexity observed in real-world justice outcomes.

Hagan put forth a "provisional base" for the development of a structural-contextual theory of criminal justice. This provisional base contained the following elements:

Orienting Premises:

1. North American criminal justice systems tend to be loosely coupled, with low levels of explained variance in outcomes across subsystems.

2. To the extent that these outcomes can be explained, they are explained by different variables within different subsystems.

Consider sentencing decisions, for example. In an analysis of sentencing decisions, Hagan, Nagel and Albonetti (1980) looked at the behavior of a federal jurisdiction that proactively pursued white-collar crime. The problem in prosecuting crime in many courts, they observed, was the absence of complainants who could knowledgeably assist enforcement efforts. The proactive problem was viewed as ways to obtain leverage on witnesses. This was accomplished by forging a connection between negotiations, coercion, and sentencing concessions. By forging this connection, the agency overcame the "loose coupling" that tended to accompany plea negotiations and sentencing decisions in white-collar cases. This example suggests that internal court processes determine outcomes, and by tightening the linkages between negotiations and sentencing, court processes become more predictable and effective. Hagan provides the following propositions:

> Propositions:
>
> 1. The flow of crimes with complainants is more resistant to political forces, so political initiatives to increase levels of law enforcement activity most often increase the prosecution of crimes without complainants.
>
> 2. The prosecution of crimes without complainants increases the use of proactive prosecutorial techniques, including plea negotiations, charge bargaining, and sentence reductions.
>
> 3. Increases in the use of proactive prosecutorial techniques lead to increases in levels of explained variance within and across subsystems, as the connections between these subsystems are tightened.
>
> 4. These increased levels of explained variance are reflected in the increased influence of organizational (i.e., plea and prosecutorial recommendations), legal (i.e., offense and prior record), and extralegal (i.e., race, class, and status) variables.

Hagan (1989) makes a persuasive argument for the loose coupling of the prosecutorial system in justice practices. His view of loose coupling is a structural argument, aimed at understanding the way in which parts of the criminal justice system tie together. Because the loose coupling is also linked to the overall effectiveness of justice system processes both within and across subsystems, it can be considered a functional theory of justice system processes. Interestingly, it is a theory of dispersion—it seeks to explain variability in courtroom outcomes, not specific kinds of outcomes.

His idea of loose coupling is different from Meyer and Rowan's (1992) idea of loose coupling, discussed in the section on institutional theory below. Hagan perceives loose coupling as an organizational problem that can be addressed through proactivity and innovation in the delivery of justice services. The condition is taken as a particular kind of organizational problem, and proactivity offers a way to deal with it. Meyer and Rowan (1992), on the other hand, perceive loose coupling as a derivative phenomenon, a consequence of environmental demands on institutionalized organizations.

Duffee: Criminal Justice and Community Theory. Duffee's (1990) theory of criminal justice stands out as a development of functional theory in criminal justice. Duffee began with a discussion of prevailing ideology in criminal justice policy and practice. Ideological differences in popular conceptions of justice are described by the umbrella terms *retribution/deterrence* and *social welfare*. Each of these ideologies are carried by advocates who argue that their view should prevail as the primary goals of the criminal justice. Policy in the United States has tended to flow from these perspectives. They are summarized below.

Retribution and Deterrence. This is the predominant perspective of those who support "retributive or criminal" justice. This is the administration of the penal sanction as the "official reaction to the commission of criminal offenses" [17]. According to this position, punishment is unavoidable, and only those purposes associated with punishment are appropriate for criminal justice. It is important that justice deal with objective acts of wrongdoing, rather than objectionable behavior. Packer (1968) focuses, for example, on the objective social harm of individual acts. The criminal sanction is best applied where ideas of incapacitation and deterrence are most likely to be effective. And Van den Haag (1975), retribution should be the prevailing purpose of the judicial process. Sanctions are essential, simply because some people want to do that which is illegal.

Social welfare and distributive justice. Distributive justice, Duffee notes, is the broad range of "political and economic processes by which goods, services, and symbolic rewards are distributed to classes and groups of people." [17]. The common theme in this perspective is that the criminal justice system should be assessed for its ability to improve the conditions as well as the behavior of those individuals in whose lives it intercedes. The coercive effect of the penal sanction does not help deal with crime, but instead perpetuates existing societal injustices. The primary goals of the criminal justice system are treatment and rehabilitation, since the welfare of criminals is inexorably tied into the welfare of the rest of society.

Both perspectives disagree on fundamentally ethical issues. The retributists support a strengthened system of justice focusing on effectiveness in the distribution of penal sanctions. The social welfarists support a reconsideration of the inequities in the distribution of societal resources that, they believe, cause crime in the first place.

Duffee also contends that both perspectives are flawed. He identifies three important areas where the two perspectives are in error. First, both have a misconception of the current nature of the criminal justice system. Both groups envision a network of agencies at the societal level that can control or guide the criminal justice system. This is not a plausible goal, Duffee observes. More reasonably, can either a criminal justice or welfare alternative "contribute to societal control?" The problem with both perspectives, simply stated, is the belief that there is a unitary group to be steered or maintained. The idea of a unitary society or group suggests a highly integrated notion of American society, and the criminal justice system as a controlling or steering agent as a component of this unitary vision. This vision, however, describes neither the criminal justice system nor society.

Consider society. The substantial differences in status and class across American society act against the notion that society is some sort of unitary whole. Politically, it is highly decentralized, with local autonomy, rather than central state control, serving as the basis for integration. This is reflected in the tens of thousands of criminal justice agencies scattered across the United States. Even within local communities, conflict over scarce resources is more likely to describe intergovernmental relations rather than mutual aid and support. Indeed, the political debate over deterrence and rehabilitation is itself evidence for the lack of justice system integration.

Next, consider the criminal justice system. Many writers have challenged the idea that the criminal justice organizations in the aggregate should be thought of in systematic terms (Walker, 1998). Goal conflict, rather than coordination, sometimes describes relationships among criminal justice organizations (Wright, 1990). Many interorganizational relationships in the public sphere represent the institutionalization of conflict. What the public perceives as inefficiency and ineffectiveness actually represents the way in which local autonomy is maintained (Litwak & Hylton, 1974, in Duffee, 1990:111). Efforts by individuals in the criminal justice system to create a unitary responsiveness represent efforts to impose unitariness over a system of local and national governance better characterized as differentiated. The behavior of criminal justice agencies, Duffee concluded, are heavily influenced by factors or "constraints" at the local level and local actor's notions of public order.

Duffee develops a functions theory of criminal justice organizations, in which the behavior of agencies depends on local community characteristics. By functions, I mean the way in which justice organizations contribute to community social control. To understand the behavior of criminal justice systems, one has to develop a meaningful picture of the communities in which they operate. By community, Duffee uses Warren's (1963) idea of community, according to which community is said to exist whenever people have access to those activities necessary for daily living. Communities represent particular arrangements of organizations and groups that provide locality-relevant (local) functions for individual members. Local communities differ from each other on two practical dimensions: The first is the degree of local autonomy, or the extent to which the local area is independent of outside sources. The second is horizontal articulation, or the extent to which different community groups interact or are in some way tied to each other.[2] by understanding where communities are located on each of these two dimensions, Duffee argues that one can predict what kind of social control system they will have and how their criminal justice system will operate. Figure 4.1 below is a typology of Duffee's model of communities and the social control function.

Figure 4.1
Community Structural Axes and the Social Control Function

High	Fragmented community, norms unclear, responsibilities for functions parcelled to various organizations that quibble over turf. Welfare law management, with legitimacy of organization over individual.	Interdependent community, organizational jurisdictions blurred, with formal mechanisms used to coordinate activities. Legitimacy dependent on interactive capacity.
Vertical relations		
Low	Disorganized area, or mass society. Norm observance low, offender and victims treated individually; formal law keeping, with little legitimacy granted to officials of state.	Solidary community, norms unified and concrete with few local organizations responsible for many functions, informal norm enforcement based on membership and peer pressure.
	Low	High

Source: David Duffee (1990). *Explaining Criminal Justice: Community Theory and Criminal Justice Reform*, Revised Edition, p. 155. Prospect Heights, IL: Waveland.

Duffee's functional model of justice organizations does not deal directly with the question of free will or of determinism. However, his argument—that justice should be understood as a locality-relevant function—is more of a deterministic argument than a free-will argument. His argument is functional—justice should be understood as local-relevant, and criminal justice organizations play a functional role in the well-being of communities. Local communities differ in the extent to which they are integrated horizontally across their member organizations, and vertically with their regions and nationally. Certain types of social control correspond to the extent to which local areas have autonomy from the central government and the extent to which their various economic and governing organizations are integrated. That is, their functional roles differ according to the community types in which they occur. This is a deterministic argument, and is based on the idea that community type determines kind of social control, of which criminal justice organizations are an important type.

On the other hand, Duffee's model emphasizes the importance of local decisionmaking in justice processes. In this sense it also incorporates ideas of free will, in that it seeks decisional processes that are locally based rather than centralized in large government.

The model has been extended to understanding the functions of the police as well. Langworthy and Travis (1994) used Duffee's model as an underlying schema to describe the nature and contemporary changes in the police. Though written as an introductory text in policing, Langworthy and Travis's book provides a sophisticated view of policing that is a blend of functional theory and historical perspective. Presenting Duffee's theory of community types they suggest how a functional model of horizontal and vertical community integration can serve as a model for understanding the nature of police authority. However, they expanded Duffee's model from a functional into a predictive model. Using Warren's (1978) idea of a "great change" in modern society, they created a model of contemporary change in social control. They then superimposed the change model over Duffee's (1990) typology of vertical and horizontal integration (See Figure 4.2 below). The strength of this presentation is that it overcame otherwise static ideas of police organization that tend to characterize functional ideas and provided a basis for thinking about police transitions in a changing world.

Figure 4.2
Effects of the "Great Change" on Community Structure

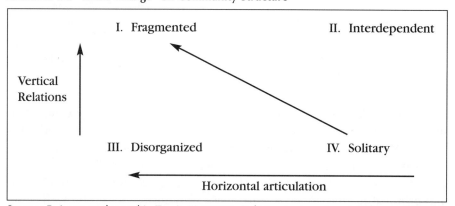

Source: R. Langworthy and L. Travis III (1994). *Policing in America: A Balance of Forces*, p. 332. Englewood Cliffs, NJ: Macmillan.

Farrell and Case: The Black Book. A quite different kind of functional perspective was developed by Farrell and Case (1995). Their research on efforts to control the mob in Las Vegas displays one of the elements characteristic of functionalsm, the presence of homeostatic mechanisms. Homeostatic mechanisms are devices whose purpose is to regulate the overall well-being of some social "whole." For example, the human body survives best at a constant temperature of 98.6 degrees. Various homeostatic mechanisms are engaged when the temperature varies too widely from this temperature. If the outdoor temperature drops, we feel the sensation of cold and seek warmth. If our core temperature drops, we shiver, which is a mechanism for increasing the level of body activity to maintain warmth.

Homeostatic mechanisms have been criticized in sociological litera-ture as little more than a metaphorical tool, appropriate for the study of living organisms and mechanical devices but inappropriate for under-standing social dynamics. However, the importance of homeostatic mech-anisms, like real tautologies (discussed later in this chapter) are important elements in the routine practice of justice organizations. Homeostatic mechanisms are routinely used by justice officials and politicians. For example, official crime rates are used by police executives as a basis for budgetary considerations. Increases in the crime rate, which can be thought of as a homeostatic change, provide a basis for increases in law enforcement, while decreases have been used to justify lower municipal investments in the police.

Farrell and Case, in their study of Las Vegas Gaming, noted the pres-ence of a homeostatic phenomenon (though they did not label it as such): The ceremonial degradation of "bad guys" and their listing in Black Book. The Black Book (officially called the *List of Excluded Persons*) is a regis-ter of persons who are excluded from Nevada casinos because of their threat to the public image of gaming. Individuals listed in the Black Book are perceived to be members of organized crime, and their entry into the book is seen as a victory over organized crime. Persons so listed are banned for life from all licensed gaming establishments statewide, and are charged with a "gross misdemeanor" (up to five years incarceration) if they enter a gaming establishment, and casinos can lose their permit to game. The Black Book was authorized by law in 1967, and 38 people have had their names entered. Officially, a person could be nominated for the book by the Nevada Gaming Commission if they are a threat to the legit-imate gaming industry. Rules of evidence are less than probable cause. Evidence has ranged from national and international arrest records and testimony of convicted informants to the mere mention of ones associates in media accounts and crime commission reports.

Of interest to Farrell and Case was the timing of the selection of indi-viduals to be listed in the book. Periods of aggressive gaming commission activity coincide with the occurrence of threats to the gaming industry in the state. The first of these threats, promised federal intervention into gaming in Nevada in the 1950s, marked the development of the Back Book. Subsequent periods of threat include the indictments of several gambling industry figures in the late 1970s, their federal conviction in the early 1980s, and questions of institutional corruption in gaming in the early 1990s.

The intensification of Black Book activity during times of threat to gaming served a legitimating function. Gaming is institutionalized in Nevada, and is central to Nevada's economic well-being. However, the legitimization is thin to the potential gaming audience, and is widely seen as immoral. Significant events, such as the indictments of prominent gaming figures, bring into question the legitimizing basis of gaming and pose a threat to audience of potential gamers. Through vigorous Black Book activity, the Gaming Commission can symbolically demonstrate that it has a firm legal control on gaming. Hence, the Black Book serves a homeostatic function: when threats to gaming legitimacy emerge, increases Black Book activity act as a reaffirmation that responsible authorities are fully in control of gaming. Farrell and Case further note that:

> In this dramatization of evil, regulators also tend to ignore or seek to discredit any ties that then individual might have to conventional society . . . Further affirming the disreputability of the nominee is the regulatory attention to the issue of aliases . . . The nominee appears to be one with deceptive intent and to have possibly committed numerous cries under other names (Farrell & Case, 1995:13-14).

Moreover, the selection of individuals for Black Book entry tends to accentuate how they are socially and culturally different from legitimate citizens. By emphasizing the degree of difference and deviance of those selected for entry, the Commission reinforces the "goodness" of gaming and the strength of conventional social norms in Gaming activity. The ritualized degradation of those nominated for the Black Book "publicly communicates the power of the state to rid the industry of even its most sinister elements" [10].

Institutional Perspective

The third perspective we are interested in is institutional theory. Institutional theory represents a profound break from normative theories of human behavior. It looks for the ways in which broad institutional and cultural values motivate our behavior. Perhaps more than any other perspective, institutional theory is interested in the unspoken and taken-for-granted value-based architecture of the justice system.

In institutional theory, agency is carried in broad social institutions and cultural values. The relationship between actors and action is tautological: actors may cause actions, but actions also crate the actor (Meyer, Boli & Thomas,1994). Our conceptions as acing individuals is a cultural myth that itself is the product of values important to us: social values link actions to outcomes, and we act out these actions to produce the outcomes (Douglas, 1986). *However, both are institutionally created, inseparable.*

Consider the punishment called "spanking." Some people "spank" children because they believe it is a punishment that will instill respect for parents, reinforce a disdain for inappropriate behavior, and teach a proper morality about individual responsibility. A means, spanking, is tied to an end, a morally responsible person. And some, perhaps many, individuals that are raised in a spanking environment grow up to be morally responsible, and continue the process. A person who grows up to be morally responsible may assert that he or she did so because of the way they were punished as children. They will not consider alternative moral accounts of spanking, for example, that they became morally responsible *in spite of* being spanked. We can also see in this example how society creates categories of behavior and assigns moral value to elements within those categories. Spanking is considered appropriate behavior and is essential to positive youthful upbringing. Violent adult victimization of young people is considered inappropriate and sanctionable by harsh punitive sentences. The distinction is in the eye of the beholder—though in this instance, the beholder is seeing spanking through the lens of institutional values and how institutions order cause and effect.

Consequently, institutional theorists look at what we take for granted in our day to day activities. It is an "unmasking" way of thinking, aimed at peering through the assumptions that undergird our taken-for-granted assumptions. It differs from functionalism in a key way. It rejects the notion that society is characterized by homeostatic mechanisms. This means that it does not believe in the idea that there are equilibrium processes at work in society. For example, we might believe that there is a link between level of crime or fear of crime and justice system activity, and that when crime or fear of crime declines we will at some point see a decline in justice system activity. This is a homeostatic argument—that there exists a level of equilibrium that insures the well-being of society. It is also an argument rejected by institutional theorists. It suggests that there is an idea of what constitutes a good society. Institutional theorists tent to counter that whatever that idea of a good society is, it represents another area of institutional values, not abstract truth.

On Individuals and Justice. What does it mean to be an individual? The term itself is full of distance and separateness: it affirms our difference, our uniqueness. We don't call ourselves *collectives*, a term that would emphasize our need for human contact and desire for friendly social inter-relationships. The phrase "What's in it for me?" is widely known: I do not recall having ever heard the phrase "What's in it for *us*?"

The importance of "individualism" as a cultural prescription cannot be overestimated. It is at the center of our ideas of democracy and lawful justice. The Declaration of Independence of the United States affirms the importance of individual life, liberty, and the pursuit of happiness. The Bill of Rights constructs a protective legal shield around citizens, with due process prohibitions of governmental intervention. But what is an individual?

Meyer, Boli, and Thomas (1994:21) capture the essence of the institutional perspective of what it means to be an individual: "the individual is an institutional myth evolving out of the rationalized theories of economic, political, and cultural action." This means that the values we carry identifying ourselves as individuals (as opposed, for example, to collectives) is grounded in highly institutionalized values and beliefs of our capacity to uniquely control our destinies:

> Modern "individuals" give expression to the institutionalized description of the individual as having authorized political rights, efficacy, and competence; they consider themselves effective choosers of their occupations, investments, and consumption goods; and they willingly give vent to an extraordinary range of cultural judgments, offhandedly responding to questionnaires with their views of the polity, the economy, even the exact properties, including being, of God. . . . they also perform a wide range of economic, political, and cultural actions—and ex post facto can explain in great detail how their activity was carefully selected as efficient for their particular purposes.

Put differently, a central organizing principle of the "individual" is the idea that we control our destinies. Hence, according to institutional theorists, the idea of individual human agency is itself a cultural product.

Being an individual also carries with it a distinctive moral standing. In Western terms, the core idea of the individual is associated with the notions of progress and justice. The linking of progress and individualism is an Enlightenment product, an outcome of the same forces that marked the transition from the middle ages to contemporary political/economic landscape in the Western countries. If we understand that, we see the tremendous organizing value the idea of "individual" has, and how it is irrevocably tied to self-determination and economic progress.

Justice is similarly associated with Enlightenment ideas of the individual. Justice is a moral property of individuals, not of governments. Both the criminal and civil laws provide an remedies justified in terms of individual equity, or deterrence, aimed again at individual citizens that might be tempted to break the law.[3] And central to the criminal law is that individuals are purposeful actors, fully capable of controlling their behavior. Individuals are rational and purposive, and should be held accountable for their behavior.

The same cluster of values that defines what it means to be an "individual" also applies to justice organizations. Organizations, like individuals are perceived to be rational and purposive. The dominant organizational form in Western society is a rational bureaucracy, organized around goals and with clearly stated responsibilities for its inhabitants (Meyer & Rowan, 1992). The complex modern organization is capable of carrying out multiple goals simultaneously, and can achieve these goals through the purposeful and systematic behavior of its leaders. Justice organizations are similarly situated in our Western landscape. Police organizations are purposeful, capable of doing something about crime. Courts can determine who is guilty or innocent. Parole and probation officers are capable of affecting the criminological trajectories of their clients. And prisons deter future wrongdoing.

A formidable challenge has been mounted against this way of thinking these "rationalizing" myths. This section explores some of these challenges by considering institutional perspective, a rapidly expanding area of empirical analysis and theoretical development.

Institutional perspectives have a modest but growing influence in justice literature. As recently as 1989, one could argue that institutional explanations of the behavior of organizations had not yet reached criminal justice circles (Duffee, 1989). In the field of organizational analysis, institutional theory had attained recognition with the publication of Selznick's studies of organizational leadership (1957) and of the Tennessee Valley Authority (1949). In 1977, studies of institutionalized organizations leaped forward with the publication of Meyer and Rowan's paper on organizational myth and rationality (Meyer & Rowan, 1992). It was not until recently that institutional analyses of justice organizations began to appear in the literature on criminal justice.

Meyer and Rowan: Institutionalized Organizations. Meyer and Rowan (1992) are often credited for the efflorescence of theory on institutional organizations. Their paper on myth and rationality in institutionalized organizations provided the spark for a large and growing body of organizational theory. The central ideas in their paper are summarized below:

1. Technical organizations survive and prosper by paying close attention to efficiency and effectiveness in the development of their core product. They turn inward, as it were. Maximization of profit is the way in which long-term organizational survival is assured.

2. Institutionalized organizations turn outward to their institutionalized environments. The development and elaboration of organizational structure and policy is aimed at satisfying values carried by important constituencies in their environments.

In any setting, an organization has to buffer itself from turbulence in its environment. However, this buffering process is different in institutional and technical organizations.

3. Technical organizations, because they have to turn inward to their technical core in order to survive, buffer themselves from their environment in order to be efficient and effective. They are loosely coupled to their environments, so that they can protect their product when the environment changes.

4. Institutional organizations, because they have to turn outward to their institutional audience in order to survive, buffer themselves from their technical core. Organizational structures are loosely coupled to the actual outcomes that they produce, so that they can satisfy demands for legitimacy from important actors in their environments.

As Meyer, Scott, and Deal observed,

> Thus, the technical organization faces in toward its technical core and turns its back on its environment, while the institutional organization turns its back on its technical core in order to concentrate on conforming to its institutional environment. A factory, to survive, must develop a well-understood process that can turn out desired products at a competitive price; then it must insure an adequate supply of raw materials, trained personnel, and market outlets, a reasonable tax situation, and so on. A school, to survive, must conform to institutional rules—including community understandings—that define teacher categories and credentials, pupil selection and definition, proper topics for instruction, and appropriate facilities. It is less essential that a school's teaching and learning activities are efficiently coordinated or even that they are in close proximity with institutional rules (Meyer, Scott & Deal, 1992:47).

Put differently, technical organizations must attend to the concrete effects of the technologies that they use. Internal control and coordination is essential for survival. Consequently, when we look at the internal organization of a technical organization, we see that it is about the product produced. However, institutional organizations must attend to the values carried by the groups who affect their well-being. They must know the institutional rules. When we look at the way in which an institutionalized organization is organized, we see that it is about the values carried in its environment. Institutionalized organizations are the enactment of values in their external environments. Figure 4.3 displays the institutional model of organizational structure.

In a democratic environment, values carried in an organization's institutional environment are often in conflict with each other. For example, the police must deal with a municipal environment whose principle authorities—the mayor and city council members, other government agencies, legal council for defendants, the press and other media, for example, carry competing values. This conflict is revealed in three ways. First, the organization will operate on a "logic of food faith," a show for its external environment of "elaborate displays of confidence, satisfaction, and good faith, externally and internally" (Meyer & Rowan, 1992:41). It should be recognized that the logic of good faith is dearly and fully believed by those who profess a belief in the rightness of the organization. "The assumption that things are as they seem, that employees and managers are performing their roles properly, allows an organization to perform its daily routines with a decoupled structure (Meyer & Rowan, 1992:40).

Secondly, the organization develops organizational units and protocols which act out the conflict through bureaucratic processes. Indeed, organizational complexity is to a certain extent a measure of the extent of disagreement and conflict in its institutional environment (Meyer &

Scott, 1992).[4] For example, elaborate hiring protocols are carried out that balance the competing claims of affirmative action supporters and police unions. Third, the organization loosely couples itself from its actual activity. It is not possible, for example, for individual officers to avoid violating values carried by some important group in their constituency. Institutionalized organizations, concerned with the way their organization looks, consequently "loosely couple" themselves to their work product (the reverse of technical organizations, who loosely couple themselves to their technical environments).

Figure 4.3
Institutional and Technical Theories of Organizational Structure

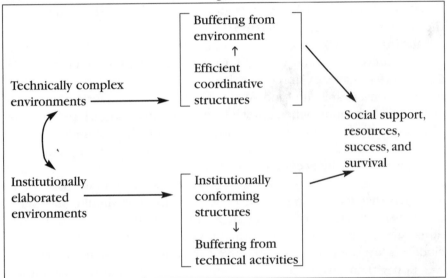

Source: Meyer, John, W. Richard Scott, and Terrence Deal (1992). "Institutional and Technical Sources of Organizational Structure: Explaining the Structure of Educational Organizations." in J. Meyer and W. Scott (eds.) *Organizational Environments: Ritual and Rationality.* Updated Edition, p. 47. Newbury Park, CA: Sage.

Institutional Theory and Justice Organizations. Institutional theory has a great deal to offer the study of justice organizations. If we agree with the ideas underlying institutional perspective, we recognize that we cannot hold justice organizations to the same "bottom line" perspective that we bring to profit-oriented technical organizations. The first area of consideration in justice organizations is values, and only after broad value considerations are satisfied can we then speak about economic concerns.

Imagine this. A police chief tells a mayor and city council that the police department has decided to allow all officers to wear blue jeans to work, because they are less expensive than a police officer's uniform. The concept doesn't work—it is inconsistent with our "image" of police. A police uniform, as some departments have learned, legitimizes police organizations. A uniform provides citizens with the knowledge that the people with whom they are interacting are, in fact, police officers. Any other manner of dress does not, and is likely be soundly criticized in a city council and the subject of ridiculing editorials in the local newspaper. The point is that we simply cannot think the same way about justice organizations that we do technical organizations. They are fundamentally different kinds of organizations—one is about profit and the other is about values.

Secondly, by focusing on institutional environments we begin to recognize the nature of the forces that affect the behavior of criminal justice organizations. An organization cannot simply "pick and choose" what it wants to do. It is constrained by some influential forces in its environments, and it is enabled by others. By studying the institutional environment of organizations, we recognize that the practice of justice is sometimes a dependent variable, and cannot simply be understood in terms of the will of its executive leadership.

Institutional perspective is beginning to make its mark in justice literature. Individually and together, Crank and Langworthy (1996; 1992, Crank, 1994) have explored the institutional characteristics of police organizations. Crank and Langworthy's (1992) paper set forth an image of police organizations when viewed from an institutional perspective. They argued that police organizations, to insure the continued flow of resources needed for long-term well being and survival, conform to broad, institutionally accepted expectations of police activity. Its organizational structures and policies are aimed at displaying to its institutional audience that it is acting like a police department should, and hence deserves legitimation as a police department. Many aspects of organizational structure, behavior, and formal policy, Crank and Langworthy conclude, are ceremonial—they are aimed outward at satisfying constituencies rather than inward, aimed at some technological core. The authors trace three myth-building processes in the institutional environment. These processes ensure that police organizations conform to institutional expectations, but also describe how the police themselves are actively involved in the construction of myths. Their work closes with a discussion of legitimation conflicts, which occur when the work carried out by police organizations violates fundamental ideas of appropriate police work. Legitimacy lost, they argue, is itself a ceremonial process, marked by the public humiliation of the organization, firing of the chief, and hiring of a new chief with a new, legitimating mandate—usually based on some notion of "doing something about crime."

Two papers have extended the institutional analysis of police organizations. Crank (1994) suggested that the community policing movement represented an institutional change in policing. The community policing movement provided a legitimating "myth"—the myth of the community watchman—that gave the police legitimacy when the previous "professionalizing" mandate of police work had failed to accomplish its own self-chosen mandate—win the war on crime. The reports of the Crime (1967) and Kerner (1968) Commissions provided the blue ribbon forums for the de-legitimation of professional policing. Community-policing has gradually emerged as a new legitimation of policing—one in which the police justify their work in terms of their linkages to local communities. And Crank and Langworthy (1996) set forth a series of propositions about the relationship between the nature of the institutional environment and the organizational structure of police organizations. In a technical paper, they argued that current changes in police organizations and their environments, designed to enhance community policing, in fact result in a growth in organizational structure and complexity in organizational design. One of the consequences of community policing, they suggest, may be an increased de-coupling of police activity from administrative oversight and the proliferation of accountability problems at the line levels.

Institutional perspective has also gained a foothold in the literature on corrections and in probation and parole. This literature had tended to focus on "loose coupling." Marquart and his colleagues (1993) argued that the Texas Prison System was able to maintain its stability in a time of environmental turbulence in the 1980s by loosely coupling its "get-tough" rhetoric on the war on drugs with the actual flow of prisoners through its prisons. In the face of accelerating police arrests and court convictions, the prison system underwent expansion. As Marquart et al. observed,

> Although the state prison system was expanded over the 1980s, authorities resorted to accelerating good time and using early parolees to accommodate increased demand in maintaining compliance with the court order. In consequence, the percentage of sentence served by released offenders declined sharply. Not only had the prison system become a turnstile but incarceration lost its significance as the state's most punitive form of punishment. Increasing numbers of convicted offenders were opting to go to prison rather than serve a sentence of probation within the free community (Marquart et al., 539-540).

In a paper on parole and probation, McCorkle and Crank (1996) challenged the "New Penology" put forth by Feeley and Simon (1992). Feeley and Simon argued that changes in corrections in the United States were broad based and constituted a "New Penology." Historically, penology in the United States has focused on individuals. Whether policy or system goals reflected a conservative or liberal orientation, its focus was on treatment or punishment of the individual offender—as Feeley and Simon noted, the unit of analysis was the individual. Criminal sanctioning derived from individual-based theories of punishment and was concerned with individual responsibility, fault, moral sensibility, diagnosis, or individual treatment of the offender.

The new penology, on the other hand, is about the treatment of classes of offenders. It, the authors observe, is "neither about punishing nor about rehabilitating individuals. It is about identifying and managing unruly groups" (Feeley & Simon, 1992:455). Its focus is actuarial, aimed at predicting dangerousness and likelihood of recidivism among populations. Its negligence standards are not individual fault or responsibility but rather strict liability. Actuarial prediction is evident in the shift from rehabilitation to crime control. For example, the return of high rates of parolees to prison has traditionally indicated prison program failure; in the new penology it represents the effectiveness of parole as a control apparatus.

McCorkle and Crank (1996) presented a different interpretation of new penology. Transformations in parole and probation were actually ceremonial responses to changes in the institutional environment of parole and probation. They argued that:

> With the demise of the rehabilitation ideal and the advent of a "get tough" philosophy, community correctional agencies, historically the rehabilitative component of corrections, had but two options—change or cease to exist. Parole and probation changed as public sector agencies do in highly institutionalized environments. They changes via organizational ceremonies of structure and behavior . . . (These changes) have brought the field of community corrections renewed legitimacy and badly needed resources (McCorkle & Crank, 1996).

The actual practice of parole and probation, they argued, loosely coupled to the actual organizational ceremonies of parole and probation. Consequently, ceremonial changes aimed at adapting to the external environment of parole and probation had little actual effect on the day to day operations of departments of parole and probation.

To be sure, McCorkle and Crank didn't state that the new penology was wrongly conceived by Feeley and Simon (1992), only that the changes associated with the new penology were loosely coupled to the daily activities of parole and probation staff. However, a case study of Intensive Supervision Probation workloads in "Midwestern County," conducted together with interviews of staff, provided tentative evidence that supported McCorkle and Crank's institutional perspective, with caveats (Bayens, Manske & Smykla, 1998).[5] While one case study cannot resolve the debate about system processes in parole and probation, this research suggests that institutional perspective has emerged as a powerful theoretical tool in the examination of parole and probation processes.

Ogle (1999) used an institutional theory of corrections to assess the problems faced by prison privatization advocates. Correctional organizations, she noted, "existed in an institutional environment composed of powerful deeply embedded social beliefs and values . . ." [598] They have to sustain legitimacy, gauged in terms of their ability to satisfy the values of powerful government constituents. Private prison corporations, concerned with profit, are consequently caught in a "catch-22." They must assure growth and profit essential for competition in the private sphere. The steps they take to achieve this end frequently places them in conflict with their legitimating audiences. Consequently, they face a:

> self-perpetuating series of legitimacy crises for both the company and the government; in adddition the taxpayers bear the expense of assisting such companies, continuously increasing the monitoring and regulation, rebidding the contracts, or returning to government operation (Ogle, 1999:599).

The perspective developed by Ogle is adapted directly from Meyer and Rowan (1977). The particular strength of the perspective is in how she uses institutional theory to assess adaptive strategies of private correctional organizations to a highly institutinalized environment.

Garland: Punishment as a Social Institution

Garland's work on punishment is not easy to pigeon-hole. It could as easily fit as an example of structuralism, though it is not functional. I have decided to keep it here, because it recognizes the role institutions contribute to values and because, like contemporary researchers in institutional theory, it recognizes the important role of historical contingency in contemporary processes.

How should we think about punishment? Garland (1990) observed that we tend to view it as a means to an ends—an instrumentality, geared to a single purpose. We assess the efficacy of punishment using the same instrumental logic, with measures such as recidivism or deterrence. This way of thinking utterly fails to understand punishment. Punishment, he argued, should be recognized as a social institution. He defined an institution as "society's settled means for dealing with certain needs, relationships, conflicts, and problems which repeatedly occur and must be managed in an orderly and normative way if social relations are to be reasonably stabilized and differentiated." [282] Institutions have their own rationality and their own way of doing things. Internal institutional logic guides how its participants think about what they do, how it is done, and the array of justifications and beliefs surrounding the practice of punishment. Institutions are worlds of their own, with their own characters, roles, statuses, and relationships.

Punishment is also a product of historical forces. Consequently, historical contingency and accident—unpredictability, in a word—affects the form and style of punishment in any particular place and time. Garland, by recognizing the role of contingency in punishment, is challenging the notion that European history should be conceptualized, as Enlightenment philosophers did, in terms of "progress" and "social evolution." These notions make nice Enlightenment philosophy, but are poor and misleading explanators of historical complexity. Large historical processes are simply too complex to be captured adequately by single idea philosophies of human nature. The particular form punishment takes and the concatenation of logical elements that comprise contemporary justifications for punishment are the result of "swarming circumstances." [285] Researchers should avoid explanations in terms of single or small numbers of principles and instead try to capture the complexity of punishment.

Garland identified three terms to evoke the range of meanings carried by the institution of punishment. Being an institution meant that punishment is *overdetermined*. By overdetermined, he meant that no single principle can explain either the causes or consequences of punishment. Institutions are also *polysemous*—they support multiple meanings and purposes. And they have the quality of *condensation*. The same object may be thee result of a fusion of several forces and contain several meanings.

> Instead of searching for a single explanatory principle, we need to grasp the facts of multiple causality, multiple effects, and multiple meaning. We need to realize that in the penal realm—as in all social experience—specific events or developments usually have a plurality of causes which interact to shape their final form, a plurality of effects which may be seen as functional or non-functional depending upon one's criteria, and a plurality of meanings which will vary with the actors and audiences involved . . . The aim of analysis should always be to capture that variety of causes, effects, and meanings and trace their interaction, rather than reduce them all to a single currency (Garland, 1990:280).

What we acquire from this institutional perspective of punishment is a rejection of the idea that straightforward, normative explanations are satisfactory. This is particularly important to political views of punishment, which tend to view it in terms of rehabilitation or deterrence. Garland advises us that punishment is often justified by either instrumentality, and that it in fact does both quite poorly.

That punishment seems to have no beneficial effects has been noted by a diverse number of observers across the political spectrum. The justice system, however, tends to respond by ratcheting up the intended instrumentality—to create more "pain" of punishment, or to increase the overall reach of rehabilitation programs within a prison environment. And it has let the "professionals" or technical experts in the field of corrections tell us how to better achieve these goals. The justice system has increased the intended "dosage" of whatever we went to accomplish by punishment, and still the desired effects aren't forthcoming. How can this be?

If punishment is seen as an institution, we move away from the perspective that it is an instrumental means for a penological end, but is an institution for the "expression of social values, sensibility, and morality" [291] We have failed to understand the way in which society—ourselves—are implicated in the penal process and its entire array of outcomes. It is clear, for example, that penal policy as deterrence is a profound failure—the recidivism rate of prisoners is astonishingly high, well beyond 50 percent for most crimes. Yet it continues to be an article of faith among justice professionals that deterrence is the primary purpose of punishment.

Garland encourages us to move beyond the narrow Enlightenment notion that penology can provide the circumstances for individual moral progress. Punishment is a tragedy, in every way, for all concerned. If punishment is a necessary evil, Garland emphasizes the word *evil.* Garland closes with an appeal to the sociological imagination.

> The tragic quality of punishment, it seems to me, is made more apparent when we approach it in a broader, sociological way. Instead of appearing to glorify punishment as a functionally important social institution, the sociology of punishment may be taken to suggest its limitations and point to alternative ways o organizing its tasks. Above all, it teaches that a policy which intends to promote disciplined conduct and social control will concentrate not on punishing offenders but upon socializing and integrating young citizens—a work of social justice and moral education rather than penal policy (1990:39).

We inherited from the Enlightenment the idea that punishment could be a rational rather than emotional societal response, and could be used on behalf of moral progress for prisoners. Punishment, Garland (1990:7) observed, could be an enlightened project, "one more means for the engineering of the good society." Penal progress, like progress in other areas of social and professional life, could be transformed from a set of ritualistic emotional practices to professional, instrumental processes devoid of emotion. This, Garland (1990) noted, was a process of rationalization, which meant that rational procedures and objective rules guided penal procedure.

> Criminology was, in effect, an expression of enlightenment ambition to cure social ills by the application of Reason, and its emergence both expressed and reinforced the developing administrative logic of nineteenth-century penal systems (Garland, 1990:185).

The culture of punishment became value neutral, pallid in its emotion, focused on the professional pursuit of good ends—the transformation of prisoners into citizens. By the same token, penal ideology became "scientized." Penal reformers provided a vocabulary that was marked by

> The rationality of value-neutral science, a technical 'non-judgmental' vocabulary, a 'passion for scientific classification,' and a horror of emotional force, into a sphere which was previously dominated by candid morality and openly expressed sentiment (Garland, 1990:186).

The ends of punishment, conceived both in conservative ideas of deterrence of future criminality and liberal ideas of rehabilitation, can be traced to the rationalization of punishment process under an Enlightenment philosophy.

The practice of punishment today, both in conservative notions of deterrence and in liberal ideas of rehabilitation, is an expression of enlightenment ideas of science and progress. And, as Garland further noted, both ideas are increasingly suspect in modern life. The capacity of punishment to deter is witnessed by the extraordinarily high rate of crime in the United States, substantially higher than any other civilized country in the world. And the notion that punishment can serve rehabilitative ends has been sharply challenged by a wide and growing number of observers of penal process. It may be that the rationalization of punishment is one of the great failures of modern society (Garland, 1990; Foucault, 1991; Christie, 1994).

Garland's vision is sweeping, a statement of the sociological imagination in the area of penology, insistent that we take a broad vision to fully comprehend the consequences of our penological decisions. It is distrustful of bureaucratic "technical" expertise and concerned with the relationship between people's problems and the social conditions behind the problems. And by recognizing the contingent nature of institutions, it reminds us that we can change what we have created.

Conflict Perspective

Conflict perspective is an earthy, practical justice perspective, not absent cynicism about the human condition, that recognizes that people are capable of immense organized violence against each other. Martindale (1960:142) traces conflict theory to the political writings of Hobbes and Machiavelli, political philosophers whose views he characterized as the "realistic analyses of mature men of affairs." Their writings on government were shaped by the personal experience of career work in government. In their dark wisdom they recognized the role that power and self-interest played in shaping human affairs.

Conflict theory can be thought of as two types. A great deal of conflict theory revolves around the central notion of class. This theory is Marxist in tradition. Class struggle for the means of production is central to all other social phenomena. The modern nation-state is set against the interests of the community and the individual (Martindale, 1960). In a widely cited quote,

It follows from this that all struggles within the State, the struggle between democracy, aristocracy, and monarchy, the struggle for the franchise, inc., are merely the illusory forms in which the real struggles of the different classes are fought out among one another (Marx and Engels, 1947:23).[6]

The criminal justice system is seen as a manifestation of the ruling elite, the upper class. Definitions of crime and the behavior of the criminal justice system are not about "doing something about crime" but about protecting the interests of the upper class. Both crime behavior and the practice of criminal justice are epi-phenomena of class structure. Occasionally, white-collar criminals are prosecuted, and many laws are concerned with the misuse of power. This occurs because, as Reiman (1998) observed, the struggle among the classes is precisely that—a struggle. The upper class holds the upper hand, but the relations among the classes continues to be a struggle. Harriman (1983), for example, described how the police preserve class relations:

> The role of the state in mediating the class struggle is a central tenant of the Marxist analysis of the capitalist state . . . .all analyses reject the pluralist notion that the state is neutral. One key element in the state's domination is its monopoly on the use of legitimate violence and coercion, a function concentrated domestically in the police institution. The capacity to use violence if other social mechanisms fail is more important than the actual violence because it is fully understood by all as a component of the state's power (Harriman, 1983:8).

Status conflict is the second kind of conflict theory. According to this perspective, society is composed of diverse groups with conflicting interests. However, these interests break down along status, not class, lines. Such status conflicts are particularly visible in legislative politics. The group that can marshal the greatest support, or obtain the greatest number of votes, will determine whether new laws will be favorable to their interests (Vold & Bernard, 1986). The winner of the conflict has, at least until a new legislative mandate is obtained, the power of the organized state to support their views. According to this perspective, conflicts over abortion, the use and legalization of drugs, the use of the death penalty, or concerning environmental law, represent status conflicts carried out from the local and legislative levels.

Status conflict and class conflict are fundamentally different notions of conflict theory. In stratification theory, they are polar notions. As Nisbet (1966:180) observed, the difference between social class and status is:

> a view of the new society resting on the assumed existence of solid, substantive social class opposed to a view resting upon the assumption of the erosion of class and its replacement by fluctuant, mobile, status groups and by status-seeking individuals.

These are profoundly different notions, with different implications for conflict and for the criminal justice system. First, they are based on different notions of economic relationships. Nisbet observed that the English landed class in the nineteenth century provided the model by which Marxist writers envisioned the future of capitalism. Its economic power and unity derived from its landed property, and it was a powerful force in the English political affairs. However, a different economic model emerged in the United States, one based on status rather than class. Conflict in the United States, consequently, occurred on fluid status lines and did not crystalize along more permanent status levels (Nisbet, 1966:177-178). Class differences atomized when faced with the leveling influence of the common pursuit of money.

Second, class and status conceive of democracy in fundamentally different ways. In notions of class conflict, democracy is epi-phenomenal to production, and is used by the rich to maintain their power. This reverses in a status system, in which democracy becomes a neutral political playing field, and different status groups compete among each other for available societal goods. The importance of this distinction cannot be overestimated. In traditional notions of Marxist theory, conflict along class lines would eventually overthrow the capitalist ruling classes. In status theory, ongoing conflicts among status groups actually serves to invigorate democracy by releasing tensions before they can crystallize into more far-reaching, cross-cutting class conflicts (Coser, 1956). Left realism is an exception to traditional Marxist perspectives. It is presented in the concluding "critical" section as a contemporary variant of class theory that views Marxist ideas of political economy as goods to be bargained for using the rules of democratic process.

This discussion is a simplification of Marxist class and status theory, highlighting some elements and glossing important theoretical nuances. In the remainder of this chapter, I will explore some of these nuances by presenting different examples of conflict theory and their implications for criminal justice practice.

Vold and Bernard: Elements of a Conflict Theory of Criminal Law.
Conflict theory is a staple of criminology studies. However, it is not a theory of individual criminology so much as a theory of the behavior of criminal law (Vold & Bernard, 1986). As such, conflict perspectives are a sharp break from normative views of justice and governance grounded in ideas of social consensus. Indeed, many contemporary conflict theorists see political disagreement and the absence of consensus as the characteristic feature of governance. In understanding the behavior of government, it is conflict, not consensus, that is normal.

The object of conflict is state power. The power of the state, as embodied in the criminal justice system, is not a "value-free framework" but state power is itself the "principal prize in the perpetual conflict that is society (Chambliss & Seidman, 1971).[7] The greater the influence and power of a group, the more likely their views will be expressed in the criminal laws. Groups will wield their power to gain and maintain control. In this political environment, the law is the contested prize—it is used by powerful groups to maintain influence and control.

The following elements of conflict theory, adapted from Vold and Bernard's "Unified Conflict Theory of Crime," represent the development of conflict perspective regarding the behavior of the law.

A conflict model of the criminal law, by recognizing the way in which policymakers, legislators, and other powerful interests affect the law, extends the analysis of justice systems beyond normative perspectives in four important ways. First, conflict perspectives permit an examination of the way in which individuals or groups are targeted by the law because of their symbolic threat to social order. For example, "politics of fear"— electoral strategies used by political entrepreneurs that demonize minority groups for political advantage—are illusive ideas within a normative context but perfectly sensible, even predictable, for a conflict theorist.[8] Secondly, conflict perspective can be used to explain how government's reaction to crime changes over time. Normative theories, focusing on elements such as norms, institutions, and roles, are poor explanators of social change. Yet change is pervasive to society—indeed, the explanation of stability over time may be more compelling and difficult. By recognizing that change is itself an important characteristic of the law and of the behavior of the criminal justice system, conflict theory provides needed realism about how justice processes and activities change over time, and forces us to focus our analytic skills on the identification of change agents.

Third, conflict theory permits a consideration of the hidden motivations of actors and the way in which people with power manipulate it for their own ends. Conflict theory carries immense capacity to be cynical about the world around us. Yet, a healthy dose of cynicism may be a needed unguent for those who view the moral rightness of justice practices uncritically. Conflict theory is the "smoke-filled decision-making back room" theory of justice practices, insisting that we look behind the scenes, penetrate the obvious, to try to find what is really going on.

Fourth, conflict perspectives are particularly useful for understanding the intransigence of poverty, particularly when minority group citizens are compared to elite sectors of the population. Normative perspective tends to view the twin problems of poverty and minority marginalization benignly, as outcomes of incidental economic forces that can be corrected with adequate training, education, and local investment. Conflict perspectives are darker, seeing in these problems the outcomes of intentional political entrepreneurship, hidden patterns of discrimination, political economies that support existing patterns of wealth among the privileged, and a justice system that uses the authority of the state to perpetuate and expand the marginalization of the poor.

Figure 4.4
Elements of a Conflict Theory of Criminal Law.

The Enactment of Criminal Laws.

1. The enactment of criminal laws is part of the general legislative process of conflict and compromise in which different groups attempt to promote and defend their own values and interests.

2. Individual laws usually represent a combination of the values and interests of many groups, rather than the specific values and interests of any one particular group. Nevertheless, the greater a group's political and economic power, the more the criminal law in general tends to represent the values and interests of that group.

3. Therefore, in general, the greater a group's political and economic power, the less likely it is that the behavior patterns characteristic of that group (behaviors consistent with their values and interests) will violate the criminal law, and vice versa.

The Enforcement of Criminal Laws.

4. In general, the greater the political and economic power of individuals, the more difficult it is for official law enforcement agencies to process them when their behavior violates the criminal law. There are many reasons for this. For example, the types of violations may be more subtle and complex, or the individuals may have greater resources to conceal the violation, legally defend themselves against official action, or exert influence extralegally on the law enforcement process.

5. As bureaucracies, law enforcement agencies tend to process the easier, rather than the more difficult, cases.

6. Therefore, in general, law enforcement agencies tend to process individuals with less, rather than more, political and economic power.

Adapted from Vold, George and Thomas Bernard (1986) *Theoretical Criminology*, Third Edition, p. 287. New York, NY: Oxford University Press.

The papers discussed below are assessments of justice system changes that carry three of the elements of conflict theory: they recognize that symbolic threats can mobilize the law, they look at justice system changes over time, and they show a recognition of how forces in the political economy marginalize the poor.

Labor Market Dynamics and Justice System Changes. Barlow and Barlow, with Johnson in 1996 and Chiricos in 1993, have explored economic determinants of justice system expansion and contraction. Labor market conditions, they observed, were consistently related to crime independent of actual crime levels (Inverarity & Grattet, 1989; Greenburg,

1977; Chiricos & Bales, 1991). Simply put, when the economy was moving in a positive direction, crime policy was more lenient, and when it was negative, policy was more severe.

Examining crime policy between 1948 and 1987, Barlow, Barlow and Johnson (1996) assessed the influence of economic conditions and crime on legislative and justice system activity. The authors focused on changes in "innovations, policy changes, and institutional developments that are related directly to crime, criminals, or the criminal justice system" (1996:228). Data included measures of justice hardening such as new laws, prohibitions, allowances, joint resolutions, and several other categories of federal crime data. They also assessed several dimensions of economic activity, including gross national product, unemployment rate, business and bank failure rate, and work stoppages.

They consistently found that legislators were more likely to pass justice system-hardening crime control measures when economic conditions were in periods of decline. Economic downturns were strongly related to the production of federal legislation aimed at expanding the scope of crime interdiction and suppression. They described this process as follows:

> When unemployment is on the rise and the economy is moving into a recession, public officials assume a posture of readiness, preparing for various manifestations of impending economic decline. New strategies for social control are sought and implemented experimentally. More research, greater attention to the criminal justice system, and perhaps increasing arrests intensify public apprehension about crime. As public anxiety around "the crime problem" escalates, pressure is applied to public officials to create a more effective, more efficient criminal justice system (Barlow, Barlow & Johnson, 1996:238).

The authors described their perspective as "political economy." According to this perspective, actors whose opinions are influential are influenced by economic indicators, and when the economy turns downward, they act against anticipated crime and social discontent. A spiraling effect occurs in which the increased attention given to crime and fear of crime by legislators is mirrored by media attention to criminal activities. Each group in turn reinforces the other's fears. Moreover, this process occurs independent of actual crime. The model is about how legislative and justice activity aims at symbolic targets who create crime fear. Indeed, actual crime is irrelevant to the model, and low levels of crime can provide elites with verification that the anti-crime policies work. This research suggests that the impact of economic conditions on criminal justice policy carries a powerful symbolic component, intended to assuage the public of its fears through justice system hardening, independent of actual levels of crime.

In a conceptually similar paper, Barlow, Barlow and Chiricos (1993) examined long economic cycles and their relationship to critical justice system activity. They assessed the extent to which the structural dynamics of economic expansion and contraction accounted for variations in criminal justice system activity. They identified four periods of economic contraction between 1820 and 1970, and noted that criminal justice system activity was heightened during each of these periods of contraction.

The linkage between economic contraction and justice system expansion occurred as a consequence of predisposing beliefs carried by powerful state managers (Box & Hale, 1982). First is that the social order is threatened by periods of economic decline. Managers feared that negative economic conditions, fostering unemployment and depression of wages, would contribute to increased labor militancy and anti-business activity. Secondly, economically depressed groups—the unemployed and poor—were thought to be more likely to contribute crime. Third, expansions in deterrent apparat, it was thought, would dissuade many potential criminals from committing crime. Managers were concerned with the development of justice strategies that anticipated and deterred potential crime among those most hard hit by conditions of economic decline. The cumulative consequence of this managerial psychology of fear was justice system expansion.

> What follows are increases in criminal justice innovations, policy changes and new institutions during the periods of economic stagnation. The increased focus on criminal justice in turn intensifies the apprehension about crime among the public.
>
> As in other aspects of the social structure of accumulation mechanisms for social control come to be seen as outdated and ineffective and state managers seek new mechanisms of control. They seek strategies which are more effective in stopping crime and social unrest, and which will, at the same time, legitimize the political economic system (Barlow, Barlow & Chiricos, 1993:163).

The consequence is both expansion of control and change in the underlying kinds of control that are deemed appropriate. In this way, economic conditions contribute to transformation in both the level and kinds of crime control practices.

Holmes: Minority Threat and Police Brutality. Characteristic of conflict perspective is the view that more powerful groups enact their authority into the criminal law. The differential enforcement of the law against less powerful groups is a measure of the "threat" posed by the less privileged. The greater the threat, the greater the differential in enforcement. This idea is characterized as the "threat" hypothesis," which states that the greater the number of acts or people threatening to the rich and powerful, the greater the extent of crime control (Liska, 1992).

The idea of threat is tied closely to elite power and authority. However, as some critics have pointed out, the police are not drawn from particularly powerful groups in American society. They often have limited educations, come from working-class families, and earn average incomes. For many of them, police work is their avenue into the American middle-class lifestyle. From a conflict perspective, we might anticipate that police are among those disadvantaged groups that the powerful take advantage of. As Holmes (2000:349) observed, "police officers are hardly automatons blindly following dominant group imperatives." How, then, can the police represent the actions of the powerful rather than the powerless?

Holmes (2000) suggested that minority-group attitudes are frequently interpreted as challenging to an officer's authority. Put more generally, minority group members aren't so much a threat to the economic order of the rich and powerful as they are a threat to the moral order (Chamlin, 1989).[9] Minority citizens, on the other hand, tend to view the police as threatening symbols of oppression (see also Locke, 1996). In this context, threat takes on a palpable meaning to all participants.

> The climate of mutual threat means that the mere presence and visibility of minorities may amplify the perception of risk among police officers, irrespective of their racial/ethnic identity. Therefore, the police should feel particularly threatened, and hence more likely to employ coercive controls, in cities with a high percentage of minorities (Holmes, 2000:351).

Assessing patterns of civil rights complaints against the police in major cities, Holmes found that urban African-Americans were much more likely to be targeted by police in cities with high minority population percentages, as were Latinos in Southwest cities with high proportions of Latinos.

Holmes observed that proximal threats to police were more important than more distant threats in the determination of police use of coercive power. In other words, perceptions of threat stem from the dynamics of police-citizen confrontations.[10] Secondly, civil rights complaints occurred when an individual filed a complaint on inappropriate police behavior and hence is a measure of informal coercive practices. This research extends our knowledge of social control to informal police practices. Holmes' research also showed that conflict is not simply a dynamic characterizing interactions between elite and non-privileged groups, but involves status and economic groups (in his research, the Police) across the political and moral spectrum.

Simon: Managing the Dangerous Classes. Penal reform—changes in the way government carries out punishment—does not arise from the "internal problems of punishing offenders, but from transformations in social and political structures" (Simon, 1993:5). With that premise, Simon discusses the formation of the "dangerous classes" and early penal reform in the United States at the end of the nineteenth century. The United States and Europe, Simon argued, underwent a transformation in the industrial working classes and in high levels of immigration. One consequence was the expansion of the capacity of the prison to punish, under the rubric of penal reform. Penal reform was specifically aimed at the "new political strength of the increasingly organized and assertive industrial working class." Innovations in punishment of criminals provided an avenue for the reestablishment of order.

> Within a short period, new programs designed to intensify the disciplinary capacity of penal regimes, and to bring discipline and order to bear directly on the "dangerous" in the midst of their communities were implemented (Simon, 1993:5).

Periods of economic transformation can cause high levels of unemployment and economic marginalization of disadvantaged groups. Coupled with the linguistic and economic disadvantages that naturally accrue to immigrants, disadvantaged groups are popularly viewed as dangerous and are ready targets of political entrepreneurs. Problems in adaptation to American life are viewed by elites as evidence of personal, moral degeneration, and prison reform is symbolically typically tied to reintroducing some notion of moral fiber or sense of responsibility. Hence, the twin effects of immigration and economic transformation create classes popularly viewed as morally and criminally dangerous, and a broad range of urban programs are aimed at reducing their threat (Rothman, 1980; Garland, 1985). The development of reforms in prison (Rothman, 1971) and in parole and probation (Simon, 1993; Pisciotta, 1994) reflect the legislative influence of elites to expand underclass control through a logic of individual responsibility and concerns of future criminal conduct.

Beginning in the mid 1970s, the process of economic transformation and prison reform was again observed. The dramatic expansion of the justice system, Simon observed, did not come about from an expanding criminogenic population but was a consequence of changes in the political economy, particularly the restructuring of the economy away from traditional industry. Economic transformation fell disproportionately on African-Americans, who were concentrated in those cities that underwent the most dramatic economic changes and who already were segregated in urban centers (Wilson, 1987). African-Americans have since become the new "dangerous class"—the target of elite fears, and symbolic politics, and have born the brunt of the intensification and expansion of justice activity.

Thus, once again, as at the beginning of the twentieth century, a wave of penal reform has characterized reforms in prison and in parole and probation (Feeley & Simon, 1992; Byrne, 1990). Moreover, the persistence of the underclass has contributed to a "management" approach, in which crime is seen as not "curable" in a medical sense but rather, a social threat to be treated with a managerial sensibility. The "new technology" is consequently managerial, aimed at classifying populations according to the likelihood of future criminality (Feeley & Simon, 1992). The expansion of surveillant technologies has particularly facilitated the growth of modern parole and probation, effectively converting non-incarcerated minority population areas into surveillant zones (Gordon, 1991).

These perspectives on penal reform are consistent with the conflict perspective because they recognize that economic factors, elite influences, and symbolic politics influence justice system practices. In the examples discussed above, immigration to the United States, urban economic dislocations that destabilized the industrial sector of the U.S. economy, and elite fears of the "dangerous classes" or "underclass" stimulated prison reform. Reform in each era was justified in terms of the popular symbols of its time, and typically involved instilling some notion of personal responsibility (McCorkle & Crank, 1996). Across different epochs of reform is an effort to make offenders "more responsible" for their behavior (Pisciotta, 1994). Hence, legislators are able to avoid dealing with the substantive causes of crime—broad social and economic dislocations—by assigning blame to those most affected by those dislocations.

Reiman: . . . and the Poor Get Prison. Reiman's (1998) critique of criminal justice practices in the United States examines crime and its control both across the social structure and in the context of various kinds of economic harms. It is a self-acknowledged Marxist critique of criminal justice, and in the fifth edition provides an appendix summarizing the Marxist view of criminal justice practices in the United States.

Reiman begins with an observation: the criminal justice system seems to behave as if it were more concerned with maintaining crime at its current level rather than trying to solve it. Reiman argues that this is indeed the case. He presents the "Pyrrhic defeat theory."

> The Pyrrhic defeat theory argues that the failure of the criminal justice system yields such benefits to those in positions of power that it amounts to success . . . the failure to reduce crime substantially broadcasts a potent ideological message to the American people, a message that benefits and protects the powerful and privileged in our society by legitimating the present social order with its disparities in wealth and privilege and by diverting public discontent and opposition away from the rich and powerful and onto the poor and powerless (Reiman, 1998:5).

The failure of the justice system to do something about crime has implications: the image that the real danger to society are the poor and minorities is created and sustained, and attention is directed away from the substantial harms committed by the rich and powerful. These other harms, in terms of death and suffering, are much more widespread than serious crime. By focusing on the poor and on street crime, attention is diverted from the real danger to life and limb caused by big business, and the rich stay rich. The criminal justice system consequently is central to sustaining economic inequities, helping the rich stay rich, and preserving the class system in the United States. Reiman provides the following information, organized into two tables, to display the relative dangers ordinary citizens face from crime and from big business.

Figure 4.5a
How Americans Are Murdered

Total	Firearms	Knife or Other Cutting Instrument	Other Weapon: Club, Arson, Poison Strangulation, etc.	Personal Weapon: Hands Fists, etc.
20,043[a]	13,673	2,538	2,650	1,182

[a]Note that this figure diverges somewhat from the number of murders and nonnegligent manslaughters used elsewhere in the FBI Uniform Crime Reports, 1995, because the FBI has data on the weapons used in only 20,043 of the reported murders.

Figure 4.5b
How Americans Are (Really) Murdered

Total	Occupation Hazard & Disease	Knife or Other Cutting Instrument Including Scalpel	Firearms	Other Weapon: Club, Poison, Hypodermic Prescription Drug, etc.	Personal Weapon Hands Fists, etc.
68,143	34,100	14,538[a]	13,673	4,650[a]	1,182

[a]These figures represent the relevant figures in Table 2-1 plus the most conservative figures for the relevant categories discussed in the text.

Source: FBI *Uniform Crime Reports*, 1995: "Murder Victims, Types of Weapons Used, 1995."

When we examine the harm of killing that occurs as a result of routine business practices, we find that it is more than twice as great as the harm caused by violent crime. Yet the focus of the criminal justice system is on the lesser problem—the problem of street crime that results in murder. By focusing on street crime, maintaining it in the newspapers on a daily basis, the image is created that the real harm facing citizens is street crime. The daily work of the criminal justice system—and big business media as well—sustains the gross economic inequalities that enable the rich to stay rich. The focus on crimes of the poor, particularly street crime, thus deflects attention of the American public away from a much greater threat to its immediate health—crimes of business. A full explication of Reiman's analyses are beyond the scope of this book; however, it should be noted that these figures are paralleled by harms that result in injury.

Th linkage of crime and poverty has two effects. First, it "paints the picture that the threat to decent middle Americans comes from those below them on the economic ladder, not from those above. [163] Second, by focusing on street crime, hostility for the poor is maintained and the more important threats to health and life facing ordinary Americans are ignored or neglected. If the justice system were to actually succeed in efforts to control crime, the middle class might recognize where their true threat lay—in the substantial benefits that go to the rich. Nothing, Reiman wryly observed, guarantees success (preserving the current economic inequalities that protect the rich) like failure (at crime control).

Reiman discounts a "conspiracy" theory to explain the advantages that the rich obtain from contemporary justice system practices. The criminal justice system provides for the rich. The system has grown piecemeal over time, and individual actors in the system have frequently acted with the best intentions, concerned for the poor and committed to the protection of victims of street crime. Yet, at the macro level the characteristic feature of the justice system is growth and expansion. Reiman calls this "historical inertia." Historical inertia is characterized by two elements: (1) The criminal justice system provides benefits to those with the power to make changes and imposes costs for those with limited power (thus further reducing their power), and (2) the criminal justice system creates the impression that what it fights are the real threats to average Americans, thus justifying more of the same—cops, money, prosecutors—especially when it is unsuccessful. The message from the justice system is an ideological one—that the threat is from below, from the poor, and that the poor are morally defective and their poverty is their fault, and reflects their inability to take responsibility for their behavior. The end result is a system that fails to address crime, and that ignores the real farms that threaten the middle and working classes.

Reiman concludes that the failure of American criminal justice is a moral failure. By failing to address the true problems faced by ordinary citizens, the criminal justice system is no morally different from the criminals it "tries" to control. Reiman recommended several initiatives to deal with crime and to make the justice system more just.

1. Put an end to crime-producing poverty. In the long-term, Reiman argues, the elimination of poverty is the most effective crime-prevention weapon.

2. Let the crime fit the harm and the punishment fit the crime. Punishments need to be redesigned to reflect the real harms that threaten people. "Crime in the suites should be prosecuted and punished as vigorously as crime in the streets." [183].

3. Legalize the production and sale of illicit drugs and treat addiction as a medical problem. The current cure for narcotics addition—incarceration—is more harmful than the problem itself. Various dimensions of legalization should be explored and implemented.

4. Develop correctional programs that promote rather than undermine personal responsibility. Offer ex-offenders real preparation and opportunities to succeed as law-abiding citizens.

5. Enact and vigorously enforce stringent gun controls. With the easy availability of handguns, any disagreement can be instantly transformed into a fatal conflict. Allowing easy access to handguns is complicity in murder.

6. Narrow the range of police, prosecutorial, and judicial discretion. Procedures should be established to hold all accountable to the public for the reasonableness and fairness of their decisions.

7. Transform the equal right to counsel into the right to equal counsel as far as it is possible. A form of national legal insurance would enable all individuals to hire private attorneys without compromising the adversarial relationship.

8. Establish a more just distribution of wealth and income and make equal opportunity a reality. This is a call for the investment in "our most important resource: people." [192].

These recommendations contain two important themes. One is a standpoint that locates the central problems faced by people in the unequal distribution of wealth and its consequential inequalities. The second is a set of prescriptions aimed at transforming criminal justice as practiced into a system of justice based on socialist conditions in which a minimum economic well-being is provided as a basic democratic good.

Critical Perspectives: Bridging Criminology and Criminal Justice

Since the 1980s, the fields of criminal justice and criminology have experienced an explosion of theoretical development. Many observers have categorized this development under the umbrella term "critical theory" (Lanier & Henry, 1998; Bierne & Messerschmidt, 2000), and I will do the same here.[11] Critical perspectives cover a wide domain of theoretical content. Their uniting theme is that they question many taken-for-granted elements of the criminal justice system. Bierne and Messerschmidt (2000) identify the following elements that are challenged by critical theorists:

1. The legalistic definition of crime.

2. Positivistic methods based on simple causal modeling

3. Contemporary penal policies

4. Increased punitiveness

5. Police targeting of particular groups

6. Political failures to considering the social and economic bases of crime

7. Systemic practices of sexism, racism, and classism.

An inspection of these elements of reveals a focus on the ethics and practices of the criminal justice system rather than on crime per se. Critical criminology is in this sense has much to say about the behavior of justice systems. Indeed, from some critical perspectives, explanations for crime are indistinguishable from explications of justice system practices. Much of critical criminology, consequently, is probably better described as critical criminal justice, or as critical inquiry into the nature of justice itself. An investigation into the various forms of critical criminology will consequently expand our understanding of theory and practice of criminal justice.

In this section I will review three perspectives commonly linked under the critical rubric: left realism, postmodernism, and theory integration. Feminism criminology is often included as a category of critical criminal justice. However, in this book, I have devoted Chapter 7 to the discussion of feminist criminal justice, believing that women have more to offer the field of justice studies than as a sub-component of a particular perspective. Peacemaking is also widely identified as a critical perspective, and it is discussed in Chapter 8 on morality.

Left Realism. Left realism emerged in the mid-1980s as a contemporary, activist form of radical criminology. It is a Marxist-tradition perspective that is highly critical of capitalism, which is believed to sustain the inequalities that are the source of criminal behavior. Because the criminal justice system is itself one of the mainstays of inequality, left realism can be considered as theory of criminal justice as well.

Left realism carries many core elements of Marxian tradition: it focuses on the way in which the political economy or class structure contributes to broad inequalities, and suggests that crime problems resulted from those inequalities. However, realists differ from those whom it called left idealists in that it (1) takes seriously victims' concerns, and (2) provides practical remedies for the inequalities it thought caused crime problems.

Advocates of left realism view themselves as different from the traditional left, or what they call "left idealism." Left realists do not believe in "waiting for the revolution" (Lanier & Henry, 1999:267). By being uninvolved in policy, realists contend that idealists abandon policy to the political right. Left realists located their "niche" in the development of social policy. They argue that important issues have been largely ignored by radical criminologists. Working- and middle-class crime is often not particularly romantic and victims often suffer substantial harm that should be addressed by the criminal justice system. Left realists advocate concrete reforms for criminal justice practice (Lea & Young, 1986; Young, 1986). However, they view contemporary criminal justice practices as a source of harm. The working and middle classes are thus victimized both from above, from the criminal justice and economic systems, and from below, by those who have limited resources and for whom crime is a way to secure a livelihood.

Policy recommendations are intended to ameliorate the way in which the criminal justice system intensifies class boundaries and disadvantages the poor. Lea and Young (1986) note the following elements of a program of left realism (discussed in Bierne & Messerschmidt, 2000:231):

1. Offenders should be demarginalized. Programs such as decarceration, community services and victim restitution should be used instead of prison. Bonds to society would thus be preserved rather than destroyed through the incarceration experience.

2. Preemptive deterrence should be carried out by citizen patrols and other community groups. This is crime prevention at the community level.

3. Prisons should only be used when an offender is an extreme danger to the community.

4. Police forces should be transformed into general police service organizations. They should also be held accountable to community groups.

5. Mobilize working class individuals so that they can act politically.

The left realist movement emerged in Great Britain, and has been sympathetically received in academia and to a lesser extent in the Labor party. In the United States it has been largely marginalized both in academics and in government, though it is slowly taking "traction" in academia as a coherent and substantive policy-oriented theoretical perspective.

Left realism represents an eclectic turn in Marxian theory. It incorporates other elements of social theory—strain theory in particular—into perspectives which accept as fundamental the inequalities caused by class structure. Its theoretical base is broadened to include macro-micro linkages in the analysis of justice system behavior, as well as social ecology theory and mainstream sociological criminology (Lanier & Henry, 1998; Shoemaker, 1996).

Left realists reveal a willingness to bring to the table Marxian notions of class inequality as bargaining chips in the fight over the future of democracy (Matthews, 1987). This engages Marxist advocates into the ongoing debate over current policy. The importance of this subtle point cannot be overestimated: it locates Marxist ideas of political economy into the grabbag of "goods" over which democratic institutions contend.

Left realism re-empowers a political perspective of economic equality that, in the United States if not in the other Americas and in Europe, has been seemingly discredited. Left realism, combined with a practical concern for the inequalities affecting minority groups, carries enormous political mobilizing potential in the Americas (Gilly, 1997).

DeKeseredy and Schwartz: Elements of Left Realism. Issues regarding left realism were sketched in two papers by DeKeseredy and Schwartz (DeKeseredy & Schwartz, 1991; Schwartz & DeKeseredy, 1991). Schwartz and DeKeseredy (1991) identified the following fundamental principles of left realism:

1. Working-class crime is a serious problem for the working-class. Left idealists tend, the authors note, to idealize the conditions of the working class and crime among working class people. This is unacceptable. Working class people "are victimized from all directions in capitalist societies[52]. Working-class people are vulnerable economically and socially, and are consequently more likely to experience both working class and white collar crime (Young, 1986).

2. Any theory of crime and crime control should contain four factors: the victim, the offender, the nation-state, and the local community. At the most general level, the perspective is influenced by Marxist theory; however, other perspectives such as strain and subcultural theories are also used to explain local and individual crime.

3. Abstract empiricism is unaccepted, though quantitative methodologies are not altogether rejected. There is a preference for a blending of qualitative and quantitative methodologies.

4. Advocates " try to answer Taylor's 1981 call for the "reconstruction of a socialist criminology. They try to provide practical, progressive crime control strategies that challenge the right-wing law and order campaign and address working class communities' fear of street crime.' [52-53]. These policy alternatives include "de-marginalization, preemptive deterrence, democratic control of the police and community participation in crime prevention and policy development." [53].

The four elements of left determinism described above are concerned with criminal activity. However, because the state is inserted as one of the central elements in crime causation, the practice of crime control becomes central to left realism. Crime and the practice of criminal justice are interwoven, spuriously related to each other through the influence of the state and conditions of inequality. Because the state is itself implicated in the genesis of crime, any effort to do something about crime requires that the state remedy the inequalities that spur crime. These inequalities are economic, and they include the way the justice system differentially disadvantages the working and middle classes.

Characteristic of left realism is the advocation of concrete policy recommendations. The authors cite the recommendations of Michalowski (1983) and Currie (1985), stated below.

1. Tax surcharges on industries that attempt to close plants or reduce a community's workforce.

2. Government laws that provide employment for all individual replaced by new technology.

3. A minimum wage level 150 percent of the poverty level.

4. Increased wages for women.

5. Publicly supported and community oriented job creation.

6. Upgrading the quality of work for disenfranchised people.

7. Paid work leaves.

8. Job creation in local communities.

A review of these recommendations reveals a common theme—they are about the economic conditions facing individuals, not about how the criminal justice system can be more effective in the "war on crime." The recommendations are beyond narrow changes in the delivery of criminal justice. They are far-reaching and complex, involving changes across the delivery of social goods.

Are the recommendations realistic? Barak (1986) suggested that citizens and politicians in the United States are unwilling to challenge either their basic assumptions about individualist crime causation or the importance of punishment as a remedy for crime. Barak's suggestions seem to have been on target. In the nearly two decades since Barak made his observations, the criminal justice system has more than doubled the number of citizens incarcerated and dramatically expanded the criminal justice system in diverse directions, enhancing sentences, prosecuting children as adults, and expanding the use of the death penalty.

Schwartz and DeKeseredy (1991) identified several dilemmas facing left realism. Community crime prevention, they noted, is central to left realism, and a decentralized and de-structured community can provide the solution for street crime. They point out, however, that such an approach has its own problems. The question of community control begs the question "Who in the community has control?" Community spokespersons may in fact advocate for more stringent crime control measures than those already in place. Local control may also carry all the stereotypes, prejudices, and biases that gave emergence to inequality and crime to begin with. Nor does left realism deal well with concerns over woman abuse. As the authors note,

> The problems of violence against women and woman abuse seem to bother left realism at exactly the point where it is weakest. How can one accede to the demands of many liberal and radical feminists for

increased punishment for rapists and batterers at the very moment that one is proclaiming a system based on minimal policing and a reduction in the power of the state? (Schwartz & DeKeseredy, 1991:66).

Finally, once official definitions of crime are accepted as a real concern, and crime becomes the central focus, it becomes difficult to distinguish between left realism and right realism.

Postmodernism. Postmodernism is a body of philosophy, methodology, and critical review of contemporary society that encompasses a variety of standpoints. Generally, these standpoints offer a critical look at life and the nature of meaning in the postmodern age. In the area of methods, these perspectives aim at the "deconstruction" of positivistic theories that purport to measure underlying social "truths." Postmodernism rejects the notion of scientific rationalism, arguing that "truth" claims cannot be sustained when they are fully investigated. A rejection of rationalism and positivist method is not unique to postmodernism. Postmodernists, however, tend to look at how symbol systems used by people in the postmodern or consumerist age are no longer connected to any "signifier," that is, the stuff we find meaning in is unlinked with any identifiable underlying reality at any level. Postmodernism is consequently highly relativistic, and proponents often argue that any effort to find underlying truth is simply an attempt to replace one symbol system with another.

Postmodernism juxtaposes itself against "modernism," which refers to the positivistic theory that emerged from enlightenment thought. Postmodernism critically challenges every element of positivism, determinism, and claim-to-truth. Lanier and Henry (1998:280) describe postmodernism as follows:

> Postmodernism refers to a school of thought that has emerged out of a period of intense skepticism with science. Scientific method and rational thought were . . . an outcome of the eighteenth century Enlightenment and have prevailed until the late 20th century. Disenchantment with modernism, linked to the suffering that its hierarchies, divisions, and exclusions have brought to many (through imperialism, sexism, racism, and class oppression), together with its increasing inability to solve society's problems (e.g., pollution, poverty), has led to a questioning of its values, particularly the value of scientific analysis and rational thought . . ."

Postmodernism can be traced to the philosophical writings of Baudrillard (1981, 1983A & B) and Derrida (1973, 1978, 1982). Below is a brief overview of the ideas of these authors and a discussion of how they apply to the field of criminal justice.

The object of Baudrillard's investigation, particularly in his later writings, is into the nature of postindustrial society. In industrial society, humans found meaning in their relations to production, and their symbolic universe was made up of meanings tied to their work. There was an underlying linkage between human production and material goods: The work carried out by people carried substantive value and provided a basis for our assessments of social and personal value. In his position that production preceded meaning, Baudrillard's Marxist roots (which he later rejected) can be seen.

In postmodern society all this changes. Consumption becomes the economic basis of the modern, postindustrial order. Production lose its value as a referent for values, and becomes meaningful only in its ability to facilitate consumption. How do we decide what to consume if we no longer have a value system based on some notion of production? We consume meanings. When we buy a fishing reel, a set of philosophy books, or a new 9mm handgun, we are acting consumptively, and we are providing meaning in our lives. These meanings are presented to us by powerful groups, politicians, and the mass media. Effective producers do not simply sell goods—they affix powerful ideological meanings to those goods. When we buy a product, we are thus purchasing meaning. The more money we have, the more meaning we are able to purchase, and the more meaningful our lives are.

For example, if we are runners, we find meaning in the purchase of expensive shoes, wick-off running gear, cloths that reflect light at night, water containers, and we participate in runs, often at considerable distance from our homes. The meaning that running has for our lives depends on our ability to consume running products. We buy running magazines, vitamins, pre-run warm-up clothing. We eat particular foods, especially products that are digestible during running. Consumption becomes the basis for identity. Because, of this, Baudrillard argued, there is no longer any reality—there is only a sort of hyperreality, produced by our consumptive patterns, which is manipulated by those who provide us with desired products.

In the field of criminal justice, we consume clusters of meaning provided by dominant patterns of justice practices. What we receive vis-à-vis the mass media are clusters of meaning surrounding the word "crime." These clusters tend to be of two types: the "corrupt system" or "tough on crime." As consumers of crime media, we want justice practices to be conducted in a way consistent with one or the other of these clusters of meaning. The presence of crime sustains both perspectives. If Baudrillard is correct, and were we actually to significantly lower the crime rate, we would have to find new behaviors to label as crime, so that the symbols could be sustained.

The distribution of clusters of symbols around various loci of meaning are called simulacra. Simulacra are controlled by marketers of symbols—media and government. Social science efforts to uncover some sort of underlying truth are doomed—truth is no longer relevant to the conduct of post-modern consumerist society. In the current era, simulacra are dominated by models and polls. Models and polls become hyper real and reality is re-constructed through them to become even more real. DNA, for example, leads the way to a more perfect human. Public opinion polls that measure attitudes toward education tell us how good education is.

If Baudrillard provided us with an image of post-modern society in which the link between symbols and what they signify is manipulated, Derrida provided a method to "deconstruct" post-modern society and understand its symbolic dynamics. In modern society, we act as if our actions had underlying meaning, and we justify our actions on the predictability of ends. However, the world is more unpredictable than our way of thinking recognizes. We are embedded in a world full of uncertainty and unpredictability, what Cooper and Burrell (1988) called a "chameleonic" world. Our meanings are not tied to some underling reality, but to dominant social ways of organizing meaning. This meaning is embedded in our language itself, and creates the illusion of order in human relations. For example, central to our way of thinking is the notion that we are fully capable of self determination, and that we can take full responsibility for our actions. However, this is a social illusion. We are actually foci through which ideological, economic, and social forces move. We do not tend to recognize these forces. The role of social science is to unmask our illusions learn about the social roots of our ways of thinking and organizing values.

Central to Derrida's method is the concept of "difference." This illusive concept is described by Hassard (1993) along the following lines. We tend to view ourselves at the center of our actions—we believe that we are individuals, and our actions are the product of our self-responsibility. We, in effect, create a language that isolates us from the surrounding world. This language is full of metaphors, common sense, and rational terms that create individual identities for humans, separate from the world they inhabit. This process, of seeing ourselves outside the many contexts in which we are embedded, is a process of differentiation. 'Differance' is an intellectual process in which we ourselves as actors self-directed and independent of our contexts. It is a product of language, and its used to categorize the world into us-them phenomena. We are able to believe that we are independent actors with agency—free will—only after the act of differencing, or separating ourselves from the many linkages we have to the world around us. In fact, we are not independent agents, but are embedded in "texts," a term that refers to the language of the various social, philosophical, and economic contexts in which we find ourselves. We are actors within these texts, not creators of them.

We act within the dynamic context of our own presence, but this dynamic identity is produced by differencing—that is, by viewing ourselves in contrast to the background against which we move. Presence is created by how we see ourselves different from the world. This presence is a linguistic construction, a product of the language we use. By the act of differencing, we as individuals become more real. But the background, the forces that move us, fades. We create the illusion of separateness to provide self identity, but in doing so we lose a sense of the extent to which we are embedded in the many contexts in which we find ourselves.

The purpose of social science is to peer through this illusions of identity created by differencing, so that we can better understand the forces that animate us. To overcome the effects of differencing, we attempt to "decenter" the subject. Instead of looking at self-directing individuals, we attempt to identify the symbols in the world occupied by the subject and that organize his or her meanings. We "deconstruct" the "individual," in people so that we can see what symbols move them and how they respond to the forces in which they are embedded. Put differently, instead of seeing ourselves as self-directed, we imagine ourselves as locations through which forces (and discourses) move (Hassard, 1993).

What does postmodernism have to offer criminal justice? To answer this, Lanier and Henry (1998) suggest that there are two types of postmodernisms, skeptical and affirmative. Skeptical postmodernists are those who reject the idea that truth can be discovered. Deconstruction is a method for underlying the falsity of truth claims and identifying its underlying assumptions. Affirmative postmodernists, on the other hand, couple deconstruction with reconstruction. Affirmative postmodernists believe that humans can actively reconstruct their world once it has been deconstructed.

The language of postmodernism is exceedingly difficult to grasp (Schwartz, 1991). This is for several reasons. It has emerged in philosophy, and its relevance to social studies is only now being explored. Hassard identifies five central concepts of postmodernism in the following table.

Figure 4.6
Five Central Concepts of Postmodernism

Concept	Argument
Representation	"Attempts to discover the genuine order of things must be regarded as naive and mistaken."
Reflexivity	"We must possess the ability to be critical of our own intellectual assumptions."
Writing	"The logocentric image of writing (which sees language as a sign, system for concepts which exist independently in the object world) must be overturned."
Difference	"We must develop a strategy which reflects but does not capture the process of deconstruction."
De-centring the subject	"The grand isolation of the modern subject must be replaced with the notion of agency as a system of relations between strata."

Postmodernism cannot be fairly accused of providing knowledge, which is a truth claim that any postmodernist would deny outright. What postmodernism provides is a method for critical analysis of the methods that are used in justice studies. It can be thought of as a method's method. Consider each of the five elements in Figure 4.6.

Representation requires that we peer beyond the order of things as we receive them. Neither common-sense nor scientific knowledge are adequate to present a world that is much more phemonenologically arbitrary than many would like to believe. We are directed to look for the unpredictable and uncontrollable elements that underlay many justice system processes—for example, how discretionary decisions are embedded in virtually all so-called "rational" justice system processes. However, the concept "representation" is extended one step further. We must abandon the illusion that our constructions of reality measure anything real. All our empirical methods show us is how academic "simulacra"—its particular symbol systems—interact with various "simulacra" in public life—symbol systems used by the public or in the practice of criminal justice. Much of our research is simply reinterpreting one symbol system with another, neither of which has any underlying reality.

Reflexivity requires that we examine the way in which we interact with the objects of our study, and rejects the notion that we can be independent observers of the world around us. Justice researchers should consciously attempt to assess how they affect and are affected by the object of study, instead of asserting an impossible-to-achieve neutrality. Kraska (1996:416), for example, reflected on how his study of a paramilitary police unit created a sense of power and autonomy from the law—how being a "beneficiary of state-sanctioned use of force" created a sense of "autonomy from the law." Emotions and transitory feelings are interjected as central elements into the social science process.

Difference demands that we look into the background, that we know our subject-matter much more deeply than simple empirical abstractions for the purposes of measurement and testing. We need to become familiar with the contexts in which the causal pattern we (think we) see emerge. It is an absolute rejection of the abstracted empiricism frequently found in many quantitative journals.

However, differencing is more than looking into the contexts that affect our behaviors. The act of writing is, itself, a process of differencing. When we write our research findings, we tend to presume that our words are signs for things that exist in the real world. Writing itself, however, embedded us in a linguistic process that creates difference. Hence, the act of writing findings should be recognized as a research tool that is as likely to create illusions as to reveal truths about the world. Put differently, the language of our research carries its outcomes built into the language of research, which *in itself* may create an order to things which is not truly present.

Finally, *de-centring the subject* reminds us not to isolate humans from their conditions. In the world of law, we reject the idea that humans should be viewed as self-determining and instead consider how they are the focal point of a whirlwind of forces, often arbitrary, out of their control. In criminal justice, this suggests that we attempt to peer bring the "background" — those forces that move humans—into the foreground and place the individual into the background. We identify symbols of "individualism" and "responsibility" and try to remove them so that we can see what really is going on. Individualist notions of behavior are rejected. What we look for are the forces that move us to use terms like responsibility.

Postmodernism, as a method for dissecting the assumptions embedded in contemporary methods, provides a brutal assessment of positivistic glosses and statistical procedures. It forces us to consider elements substantially beyond simple causal models built on ideas of dependence and independence. It doesn't answer questions, but provides us with a method that enables us to think about our research questions much harder than we might otherwise.

Postmodern research is still in its infancy in the justice studies field. It is so different from conventional ways of thinking that we cannot begin to guess where it might take us. Yet, it addresses old and known problems. As we will discuss in detail in the following chapter on methods, our empirical methodologies are beset with philosophical problems (DiCristina, 1995). Nor are these problems inconsequential. Problems such as the interaction of the observed and the observer and of intentionality (discussed in the following chapter) profoundly undermine the validity of research conducted in the positivist tradition. Yet these and related problems tend to be either ridiculed or ignored to such an extent that graduate students rarely have even a marginal familiarity with them. It may be that the seeming alienness of postmodernism to us as social scientists is not so much a statement of its research value as it is a reflection of our ignorance of the problems it addresses. At some point, for the field of justice studies to come of age, it may have to address the complex and occasionally unnerving problems presented by postmodernism.

Integrative Criminal Justice. The field of criminal justice is diverse, and researchers come from a variety of intellectual traditions. One of the consequences of this interdisciplinary intellectual heritage is that the field is characterized by a diversity of theoretical perspectives and concepts. This diversity appears to be a rich heritage to some observers, while others are concerned about field fragmentation, absence of focus, and lack of a clear message that can contribute to policy at the local or national level

Integrative theory is a topic of considerable interest in the field of criminology (Lanier & Henry, 1998; Barak, 1998; Akers, 1994; Messner, Krohn & Liska, 1989). By integrative theory is meant "the combination of two or more pre-existing theories, selected on the basis of their commonalities, into a single reformulated theoretical model with greater comprehensiveness and explanatory value than any one of its component theories" (Farnsworth, 1989:95; cited in Lanier & Henry, 1998:290). Integration holds the promise of clarity and parsimony. By reducing the current list of bewildering ideas to a few succinct and relevant concepts and perspectives, the field should be able to more clearly state its core ideas.

Integration, though holding the promise of parsimony, presents particular problems. Lanier and Henry identify the following problems regarding integration.

1. What is to be integrated? When theories are integrated, do we look for concepts with similar meanings? How do we decide whose meaning is the most accurate? Further, such an approach presumes that a concept has meaning and identity apart from the theory from which it is abstracted. If we pare and recombine meanings, to what extent will we retain the intent of the original author? Put differently, will such an approach clarify or impoverish the field's theoretical heritage?

2. How are propositions and concepts to be integrated? The issue here is causal order. For example, should the behavior of criminal justice agencies be seen as causal to the behavior of criminals (normative theory), or both spuriously related vis-à-vis economic conditions (class theory)? The ordering of concepts itself is central to how we think about justice theory.

3.   At what level should concepts be integrated? Are we going to focus on the individual level and conduct micro-integration, or on structural/cultural relationships at the macro-integration level? Researchers have identified three levels of integration: kinds of people and their behavior, organizations and organizational processes, or cultural and structural processes. Any effort to integrate theories must carefully distinguish which level integration is to occur.

Barak and Henry (1999:167) identify two kinds of integration—modernistic and post-modern. Modern integration is based in positivistic method, and is concerned with the identification of predictors for criminal behavior. Modern integration is propositional, predictive, particularistic, and static. It tends to take a clear, narrowly defined notion of harm in terms of violations of the criminal law. Postmodern integration, on the other hand, holds that "everything affects everything else," and effects are in a constant state of change. These models are conceptual, interpretive, holistic, and dynamic (Barak, 1997). They involve a wider concept of harm, including the harm of inequality and injustice. In the following section, I discuss a model of modernist integration, developed by Bernard and Engel (2001).

Bernard and Engel: Toward Criminal Justice Integration. The field of criminal justice, Bernard and Engel (2001) observe, emerged as a practical field and has developed theory slowly. At the present time, theory is necessary for the further progress of the field as "an academic and scientific discipline" [2]. Perspectives in criminal justice are diverse and tend to reflect various stages of growth of the academic field of criminal justice. These perspectives can be classified in three ways. First is normative, in that classification reflects the different components of the criminal justice system, such as the courts or the police. Second, classification occurs on the basis of underlying assumptions and propositions of particular theories. That is, various writings are organized according to whether they are an example of consensus theory, or of conflict theory, or of postmodernism. Third are efforts to group research by dependent and independent variables.

It is a version of the third approach that Bernard and Engel propose. Criminal justice theories, they state, should be grouped first by their dependent variables, and then according to their independent variables. There are three broad types of dependent variables:

> The first type focuses on the individual behavior of criminal justice agents (e.g., the behavior of police officers, courtroom officials, correctional officers). The second focuses on the behavior of criminal justice organizations (e.g., the behavior of police departments, court organizations, correctional organizations). The third type of dependent variable focuses on the characteristics of the overall criminal justice system and its components (e.g., police killings, "get tough" sentencing, incarceration rates) (Bernard & Engel, 2001:5).

The authors state that this kind of approach has three advantages over the other two. First, it facilitates competitive testing and the identification of generalizations across the various dependent and independent variables. Secondly, it allows for the assessment of the relative explanatory power of each of the variables: hence, it is not only integrative but offers parsimony. Third, it facilitates theory building. We can observe how different variables have commonalities across the criminal justice system.

The approach proposed by Bernard and Engel is intensely empirical. The approach locates the legitimacy of conceptual relations in their ability to fare well in statistical testing. While theories are not falsified, "they may be found to possess so little utility (account for so little explained variation) that they can be discarded." [25].

The objective of empirical unification through empirical testing occupies an important place in that part of the field of justice studies that is empirically focused. Undoubtedly, there is a great deal of loose theorizing and questionable measurement in the justice studies field, and a systematic analysis of the conceptual interrelations of various theories will contribute much to our understanding of their empirical utility in specific situations.

Yet, there is something unsatisfying about the astringently empirical approach to theory-building proposed by Bernard and Engel. Consider, by way of comparison, the following passage from Toch's (1990) splendid essay "Falling in Love with a Book."

> If books are not read, is anything lost beyond the authors' or publishers' royalties? The truth is that much is inevitably lost, and the assumptions we make about what is preserved are unlikely to be realized . . .
>
> If the progenitors of any field are in fact consequential, we hope they have written meaty books that defy easy summaries. Meaty books tend to be complex, multi-thematic works that make points in throw-away fashion. They are also apt to be beautifully written, with phrases that sparkle and amuse. Where there is one salient theme, we expect the argument that leads to it to be subtle and leisurely developed (otherwise, why write a book?). We expect the theme to follow neatly from the argument, but—like any punchline—to look unprepossessing out of context (Toch, 1990:246).

At first, these two writings appear to have nothing in common. Yet, they are both about the great ideas that animate the field of justice studies, and particularly how we decide what ideas we should retain to develop the field and to pass on to our students.

Were we to assess the great ideas regarding justice studies that derive from the written word using Toch's recommendation, we would carefully read the books in which they were contained. Were we to carry out a similar assessment using Bernard and Engel's recommendation, we would strip the books down to their central independent and dependent variables, and then we would carry out empirical analyses. Focusing on dependent variables and their measurements, we would systematically work across the field of independent variables. Clearly, these are sharply different modes for advancing the body of knowledge about justice studies. How can we reconcile Toch's notion of books that "sparkle and amuse" with Bernard and Engel's distillation of theory (theory, after all, does come from books) to measurable concepts and articulated linkages? We cannot. One is profoundly empirical, and reflects the positivist base of the social sciences. The other is grounded in the humanities, and is a recognition of the uniqueness and fecundity of each work. Yet, both views are of central importance to the field of justice studies.

One of the central themes of this book is that the field of justice studies is as much of a humanities as it is a social science. In our field, both perspectives carry heft. It is not as important that we endeavor to reconcile the perspectives suggested by Bernard and Engel, on the one hand, and Toch, on the other. Through the positivistic tradition, we learn about the immediate applicability of specific measures of middle range concepts in specific circumstances. In this part of the field, Bernard and Engel provide us with a way to correct often sloppy and confusing theorizing. Through the humanities, we learn about justice through the unique contribution of great writers. We grow intellectually through our understanding about how great books increase our capacity to imagine justice.

Notes

[1] A fifth definition of functionalism is stated by Turner (1982) who argues that the term functionalism ought to be abandoned altogether and replaced with the phrase "parts to whole" analysis.

[2] Duffee identifies two other dimensions of community variability but does not develop them. These are (1) overlap between local service areas, and (2) psychological identification with the local area.

[3] To be sure, the law carries a broader mandate than the protection of individual rights. To be sure, collective rights are sometimes recognized in tort cases, for example, where class-action suits are brought against businesses, and in cases in which governmental units bring suits against other units or individuals. However, the idea of a law without a notion of individual rights is not conceivable in our justice system as currently constituted.

[4] Meyer and Scott note that organizational structure does not develop from all kinds of conflicts, but rather conflicts that stem from legitimating questions, or questions concerning the fundamental identity and purpose of the organization and its various subunits.

[5] Intermediate risk offenders received more ISP supervision contact per week than either of the high risk categories. Drug testing among high-supervision offenders was also the lowest for all groups during the testing. Both of these findings support McCorkle and Crank (1996). Caveats were that the risk/needs assessment test given offenders was based on the general parole population, and the instrument needed to be refine for the ISP population. This caveat itself could, Bayens et al. note, arguably be considered additional support for McCorkle and Crank.

[6] Cited in Martindale, 1960: 159.

[7] Cited in Vold and Bernard, 1986: 283.

[8] Tonry (1995: 11) describes a particularly biting example of political entrepreneurship.

> Lee Atwater, George Bush's campaign strategist, decided in 1988 to make Willie Horton (an African-American on prison furlough who broke into a woman's home, and raped and stabbed a woman) a wedge issue for Republicans. He reportedly told a Republican gathering in Atlanta "There's a story about a fellow named Willie Horton who, for all I know, will end up being Dukakis' running mate."

Subsequently, many adds were run on television associating Dukakis' furlough program with the murder, and showing Willie Horton's very black face. Atwater died of cancer a few years later. On his deathbed, he

> . . . apologized for the naked cruelty of the attacks on Dukakis. "In 1988, fighting Dukakis, I said that I would 'strip the bark off the little bastard' and 'make Willie Horton his running mate.' I am sorry for both statements.

This example does not intentionally target Republicans. Clearly, the history of the Democratic party is equally (if not more) filled with such tragic examples of political entrepreneurship—after all, the Democratic party was at one time the party of slavery. The historical recency of this example, combined with its trenchant importance for contemporary policies clearly targeted against African-Americans, make it particularly relevant for current justice activities.

[9]   Crank and Caldero (2000), in their study of police ethics, argued that the police should be understood as representatives of a moral order, and that they use the law to enforce that morality.

[10]   This does not mean that police officers to not contribute to the circumstances in which they find themselves threatened. Crank (1998) argued that police sometimes operate from a tautological framework, in which beliefs about the dangerousness of minority group members mobilize a police officer's behavior. The officer's behavior, in turn, channels the behavior of the other actors in the interaction towards what it is expected to be. The outcome is taken as further proof of the potential dangerousness of minority group members.

[11]   Others refer critical criminology specifically to the broad body of literature that has emerged from or been influenced by the writings of Karl Marx (Cullen & Agnew, 1999).

Chapter 5

The Methodologies of Justice

The truth is out there.

FBI Agent Fox Muldur to his partner Dana Scully,
concerning his search for his sister, kidnapped by
aliens.

FBI Agent Fox (a.k.a. Spooky) Muldur is known to aficionados for his statement that the truth is *out there*. One of the two protagonists on a television show called "The X-Files," Muldur was in charge of unusual cases. Muldur's sister had been kidnapped by (otherworldly) aliens when she was a child, an event witnessed by Muldur, and he believed that the United States Government was covering up a history of extraterrestrial contacts. In each episode of the show, Muldur would uncover compelling (though sometimes misleading) information that the government was hiding evidence of their contacts. The truth about the government's behavior was *out there*, real but hidden. He was determined to find the hidden truth.

This chapter is about the *out there*.[1] We have many different terms for the out there; reality, noumena, truth, facts, certainty, objectivity. When we conduct research, our ostensible purpose is to find out what's really going on *out there*. We use various methods to identify the *out there*. Most typically, we conduct our research in the belief that empirical methods grounded in statistical procedures will provide a sensible way to look at the world. Would Muldur use statistical methods? Probably not: lawyers are notoriously distrustful of statistics, and criminal justice professionals tend to embrace the philosophy of individual self-determination. Does Muldur have a weaker grasp on the out there—his underlying reality—than social scientists do of their statistically produced vocabularies of crime and justice? That question is surprisingly hard to answer. If you disagree, answer the following question: How much crime is going on out there? (Answer: It depends on how you measure it—which is really no answer at all, just a statement of relativity. Now answer: What is crime relative to?)

Criminal justice research tends to take the *out there* for granted. The way in which researchers develop knowledge about the *out there* are typically defined as methodological and definitional ones—what methods will provide us with the best overall picture of what's going on in crime, justice, or justice organizations? The most commonly used methods are designed to provide researchers with ways to learn about the *out there.* But, when all is said and done, when research process is concluded, hypotheses tested, and findings evaluated, is the research-derived *out there* any more believable than Muldur's? More importantly, should it be more believable? That is, can we place more trust in scientific methodologies than Muldur did in his inferential hunches about governmental cover-ups?

One of the central arguments in this chapter is that the various methods and tools we use to tell us about the *out there* don't achieve that goal. The use of statistical procedures and scientific methodologies for gathering information have held hegemony as the *out there* tool of choice in the academic fields of criminology and criminal justice, but that hegemony is widely challenged (DiCristina 1997; Cohen, 1988; Williams, 1984). Alternative methodologies that do not use statistical procedures provide creative and fertile ways of thinking about the justice fields. This chapter discusses the principles of scientific research using quantitative (statistically based) strategies, the problems associated with quantification, and alternative ways of conducting justice research.

I will give away the conclusion to this chapter ahead of time. It is that there are many *out there's*. The underlying premise of this chapter is that there is no single, Platonian truth that can guide our search for knowledge about humans and their ethical, legal, social or moral systems, or about the important words that fill their language, such as crime, morals, and law. This does not mean that all is abandoned to complete relativity. Social scientists may intellectually recognize the relativity of things, but can act on the conviction that some things are certain enough. Humans are intentional creatures, and we select what is meaningful to us. There are many different truths *out there,* some of which compete with each other, and many of which we will discuss throughout this book. Each has a role to play in the understanding of justice. Wisdom lies in the desire to assemble breadth of perspective, but also in the ability to cut through the chaff and *act*.

This chapter promotes the use of a diversity of methods, believing that the process of discovery creates, shapes, and sustains our interest in that which is discovered. Different methods provide different ways of looking at the nature of wrong and the way we link notions of wrong to ideas of justice. Any single method limits justice perspective and increases the likelihood that a particular influence will control the way information is interpreted, be that influence the government, the scientific community, or personal biases. A combination of methods acknowledges that the world carries an abundance of visions and a variety of moral and ethical realities. Method diversity, by probing the *out there* from several different vistas, provides us with a more nuanced and richly textured understanding of what justice is and how we come to terms with it personally and professionally.

Part I: Philosophical Problems
in the Study of the *Out There*

In Part I, I present a discussion of philosophical dimensions of social science research. Empirical research in the domain of justice is always controversial, for the spirit of empirical analysis is to challenge widely held values. Yet, at the same time, it confronts its own dilemmas. The field of justice studies is as much a humanities as a social science, a legacy it cannot and should not abandon. It is also an intentional science, which means that the object of its study is created by humans. Its meanings are consequently in a constant process of interpretation and creation, and not amenable to rule-like prescriptions associated with empirical methods.

Positivism and the Out There. We observe, and we learn. This simple premise is central to the idea of social science. It is a premise that quickly becomes enormously complicated, but for now let's think only about the premise.

How do we know if what we think is consistent with what is going on in the real world? People, after all, are full of opinions (that they all too frequently share). Anyone who has ever read the "letters to the editor" section in their local newspaper quickly discovers the astonishing non-sense that passes for some people's reality. (Did Muldur write letters to the editor?) There are flat-earthers out there, and at least monthly one can read "letters to the editor" written by people who think that the holocaust was a Jewish myth. People hold perspectives that have no legitimacy, others hold perspectives with high legitimacy among some groups and no legitimacy among the general population. On the other hand, perspectives are sometimes widely shared by the general public that have no legitimacy among the scientific community. And scientific perspectives, however well grounded in research, are sometimes rejected by the public, as we witnessed when the Kansas Board of Education in 1999 abandoned the required instruction of scientific principles of evolution.

Values and the Out There. Many people view the world through the prism of cultural values. They see the world primarily from a cultural point of view, interpreting events in terms of an array of specific ideological and moral values. Consider a widely publicized event at Columbine High School in Littleton, Colorado in 1999. Thirteen high school students were killed by two other students who used semi-automatic weapons, and who then turned the weapons on themselves in a double suicide. This tragic event was widely viewed through the values prisms of democratic and republican political beliefs. Many republicans described the murders as a collapse of family values and the influence of media violence. Many democrats blamed the murders on the easy availability of semi-automatic weapons. Both groups interpreted the event in terms of values central to the world-views they represent. And members of both groups complete-ly believed in the rightness of their views and he wrongness of the views of the other side.

Culture is like a candle: it illuminates and creates shadows at the same time. The value perspectives of democrats and republicans reveal how culture selectively highlights elements of events and fades other, perhaps equally important, elements into the background (Manning, 1989). Democrats knew that young people could easily acquire deadly weapons. Republicans correctly recognized that many elements of popular media are aimed at young people, and advertisers won't hesitate to use graphic displays of gratuitous sex and violence to sell their products. Democrats carry a distrust for gun-users and fail to understand how guns are integral to some North American subcultures. Republicans do not trust popular media and do not acknowledge how it is tied to large business, which they very strongly support.

The values of both groups act as spotlights and blinders. Through the values that people carry, we can see aspects of some situations too well, and we utterly fail to see other aspects that may be more important. Unfortunately, neither perspective—gun control or media control—has provided a great deal of illumination about the events at Littleton. They both cast shadows, misdirecting rather than clarifying. If we try to under-stand the *out there* by analyzing how events match our values, we end up where we started, with perhaps a deeper conviction about our values—but we learn nothing about the world around us, certainly nothing of use about the Littleton Massacre.

Empiricism and the Out There. Let's think about another way to assess the Littleton incident. We could undertake a systematic analysis of all the events and circumstances surrounding the shootings. We approach the situation as if we didn't know why events occurred (instead of assum-ing that it is tied in some ways with some value set having to do with guns or family morals), and ask questions that will give us measurable informa-tion. We might begin with a moment by moment analysis of the events as they unfolded. When did the shooters approach the school? What did they do? How did they enter? Let's also look at the design of the school. Are there design elements that seem to have contributed to the incident? That facilitated or slowed the shooters? And the SWAT teams—how quickly did they arrive? How was leadership coordinated among the four teams? Could they have conducted themselves in a different way? Let's look at the suspects' backgrounds as well. Was there a history of problems, and was there a realistic way to interpret any identified problems as a potential threat to their classmates? Where did they obtain their weapons?

After we have acquired as much practical information on the incident and the background of the participants, we could reconstruct the flow of events and see if there was anything—building reconstruction, policy, changes in communications systems in the school, SWAT training, availability of timely information about the school layout, training for students, etc.—that could have realistically avoided or mitigated the outcome. If we are so fortunate as to identify contributing items, are changes feasible? They might not be. If they are, then can we create a policy or implement a plan for that particular school? Then, perhaps a broader study might provide us insight into whether such a policy or change would be feasible in other schools.

This second way of thinking about the events at Littleton is what we call *empirical.* By empirical, I mean that we form our ideas of the causes and consequences of events based upon what we see. Empirical means that we use our own observations to assess events. Further, it means that we apply rules of procedure to what we see.

Social science research is founded on empirical principles. The idea of empirical research, that we use principles of scientific rigor to systematically organize our observations, sounds dry and lifeless. The idea that "truth" can be determined from our observations and not from some culturally based value-system may be a simple idea. Yet on it rests the scientific revolution that undergirded the Enlightenment.[2] The threat of science to the medieval order of church and state was a fundamental element of the Enlightenment. The findings derived from scientific methods undermined the orthodoxies of church and state. Method itself was suspect—only God could determine truth, not methods used by people to assess the merely observable. The traditions of state and church were not to be taken lightly, as Galileo discovered:

> As the world knows, he was summoned to the bar of the inquisition first in 1616 and five times in 1633. . . . It (his work) was too much for the Church. He was required to recant, threatened with torture if he refused to do so, and sentenced to life imprisonment—a sentence that was enforced with some leniency in that he was permitted to receive foreign visitors, one of whom was John Milton. Bottomore and Nisbet, 1975:3-38.

Today, scientific methods are used in the justice fields to inquire into (and by implication to hold accountable) the behavior of the state and of suspected wrongdoers alike. Empirical research is considered central to the development of knowledge in the field of criminal justice. Yet, when research challenges strongly held values, it is often research that is neglected. This can be seen in the history of the Uniform Crime Reports (UCR) and National Crime Victimization Statistics (NCVS). The UCR has been widely accepted as a measure of crime, even though it is a measure of police behavior. In spite of NCVS data that clearly showed a decline in almost all kinds of crime from 1973 to 1990 and dramatic declines in many kinds of crimes, public perceptions were dominated by legislators and crime control advocates who capitalized on the UCR data, that crime was going up.

In the field of justice studies we encounter strongly held moral predispositions and values about people, how they should act, how they can be compelled to act, and what to do when they don't act right. The agencies of criminal justice enforce our most strongly held moral sentiments. They deal in values so potent that the state or federal government can justify the punishment, incarceration and occasional killing of people who violate them. This makes empirical research inescapably controversial.

Just as Galileo used empirical research to challenge the authority of the Church, justice studies researchers sometimes use empirical research to challenge traditional or common-sense values. And they are sometimes chastened for their work—the use of scientific methods to challenge strongly held moral positions frequently results in questions raised about the morality of the scientist, not the legitimacy of the traditions she or he questions. As a social science grounded in empirical methods, justice studies sometimes finds itself at arms length from the criminal justice community. The nature of science is, after all, to question that which is taken for granted. It is very difficult to think against the moral grain in this field, where strongly held values tend to preempt scientific findings.

Dilemmas of Value-Free Research. The previous discussion presented observationally based empirical methods as fundamentally different from value-based conservative and liberal ideologies. This is fine for science, but in justice studies the distinction between empirical methods and ideology is muddy. The scientific enterprise has as a central goal the ability to conduct research unhampered by political pressures to produce (or hide) particular findings. Findings are not an arrangement in which research and politics each get equal weight in determining outcomes. Galileo, after all, didn't conclude that sometimes gravity was controlled by the laws of the universe and sometimes by the church. Yet, in the field of justice studies, we immediately encounter a contradiction. Those of us who are justice workers, whether in agencies or in the professions, carry an ideal of justice that stems from the values we carry. We desire to change the practice of justice in some way, and we want to create a more just world. Justice is more than a dry statistical exercise. It is a moral commitment toward a better world, grounded in our ideas of valued end states that constitute "justice." How can we then conduct impartial scientific research? Aren't our findings likely to be biased by our predispositions, by the very values we carry?

In some instances, our commitment to a particular vision of justice may bias or corrupt researchers. Researchers may be already committed to a particular perspective and conduct research in order to champion their perspective. They are not interested in research that disagrees with their views and do not seek or try to explain anomalies in their own work. In extreme cases researchers have manipulated data in order to confirm their findings and ignore contradictory outcomes. Students who regularly work with criminal justice faculty will inevitably encounter those who conduct research only to assert their point of view, not in order to advance knowledge about the field. This kind of researcher is an *empiric* in the original meaning of the term—a person who rejected science in favor of his or her own common-sense views.

Another dilemma is the nature of social science itself. The social sciences are different from the physical sciences in a fundamental way. In the physical sciences, researchers seek an underlying order in the universe that can be mathematically modeled. Empirical research conducted at subatomic and cosmic levels has provided a means to identify elements of that underlying order and to fill in the gaps in our knowledge. To be sure, the physical sciences do not conclude that the universe is orderly, to the contrary. Chaos and quantum theories identify fundamental discontinuities in the way the universe seems to work. However, the nature of the research process in the physical sciences is to seek patterns and rules that can be used to describe phenomena, a task that has been generally successful.

Can social scientists make similar assumptions of underlying order about elements of the human condition? For example, can sociologists identify fundamental, invariant principles of social structure? Can psychologists identify fixed elements that explain patterns of individual behavior? Similarly, can culture, the great anthropological concept, provide us with rule-like prescriptions of human conduct? And will criminologists someday determine the causes of crime? The answer to all of the above questions is likely to be a resounding NO. Indeed, the trend in the social sciences since the 1940s has been away from deterministic models and toward a recognition of the unique and indeterminate nature of human situations. This was discussed at length in Chapter 2.

The problem of underlying order is particularly acute in justice studies. In important ways, justice studies is not a social science but a humanities—it is about human values and the meanings humans give to their predicaments—how problems emerge, and how they are solved. It encompasses imaginative stories aimed at finding the underlying humanity in justice dilemmas—*The Brothers Karamazoff* (Dostoevsky, 1991) comes to mind. In a word, justice is a creative endeavor whose breadth is limited only by the imagination of its creator and the moral constraints of social entities.

As a social science, justice studies is about the investigation into underlying order, much like the so-called "hard sciences." That investigation is for rules that describe individual and organizational behavior in matters having to do with crime and the practice of justice. And it is here that the social science and humanities dimensions of justice studies part company, for several reasons.

First, all of the terms that make justice an important endeavor—equality, victimization, justice, and the like—have no underlying reality. They are wholly about value, and constitute part of the language that makes the field of justice studies more of a humanities than a social science. Try to imagine these terms in value-neutral terms and they lose all meaning. Can one imagine punishing someone for assault, for example, without recognizing some harm committed against a person? We cannot identify underlying order "out there" for these terms because they don't exist apart from the values we apply to them.

The second point is closely related to the first, that we are not finding some truth "out there." Our findings are wholly embedded in value judgments, and we are consequently implicated in our work. We cannot adopt the position that we are independent investigators seeking truth. In the justice fields, so-called facts are subjective and inseparable from our values, which are in turn tied to our culture in which values acquire meaning and language in which values are expressed. The selection of research topics, the identification of methods, the level and kind of analysis, the identification of methods, and the interpretation of findings are all driven by value judgments.

Third, the scientific and political endeavors are inexorably intertwined, with important implications for any search for underlying order. Efforts to identify order are tied to efforts to exert technical control, described by DiCristina (1995) as "identifying (inventing or discovering) ways to make the world do what we want it to do." DiCristina further observed that this endeavor "translates into the overt goal of identifying technologies that can be used to control crime—especially strategies for reducing crime and the suffering it causes" (1995:56). The scientific search for order is tied to efforts to transform science into policy, and to use identified patterns of order as a basis for social control. Hence, the scientific practice of justice cannot be separated from the politics of social control, and we as social scientists are implicated in existing social control practices, like it or not.

Fourth, the science—policy link raises an important question. Do we as social scientists in the field of justice studies discover underlying order—or are we creating it? For example, when we engage in research on the effects of deterrence, are we thereby legitimating the use of deterrent strategies for social control? An observer might respond that a great deal of research shows that deterrence is a flawed idea of human behavior. However, this is a scientific response that fails to understand the relationship between politics and research. If there are 100 papers that show no effect, and five papers that show effects, those committed to as philosophy of deterrence will focus on the five supporting papers. The same logic, of course, holds for rehabilitation. In our efforts to provide a large body of research from which to identify underling order, we provide grist to the politically powerful to justify their governmental policies.

There is an answer to these dilemmas. It is an answer that is value based. In our search for justice, we conduct research, we participate in community activities, and we select career tracks involved in justice. If we are educators we are in frequent contact with students who share in our interest in justice. The answer to the dilemma lies not in the righteousness of justice goals, for value-neutrality truly is an impossible goal and "right" has many meanings. We find the answer in our professional integrity and in our willingness to accept new ideas. We explore alternatives. We see the other person's point of view. We expand our concept of justice. We contribute to the colleges and communities that provide the environments of our social and spiritual lives. Perhaps, in the justice field that is more humanities than science, the best substitute for value-neutrality is open-mindedness to other perspectives and a willingness to recognize that justice takes more forms than we can know.

Method and Positivism. When we conduct research, we select a method. The purpose of the method we choose is to provide a systematic way to find out about the *out there*. In the social sciences, we are guided in our inquiry by rules, and the body of these rules constitutes a method. Generally speaking, these methods can be classified as quantitative and qualitative. Quantitative methods are the "scientific" methodologies that incorporate statistical procedures into the search for regularities "out there," and qualitative methods focus on the unique properties and idiosyncratic properties of their object of attention. Quantitative methodologies usually are used to examine the properties of aggregates or groups of cases, and qualitative methods tend to focus on a detailed examination of single cases.

This section presents a philosophical discussion of methodologies. Carried in the ideas discussed below is the idea that there are many competing perspectives on the "out there," and that each is legitimate in its own way. Scientific methods represent a particular set of values, and should be balanced with other kinds of methods. The employment of a diversity of methods is the best way to endow the field of justice studies with breadth of justice perspective.

Scientifically based research methods are not value free. They are grounded in the powerful values of egalitarianism and every-person common sense, that what a person can plainly see is the foundation upon which science should be constructed. Scientific methods embody important values about what it means to be human. To understand the value basis of quantitative analysis in criminal justice, one must cast one's gaze to the Enlightenment. Enlightenment philosophers frequently contrasted the liberated, free individual against historical traditions. Intellectually free individuals were those who could resist traditions, who could break with the past and force a new world. Liberation was embodied in citizens' abilities to freely choose their destinies, unhindered physically and intellectually by state and church, and liberated from the burden of beliefs that bound them to their past.

In phrasing at once colorful and sternly individualistic, the philosopher Nietzsche[3] (1982) proclaimed that *God was dead*. God was a metaphor for the traditions, customs, and superstitions that embedded individuals in their past. In this phrase, Nietzsche was celebrating the emergence of a modern citizen, unshackled by tradition and history, using the tools of reason and rationality to construct a world of her or his choosing. Through the systematic study of the world around us, we can learn about those factors that otherwise are hidden to us. The systematic collection and study of information, in a word, will set us free.

Empirical methods were the tools that enabled scientists to distinguish between truth and the customs and habits of the past. The path to understanding reality was through the testimony of our senses. Our traditions and beliefs only shackle us. Schneider (1965:85-86) bluntly states the spirit of the positivist concept of reality:[4]

> There is no supernatural. Ghosts do not exist. Spirits do not in fact make storms, cause winds, bring illnesses or effect cures. The gods in the heavens do not really make the stars go around and neither do they decide each man's fate at his birth . . . Whatever unity there is to man's beliefs about the supernatural derives, therefore, from the nature of man himself and not from the nature of the supernatural.

According to positivism, knowledge of the world does not come from our traditions or values. The only way we can know about the world is by applying rules of logic and rationality to its study, balanced with the systematic observation of the world around us. Both the social sciences and the natural sciences are grounded on the principles of empirical method. In the social sciences, we tend to believe that, by applying empirical rules to the chaos of everyday behavior, we can identify statistical regularities that provide us with an understanding of the underlying laws that guide human behavior. Hence, a positivistic social science, in the field of justice studies as well as in its many companion fields, is carried out in the identification and analysis of statistical regularities in human behavior.

Giddens (1978) argued for a narrower definition of positivism, a definition that focused on the writings of Comte.[5] His definition carries the same philosophical tenor, however; that empirical methods represented a way of thinking about the world superior to taken-for-granted social traditions. Giddens describes Comte's positivism below:

> The reconstruction of history as the realization of the positive spirit. In this scheme of things, religion and metaphysics have a definite place, but only as prior phases of mystification to be broken through by the advent of science. With the development of the scientific outlook, the "prehistory" of the human species is completed . . . Giddens, 1978:246.

In Comte's view, the difference between positive science and other ways of knowing derived from systematic observation. Certainty in knowledge could only be derived from the evidence provided to the senses. Empirical science was necessary for the moral and material progress of society.

Positivism is a multifaceted term and carries a surfeit of meanings (Halfpenny, 1982). Giddens (1978:237) identified the following dimensions of positivism.

> . . . phenomenalism, the thesis, which can be expressed in various ways, that "reality" consists of sense impressions, an aversion to metaphysics, the latter being condemned to sophistry or illusion; the representation of philosophy as a method of analysis, clearly separable from, yet at the same time parasitic on, the findings of science; the duality of fact and value—the thesis is that empirical knowledge is logically discrepant from the pursuit of moral aims or the implementation of ethical standards; and the notion of the "unity of science"—the idea that the natural and social sciences share a common logical and perhaps even methodological foundation.

It can be added that positivism is closely tied to a theory of progress. Positivistic science can contribute to technological development, bettering the material conditions of life. In the social sciences, positivistic science is aimed at the acquisition of happiness and security. The term "empiricism" carries a similar meaning to positivism, and the two terms have sometimes been used interchangeably. It is often used as a gloss for the "real world," as in "the empirical world."

The development of the positivistic social sciences has been the subject of a wide historical literature. The development of the fields of sociology, psychology, anthropology, criminology, and political science are all traced to eighteenth-century positivism and its advocates. Today researchers tend to take empirical methods for granted. They believe that, through the systematic study of the world around us, research can achieve an accurate image of the practice of justice. And they tend to carry the same moral fervor that positivists expressed centuries ago—that by peeling back the occulted practices of the justice system, we can develop a clearer understanding of crime, or the police, or the courts, or of victims, or the like.

Justice studies today is frequently taught and conducted in the same moral fervor that characterized early positivists: its practitioners *believe* in the rightness of the empirical method. This righteousness is expressed in two common ways: through the acquisition of "facts" that describe the practice of crime and justice, and through the "debunking" of justice traditions as superstitious residue of unenlightened thinking.

Yet, scientific method may be too taken-for-granted. Its problems are well-studied in the philosophy of science, and they are important enough that students of justice should also be familiar with them. However, when students learn about them it is typically through a philosophy or a history course, and they seem to be abstract philosophical problems, unrelated to the practice of justice. Quantitative researchers tend to take the data we use for granted. But should they?

Objectivity, Intentionality, and the Out There

Embedded in the methods of empiricism is a problem central to the philosophy of science. We believe that there is an objective world out there. We can learn about the objective world if we look at it in the right way through our senses, or by using the right methodological tools to guide our senses. The issue raised here is not the correspondence between theories and observations, an issue I will discuss at length later in this chapter. The issue here is more fundamental—whether there is a real "out there" that can be identified and measured vis-à-vis positivistic methods.

The relationship between methods and the "out there" is unclear in the hard sciences, and is sometimes baffling in the field of justice studies. Consider, for example, a mountain discussed by Persons A and B. Person A tells Person B to look at a mountain and Person B does so. Person A is willing to accept that Person B is looking at a bona-fide, large, Matterhorn of a mountain in all its steep-faced, snow-capped grandeur. Now person A continues "look at that climber" and Person B says "where?" Person A responds "On the front of the mountain."

Front? This is where things get tough. Person B can claim that a mountain has a front, but when he or she does so she is using a term that only has meaning from a cultural standpoint. Front-back is a culturally accepted metaphor that tells a person that their companion is speaking about the side of the mountain facing us (Lakoff & Johnson, 1986). Other cultures may orient the front of the mountain, not according to where they are standing, but according to where their settlement is located. By the same metaphorical reasoning, the mountain also has a top and sides. In this example, we see that the way we see and interpret the world is partially understood in terms of other concepts, in the form of socially accepted metaphors. To take the example one step further, mountains are steep and plains are flat. Well, then, where do plains become mountains? The distinction between plains and mountains is a part of a cultural apparatus, made meaningful by common metaphors.

Are there then any concepts that are not understood in terms of other concepts but are perceived directly from the real world? Probably not. Systems of cultural meaning provide a diverse array of metaphors for interpreting and organizing the information provided by our senses. The implications of this are immediate—when we describe things "out there," we are describing them in a metaphorically based socially constructed language. Language is itself a barrier to understanding the actual condition of things "out there."

DiCristina (1995:47), paraphrasing Rorty (1989), states the problem as follows:

1. Descriptions of the world are confined to sentences.

2. Sentences can only be coupled to each other, not to something beyond language called reality.

3. Therefore, statements concerning the truth and falsity of descriptions of the world are constructed by coupling sentences with each other, not by comparing them against reality. In other words, truth and falsity only exist in sentences.

4. Sentences are properties of languages.

5. We create languages.

6. Therefore, we create truth and falsity.

These propositions do not refute the existence of a reality "out there," only that our perceptions are culturally predispositive and we cannot communicate a reality in its actual state.

Consider another example. If a person clambers over a six-foot concrete wall with glass shards embedded on its metaphorical top, he likely to eviscerate himself, whether or not he knows about the shards. This example might on its surface might seem to argue for the persistence of the "out there" in spite of our efforts to philosophize about it. However, the opposite is the case. The person has probably clambered on top of the wall (for whatever purpose) because they carry a cultural conception of walls without inset shards of glass. Certainly in the United States we are unlikely to encounter a sharded wall because of potential litigation that could be taken against the wall's owners. However such walls are commonplace in central and south America, where a person would never consider clambering over a concrete wall. One's evisceration flows from one's cultural predispositions.

The reality issue is much more complex in the field of justice studies, where the most important "sentences" are about human qualities like personal responsibility, justice, deterrence, criminals communities, and the like. The language of human qualities is what makes the field of justice meaningful and is central to why most justice workers commit themselves to the work of justice. However, this language is intentional—it exists as the result of human desire. Shweder (1991:74) describes intentionality as follows.

> Intentional things are things that have no existence apart from human understandings and activities. Practitioners and practices, people and their social environments, interpenetrate each other. One part cannot be

studied without borrowing from another part. Intentional worlds are human artifactual worlds, populated by products of our own design. An intentional world might contain such events as "stealing" or "taking communion," such processes as "norm" or "sin," such stations as "in-law" or "exorcist," such visible entities as "weeds" and invisible entities as "natural rights . . . " What makes their existence intentional is that such things would not exist independently of our involvements with and reactions to them; and they exercise their influence in our lives because of our conceptions of them."

Take the word "weed." We share an idea what a weed is. It is a pernicious plant that grows where we do not want it to grow. However, in the *out there,* there is no such thing as a weed.

The word "weed" is a reality-posit. A reality posit means that it is a word for describing some class of thing "out there." The "reality" part of reality posit refers to another (exteriorized) realm beyond our immediate senses. The weed is a phenomena that we use to categorize. But in the objective *out there,* there is no such thing as weed. It has meaning in relation to human activities—in this case, gardening. The "posit" part of reality-posit is the symbolic term we use that describes the class of phenomena. Weed is the posit. What is the reality?

The word weed is intentional. This means that a "weed" exists because of the desires and emotions we have about it. With intentional terms, there is no *out there,* and there is no actual, objective thing called a "weed." A weed is simply a classification of another classification (plant). Yet it is a special kind of classification: A weed is an "intrusive, interfering, or improper plant that you do not want growing in your garden." (Shweder, 1991:75). It has no natural identity apart from human understandings and activities. That we make a distinction for something called a weed describes our symbolic, value-based universe, but doesn't tell us about the *out there.*

Now compare a weed to a plant. A plant is a reality posit for something out there. It is not intentional—or not to the same degree as weed. It is taxonomic, and what we call plants would continue to exist independently of their relationship to us. It should be pointed out that the reality of plants is not as clear as we might like to think—some biologists question the taxonomic distinctiveness the plant kingdom and suggest that the relationship between plants and animals is muddy and unclear. So even the *out there* of our reality-posit "plant" may not be as clear as common sense and a lifetime of habitual thinking might suggest.

Let us return to the language of the justice fields. The idea of crime is like weed. Crime is part of our valued, intentional world. It refers to behavior that we find unacceptable. It has no meaning apart from our human activities. We will never identify Platonian, rule-like laws about crime because crime is a creation of our intentional world. When we study crime, we are studying the way our intentional world works, but we do not uncover truth. If our intent changes, so does crime. And observers of the law know that the constitution of "crime" changes frequently. In the intentional world, and crime is a part of the intentional world, there are no truths out there to uncover. We are only studying unstable distributions and relations among our values in our sociocultural environment.

The problem of intentionality is captured in the following editorial from the *New York Times*.

> The same week that a Republican candidate for President spent struggling to compose ever more tortuous non-denials of his drug use as a young man, a former Republican Presidential candidate could be seen in full-page advertisements forthrightly acknowledging his own use of another drug. Of, I know: two completely different and incomparable situations; how unfair to Robert Dole and the Pfizer pharmaceutical company even to mention them in the same paragraph as George W. Bush and cocaine. One concerns an illegal drug that people take strictly for pleasure. The other concerns a legal drug that people take . . . well, also strictly for pleasure, but (almost) always with a prescription.
>
> The ability to draw and patrol distinctions of this kind becomes critical in a society like ours, with its two thriving multi-billion-dollar drug cultures. How much easier things would be if, instead of lumping them all under the rubric of "drugs," we had one word for the beneficent class of molecules to which Viagra and Prozac belong, and another for the pernicious class that contains cocaine and cannabis.
>
> The problem is that there is a long history of molecules getting switched out of one drug culture and into the other. Alcohol, for instance, has spent time in both cultures in this century. for part of the time that alcohol resided in the bad drug culture, opium now evil, occupied a place in the good drug culture, where it was dispensed by reputable pharmaceutical firms. More recently LSD and MDMA (a.k.a. ecstasy), both born of the good drug culture, have found them exiled to the bad. Occasionally the drug traffic flows in the opposite direction. After spending the last few years firmly ensconced on the demon side of the drug divide, cannabis has lately got a toehold on the therapeutic side, at least in a half-dozen states that have legalized medical marijuana. Earlier this year the Institute of Medicine announced that for a small class of patients, cannabis did indeed have a therapeutic value.
>
> What we have here, then, is a drug war being fought on behalf of a set of distinctions—a taxonomy of chemicals that, far from being eternal or absolute, has actually been shaped by historical accident, cultural prejudice and institutional imperative. You can imagine an alternative history in which Viagra would show up on the other side of the line—had it, say, been cooked up in an uptown drug lab and sold first on the street under the name Hardy Boy.
>
> You would be hard-pressed to explain the taxonomy of chemicals underpinning the war to an extraterrestrial. Is it, for example, addictiveness that causes this society to condemn a drug? (No; nicotine is legal, and millions of Americans have battled addictions to prescription drugs.)

So then, our inquisitive alien might ask, is safety the decisive factor? (Not really; over the counter and prescription drugs kill more than 45,000 Americans every year while, according to the New England Journal of Medicine, "There is no risk of death from smoking marijuana." Is it drugs associated with violent behavior that your society condemns? (If so, alcohol would still be illegal.) Perhaps, then, it is the promise of pleasure that puts a drug beyond the pale? (That would once again rule out alcohol, as well as Viagra.) Then maybe the molecules you despise are the ones that alter the texture of consciousness, or even a human's personality? (Tell that to someone who has been saved from depression by Prozac.)

At this point our extraterrestrial would probably throw up his appendages and ask, Can we at least say that the drugs you approve of all have a capital letter at the beginning of their names and a TM at the end?

To listen to the storm of comment surrounding George W. Bush's "irresponsible youth," one might reasonably conclude that no upstanding American has taken an illicit drug since 1974 or so. Illegal drugs have been so thoroughly demonized that the only way a person can talk about his drug use in public (in private is a different matter) is by drawing bright lines in time: *It was a different moment, I was a different person.* (Italics in original) Thus we have a tortuous taxonomy of self to go along with our tortuous taxonomy of chemistry.

Source: Pollan, Michael (1999) *A Very Fine Line.* New York Times Magazine, Sept. 12:27.

This editorial is not included to belittle those who are concerned with harmful consequences of drugs, nor to criticize a political point of view. I use the editorial because it brings out in graphic relief the intentionality of the term "illegal drug." What is the reality behind the reality posit "illegal drug?" As Pollen has so eloquently shown us, it is indistinguishable from the reality-posit for "legal drug." "Illegal drug," an intentional term, has no underlying, uniquely identifying reality. Yet, we act as if it does, and many, many people are serving harsh prison sentences because of our actions. In this instance, we see that the practice of criminal justice operates in an intentional world, in which an underlying "reality" is simply absent.

Intentionality and Methods. The issue of intentionality bears directly on the use of quantitative methods. Advocates of the use of quantitative methods sometimes argue that only scientific method should be used to study the world around us. With scientific method, the argument goes, we can set about the practical work of debunking witchery, ghosts, hidden meanings, false consciousness, taken-for-granted meanings, and the like, in order to identify true underlying patterns of our social worlds. We can select operational measures as our real-world markers, confident that our measures in fact match some underlying reality *out here*, and then we can measure the relationships among them. We can then develop a theory or perspective about what the relationships mean. And we can draw conclusions about the "out there" from the relationships among our operational measures, which are the "reality posits" for our theoretical terms.

The relationship between reality and reality-posits can be described by considering the way in which we construct theory in the social sciences. The theories we create are ideas of the relationships between people "out there." But how do we know which are the best? We have many, many perspectives on crime and justice. Which one is right? Which reality-posits do we accept? The problem is that they are all drawn from the intentional terms.

Shweder describes it this way:

> Since no reality-finding science can treat all appearances-sensations-experiences as revelatory of the objective world, and since, at least for the moment, no infallible way exists to decide which reality-posits are signs of reality and which are not, much is discretionary in every portrait of the objective world out there beyond our symbolic forms. Reality, after all, for all we can ever really know, may be far away, or deep within, or hidden behind, and thus viewable only "as if through a glass darkly"; or perhaps the really real really is available only through a privileged state of mind (such as deep meditation) attainable only to a privileged few (Shweder, 1991:64).

Herein lies the dilemma of social science. We can only know our reality-posits. We can never know their actual correspondence to the *out there*. There is no way to self-validate reality. There is no justice out there, at least none that we can know about. There is no crime out there. It is all values, through and through. And it is whatever we want it to be.

Intentionality and Justice Studies. Intentionality means that something does not exist independently of its being the object of our intent or will. Justice does not exist independently and would cease to exist in any form if all humanity ceased tomorrow. There is no "out there" that is separable from the mutable human condition. This has several implications for the field of justice studies.

First, intentionality carries the recommendation that justice is more correctly represented by the notion of "standpoint" than a hard notion of "objectivity." The underlying issues that inform and excite our field, the reasons we are justice workers to begin with, animate the discussion and interpretations of any findings generated by social science methods. And, importantly, they animate it with value-based standpoints. It is, after all, our individual standpoints that motivate us to become justice workers.

Let's say that I am measuring a population of ex-prisoners and I find that 50 percent of them recidivate. Well, is the cup half-full or half-empty? Is it a mark of prison effectiveness that only 50 percent will recidivate? Is it a mark of ineffectiveness? Is the finding a measure of natural human tendencies that cannot be affected by the prison experience? The failure of rehabilitation? The success of prison-based rehabilitation programs? The successful ability of humans to adapt to new post-prison settings? The failure of people to adapt? Random occurrence? What does the finding mean?

Think of the array of judgments surrounding research on recidivism and one immediately recognizes that they are value-based. We can't make independent, purely rational judgments about rehabilitation because there isn't some objective "thing" out there against which we can scale rehabilitation. All this talk about independent, objective social science is bunk. Social science findings only acquire value within human standpoints.

Second, if social science of justice acquires meanings only within a "standpoint" perspective, what is the appropriate context in which to think about justice issues? It may be that justice systematically organizes the meanings for "social science" findings. Consider rehabilitation again. Rehabilitation is intentional, and its meanings and interpretations emerge in relation to our values. Notions of right and wrong are embedded in every action we take with regard to rehabilitation. Certainly, we can empirically measure changes in behavior—frequency of drug use, for example—and use those changes to assess the extent to which they are using something. The issue of intentionality emerges when we try to give some meaning to that behavioral change. These meanings are articulable within a moral and political philosophy.

Third, the prevailing values and sentiments about justice issues are unresolvable through the use of social science. Policies will ultimately be determined by whichever group is most adept at linking justice values to their findings. And these values are a product of the political climate, in which ideological predispositions—value clusters—guide decisionmaking. The prevailing predispositions are organized around conservative and liberal philosophies. One of the lessons of political science is that a "third tradition" based on objective social sciences (see Chapter 2) will ultimately fail to achieve legitimacy as a way of thinking better than subjective politics.

Fourth, once we recognize that the "social science" of justice, to become meaningful, occurs through a standpoint, we also acknowledge that the way we think about our research is relative to the values we carry at any point in time. Put differently, research will not provide us with solid truths. Research should always be recognized as tentative to place and time, and to the moralities of the people who carry out the research. This may seem to open the door to extreme relativism, but it does not. There exist a limited number of methods for the study of empirical information, and whatever method is chosen, underlying considerations of validity and reliability are still important. Moreover, the issue of standpoint does not directly challenge the methodology of social science. Because it is primarily concerned with interpretation, its challenge is in the interpretations of findings, not the findings themselves.

Consequently, the acknowledgment of intentionality should not be taken as a rejection of social science methods for the field of justice studies. Social science plays an integral role in our efforts to find justice. But many different roles are needed to broaden our horizons about the inquiry into justice.

A Beneficiary of All Traditions, a Slave to None. Are we to give up and conclude that all is relative? That is a conclusion particularly unsatisfactory for justice studies—and indeed for most of us. A justician committed to victim protection might respond as follows: *I don't care about this. What criminals do to victims is important to me, and I will do whatever I can to stop them.* What counts for this justician is not that the values he or she carries are relative (which many of us might concede) but that they are personally meaningful. Two responses to this justician are appropriate.

First, accepting the legitimacy of this justician's feelings is to acknowledge the limitations of the social sciences on the field of justice studies. When we recognize that values are important and meanings are central to our work, we are locating our field in the humanities. Education for morality and ethics becomes as important as the search for underlying order characteristic of the social sciences.

Second, the arguments presented above are not intended to suggest that concerns over victims are misplaced. But justice is nevertheless intentional, a product of human desire, and is diverse in its forms. One must temper one's values with the recognition that many different values and perspectives inform justice. The relativity of values is not an intellectual trap that renders values unimportant. To the contrary, it is a gate through which justicians pass in order to more fully understand the world around them.

Truth may not be ours to know, but we must act in order to participate in the world around us. Those of us in justice studies are not permitted the luxury to think abstractly while ignoring the practical consequences of our ideas. We interact with criminal justice agencies, we are involved in policy, and we deal with many students who will one day carry the authority of the state in considerations of the life and death of citizens. We make decisions that affect other people's lives in an immediate way. We cannot abandon the responsibility for our prescriptions and decisions to cynical relativity.

We cannot know yet we must act. Where does this dilemma leave us? As social scientists, we must recognize the limitations of positivism and move forward. We must seek a just path between the extremes of a single method and total relativity. The objective world "out there" is incapable of being represented from any particular point of view. But neither can it be presented intelligibly if we try to present it from all viewpoints at once. The aim is for us to be a "good student and beneficiary of all the traditions, and a slave to none" (Shweder, 1991:68).

> Transcendence without scorn is the kind of transcendence that comes from constantly moving from one objective world to the next, inside and then out, outside and then in, all the while standing back and trying to

make sense of the whole journey. It is a state of mind in which there is a detached engagement with each of the several traditions, which promotes an engaging detachment from each of one's many selves. [68].

The philosophy of science is in what Shweder (1991) calls a "post-positivistic"state. It is retreating from the idea that a single method can give us a realistic picture of the forces that move the world. The post-positivist era is marked by a return of the gods denied by Nietzsche. There are realities, but they are plural. The path of justice lies in the recognition that many different perspectives legitimately lay claim to the truth, and that we approach justice by gathering together a wide conception of these perspectives.

Shweder concludes with the following observation, intended to quell the fears of those who think a plurality of methods promotes anarchy:

> As for those who fear that truth is not unitary, that nihilism will reign and that polytheism is merely a code word for anarchy, it is comforting to remind ourselves, again and again, that the fact that there is no uniform reality . . . does not mean that there are no realities at all (Shweder, 1991:69).

Today, justice studies is primarily an empirical field within the social sciences. Its practitioners are involved in the search for truth vis-à-vis quantifiable, statistical regularities in data (Michalowski, 1985; Bernard, 1990). The classes most likely to be found in graduate justice curricula are statistics and methods courses that integrate statistics, data collection procedures, and the formal presentation of findings (Flanagan, 1990). We collect information that is relevant to important issues in the operations of criminal justice organizations.

The use of scientific methods in the justice field has been described as privileged (DiCristina, 1995). Citing Wolfgang (1989, vii), DiCristina observed that "the cannons of the scientific method form the belief system of this discipline." Though both were referring to criminology, the point is equally applicable to justice studies. DiCristina further noted that:

> Many criminologists are obsessed with being scientific, and this obsession has resulting in the privileging of the scientific methods in criminology. The [privileging of these methods is enforced through definitions, curriculum, promotions, publication, and grant decisions (DiCristina, 1995:63).

Statistical procedures allow us to collect only a narrow slice of the informational pie. What we learn with our positivist methods is a form of intentional truth. It is our *out there,* important because we believe in it. But our selection of it is based on faith, not on fact or truth. And it is not the only *out there* that we should pay attention to. As Shweder recommended, we should proceed as if reality is a plurality and truth has many meanings.

Justicians will learn more truths with a diversity of methods. It is not only through positivistic social science that justice studies should approach justice and crime. The large body of methods described under the term "qualitative" also provides a vehicle for the discovery of the *out there*. Qualitative methods are an specially vibrant methodological form for studying out there, because correctly applied they require that we learn about the groups that we study from the standpoint of *their* values and beliefs, not ours. They broaden the base of our knowledge in immediate ways—they increase our justice vocabulary, helping us to make sense of group or organizational processes human though alien to us.

To Comprehend the Human Variety. What does it mean to say that we will learn more truths with more method diversity? Recall that the study of justice and crime is the study of intentional terms, which means that the object of our study has no correspondence in the *out there*. The truths that we learn are the perspectives of others. We gain breadth of vision. We learn a wider repertoire of meanings for justice. By acknowledging that ours is an intentional field, we begin to recognize that there are many ways to imagine justice. No method provides hegemony, no world-views more right than another. Our responsibilities as social scientists are to look at all visions, to try to understand the breadth of this very human endeavor, which after all is what justice is about. Justice is our creation, our intention, not reflective of truth out there, but of what we hope we can achieve.

To use the language of Mills (1959:132), diversity in methods increase our capacity to comprehend the human variety. By human variety, he meant all the social worlds in which people have lived, are living, and will live. It is the human variety, Mills argued, that is the proper study of sociology. This is equally true of the justice fields, for the consequences of our study have a very real impact on people's lives. When we are slaves to a single method, we are able to see only that which we are trained to see. Knowledge is predetermined by those who collect the data—by the way they conceive problems, by the methods they use, and by the implicit assumptions they make about the human variety. When, on the other hand, we are agents in the production of our own methods, we add to the breadth of our field. And the field of justice is enriched for our effort.

Part II: Quantitative Analysis in Justice Studies

In Part II, I explore the principle way in which we conduct research in justice studies. Statistically based methods are dominant in our field today, though a small number of researchers are using qualitative methods to identify the social worlds that lay claim to heir various *out there's*. This part discusses the nature of quantitative analysis, its strengths and its weaknesses, and its implications for the way we perceive justice in the United States.

Quantitative Methods in Positivistic Analysis

The preeminent method in the field of criminal justice is the quantification of data and testing of hypotheses. If we are social scientists accustomed to the methodologies of quantitative analysis, we proceed as follows.

1. We develop a theoretical hypothesis. An hypothesis is a statement of relationship between two variables. For example, I might be interested in crime and its etiology. I have read all the books on crime causation, and I have seen that many people think that crime is related to a person's wealth in the following way: the less wealth a person has, the more likely that person is to commit crime. So I have two variables, *crime* and *wealth*. These are theoretical variables, because they were taken from a theory of crime causation. The hypothesis is a theoretical hypothesis. It is also causal, because it states that wealth is the determinant of crime, not vice versa. The hypothesis is stated as follows:

    Increases in wealth are negatively associated with increases in crime.

2. We develop empirical measures of our theoretical variables. We call this our empirical hypothesis or in DiCristina's terms, an observational theory. For example, crime can mean many different things. Am I interested in misdemeanor crimes? In reported crimes? In the total number of crimes a person has committed? In this example, we will settle for the number of times a person has been arrested as our measure. Now we do the same thing with wealth. What represents a person's wealth? I might measure wealth with any of the following: the amount of money they have in the bank, their personal income, the value of their property, the total family income, or investments in stocks and bonds. Any one of these might be my measure. The measurement hypothesis is consequently:

    Increases in a person's total family income are negatively associated with increases in the number of times the person has been arrested.

    Note that I specifically state "a person." I could have stated a family, or a city, or whatever. In this case, the "person" is the unit of analysis.

3. We develop a specific measurement strategy for these measures. This measurement strategy is called our "methods." For our measure of crime, we might take a random survey of all citizens in a community (recall that persons are our unit of analysis), and then ask them about the number of times they had been arrested. It might be that respondents are not forthright about their answer, but this kind of problem happens all the time. Then we ask them what the annual household income of their family is. So now our methods have produced something that we can specifically measure.

Information we have collected is coded on a sheet, and the findings are tabulated and entered into a statistical spreadsheet. After the information is coded, we conduct a test of the statistical hypothesis and we select a statistical procedure. A test of significance is used to tell us whether the relationship between the variables in the statistical hypothesis is statistically significant. If we find that the relationship between the two variables is strong enough that it is likely to occur by chance less than five percent of the time, we conclude that the relationship is significant.

4. We select a procedure to collect our data. We probably want a random survey, in which all members of our population have an equal chance of being included. We are likely to conduct a telephone or a mail-out survey. Telephone surveys are costly, so we decide to do a mail survey. Using a phone directory, we select a random sample of 500 citizens from our city. We mail them a questionnaire. We receive 200 back, and mail out another round. We receive 100 more, and decide that we have received enough to be confident that our survey represents the overall population.

A review of these four steps reveals the following: We have a hypothesis, which is a statement of relationship between two concepts. These concepts are linked to each other both horizontally and vertically, across all four levels. We can diagram these relationships in the following way:

Figure 5.1
Model of Research Hypotheses

Theoretical Hypothesis	Wealth	→	Crime
	↕		↕
Operational Hypothesis	Income	→	Arrests
	↕		↕
Methods Hypothesis	Citizen's response to question on household income	→	Citizen's response to question on arrests
	↕		↕
Statistical hypothesis	Tabulated data on Household income	→	Tabulated data on number of arrests

The model presented above is a form of an inductive-deductive model (Hagan, 1982). According to this model, I have described variables at each of four "hypothesis" levels. These variables are related to each other both horizontally and vertically. The horizontal relations between the variables is determined by a logical, deductive process. At the lowest level the relationship is assessed statistically. The vertical relations are related by an inductive process, and require an assumption of correspondence. The purpose of the model is to test the concepts used to develop our theories.

Horizontal linkages. The horizontal components of this model are important for our discussion because they represent the deductive elements in it. The horizontal linkages are stated as cause and effect. The idea of causality is embedded in positivism. All of the social sciences—psychology, anthropology, sociology, justice studies, and the like—are historically grounded in notions of causality. Sociology, for example, is predisposed to assume that social factors are causal to behavior. Psychology makes similar assumptions about the mental determinants of behavior. So these fields look for reasons for why someone acts the way they do, and tends to locate the explanation in the overall field perspective.

A word about "causality" is in order. Many social sciences reject the word "causality," because of philosophical problems with the notion of cause. In the place of the word "cause" are substituted logical notions like "sufficient conditions" and "necessary conditions," techniques such as "path analysis," "regression," and "LISREL," the language of "dependence" and "independence," "time series," and experimental methods with terms like "dosage" and "stimulus." These terms are all complicated ways of permitting us to talk about causation without using the word cause.

The fields of social science tend to be deterministic—they look for determinants of human behavior. They are not rigidly deterministic. They all allow for uncertainty, recognize that volition is involved in the production of human behavior, and acknowledge that individuals may sometimes act rationally. Yet, the idea that people's behavior is a consequence of some aspect of their physical social, moral, psychological, or biological environment is central to the social sciences. Without this assumption the idea of statistical analysis to measure predictors of human behavior is meaningless. This is one of the reasons the social sciences fundamentally differ from the law—the law is grounded in a presumption of the free choices of the individual, while the social sciences, while acknowledging uncertainty, look for causes of behavior.

Second, only two variables are tested at a time. There are many statistical procedures that allow for the testing of multiple variables, and these procedures are lumped together under the taxonomic term "multivariate analysis." However, most of the procedures are reducible to the core ideas stated in the figure above.[6] If the relationship holds when I conduct statistical tests, (the lowest horizontal linkage) I can state that the theoretical relationship in this aspect of the theory (the highest horizontal linkage) is supported. The test of a single hypothesis is never considered to be a complete test of a theory.

Third, the assessment of the statistical hypothesis is not taken as a proof of the theoretical hypothesis. It is considered only as evidence in favor of it. Principles of research require that a theoretical hypothesis is tested with different measures and in different research settings before it is accepted. A single research project is never considered definitive, only supportive. Researchers consequently tend to look for evidence of falsifi-

cation (Bernard, 1990). This means that the accumulation of non-significant findings at the operational level of the model can result in the rejection of the theory. Put another way, although a theory can never be
proven true, through the principle of falsification it can be proven false.[7]

Vertical linkages. The model's vertical linkages also reveal important
strengths and weaknesses. The vertical linkages represent the "spirit" of
positivism. They are the means used to connect ideas to the real world,
the "out there." The principle strength of the model is that it does not permit us to rely on tradition, ideology, or untested belief in order to explain
the world around us. A justician cannot simply say "Poor people are lazy
and don't want to work, they want to take someone else's hard-earned
money" and pat himself on the back for such sharp insight. The idea of
positivism requires that a person systematically test any such idea using
the model above. A social scientist can use the model to test traditions, or
superstition, or ideology. The verification or refutation of an idea must
come from the observable world, not from a crowd of yea- or nay-sayers.

The vertical linkages are decidedly non-positivist in one important
way. The vertical linkages all require a leap of faith—that each lower level
represents a higher level. The linkages are representational—each is seen
to represent at a more concrete level of reality the idea stated at the higher or more theoretical level. Yet, representativeness is always an assumption of correspondence.

Vertical linkages are inductive and are based on congruency. This
means that we identify an equivalence between comparable levels in the
hierarchy of hypotheses. We cannot logically deduce the congruence, nor
can we prove it empirically. To a certain extent, our acceptance of the
congruence is a matter of faith. For example, we cannot prove that
income is a measure of wealth. Indeed, there are those who argue that
income and wealth are fundamentally different ideas (Oliver & Shapiro,
1995). The connections across vertical levels stem from our knowledge
of the specific environment studied, common sense, convention, and
insight. But they are inductive linkages, and are hence unprovable.

The vertical linkages are the "bridges" by which we construct a model
from the conceptual world to the *out there.* Each vertical step down in
the model progressively restates our idea, in the form of an hypothesis, in
a more concrete form. Let us think about these linkages across each of the
hypothesis. The first or highest linkage is from the theoretical to the operational hypothesis. In Figure 5.1, "arrests" is used as a more concrete idea
of "crime." Yet, it is reasonable to argue that this is an inappropriate
assumption—arrests are police behavior, while crime is tapped by a perpetrator's behavior. In justice research today, we generally do not find
arrests to be a satisfactory measure of crime. The Uniform Crime Reports,
however, were established for the express purpose of measuring crime
nationally, and the use of arrests as a measure of crime was commonplace
in research on the etiology of crime until only recently. This tells us that

the appropriateness of a measure of a concept—the concept's representation—is very much a matter of convention, and finds its meaning in historical context. This is a most unsatisfying conclusion for researchers who believe that positivist method can provide some sort of "truth," for it suggests that operational measures tend to be matters of historically situated convention.

The next set of linkages are from the operational hypothesis to the methods hypothesis. One might contend that the linkage between the operational hypothesis and the methods hypothesis is a matter of technical detail; that with appropriate procedures this linkage can be measured for its accuracy and tested for reliability and validity. However, we have to make a fundamental assumption in order to conduct such tests: that the question the citizen responds to is the same as the question that the interviewer asks. And this may not be a valid assumption. If the researcher exploring the model above, for example, asks a person if he or she has been arrested, he or she means "arrest" in terms of the formal legal code. Is that what they hear? They may think that the researcher is asking them if they have had previous encounters with the police. They may think he or she is investigating their backgrounds. They may not speak English well and completely misunderstand the question. They may have been handcuffed as a material witness to a crime—not technically an arrest, but it sure feels like one. This is a long-winded way of saying that one never knows if what someone hears or reads stated is actually what is intended, or if it means the same thing to them. What we hear and what it means to us is inseparable from our own experiences. To the extent that the sum total of our experiences differ, we perceive the world differently. A researcher's hopes for response reliability is based on common cultural understandings, not truth value.

Third, we consider the inductive linkage between the methods and the statistical hypothesis. Of all the linkages, surely we can consider this one as a technical matter. Unfortunately, even this linkage is highly interpretive and a matter of conventional understanding. When we consider the relationship between our sample and the population from which we drew it, we use sophisticated statistics to assess its representativeness. This is in turn incorporated into an assessment of the relationship between the variables in the statistical hypothesis. When we assess the hypothesis, we use tests of significance. A test of significance assesses the likelihood that the relationship between the variables is a matter of chance. We commonly say that a relationship between two variables is not a matter of chance is we encounter it less than five times in 100, which is called a 95 percent level of significance. Sometimes we use a 99 percent level of significance. Yet, as every statistician knows, the selection of levels of significance is purely a matter of convention. It has no independent "truth" *out there.* Moreover, in order to test for significance, particularly at the interval level (where we like to conduct most of our analyses), we have to make assumptions about the normalcy of our population. His means that we have to assume that the distribution of values in our population matches a normal curve. This also is no more than an assumption. Frequently, it is an erroneous assumption. Some values, for example, the loudness with which we hear sound, may fit a different kind of curve altogether. Attitudinal values frequently form bimodal distributions. Population-based size curves, such as city size, typically are highly skewed distributions more similar to chi-square than a normal distributions.

In sum, we make inductive assumptions through each level of our hypothesis-testing. All of these assumptions are problematic. They rest, not on fact nor on clear logical deduction, but on convention and common-sense. By the time we look across all levels of our induction, we have a string of conventions that allow us to link our "theory" to the *out there.* A critic can reasonably argue that, in the end, our conclusions are predisposed by our conventions. We see what we expect to see, but we learn nothing about the *out there.*

We might try to recapture a bit of scientific ground with the following argument. Our various communications and statistical procedures are capturing the rough, indistinct image of an underlying reality out there. This Platonic notion can be stated as follows: there really is something *out there* and our measures somehow capture indistinct parts of its essence. We capture fuzzy *out there's.* With enough concrete measures in a variety of research settings, we eventually can validate a concept. However, this argument makes the problem of induction worse, not better. Let's return to our dependent variable, crime. Crime is by definition a state product—there is no crime without a corresponding law. And every state and nation has different laws. Crime is an eminently human creation, a product of time and place, changing from year to year. There is no ideal "crime" in the "out there," it is all intentional, whose meaning only exists in relation to people, and whose meaning ceases to exist in all other circumstances There are consequently no rule-like regularities that can model crime with other variables. Its existence and meanings are wholly defined by their space and time relationship to populations, states, and values. Hence, underneath all our inductive connections are nothing except sentences and relations among words whose meanings overlap.

If we're not measuring some underlying truth or fact that we can call "crime," what then are we measuring? That is a good question—and one without an answer. Or rather, it is a question without a single answer. The correct answer is that there are many possible answers—certainly crime, but also we can say with equal merit that we are measuring state intervention, bad behavior, poor social skills, adaptation, morality, innovation, resistance to the state, terrorism, meanness, police behavior, and elite control. All of these are reasonable interpretations of what we are measuring, all are held by different groups, yet all have sharply different implications about the hypotheses we are testing. Whatever term we use, it is a term of our creation, and all we can be confident in is that its meaning will change in time.

Put simply, the very thing that positivist method tries to get at—the "out there" of empirical reality—can only be achieved by several leaps of inductive faith. The underlying reality remains unknown, probably unknowable, and possibly nonexistent.

In order to refute my concerns that we cannot know about the *out there,* a positivist might reasonably invite me to kick a rock with my bare foot and then assess whether or not I feel pain. For anyone who attempts this empirical test, one will find that it is a compelling argument and painful lesson that there is indeed something going on *out there.* Kick a rock, prove positivism. But the exercise is too simple. The field of justice studies is about something more enigmatic than a rock. Our most fundamental issue—justice—is a product of our creation, variable, located in time and place, a consequence of our living arrangements, our culture, and our sense of right and wrong. A rock is not, at least not in the same way.[8] Justice is intentional—it cannot be removed from the domain of human purpose, and it has no independent existence apart from humans. It has no *out there.* Indeed, the practice of justice may be more layered in convention as are our statistical methods. We study one set of conventions with another.

On Being a Data-Jock in Criminal Justice. Of all the ways of assessing the world of crime and justice, quantitative techniques are the most popular. Yet, for those (many) individuals and students who are fearful of numbers, statistics is a dry, tedious exercise bereft of substantive value. Few classes generate more terror in students than statistics. Statistics is so, well, mathematical. It is very unlike other criminal justice classes. It has problems that have right and wrong answers—a student cannot simply think imaginatively about the topic and get a good grade. One actually has to study every week! Yes, a statistics course has brought the academic careers of many a criminal justice student to an ugly end.

For a small number of students, statistical analysis is bewitching. There is an exhilaration to the statistics game, as anyone who has ever attended the quantitative summer programs at the University of Michigan knows. It is a feeling not unlike gambling, a throw of the dice, and who knows what you might find? Imagine sitting in front of a computer screen, running a correlation matrix, looking for patterns of significance, running another matrix, trying to interpret the patterns, anticipating that special publication from the findings. You see something in the data— what is it? You rub your eyes, run the data again, try to tease out the pattern, and again, and again.

Welcome to the world of a data-jock.

There is a heaven for criminal justice data jocks. It is the Inter-University Consortium of Political and Social Research (ICPSR). Located in the magisterial setting of the University of Michigan, it is a summer program devoted to quantitative analysis. It offers a special program for invited criminal justice students and faculty, and it provides participants with a stipend, a data set of their choosing, a living quarters, and an educational environment that includes the brain trust of criminology and criminal justice. Anyone who participates in the program feels as if they have arrived—they are in the mecca of justice research.

The ICPSR is the exemplar of the cardinality of quantitative analysis in criminology and criminal justice. Quantitative analysis takes many forms, from relatively straightforward frequency counts to sophisticated procedures such as Latent Structural Analysis (LISREL). Quantitative analysis is so central to justice studies that a class on statistical procedures is a normal part of the required course-load in undergraduate and graduate programs in justice studies.

Quantitative analysis is widely practiced in the justice fields. A young professor is more likely to be published if he or she produces research using quantitative techniques. Though some journals emphasize other ways of conducting research, they are infrequently considered "top-tier" journals. A content analysis of refereed publications in the field of criminology found that 72.8 percent used statistical methods of some kind (Wolfgang, Figlio & Thornberry, 1978). A young data-jock, wishing to make her or his reputation in the field, knows that they must publish in respected journals, and the most direct avenue for publication is through quantitative analysis. Quantitative research in the justice field is a highly institutionalized form for academic success.

Statistics and statistically based methods are a central component of many justice departments' curricula. A study of justice programs found that 61.3 percent of the four-year programs contacted required a course in statistics. An additional 12 percent provided an elective statistics course (Fields & Robertson, 1988). Statistics courses are sometimes required in two-year programs, though the frequency is less, at 18 percent.

Statistics are also a common offering at Ph.D. granting institutions. A study of 16 Ph.D. criminology/criminal justice institutions revealed that 15 of the 16 required at least one class in quantitative analysis. Thirteen of these programs required the completion of two quantitative analysis courses (DiCristina, 1997). These data reveal a pattern—the higher the degree, the greater the likelihood that quantitative analysis will be required among students. This is consistent with the institutional missions of colleges, in which two-year programs tend to be applied, with a behavioral emphasis increasing as programs offer higher degrees.

Data and Value-Neutrality. To conduct statistical analyses, a young data-jock has to acquire data. One source of data is what is called "official" data. This is data, collected or funded by the government, aims at providing knowledge about crime and/or criminals. The best known data sources are the Uniform Crime Reports (UCR) and the National Crime Victimization Study (NCVS). The UCR is information collected by police departments semi-annually about reported and cleared crimes. The information is turned over to the FBI for collation. The NCVS is data about crime collected by the Census Bureau from victims of crime about characteristics of crime and of the perpetrator. Though the UCR and the NCVS are the best known sources of official data, there are many, many other sources of data available. Those interested in the courts have used the Offender Based Transaction Studies, those interested in prisons and jails can turn to prison and jail census; those who focus on drug use and delinquency can use the Drug Use Forecasting data (recently renamed ADAM), and so forth. These and more data are readily available from university and governmental sources.

Researchers endeavor to be value neutral toward their work. This means that they are expected, and many sincerely try, to keep their predispositions from affecting the outcomes of their research. They may have powerful beliefs about right and wrong. These beliefs can affect the selection of research areas, but should never affect the outcomes of research.

Governmental agencies are not value neutral towards crime. Government agencies actualize the state's interest in maintaining internal security, suppressing crime, and acting against symbolic threats that could mobilize discontent. Some fear that the government focuses on the crimes of the poor in order to obscure and misdirect middle-class attention away from the more widespread harms caused by big business. Does the data produced by governmental agencies carry subtle biases that are likely to encourage a particular view of crime? For a researcher, the practical question is this: can the data be trusted to have been faithfully collected and presented in accordance with ideas of value-neutrality? Put differently, can we trust government agencies not to collect or adjust data in a way that presents agencies in the most favorable way? This issue has been frequently raised with regard to the UCR. UCR data, for example, is presented as an objective measure of police clearance practices and crimes reported to them. But does it? Concerns have been raised that agencies sometimes manipulate the clearance rate to promote their pubic image and position themselves for budgetary considerations. Lanier and Henry (1998) observed that:

> Police agencies may deliberately alter crime data to improve their department's clear-up rate. They can do this by failing to count ambiguous or lesser offenses, lowering the value of goods stolen below the level necessary for the offense to be singled out as an index crime, and counting multiple offenses by single offenders as one offense. Indeed, if multiple offenses are committed during the same incident, the FBI only counts the most serious offense (Lanier & Henry, 1998:46-47).

Expressing this concern, Silberman (1978) described one agency that maintained a separate "File 13." In this file were stored crime reports that were not forwarded to the FBI, yet retained so that the department could answer questions for insurance companies. Why would an agency do this? So that critics would not think that crime was out of control.

The issue of value-neutrality has also been raised regarding the collection of federal data. Regarding the Bureau of Justice Statistics (BJS) data in the 1980s, Tonry (1998) noted that:

> . . . confirming the Wickersham's worst fears about the credibility of government-sponsored statistics, some directors of BJS became active spokesmen for various Attorneys General's political and ideological positions and distorted statistical data to that end. One director in the early 1980's ,for example, claimed that 95 percent of all prisoners ere violent offenders, repeat offenders, or violent repeat offenders. That director's successor made similarly hyperbolic statements at the 1991 Attorney General's summit on Law Enforcement Responses (U.S. Department of Justice, 1991). Not surprisingly, in many circles, BJS statistical reports issued in the Reagan and Bush administrations were suspected to suffer from similar distortions (e.g., Hughes, 1992) (Tonry, 1998:103).

To say that some governmental statistics are biased is not to say that government agencies are inevitably corrupt, or that they cannot collect data responsibly. To date, the UCR is the only source of national data that permits comparisons on police response to crime at local and regional levels, and it is unlikely that there is a way to routinely collect important data unaffiliated with the federal government. Nevertheless, integrity in the collection and interpretation of data is a reasonable concern that requires vigilance among agency leaders and acknowledgment by those involved at all levels of the data collection, analysis, and publication process.

Value-neutrality issues emerge in other ways. Official data also carry with them the morality of the state. Consider someone who wishes to study, for example, patterns of gun violence. One source of such data is ADAM. ADAM is a data set for studying the attitudes and self-reported behaviors of jailed misdemeanants or imprisoned felons. The data is derived from annual grants solicited by the National Institute of Justice. However, a condition of the grant is that the participants submit to drug testing. Those working with ADAM data consequently are implicitly encouraging the use of drug testing as a routine state practice for people housed in its jails and prisons. In the minds of many people, drug-testing is a controversial practice, a violation of privacy and democratic protections. The use of data collected under these circumstances carries with it an implicit acceptance of the practice, and places researchers in a pro-drug testing policy, whether they acknowledge it or not. Generally, researchers who use state derived data are implicitly accepting state-based values that undergird crime control practices. This is not to say that the state values are wrong in some absolute sense. It is to say that researchers cannot claim value-neutrality in their work.

DiCristina (1995) describes the problems associated with value neutrality when using official data.

1. By accepting large data sets as objective, we endow them with political power. Consider UCR data. UCR data identifies index crimes—the supposedly worst crimes from a moral sense—primarily as street crimes. Other areas in which significant harm occurs to citizens such as white-collar crime lack political relevancy. Whoever heard of a politician running on a platform to get the predators out of the insurance companies? Justicians consequently are implicitly accepting the government's idea of what constitutes morally offensive crime.

2. By laying claim to objectivity, justicians can shield themselves from the charge that they are implicated in their findings.

3. Governmental data should be understood as an effort to produce knowledge that expands the technical control of the state. Research tends to be functional—about operational, strategic, and informational needs of justice system organizations. Research on these needs facilitates the ability of the state to extend its control over citizens.

In the ways described by DiCristina above, researchers who use governmental data-sets or contribute to functional research fulfill a crucial link in the state's control apparatus, *regardless of the findings of their research*.

Secondary data-sets can stifle the creative process. When working with federally produced data, data that were intended to solve a problem collectively defined is often used to address a different research question. We work within collective definitions of problems embodied in secondary data-sets. The creative contribution of individual research entrepreneurs is proportionally restricted. This is not to say that no new ideas can emerge from the use of secondary data-sets—it is not unusual for original researchers to fail to understand the full implications of the data they collect. Yet, innovative research is often linked to the data collected. The ability of researchers to separate themselves from collective definitions of problems and conduct creative research is facilitated by gathering one's own data. The generosity of the government in contributing to the justice fields by providing grants for the collection of data in important substantive fields should not be disdained; yet the importance of creative, fresh, innovative work should be recognized to equal degree.

Finally, when one uses official data, one undergoes an experience not unlike hiking in the desert. One is never quite sure where they are. There is always a sense of being slightly lost—only with data, the sense of "lost" is interpretive. Many steps are involved in the collection and preparation of data, from conceptualizing the variables used to refining the data for analysis. Many sources of interpretation and error can creep in that a subsequent user will not know about. The sense of being "lost" tends to accompany a researchers understanding of the data collection procedures he or she is using—the more one learns about it, the more troubled one becomes about the quality of the data.

With these problems associated with state-based data systems, what then is the young data-jock to do? Certainly, she can plow ahead, writing away and conducting analyses. The problems associated with governmental data can be allocated to a paragraph at the end of a paper, in which the author offers caveats (admonitions about the data process, product, or interpretation of findings), as if their importance is little more than a footnote in the grand process of empirical knowledge acquisition.

Alternatively, a data-jock can decide to collect his or her own data. Many students and faculty collect their own data by conducting local or national surveys. Collecting one's own data has advantages—one can formulate a research problem and then tailor the population surveyed and the survey questions asked to the specific demands of the research problem. Mail surveys are convenient for this kind of research. Mail surveys are also often within the financial reach of faculty. Also, many measurement scales are easily available in journal article appendices where they are used. A student will also find that many measures popular among government agencies are lacking in sophistication or are poorly designed. A corollary is that a measure should not be used simply because it is widely used.

The costs of telephone surveys are prohibitive, substantially more than the meager stipends that typically constitute university-based faculty research support in the social sciences. And the construction of new measures can be hazardous. Few things are more frustrating than to collect data, submit a paper for review, and then be rejected by peer reviewers because there are fundamental flaws in the way the data was collected or measured. The collection of data is time-consuming, taking a person's time away from other work. In the current age in which a researcher frequently has to establish a significant publication record in order to acquire tenure and promotion, the collection of original data is often abandoned in favor of the ready and easy availability of other, already existing sources of quantifiable information.

Quantification in Action: An Evaluation Research Model in Corrections. With the many criticisms that have been heaped on quantitative analyses, the reader might conclude that they should be abandoned by the field of justice. This is an incorrect conclusion. The statistical analysis of large systems occupy a powerful role in the justice fields, a role that cannot be filled by any other method. Statistical and evaluational analyses of the behavior of the justice system are the only way that generalized assessments of state behavior can be acquired. The critical contribution of large-scale empirical analyses is that they represent the best way to impede the ideological control of state justice systems.

Empirical analyses can tell us about the behavior of the state and can provide a tool to change or modify that behavior. Consider the following example, drawn from evaluation efforts carried out by the Federal Bureau of Corrections. In this example, we can see how empirically based quantitative analysis illuminates the justice process.

Federal Bureau of Corrections: Ongoing Evaluation of State Prison Systems. Why do we put people in prison? Because they deserve it? In fundamental ways, our views on prisonization reflect the values we carry, and Western rationality is heavily desert-oriented. Some justice workers believe strongly in prison as a way to deal with bad people. Others are horrified at the prison experience and its effects on prisoners. Our views on prisons and prisoners reflect our most basic views of how we as humans believe others should be treated.

In response to conservative trends in electoral politics, the justice system has undergone dramatic expansion in the 1980s and 1990s. Much of this expansion can be seen in U.S. prison systems. In 2000, the total jail and prison population in the United States exceeded two million persons. Political concern focused on punishment for wrongdoing, and scant attention was given to the eventual release of prisoners. High recidivism rates have marked prison releasees, with estimates ranging from 30 percent to 70 percent, depending on institutional type and specific measure of recidivism used.

In the 1990s, the Federal Bureau of Corrections initiated an evaluation effort aimed at assessing and strengthening existing prison programs. The evaluations focused on the success of programs inside prisons, with outcomes measured in terms of recidivism. The program's authors wanted to find out if state rehabilitation programs did what they were supposed to do, provide recommendations for programs not achieving their goals, and to initiate measures designed to assess whether these programs lowered recidivism on subjects who completed them. Evaluation teams were assembled to meet with representatives of state prisons and provided an initial discussion of program purposes.

The evaluation team held initial meetings with correctional personnel in each state. This meeting lasted for three days and was characterized as a series of presentations by the evaluation team on the purposes of evaluation. During the meetings, program staff met with a broad range of professionals in the state, discussed current correctional programs, described kinds of programs that worked and that didn't, and determined whether there was an interest in a deeper evaluation of statewide correctional programs. If the state decided to continue with the program, the evaluation team would return at a later date, conduct an evaluation of existing programs, and provide recommendations for change. The evaluation teams focused on the following issues.

Recidivism. The program review was structured as followed. The first presentation discussed existing research on prison recidivism. Research assessing the relationship between treatment programs and recidivism were discussed. Building on the tradition of research evaluation, a group of principles of effective intervention were presented.

Risk. Following the discussion of interventions, a discussion of risk factors (characteristics of prisoners associated with recidivism) were presented. An overview and statistical summary of the findings of several hundred surveys was used to document known risk factors. From this were assembled a "major" and "minor" list of risk factors.

Program assessment. The evaluation team discussed the specific elements of assessment needed. Each program was assessed for:

1. Program implementation and leadership.

2. Client assessment.

3. Program characteristics.

4. Staff characteristics.

5. Evaluation.

6. Other—ethical guidelines completion of files, and community support.

The central criteria underlying these categories of assessment was "Is the program actually doing what it states it will do?" By examining each of these elements, any misalignment in the programs formal goals and its actual behavior can be identified. Information is gathered through structured interviews with staff, policy manuals, program curriculum, review of case files, and other materials as requested by the evaluator.

Sometimes the evaluation team are asked to recommend or evaluate a specific program that will be implemented. For program implementation evaluations, it recommends the following steps:

1. An assessment of the skills, background, and involvement of the program leader.

2. The staff selection and training protocols.

3. The way in which the program is conducted.

4. A literature review: Did the individuals who developed the program review the available scientific literature on similar programs? Are they familiar with known problems in the program?

5. A pilot program. Was a pilot program carried out first in order to debug potential programs that might occur when the program is fully implemented?

6. A documented need for the program.

7. Assessment of the fit of program and community values and goals.

8. Cost-effectiveness of the program.

9. Sustainability of funding.

Classification. Classification of prisoner risk is central to prison program success. Programs are designed for particular prisoners who had specific kinds of problems. In practice, prisoners are sometimes assigned to programs without thought to their specific needs. Effective programs are those that assess the specific risk factors of prisoners prior to assigning them to a program. The program evaluation team discusses risk, provides a summary of the history of risk assessment, and provides a presentation of the kinds of factors amenable to change. The evaluation team looks for the following specific factors:

1. Is the program receiving the appropriate clients?

2. For clients who are excluded, what is the rational for exclusion?

3. Offenders are assessed for their risk, their need for the treatment, and their likelihood of responsiveness to the treatment.

4. The treatment method should be clear and objective.

5. What constitutes levels of risk, need, and responsivity needs to be objectively defined (not determined by subjective judgments of staff.)

Treatment models are discussed and recommended for the problems clients face. For example, a social learning model is appropriate for developing particular skills. For individuals with radical behavioral problems, conditioning models may be appropriate. The evaluation team also discusses the least effective programs, such as popular boot-camp programs that mix first offenders with offenders with extensive criminal histories. Finally, the team discusses research on recidivism and programs. Some kinds of workable, tested programs are known to contribute to recidivism. Others do not.

The presentation concludes with a discussion of the factors that can disrupt the success of otherwise good programs. For example, an overuse of punishers as program personnel can undermine efforts to reward good behavior. Programs sometimes need booster sessions—this is particularly the case when the program intervention is conducted a long time before the person is released and the effects of the program intervention have worn off. Or the family was not involved in the treatment process. The team concludes with an insistence that all implemented programs be rigorously evaluated for their successes.

The evaluation research presented above is research-based and positivistic. It is intended to provide insight into correctional practices by examining current practices that have been systematically evaluated elsewhere, and by evaluating programs whose success has not yet been systematically assessed. It is based on positivism—by assessing the programs, we can know about the extent to which they contribute to the post-prison adaption of clients to civilian life.

Empirically based research is central to many aspects of the review process: (1) the review of existing programs, (2) assessment of offender risk, (3) assessment of program practices, (4) assessment of program outcomes, and (5) measurement of recidivism. Every aspect of the program is subjected to inspection and rigorous review using measurable assessments of success. The evaluation methodology developed by the Federal Bureau of Prisons is an example of positivistic evaluational methodology at its finest. Every program juncture, where opinions or predispositions might misdirect program activities, is screened by an empirical assessment or review. The focus on the *out there* is relentless.

This example is presented to show that quantitative analysis is a powerful tool that contributes a great deal to justice inquiry. In the example above, evaluation is a tool for the assessment of existing conditions in terms of a clearly articulable standard—do the programs offered by corrections have an impact on recidivism? It is unlikely that another method could provide the broad information needed to assess this important outcome. Empirical methods allow researchers to gauge the success of their endeavors in terms of measurable outcomes rather than in vague, ideological, or moral terms. Empirical methods may be the only way that ideologically entrenched views can be reasonably challenged.

Part III: Qualitative Research

In this part, I examine qualitative analysis. I focus on ethnographic methods as an alternative to traditional scientific methods in the field of criminal justice. First, I review a problem Mills associated with quantitative analysis—abstracted empiricism. His criticisms are particularly apt for the justice inquiry. Ethnography is presented as a congeries of methods that can serve as a methodological counterweight for some of the problems associated with abstract empiricism.

The Problem of Abstracted Empiricism

There is in the justice fields today an alarming trend: researchers who conduct analyses and author publishable papers, yet lack fundamental knowledge of the topic they study. Young and capable researchers, trained in quantitative methods, launch into survey research projects where they assemble indices, assess factor congruity and develop factor scores, test for reliability, and build scales to plug into causal analyses. Yet at the end of the project, they may have scant knowledge of the object of their research and no understanding of the people or organizations behind the data. They are abstracted from it; not simply because they were outsiders—being an insider can be equally blinding from predisposing cultural biases—but because they were uninformed outsiders. They seemed to lack a sense of the fundamental nature of the object of their study. Their absence of understanding is particularly compelling in the conclusions sections of their research papers—they did not grasp either the local or the national the implications of their research.

Consider a hypothetical example. A researcher might conduct a survey in which she or he uses pre-structured (closed-ended) measures in order to assess and contrast particular occupational characteristics of prison guards in a maximum-security and minimum-security institution. The researcher might be interested in their feelings of cynicism, psychological feelings of work stress, role conflict, and job ambiguity. A quick review of the literature provides established indexes for measuring these constructs. Analyses are conducted, and lo and behold, stress is found to be higher for guards in minimum security institutions than in maximum security institutions. Controlling for task ambiguity, the relationship between stress and institutional type drops below significance. The researcher concludes that role ambiguity intervenes between stress and institutional type. The paper is published and the researcher celebrates, knowing that six more publications will provide the quantity of scholarship necessary for tenure and promotion.

What has the researcher actually learned about the population studied? If he or she had simply looked at mean averages, she might have found out that they weren't particularly role conflicted, stressed, or cynical. What has the research actually told her about guards? The point is this: statistical analysis, to be meaningful, needs to be accompanied with a nuanced sensibility of the group being studied. By a nuanced sensibility I mean a personal knowledge of the values, beliefs, problems, and meanings carried by guards either generally or in this particular setting. Does a researcher really understand what is going on in the minds of my respondents when they looked at these questions? Is his or her awareness of the problem limited to intuition concerning the scales, created independently of any knowledge of the prison guards studied? Does the researcher have any fragment of understanding that allows her to see the scales through their eyes—to understand what the words mean to them? If not, then a published paper is no more than an exercise in abstracted empiricism.

Mills (1959) described the problem of abstracted empiricism as follows:

> In abstracted empiricism, what to verify often does not seem to be taken as a serious issue. How to verify is almost automatically provided by the terms in which the problem is stated: these feed into correlational and other statistical procedures (Mills, 1959:125).

Abstracted empiricism tends to take as given many elements of the research setting: its focus is so narrow that it fails to recognize how the findings are embedded in the working and life circumstances of the people studied. We carry the potential to construct an illusory set of meanings for what we see, meanings that are independent of the actual dynamics we're trying to explain. Mills' work is meaningful for justice studies today, where our research, especially that part of it which comes from secondary data analysis—carries with it underlying assumptions about the way the data was collected, what the data means, and by implication the rightness of contemporary justice practices. The meanings that we write about, abstracted from the nuanced social environment from which they derived, default to the meanings and ideologies of those who collect the data. In this way, abstracted empiricism can be thought of as the substitution of the means of research method for the ends of learning about the people studied.

> The everyday empiricism of common sense is filled with assumptions and stereotypes of one or another particular society; for common sense determines what is seen and how it is to be explained. If you attempt to escape from this condition by abstracted empiricism, you will end upon the microscopic or sub-historical level and you will try slowly to pile up the abstracted details with which you are dealing (Mills, 1959:123).

and elsewhere:

> In bureaucratic social science—of which abstracted empiricism is the most suitable tool and grand theory the accompanying lack of theory— the whole social science endeavor has been pinned down to the services of the prevailing authorities. Neither the old liberal practicality nor bureaucratic social science handle public issues and private troubles in such a way as to incorporate both within the problems of social science. The intellectual character and the political uses of these schools (for that matter of any school of social science) cannot readily be separated: it is their political uses as well as their intellectual character (and their academic organization) that has led to the position they occupy in contemporary social science (Mills, 1959:129).

Mills' recommendation: *Every man his own methodologist!* Although in the current age we would make this impassioned statement in a gender neutral way, its importance is no less significant for justice researchers in the contemporary era. Mills recommended that we think through the problems people face and how the problems link to broader social conditions—what he refers to as "milieux." He advocates that social scientists become craftspeople who reflect on the nature of the problems they actually work on.

In order to identify the problems people face, we need to have some sense of what they think is important, how they see the world, and what their daily concerns are. Yet it is this—our knowledge of people's sensibility of the world around them—that is lost in abstracted empiricism. A person's problems emerge in he context of broad threats to their values and meanings, and in order to understand these problems the social scientist has to familiarize herself with what people care about as well as the historical and social context in which they live.

When research is abstracted from the cares of ordinary people, our attention is diverted from what is actually going on in their lives to the methods we use and the outcomes we, not they are interested in. We allow others to define for us what those values are and what threatens them. This is particularly important in criminal justice, where abstracted empiricism can result in a bland assumption of the rightness—or wrongness—of the behavior of the criminal justice system, and a failure to understand the complex ways in which the criminal justice system intersects with people's lives or in the factors associated with individual deviance and criminality.

How can we rise above abstracted empiricism and inform our research with meaningful and creative insights regarding the justice enterprise? One way is by working as a justice professional. Professionals often deal with the harsh reality of lives ruined by the ravages of crime and incarceration. Justice professionals, however, are sometimes committed to an ideological perspective of the rightness of the way normative practices, and are unwilling to consider ideas openly critical to justice as it is practiced in the United States. The task for justice professionals is to recognize the limitations of experience, that experiential knowledge is both a candle and a shadow. The brighter the candle burns, the deeper are its shadows. The central problem facing justice professionals is to set aside the experiences and meanings accumulated from their work so that they can comprehend the meanings and behaviors of others.

A second way is to study justice as an outside observer, and become informed about justice agency and employee behavior through service activity. This is a path followed by many academicians. If the problem of many justice professionals is that they see too closely and lose breadth of perspective, the problem of many academicians is that they see from too great a distance to acquire perspective. Many individuals are interested in justice work, yet have limited knowledge of the justice system and lack the insights into the practice and values of the justice system. Knowledge of justice organizations cannot be acquired in the abstract, although abstract critical thinking informs any good work. For such individuals, committed to a vision of justice, knowledge comes from participating in justice organizations, be it at the local or national level. Through service, we participate in and contribute to the life of a just community.

A third way lies in work that affiliates the researcher with others who are working on problems of personal interest. This work tends to be carried out in voluntary organizations. Amnesty International, or the Southern Legal Foundation, for example are organizations dedicated to human rights. Through this kind of service commitment, the kinds of knowledge that provide meaning and substance to an otherwise dry research paper can be acquired. Service will afford those who participate with the opportunity to seek those changes they think are just. But it will also change those who participate.

The fourth way is research based, and lies in the methods we choose. Just as service is important for students seeking a justice career, training and research in ethnography will provide a set of skills both for the conduct of research and through which to think about the nature of justice work. A trained ethnographer learns about the values of the organization she or he studies, and also learns about his or her own.

Ethnography is an inquiry aimed at finding out how the world appears from the perspective of the group being studied. The challenge of ethnography is that we, as ethnographers, set aside personal judgments so that we can learn about the views and sentiments of other people. The lesson of ethnography is that the way we think about the world is in relation to other values, and that there are many values, all with a meaningful claim for understanding the *out there*. Ethnography, correctly carried out, avoids the problem of abstraction by embedding researchers in the lives of the researched. The use of ethnographic methods provides researchers with previously unknown insights into group dynamics. In this sense, ethnography contributes to the justice enterprise—it enables to see justice through the perspectives of those we study.

Qualitative Analysis: What Is It? Qualitative research is an alternative to statistically driven quantitative methods. DiCristina (1997) describes the scope of qualitative research as follows:

> . . . qualitative research may be conceived as any serious attempt to describe a single or recurring phenomenon that does not require reducing to numbers the phenomenon under investigation and the factors that may explain it. Qualitative research has no general model in the same sense as quantitative research. It is "inherently multimethod" in focus and "as a set of interpretive practices, privileges no single methodology over any other (Denzin & Lincoln, 1994:2-3). Researchers of this orientation use "ethnographic prose, historical narratives, first-person accounts, still photographs, life histories, fictionalized facts, and biographical and autobiographical materials, among others (see also Denzin and Lincoln, 1994: 6) (DiCristina, 1997:186).

Qualitative research tends to focus on the unique attributes of individual settings, and does not seek the identification of underlying regularity or order across multiple cases. Qualitative research typically requires an involvement of the researcher into the life of the people they are studying. The sense of detachment from the object of study, characteristic of a great deal of quantitative research, cannot survive in qualitative work carried out correctly.

Qualitative research is a methodological unguent for the problem of abstracted empiricism. In statistical research there is a tendency to view data in a very abstract unidimensional sense. The stimulation that comes from interacting with the subjects, from having to communicate with them, to get along, to understand, is absent. If a researcher is using ethnographic methods to study a group or organization, he or she is not permitted the lethargy of abstract detachment. The method requires interaction, that the investigator learn the language they use and what the world looks like through their eyes. Ethnographic work requires that a researcher interact with subjects as multidimensional individuals, not as abstracted data. If ethnography is carried out properly, the researcher will find him or herself identifying with subject's cares and problems, relating to them emotionally as well as research subjects, and will find it difficult to separate objective work from subjective feelings. Qualitative research accomplishes a goal central to the justice enterprise: It increases the scope of knowledge about the different forms justice can take.

Qualitative research is not widely represented in today's academic marketplace, particularly for departments in colleges and universities that push grants-work. Yet, it contributes to the creative research process in ways that grants-work cannot. All grants-work locate the active grants writer as an element in the criminal justice system with a focus on functional research. The review process for grants, though often exacting, focuses on the application of existing knowledge to problems in the practice of justice organizations. Grants reviewers do not look for creativity in grants—they assess the extent to which the grants writer has correctly identified a justice problem, has a contemporary literature review, obtains letters of support from local agencies, offers a proposed solution, and has framed a sufficiently rigorous evaluation methodology. Grants-work is not conducted in order to add to basic knowledge—it looks for problem solutions.[9]

Qualitative analysis is more difficult to apply to policy. The requirements of qualitative research tend to focus on unique cases, hence their analyses are not readily adaptable to policy aimed at a class of organizations. The sorts of insights that derive from qualitative analyses often require the reader to suspend his or her sense of "belief" and when they enter the habitat of the group studied.

Important policy insights may derive from qualitative research but this is not its primary goal. Qualitative research develops a story about the unique and particular characteristics of groups, not generalizable knowledge. This kind of research is a fundamentally different approach to knowledge acquisition. Through the use of ethnographic methods, researchers trace out the actual structure of events and the meanings associated with those events. Through intensive analysis of group activities and events, researchers develop an understanding of their significance in a particular cultural setting.

Ethnography and Thick Description

Perhaps the most eloquent statement regarding ethnography is Geertz (1973a) paper titled "Thick Description." He opened with a discussion of the relationship between methods and the concept of culture.

> Believing, with Max Weber, that man is an animal suspended in webs of significance he himself has spun, I take culture to be those webs, and the analysis of it to be therefore not an experimental science in search of law but an interpretive one in search of meaning (Geertz, 1973a:5).

In this brief statement, he marked the territory of investigation distinct from the operational methods commonplace in the other social sciences.

Geertz used he term "thick description" to describe the work of ethnography. To distinguish between "thick" and "thin" description he used the example of a "wink." Suppose, he queried, a boy rapidly contracts his right eyelid toward a friend who is looking at him. It could be an involuntary twitch. It could also be a conspiratorial wink. The behavioral movement of the eyelid is identical in both interpretations. The difference in meaning, however, is great. If it is a conspiratorial wink, it is carrying a great deal of information: it is (1) deliberate, (2) aimed at someone in particular, (3) imparts a particular message, (4) uses a socially acceptable code, and (5) without the knowledge of the rest of the group. Moreover the other boys in the group may be in on the conspiracy, and the wink is meant to trick the other boy into being an unwitting burlesque. At the level of thin description, the winker is carrying out an observable behavior, contracting his eyelid, and that is all. At the level of thick description, he might be faking out a friend to deceive him into thinking that a conspiracy is in motion when the conspiracy is actually against him.

The object of ethnography is thick description, aimed at acquiring the full array of meanings behind the visible behaviors. Geertz (1973a:5) described ethnography more as an art of writing than an investigatory science:

> . . . the sorting out of structures of signification and determining their social context and meanings. Doing ethnography is like trying to read (in the sense of constructing a reading of) a manuscript—foreign, faded, full of ellipses, incoherences, suspicions emendations and tendentious commentaries, but written not in conventionalized graphs of sound but in transient examples of shaped behavior.

VanMaanen (1988) describes the difference between ethnography and quantitative research as follows:

> To write an ethnography requires at a minimum some understanding of the language, concepts, categories, practices, rules, beliefs, and so forth, used by members of the written-about group. These are the stuff of culture, and they are what the fieldworker pursues. Such matters represent the ways of being and seeing for members of the culture examined and for the fieldworker as a student of that culture. The trick of ethnography is to adequately display the culture (or, more commonly, parts of the culture), in a way that is meaningful to the readers without great distortion. The faithful hold that this depiction must begin with intensive, intimate fieldwork during which the culture will surely be revealed (VanMaanen, 1988:14).

Ethnographic analysis has a rich tradition in anthropology (Geertz, 1973b). Ethnography, in the Geertzian model presented above, is tied to a way of thinking about human culture. Ortner (1984) describes the way in which Geertz tied ethnography to a particular conception of human culture:

> Geertz's most radical move (1973c) was to argue that culture is not something locked inside people's heads, but rather is embodied in public symbols, symbols through which the members of society communicate their world-view, value-orientations, ethos, and all the rest to one another, to future generations—and to anthropologists . . . the focus of Geertzian anthropology has consistently been the question of how symbols shape the way social actors see, feel, and think about the world, or, in other words, how symbols operate as vehicles of "culture" (Ortner, 1984:129).

In order to understand the meaning of symbols, one studies culture "from the actor's point of view." Through interviews, detailed note-taking, observing rituals, tracing the various dimensions of human action and individual practice, what we might call the art of thick description, we can comprehend the cultural dynamics of particular groups.

In order to train students for the study of culture, the field of anthropology has made observational methods associated with fieldwork central to graduate and undergraduate methods. Fieldwork is an essential ingredient of all academic training, and often involves a lengthy stay in some location out of the United States. Anthropologists seeking a Ph.D. must prepare themselves for the rigor of living in uncomfortable settings and experiencing the world in a less protected and clean state—sans air conditioning, hot water, and with food that derives from occasionally surprising sources. In the field of anthropology, the fieldwork process is as much rite of passage as it is a source of data.

The Elements of Ethnography. When we talk about ethnography, we are referring to a process that begins with the selection of a group and ends with the presentation of findings to some audience. VanMaanen (1995) identifies three distinct activity phases in the ethnographic process. These phases are as follows:

Phase 1.   The collection of information or data on some culture. This phase refers specifically to the fieldwork carried out by researchers. Practices, VanMaanen (1995:6) notes, include techniques like intensive and representative interviewing, working closely with a few key informants, designing and administering local surveys, observing and participating in everyday routines and occasional ceremonies, and collecting samples of discussions across a range of situations.

Phase 2.   Phase two is writing up the findings. This phase has been historically marked by "ethnographic realism:" the provision of as clear an image of the world and its elements as possible as experienced by its members. In the current age, realist ethnography has been expanded by other ethnographic forms.

Many contemporary ethnographers have noted their own cultural biases in the identification of what constitutes "real." A genre called "confessional ethnography" has emerged in which the observer assesses his or her own sentiment and reactions to the group studied. A second type of ethnographic writing, "critical ethnography," attempts to locate the studied culture within larger social, symbolic, and historical forces. Third, "dramatic ethnography" focuses on the narration of a significant event (or events) and are presented as unfolding stories.

Phase 3.   Phase 3 refers to the audiences to which the ethnographer writes. Collegial readers are the most ardent readers of ethnography, and are the most careful readers as well. Outside of this small circle are general social science readers, who follow particular ethnography because it furthers their own research. Third are those who read ethnography for entertainment. These audiences sometimes have different expectations. VanMaanen observes that "Ironically, the ethnographer charged with being a novelist manque by colleagues is likely to be the ethnographer with the largest number of readers." [11].

Ethnographic Process, Culture, and the Out There. Ethnographic process and product (Phases 1 and 2 above) are intertwined. The process of fieldwork requires constant reordering and editing for the presentation of the findings. Fieldworkers "observe, participate, conduct interviews, make their audio and visual recordings, or pursue archival research" (Wolcott, 1995:83). The product is the written conclusion to the research.

One way to think about ethnography is as a theory of cultural behavior in a particular setting (Frake, 1964:112). The process of writing up the ethnographic account is a process of creation. The written account is the ethnographer's perceptions and interpretations of what members of the group are doing. The ethnographer learns about the culture of the group, and the group develops a record of its identity from the ethnographer.

The act of writing authenticates the culture. The cultural characteristics identified by the ethnographer exists precisely because they are written down. Culture is not an "out there" but is inescapably intertwined with accounts of it: culture exists because the ethnographer puts it there. Culture, in other words, is the record of concrete events, rituals, ceremonies, behaviors, talk, and the full panoply of human action that describes the group. It is given life by the ethnographer. One cannot separate the observer from the observed. Hence, in anthropology, the method of ethnography and the object of ethnographic research—culture—are fused, indivisible.

A cultural record becomes richer as the ethnography becomes elaborated. But at some point, the field-note-taking has to stop. At what point does the ethnographic process end? Put differently, where should the ethnographer, making detailed notes, simply stop and write up the findings? This is always a subjective decision. Geertz (1973a) provides the following story to describe the "intrinsic incompleteness" of ethnographic research:

> There is an Indian story—at least I have heard it as an Indian story—about an Englishman who, having been told that the world rested on the back of an elephant which rested in turn on the back of a turtle, asked (perhaps he was an ethnographer; it is the way they behave) what did the turtle rest on? Another turtle. And that turtle? "Ah Sahib, after that it is turtles all the way down" (Geertz, 1973a:29-30).

For Geertz, the ethnographic process was always incomplete. Yet, at some point the ethnographer had to organize what she had and write it down. Consequently, the extent to which any cultural group was known or its culture specified was subjective and incomplete. It was subjective because the people studied were given cultural identity and unity by the ethnographer—they didn't exist as a culture apart from the observer. It was incomplete because the recording had to end, yet the group's activities continued. And the patterns found by the ethnographer represented treaties, conditional relationships and conveniences of mind that made group life possible. It did not capture the full panoply of detail that lead to those treaties, nor the disagreements, nor the minutiae that encompassed every group member's everyday life.

Culture is in this sense a written record of an abstraction of the minutiae of everyday life, in which the author focuses on various areas of shared behavior. How much minutiae should there be? Do we need to know about "turtles all the way down?" How many turtles are enough? A variety of ethnographic strategies produce different levels and kinds of data. Some ethnographers use strategies such as "domain analysis," a set of rigorous field-note-taking procedures designed to clarify central cultural elements (see Spradley, 1979; 1980). Other ethnographers have a more flexible view, believing that one need only attempt to develop and sustain an "ethnographic" focus. Yet the conclusions and implications for the *out there* are the same—culture is a product that only exists in its relation to the observer. It is the ethnographer's imagination for linkages superimposed on some group's dynamics. Nor does the "thickness of description" in some way improve on its truth value. To the contrary, the thicker the description, the greater is the need for interpretation. Ultimately, in any account, there are three standpoints that are inexorably intertwined: (1) the standpoint of those studied, (2) the predispositions of the observer, and (3) dear reader, yours and mine when we read the account.

Contemporary Issues in Ethnography. Ethnography has changed over the past 40 years. Most of these changes are at the periphery; the "realist" core, with its emphasis on the identification of local cultural dynamics for their own sake, continues to dominate ethnographic research. Manning (1995) identifies several contemporary issues faced by ethnographers.

> *Genres.* There are many available genres for the representation of findings. In addition to the traditional anthropological monograph, these include the literary report, the novel, photographic essay.
>
> *Unpredictability.* Ethnographers should recognize the fundamental unpredictability of human behavior. Chance and indeterminancy, not causality, often characterize human behavior and sometimes are central to it.
>
> *Reflexivity.* Traditional "realist" ethnography attempted to characterize the world from the perspective of the native. Contemporary researchers recognize the interplay between the subject and the observer. These can take the form of reflexivity (integrating the reaction of the observer to the subject into the text) or intertextual integration of the roles of the subject and the observer (assessing how the role of observer affects the subject and vice versa).
>
> *Space and time.* By space and time, Manning refers not to universal notions, but to cultural uses of them. Pauses, for example, may have linguistic or ritual meanings, emptinesses are not hollow, but contribute to local meanings.
>
> *Image.* This refers to the way in which the other experiences reality. But it also depends on the ability of the author to evocatively express his or her perceptions of the other's reality. If "turtles all the way down" express the depth of reported culture, then imagery refers to the breadth of the native's world view through the lens of the observer. At once, it expresses the richness of local dynamics and the communicative skills of the observer.

These issues are a part of the contemporary landscape for the conduct of ethnographic analysis. They prescribe methods that are aware of the values affecting social analysis at the end of the twentieth century, and embody trends in the social sciences discussed in Chapter 3.

As methodological devices, do these issues bring us closer to the development of knowledge about the *out there*? To the contrary, they encourage the methodologist to recognize the limitations and uncertainty in any information gained in the research process and product. They expand knowledge of the diversity of human activities. They balance the quantitative quest for predictability with a qualitative recognition of uncertainty in human endeavors and reflexivity in their study.

Ethnography and Justice Studies. To what extent can ethnography, a method oriented toward the individual case, contribute to the kinds of knowledge needed in justice studies? It is one thing to gather ethnographic knowledge for the purpose of understanding the local dynamics of a particular social setting. It is quite another to gather information with the idea of using it in some practical or policy-oriented way. Ethnography as practiced by anthropologists identifies local group dynamics and interprets their meanings. The accumulation of knowledge occurred gradually, with each case adding to the store of lore about human culture, behavior, and communication. Instead of generating general principles of group behavior that might have policy applications, the method of ethnography emphasized the unique characteristics of groups. Its purpose is to add to the breadth of literature about cultural diversity.

The field of criminology has a rich tradition of ethnographic analysis. In its heyday in the early 1900s, the Chicago School of sociology used participant and nonparticipant observation techniques, focusing on individual cases. It differed from the ethnographic style discussed above in that it had an issue-oriented focus (Manning, 1987). It identified problems to focused on rather than allowing the groups studied to define their own problems. This style tended to encourage sympathy for the underdog and produced works such as *The Gang* (Thrasher, 1927). This ethnographic tradition has provided core ideas of criminology. VanMaanen described the sociological tradition in fieldwork as follows:

> The Chicago School (of urban ethnography) is usually regarded as the main force behind sociological fieldwork. What Jules Henry (1963) calls "passionate fieldwork" emerged at the University of Chicago just before the great depression as Robert park, W.I. Thomas, Ernest Burgess, and others pressed their students to begin exploring the city as if it were a remote and exotic setting. Students were to bring ethnography home by learning of the vigorous, dense, heterogenous cultures located just beyond the university gates. The method stressed direct participation in these cultures and the discovery of the particular (VanMaanen, 1988:17-18).

Two forms of ethnography were used by the Chicago School. One form, called community studies, was carried out by a team of researchers gather as many facts as they could about some group or area of the city. Community studies have been likened to the early expeditionary work of anthropologists. The second form of ethnography was the use of life histories. To conduct a life history, interviews were carried out of members of so-called "deviant subcultures," or more simply, the Chicago down-and-out. Interviews were intensive and serial, carried out in natural settings, and accompanied by close observation and sometimes participation "in the settings—pool halls, brothels, street corners, tenements, mission shelters, bars union halls and so on" (VanMaanen, 1988:20-21).

The spirit of ethnographic tradition is alive in contemporary justice research. Manning's (1997; 1995;1989; 1988) diverse work on semiotics and police culture are in the tradition of Geertz, and have positioned him as heir to the Geertzian tradition in the justice fields. In the sociology of law, Milovanovic (1994; 1988) has studied linguistic systems in the courts. It has contributed through historical-comparative research (Foucault, 1991). Kraska's (1996) paper on police and paramilitary force was conducted through interviews conducted with officers and focused on the way in which his informants thought about the use of force. Gilsinan's (1988) study aimed at uncovering the sensibility from which dispatchers engage in meaning construction based on the 911 calls the receive. McNulty's (1994) analysis of linkages between story-telling and on-the-job training for police officers identified the way in which officers are trained for uncertainty. Shearing and Ericson (1991) have looked at story-telling and how it provides a sensibility out of which the working environment is understood. Hunt's (1985) study of the practice of police force showed how cultural standards of "normal" force sometimes supplant legal definitions of use-of-force. Historical narrative has been used to describe the history of the Academy of Criminal Justice Sciences (Morn, 1995). Crank's (1996) analysis of story-telling in a parole and probation department showed how local cultural standards adapt to changes in the institutional environment. These papers all use ethnographic fieldwork to identify metaphorical and semiotic dimensions of organizational activities, beliefs, and communications.

The Ethnographer in Action: An Analysis of Gender and Prison.

Daly's (1994) analysis of gender issues in prison are an example of how ethnographic methods contribute to understanding of justice processes. It is presented here as an exemplar of ethnographic analysis.

Daly begins with a paradox. Statistical studies of women have shown that they are treated more leniently in sentencing than men, a finding inconsistent with the subordinate position of women in the male-female status hierarchy. Analyses of income comparing men and women consistently show that women earn lower salaries for equivalent jobs. Why are women then favored in sentencing practices, if women are indeed disfavored in virtually all other circumstances? The paradox, she suggests, is an illusion that stems from the quantitative methods used to measure sentencing. Researchers adopt an "add women and stir" approach to quantification—they measure the relationship between criminal outcomes and sentences, and then include a measure of gender to assess categoric differences (See Chapter 8).

The problem with this approach is that measures of crime presume that the quality of men's and women's lawbreaking is the same. This is an erroneous assumption for two reasons. First, quantification cannot capture "the content and context of an offense, its perceived seriousness to victims and court officials, and the relation of a defendant's prior record to the current offense" (Daly, 1994:7). By simply adding women to quantitative studies of male offending and sentencing, nuanced gender differences in actual behavior are overlooked. The subtle, contextual features of the circumstances of the offenses or the offender are unrecognized. Second, the interpretation of measured differences between men and women lack political referents. How much difference in sentence disparity between men and women should we regard as significant before we take corrective action? What constitutes a small or a large difference? Quantification cannot answer this very important question.

In the current era, policy has attempted to make sentencing "fair" through equalizing justice. Retributive sentencing, aimed at providing equal sentences for equal crimes, appear to be a way to insure that all offenders receive equivalent sentences. But, as Daly notes, judges have in the past used leniency in sentencing in order to keep families together, to avoid punishing innocent children, and to implicitly acknowledge real; differences in harm committed by offenders. Efforts to equalize sentencing for men and women may take away this option from judges. Uniformity is thus imposed by giving women longer sentences.

Sentence equalization may have other implications not fully understood. By providing equal sentences for similar crimes, women may be in fact receiving relatively harsh sentences for behaviors that, if fully understood, are not as severe as men. Equal sentencing practices thus might "lock in" gender differences that are disproportionately harsh on women while creating the illusion of fairness.

Daly carried out both quantitative and ethnographic analyses. For the ethnographic analysis, she selected a narrative method that would give her a "thicker" description of the cases. The narrative was intended as a complement to the quantitative measures of lawbreaking, to see if it produced a different way of thinking about gender differences in sentencing (Richardson, 1990). By moving back and forth between narrative and quantitative analysis, she sought to uncover the broadest possible image of justice as practiced in the criminal court she examined.

Quantitative measures were used to describe overall patterns of sentencing practices in the court. She used narrative for her "deep sample" of 80 cases, 40 each of women and men. For these cases, she examined their pre-sentence investigation reports and their court transcripts at the time of their sentencing. The two methods produced different results. She describes the relationship between the results as follows:

> Are men and women sentenced differently for like crimes? To this core question my answer is no—not in the court I studied in the 1980s, even though a statistical study might suggest otherwise. When I carried out a traditional disparity study, analyzing a large data set with control variables, I found statistically significant differences that apparently favored women. But when I used my comparative justice metric, analyzing pairs of cases and using narrative materials, gender differences were negligible. Although the traditional disparity study can be improved by better measures, the narrative materials have an integrity and meaning that cannot be captured by quantifying their parts (Daly, 1994:258).

Quantitative studies, Daly observed, look at the effects of gender on crime within categories of crime severity, for example, how sentences for men compare to women when we examine burglary. By looking in categories of crime severity, researchers can assess if men and women are sentenced similarly or not. This way of looking at the effects of gender appears to remove the effects of severity in comparing sentencing among men and women. However, it can inadvertently have the opposite effect. It does not distinguish between real differences in the behavior of men and women that actually occur within "objective" categories of crime seriousness.

In many cases, when Daly examined what men and women actually did, she found that male involvement was much deeper and their behavior more violent. Judges would consequently give men more serious penalties, even when both might be charged with the same crime. Differences in sentencing consequently reflected real differences in harm. It only appeared that women were being treated lenient to outside observers unfamiliar with the actual criminal conduct of the men and the women. Quantitative research, looking only at crime categories and not at actual behavior, was unable to identify these subtle yet substantively important differences.

This finding had implications for policy. If crime policy seeks to ensure that legally equal crime categories result in equal time, then women will end up doing equal time for what is actually less serious harm. Desert-based crime policies based on categoric equality would be disproportionately severe for women. Efforts to make sentencing fair, in other words, locked in unfairness.

Daly selected the method of narrative to provide detailed, qualitative information about gender and criminal activity. This method, she intended, would provide the kind of information needed to provide an objective understanding of differences in male and female criminal activity. Narrative enabled her to identify pathways to crime—more or less predictable elements of backgrounds that led to the criminal incident which landed criminals in their current circumstances. These pathways were gendered—the background for women was different than that for men. Among women, pathways were described as follows: abusive households, motherhood and child rearing, a woman's ability to make money by sex, and gender factors in their street and intimate lives that increased the likelihood off victimization. For men, the importance of aggressive-masculine themes were noted—explosive violence, masculine forms of street "gaming," and hardened through histories of incarceration.

Daly also observed gender-common themes. One of these themes was the "reproduction of physical and emotional harm" affecting both men and women, though more prevalent among women. [260]. This theme implied a dual status for criminals; that of "victim" inside that of "criminalizer." In these cases Daly noted a social construction effect. She relied on pre-sentence investigations (PSI's) to provide a discussion of the crime and its history. Yet, she was concerned that the probation officers who wrote the PSI's themselves were predisposed to view women in terms of the blurred "victim-offender" status. Consequently, when they wrote a PSI, they accented their background as victim in order to prescribe a course of treatment.

Daly's analysis should be interpreted in the tension between the quantitative analysis and narrative perspective. The narrative both fills in the quantitative analysis and provides details and new meanings otherwise obscured. By providing a "thick" description of the adjudication process, one can see how justice—as this court practices it—emerges from the diversity of information available to it, not simply from rough, one-size fits all categories of crime. Her analysis is a refreshing change from quantitative efforts to study justice processes externally. By providing the discussion of "gendered" pathways to crime, she captured the full panoply of court dynamics, and perhaps, a more realistic understanding of the *out there* of courtroom practices. Table 5.1 below displays and summarizes the tension between narrative and quantitation.

The most comprehensive image of justice processes, Daly asserted, derived from the "oscillation" between the narrative and quantitative approach (See Table 5.1 above). By oscillation is meant that the findings of each methodology is considered in light of findings produced by the other methodology. Her analysis demonstrated this oscillation as a practical, multi-phased multi-methodology. First, she presented an image of justice processes using a quantitative analysis. It was a predictable image, with findings similar to previous research in other courts. Second, she conducted the narrative approach. The narrative approach served five purposes:

1. Narrative provided a particular way to look at the adjudication process.

Table 5.1
Tensions in Developing a Measure of Justice

	Measure of Justice	
	Quantitative	Narrative
Empirical Strategy	Quantification focused on whether punishment is the same for selected subgroups after controlling for such sociolegal elements as culpability.	Description focused on meaning and process, and on social and organizational contexts of decisionmaking.
	Types of data: large data sets, coded elements of offenses, numerical representations of cases and outcomes.	Types of data: observations of interactions and conversations, ethnographic or "thick" description; interviews of justice system workers.
	Asks: What is the outcome? Why do outcomes vary?	Asks: How does justice get done? What are participants' meanings and conceptions of justice?
	Aim: Devise an objective measure to determine whether the justice system operates on rational-legal principles.	Aim: Reveal the ways in which justice system decisions are patterned, but not necessarily rational.
Idea of Equality	Assumes proportional equality: benefits and burdens distributed on a measure of need or desert-based criteria.	Not specified. One could assume subjective equality: benefits and burdens distributed on the basis of shifting standards of need, merit, ability. Authors' evaluations of justice system process are bracketed.
Idea of Justice	Apply law uniformly.	Apply law individually.
Measure of Justice	Numerical representations of social phenomenon focused on disparity and outcome.	None outlined. The "jungle" needs to be described (Hawkins, 1986), the gestalt of decision making needs to be modeled (Maynard, 1982). Justice is contingent, multidimensional, and based on moral sentiments. A measure of justice may be premature or not possible.

Source: Daly, Kathleen (1994). *Gender, Crime, and Punishment,* p. 266. New Haven, CT: Yale University Press.

2. Narrative informed the quantitative analysis.

3. Narrative identified important patterns not noted in the statistical analysis.

4. Narrative showed where existing theory on crime causation is inadequate.

5. Narrative informed criminal justice policy while at the same time revealing the limitations of policy based on quantitative methods.

With this said, narrative methods are not a panacea for all of the problems that haunt quantitative analysis. They will not provide a full accounting of the *out there*. The PSI's, one of her central sources of data, were used as if the were an accurate accounting of actual problems facing female defendants. However, as Daly observed, they might have been social constructions that reflected the ways in which probation officers viewed female crime. Nevertheless, the narrative method provides a broad and informed set of data for policymakers. In Daly's research we witness the capacity of ethnographic methods to sharply expand our knowledge about actual justice processes.

Notes

1   Having written this chapter, I found that DiCristina (1995:31) had previously used the phrase "out there" in a similar way. His treatise on methods in criminology shares many similarities with this chapter, with the important exception that he focuses on criminology and I focus on justice studies. The two works are distinguished more by emphases than by substance.

2   The contribution of capitalism to the enlightenment should not be overlooked. Then relationship between the scientific revolution, capitalism, and the Enlightenment is reciprocal, with many interweaving influences. I recommend Pellicani (1994) for an historical analysis of the relationship between capitalism and the Enlightenment.

3   In Thus Spake Zarathustra, 1883-1885.

4   In Shweder, 1991:42.

5   See, for example, System of Positive Polity, (London, Longmans, 1875-1877), from Bottomore & Nisbet, 1978)

6   In tests of significance using global chi-square models such as LISREL, model fit is assessed by a change in chi-square associated with model simplification. In these models, non-significant change rather than significant change is the indicator of successful model fit.

7   Bernard (1990) suggested that a theory could be verified if efforts to falsify it were unsuccessful. See DiCristina, 1995:29-31.

8   A rock is a rock—or is it? Is a granite mountain a rock? Is a pebble a rock? Is concrete a rock? If so, then should we conclude that a rock is in part made of water? If a rock

is "hard," then is lava rock? Is mud a rock? How about shale? It is hard mud, pressurized, but will sometimes melt in water and flake in a person's hand. Is a conglomerate a rock, or a bunch of rocks glued together? We have to have a metaphor of individual identity in order to distinguish the rock from its surroundings (Lakoff & Johnson, 1980). Even a seemingly obvious term like a "rock" can quickly become complicated if we seriously consider it.

9   This does not mean that grants-work does not also add to basic knowledge. The relationship between problem-solving and the development of basic knowledge can sometimes be reciprocal.

Chapter 6

Race and Ethnicity: Understanding the New Order in the United States

Thinking About Race and Ethnicity

Race and ethnicity are terms widely use but poorly understood. The term "black" is commonly used as if it were a term carrying a panoply of unalterable meanings, identifying fundamental biological and moral differences between African- and Anglo-Americans. Labels of racial and ethnic identity are used to imply causes of lifestyles, poverty in major American cities and why "our community is special," and to summarize all that's wrong with contemporary immigration policies. In astonishing ignorance at the beginning of the twenty-first century, many of us continue to speak of anyone who carries even a sliver of African-American heritage as "black," as if it were a stain that entered into the gene-pool of otherwise "white" people and cannot now be eradicated from their DNA. Similarly, the term "Latino" is often used as an ethnic marker in a way that makes the term ethnicity roughly equivalent to "race-lite." The word *ethnicity* carries the same connotations as the term *race*, but is not freighted with the same weight of difference. It is clear to me that some students understand neither the terms race nor ethnicity.

Consider the concept "race." Suppose a person fills out an employment form or a social survey. It is likely to contain on it a set of categories intended to identify my race. Now, suppose that he or she is descended from a long line of Anglo Irish, but that 80 years ago his or her great grandfather married an African-American woman. Then that person would technically receive one-eighth of my genetic material from my great-grandmother. How then does he or she respond to the employment document? Historically, the person would have clearly been African-American—Under the "one-drop" rule developed during slavery, an African-American was any person with any known African black ancestry. Suppose my grandfather was African-American—what am I? What if my father was African-American? The question is not simply one of academic curiosity, but carries powerful political and justice consequences. One of the "founding fathers" of the United States, Thomas Jefferson, has an extensive African-American lineage through one of his slaves, Sally Hemings. Many of them were so light-complected that they passed as white, and some of their descendants only recently discovered their African-American heritage. In 1918, the U.S. Census Bureau estimated that 75 percent of all African-Americans were of mixed ancestry (LaFree & Russell, 1993). It is reasonable to presume that the percentage has increased, because it could only remain the same if no additional intermarriage occurred. What, then, is an African-American?

This chapter is written in the following spirit: A student should not complete a college education in justice studies with common-sense notions of race and ethnicity intact. In the United States, racial categories are commonly used to conceptualize migration from Mexico to the United States, to think about urban problems, to level accusations of racism at "white" Americans (whatever "white" is), to attack political candidates, to construct situation comedies on television, to sell commercial products, and most importantly to this book, to assign blame to crime (political right) and to the criminal justice system (political left). It is important that students begin the hard intellectual work of peeling back the cultural veneer to understand race and discrimination. By "common-sense" notions of race is the notion that we can use skin color or cultural identity as a marker for 'race,' and from those markers, infer behavioral traits. Thompson (1989) captures the contradictions in this common-sense usage:

> The racial classification of blacks and whites in the United states has meaning and social significance only to the extent that blacks and whites are differentiated from each other on dimensions other than skin pigmentation (Thompson, 1989:16).

All of the values attached to race, in other words, are intentional. We end up transforming skin pigment from an objective characteristic of the genetic *out there* into a "master status" with dense implied meanings that have nothing whatsoever to do with objective differences in skin color. The issue of race needs to be openly addressed and treated in a straightforward way. Too often it is not.

This chapter treats race and ethnicity as fundamentally different ideas. Part I looks at issues having to do with race, and focuses on efforts to define race as well as its implications for justice system processes. Part II discusses ethnicity. To frame ethnicity, first discussed are the complex issues of ethnic identity and of justice in a multicultural society. Particular issues in crime and justice are then addressed.

Part I: Race

Race may be the most compelling issue in the criminal justice system today. Yet we tend to bring common-sense ideas of race to the table without considering what it is that we are talking about. Our failure to address race in a direct and forthright way has led us to implicitly assume its presence and look at its consequences. Many of us in justice studies, faculty and students alike, focus on the derivative questions. The derivative questions are formulated in the following ways: *Is the criminal justice system racist? Are African-Americans perpetuating a culture of poverty? What can be done to promote racial equality? Are the intellectual capacities of races different?* These are all derivative, because they are based on a presumption—that there is such a thing as race. They do not ask the important question—Do races exist? And this is the unaddressed question that should be asked first.

This chapter argues that the answer to the important question is no. There are not different races, at least insofar as we commonly think of races, certainly not in any behavioral sense. The racial categories that we use in the United States today are a reification, emerging from the development of the nation-state during the period of European colonization in many places in the world. By *reification* is meant that we have taken a concept and changed it into that which it was intended to measure. To reify is to confuse a concept or measure for the object that it is intended to conceptualize or measure. In this case, we have taken a label intended for administrative purposes and converted it into a characteristic of an individual. Race is first and foremost an administrative category.

Yet, to deny the concept of race is not to say that there are no genetic differences among population groups. Any fool can see that some people have dark skin and others have light skin, and that Africans tend to be dark-skinned and Europeans tend to be light-skinned.[1] What is this difference, if it is not race? When we see differences, what is it we are seeing, and what are the implications?

What Is Race?

In the field of justice, few if any concepts generate more controversy than race. The reasons for this are clear: Race has been used as a label through which populations have been stigmatized and oppressed. Humans throughout history have demonstrated a malevolent tendency to cruelly mistreat groups identified as different and inferior. From the Nazi holocaust in the Second World War to the North American institution of slavery, the term "race" has been used by nation-states to symbolize biological inferiority and justify brutal mistreatment.

Yet, there is more to race than the perverse uses to which it has been applied in the realm of politics. In the genetic realm, there is a vital and lively debate about the meaning of human differences and race, a debate that ultimately asks what it means to be human. Sun (1995) captures the nature and spirit of these uses of race:

> It can be argued that anyone attempting to define race scientifically is obligated to examine how the meaning of race in the social world is distinct from and related to the biological one because the concept is used in both domains and the obsession with racial problems remains a critical social issue in society. . . "

Sun further observes that race in the social world not only refers to biological characteristics but to social experiences as well, and often reflects social experiences that are independent of genetic characteristics. Readers will recognize that Sun is describing the problem of intentionality described in the previous chapter. If we view the issue of race through the prism of intentionality, we perceive it as follows. Race is a term to which we assign social meaning. The meaning is intentional. Indeed, we obsess over the term race, a sure sign that it is an intentional term. Its meaning is about values, not science.

Researchers involved in the study of biological distinctiveness among peoples sometimes fail to understand the intentional nature of the concept. A common response is that ""knowledge is neutral." This means that, although race may be an emotionally charged topic, it can be objectively studied in a value neutral way. However, others counter that knowledge cannot be neutral in some sort of objective, independent-of-human-values sense. Seemingly "objective" knowledge is filtered through the sensorium and morality of the observer. Knowledge exists in a state relative to the observer, not in an independent, abstract state.

To state that knowledge is neutral is to suggest that its meanings exist independently of the observer. Knowledge of this kind, however, is not common, and intentional concepts like race only exist in relation to the particular meanings given them by humans. Humans are cultural creatures, carriers of value, seekers of meaning. Put differently, the use of the term race is more revealing of the values and world-view of the describer than the group or individual described

Because race is intentional, researchers who use race in the conduct of research carry a particular responsibility—to distinguish between its intentional (what Sun referred to as social) and objective (what Sun referred to as biological) characteristics. When we conduct research, we carry responsibility for what we find and how it is used. This is a responsibility we must carry regardless of the extent to which we justify our work in terms of "value neutrality." Those that claim "value neutrality"are expressing their obliviousness to the emotionally dynamic, political, value-laden—in short, human—world around them. There are many good justifications for studying patterns of genetic adaptation among population groups, but "value neutrality" is not among them.

Race and Distinctiveness

Issues having to do with race are extraordinarily complex. On the one hand, race is a political term, rooted in ideas of European superiority. However, the concept of race has been of considerable interest in the genetic, social, and biological sciences as well. In this short section, we are going to explore some of these controversies, noting that *all* race-based research is controversial.

Studies of race are often linked to genetic research on population differences. Research into genetic distributions of human populations reveals the presence of broad international and geographical differences. research on genetic differences is typically carried out by studying alleles. Alleles (also called loci) are alternate forms of genes that occupy the same place on the genetic strand and which pass on specific traits, such as hair color. Some alleles are polymorphic, which means that the gene carries dominant and recessive forms. An individual's blood type, for example, is determined by the particular assortment of polymorphic alleles carried by the individual's parents. So is hair color. Many alleles are not polymorphic, which means that they are fixed in the species.

Not everyone has the same combination of alleles. Differences in allele patterns will emerge from one of four processes: natural selection, mutation, flow, and drift. Of these four modes of genetic change, natural selection alone is produced by environmental conditions (see Walsh, 1995). By natural selection is meant that human populations tend to adapt to their environments, and groups that move into new environments will adapt accordingly. The term for adaptation vis-à-vis natural selection is sometimes called "Darwinian fitness," which refers to the degree to which a particular allele enhances the survivability of its host.

Human groups display different frequencies of allele patterns, and these frequencies correspond to geographical areas. When groups that have shared the same geography separate, and become non-contacting, a process of genetic divergence occurs. In response to environmental challenges, natural selection will tend to select in some genetic combinations and select out others. The pattern of genetic combinations is revealed in the relative distribution of alleles.

That a process of natural selection occurs is widely held by biologists. Just as sociologists view individual behaviors as adaptations to social environments, biologists study natural selection as one form of adaptive response to the physical environment. The idea that change occurs through natural selection is an environmental theory of change. It is a way of thinking central to how we think of evolutionary processes throughout the plant and animal kingdoms and how we teach it in schools. An analysis of differences in genetic patterns, called *genetic distance mapping*, has the potential to tell us about the cumulative differences in populations in different geographic regions, and how long those populations have been separated. *Distance analysis* looks at the frequencies with which we find particular alleles in the general population. By comparing the frequencies in one population to those in another, we can form an overall estimate of differences between population groupings. Because we can estimate how frequently changes occur, we can then estimate how long groups have been apart and where and when they separated.

Genetic distance mapping has provided a great deal of information about human geography and history. For example, genetic maps of humans in sub-Saharan Africa show allele differences from Europeans, Asians (depending on the Asian population), Australians, and other groupings. Importantly, genetic mapping shows differences where we might think that populations are close—the English and the Irish are surprisingly different, for example (Cavalli-Sforza, Menozzi & Piazza, 1994). That there are differences in allele frequencies associated with current population groupings has been widely demonstrated. Studies of allele frequency distribution are tapping something in the *out there* in human genetics.

Something is going on that distinguishes population groupings, that makes populations distinctive and associates that distinctiveness with particular geographies. Assigning meaning to that *something* is difficult. First, the specific purposes of most genes is unknown, and so the significance of differences in allele distribution is unclear. This is very important, because without such genetic mapping we cannot determine if particular genes or gene clusters are associated with human traits and behaviors.

Second, the variability of the distribution of alleles within populations is greater than the distribution of alleles between populations, suggesting that genetic drift has had a proportionately small aggregate effect on human characteristics. The proportionally large in-group variability means that when we talk about differences among genetic groupings, we cannot make inferences to individuals. Group differences tell us little about individual differences.

Third, differences in allele patterns across populations are thought to reflect different patterns of fixed evolutionary choice as population groups settled into regions for long durations and adapted to the environments in those locations. If the driver of population differences is natural selection around pre-existing allele combinations, then adaptive processes are not changing us in any fundamental way. Processes of environmental adaptation through natural selection has simply highlighted particular combinations of alleles within an existing genetic framework.

Fourth, allele differences in humans are all associated with physical traits. They are not as of yet associated with behaviors. There are no known pattern of alleles that we can associate with behavior. We try to infer behaviors from traits, but this inference is contaminated by real-world experience. Until we map the genetic structure and know the purposes of individual genes, we will be limited in what we can infer from genetic differences among both individuals and populations.

This is not to say that genetic research is fruitless or unimportant. The findings from genetic research on populations is important for many reasons. First, advances in medicine and research into immunity are recognizing the importance of genetic structures, and many scientists think that genetic structures vary across populations. To fail to recognize genetic differences would systematically disadvantage particular populations of appropriate medical research and treatment. It certainly would be bad science. Moreover, the study of genetic change and adaptation provides insight into the nature of the human species. We begin to understand the nature of our history and our origins. And we learn about our capacity to change, to adapt, and perhaps to survive.

Race, Distinctiveness, and Diversity. We learn a lot from the study of genetics and allele distributions. But can genetic mapping provide evidence for the concept *race*? Processes in genetic drift are incremental and cumulative, leading to diversity. However, human populations don't simply drift apart—they also reconnect and merge. All this has been going on for a very long time. Consequently the idea that populations have emerged from a clear history of genetic drifting apart is misleading. Humans have an enormous capacity to migrate to new places and to return home, separating and re-pooling their differences. We witness this happening today, among African- and Anglo-Americans in the United States. Such merging is inevitable.

Can differences among populations be called "race?" Put differently, is there a distinctiveness below the biological classification level of "species" into which we can catalogue humans? Cavalli-Sforza, Menozzi, and Piazza (1994) undertook a study of allele frequencies around the world. Their work, though not definitive (they could not acquire data on allele patterns for a number of regions or populations), is the most exhaustive to date. Their analysis was accomplished for 42 populations distributed worldwide. Their study is recommended for anyone interested in the study of population distinctiveness. These authors, however, question whether their findings should be used as evidence for the presence of races:

> The classification into races has proved to be a futile exercise for reasons that were already clear to Darwin. Human races are still extremely unstable entities in the hands of modern taxonomists, who define from 3 to 60 or more races (Garn, 1971). To some extent, this latitude depends on the personal preference of taxonomists, who may choose to be "lumpers" or "splitters." Although there is no doubt that there is only one human species, there are clearly no objective reasons for stopping at any particular level of taxonomic classification.
>
> It may be objected that the racial stereotypes have a consistency that allows even the layman to classify individuals. However, the major

stereotypes, all based on skin color, hair color and form, and facial traits, reflect superficial differences that are not confirmed by deeper analysis with more reliable genetic traits and whose origin dates from recent evolution mostly under the effect of climate and perhaps sexual selection (Cavalli-Sforza, Menozzi & Piazza, 1994:19).

Yet, the study of distinctiveness continues to intrigue many researchers. Some argue that, though race is a loaded term, the use of any other term to describe differences (such as distinctiveness) is semantics. Human populations are more varied than suggested by an accumulation of discreet differences. Walsh (1995) described the problem in inferring from genetic differences to categories of race with the following analogy. He discussed the concept of clines. Clines are lines of equal gene frequency. We can look at the distribution of clines across a particular geography, and the cline lines will tell us of the proportional distributions of overall genetic similarity

Clines, Walsh observed, are like contour lines on a map—they tap graduated changes. If we look at patterns of clines among different human populations, will they reveal relative smoothness as we move from population to population, suggesting gradual changes? Or will some other, more sharply delineated topography emerge? If a more sharply delineated topography is revealed, we can build an argument for the concept of race.

Some research, Walsh continued, suggests that there is a "plateau-valley" topography to different human populations. This topography shows plateaus in Europe and in Africa with valleys between, suggesting a natural categorization that cannot be accounted for by simple ideas of gradual change. Yet the data are limited, and data measuring the topography between regions is scant.

Ultimately, trying to determine whether or not we should recognize the existence of different races comes down to our most fundamental questions about what it means to be human. When researchers study patterns of fixed and polymorphous allele patterns, are they studying the sum total of the possible variation of the human creature? What does this variation mean? Is our genetic code a cage, limiting our possibilities in ways that we, by design, cannot conceive? Or does our genetic diversity represent a gate, opening at each stage of our individual developments the possibility of growth in spirit and intelligence? The question "are we different from each other" inevitably leads us to ask a far more important question—what are we? In the debate over race we can see the fundamental paradox that drives the justice field: Are humans predictable creatures, whose characteristics and behavior are habitual and precoded by their genetics? Or is behavior genetically unrestrained, and humans are free to pick and choose their social, physical, and moral environments rather than be limited by them? Is the future fixed, a done genetic deal, a trick of fate, an evolutionary dead-end that carries the illusion of choice?

Or is it up to us? The answer to this question is a beginning, not an end. It is this—I decide. To an idea of race that is a product of our intent, the answer may be moral. One can opt for a belief in the future, being ever vigilant about the intellectual traps of the past.

Empire and the Reification of Race

To understand race is to comprehend the power of labeling. In the context of African-American history, race *was* an administratively created label. Our current conceptions of race can be traced to European colonialism in Africa. Colonial conquest brought with it the importation of that most powerful of political statements—the map. Territorial units were often re-drawn to fit colonial ideas of state boundaries, disregarding pre-existing sociocultural boundaries. Groups were sometimes split and combined into the same state, creating the illusion that they represented an underlying cultural identity. In many cases, Eller (1999) noted, racial categories were superimposed on existing social differences, creating racial identities for particular states in spite of cultural differences. With the stroke of a pen, race became a closed, fixed historical characteristic with biological implications. Race was yoked to territory, statehood, and culture.[2] The process of European state creation and how it led to the reification of race is described below.

In many instances racial categories were superimposed upon existing social differences, reifying those differences while often suggesting a closer racial relationship of one group than the other to the white colonizers. The very idea of race was (and to an extent still is) a European or Western preoccupation, not endemic to all societies or civilizations—not only as a method to classify peoples but also to explain behavioral differences in terms of physical differences. Like the notion of society, race too was supposedly a real, discrete, bounded phenomenon, yet the two concepts worked hand in hand, because a set of cultural traits could ideally be attributed to the group identified by its set of physical traits. Race was often linked to or established on the basis of cultural characteristics, most particularly language or territory: the thinking was "every language group a race, and every race a language group" and "every territorial group a race, and every race a territorial group." *Race* was often even something of a synonym for *society* or *nation*, as in the *British race* or the *French race* (Eller, 1999:33-34).

Unfortunately, as W.I. Thomas observed, something is real if it is real in its consequences. Having assembled "nation states" where none existed, European powers tried to assert principles of democratic governance within these states. The imposition of the bureaucratic entity "state" over preexisting populations erased fundamental differences in ethnicity and pluralism. Only the imposition of external authority could preserve these created "states" from dissolving under internal conflict. With the withdrawal of empire, efforts to cede democratic authority to many of their nation-states resulted in the awakening of ethnic identity and inter-group conflict. Confusing cause and effect, many Western observers have concluded that such groups lack the capacity for democracy, no understanding how the imposition of the nation-state concept itself guaranteed internal conflict and strife.

Making a Reified Concept Real: Contemporary Race Disparities in the United States. We have inherited a reified concept, and made of it something real. Race came about as an administrative label, a way for European expansionists to construct and manage empire. As children of empire, race appears to us as a natural part of a person's identity. We fail to recognize how our everyday world carries to this day the tendencies of European colonialism, how our labeling has consequences, how our language of distinctiveness divides peoples and creates precisely those problems we blame on those different from ourselves. We continue to use the labels today, even while acknowledging that they have no basis in fact and serve only administrative purposes. Walker, Spohn, and DeLone, for example, note that:

> The OMB [Office of Management and Budget] defines a black or African American person as anyone "having origins in any of the black racial groups of Africa." It defines a white person as anyone "having origins in any of the original peoples of Europe, the Middle East, or North Africa."
>
> The OMB concedes that the racial and ethnic categories it created "are not anthropologically or scientifically based." Instead, they represent a ""socio-political construct." More importantly, OMB warns that the categories "should not be interpreted as being primarily biological or genetic in reference" (Walker, Spohn & DeLone, 2000:9).

This statement is one of intentionality. In it, the OMB acknowledges that its racial groupings don't exist in the *out there*, but are used for administrative purposes only. One should wonder how administrative purposes are benefitted by sustaining the processes of racial labeling begun in the expansion of European empire. Moreover, however the OMB provides disclaimers, its process of racial labeling will only provides the stamp of official legitimacy on racial differences.

Race is real in its consequences. The United States today confronts profound problems of separation between its African-American citizens and everyone else. Although a discussion of the long-term history of racial relations is well beyond the scope of this book, the near-term history is disturbing and alarming. The integration efforts that characterized the 1960s have today stalled and in some cases back-slid. The racial problems of the 1960s continue to affect the United States at the beginning of the twenty-first century.

Segregation of African-American and white communities in the United States is an ongoing process. This is surprising to many who believed that the United States had "turned a corner" in the 1960s and was undergoing the hard work of integration. The reasons for continuing racial segregation are complex. The mid-1970s, Glazer (1997:127) observed, were a reversal for integration efforts: progress towards integrated schools and housing slowed and in many cases stopped. Segregation actually increased in New York and in Newark over the decade of 1970-1980 (Massey & Denton, 1993). As a means to achieve integration, busing was similarly unsuccessful. Race today continues to limit equality of opportunity.

Today, we brink on the twenty-first century, and racial integration is at a standstill. Why? Benign, non-race-based explanations are inadequate. Recency of migration, for example, cannot explain inner-city concentration, for other recently arrived immigrant groups are clearly integrating with each passing generation. Other non-white groups tend to "deconcentrate," that is, assimilate into mixed neighborhoods, by their third generation in the United States. Nor does poverty adequately explain the phenomenon. Even for African-Americans with incomes in excess of $50,000, segregation is as severe as for those living in poverty. Demographers have noted that some suburban areas are increasingly African-American. But where this has occurred, the suburban areas tend to become segregated extensions of inner-city black areas (Glazer, 1997).

The explanations for the lack of African-American assimilation are complex, yet certain themes are central. Racism is one of them. Among the working classes, racist resistance to residential in-migration of African-Americans is direct and frequently confrontational (Glazer, 1997). In middle-class neighborhoods resistance to African-American in-migration is more subtle and less confrontational. Racial biases mix with concerns for family, children, and property in ways that are not amenable to governmental intervention. The crescive, voluntary acts of citizens overwhelm efforts by local and national governing bodies to encourage integration.

Broad social factors have contributed to the concentration of African-Americans through the 1980s and 1990s. These "concentration" effects have worsened the plight of African-Americans (Sampson & Lauritsen, 1997):

> . . . patterns (of urban residence for African-Americans) underscore what Wilson (1987) called concentration effects—the effects of living in a neighborhood that is overwhelmingly impoverished. These concentration effects, reflected in a range of outcomes from degree of labor force attachment to social dispositions, are created by the constraints and opportunities that the residents of inner-city neighborhoods face in terms of access to jobs and job networks, involvement in quality schools, availability of marriageable partners, and exposure to conventional role models. Moreover, the social transformation of inner cities in recent decades has resulted in an increased concentration of the most disadvantaged segments of the urban Black population—especially poor, female-headed families with children (Sampson & Lauritsen, 1997:337).

Factors contributing to concentration are complex, and include the de-industrialization of American cities, the shift to service-based industries, the exodus of upper-income black families from the inner city, and urban renewal and subsequent forced migration (particularly the freeway networks built in many cities in the 1950s). Deliberate housing decisions to concentrate poor and African-Americans in public housing, opposition from many communities to black in-migration and public housing in their neighborhood, and the failure of many local governments to rehabilitate antiquated public housing has contributed to "massive, segregated projects which have become ghettoes for minorities and the disadvantaged" (Sampson & Lauritsen, 1997:38). The consequences of concentration have brought the civil rights movement to a standstill, and in some cases have reversed hard-fought gains. Though attitudes among white Americans toward African-Americans have improved generally, the quality of life of many African-Americans deteriorates in many urban areas.

Race: The Justice Controversy

Issues of race bring out the most complex methodological, theoretical, and ethical issues in justice today. Ethically, the study of racial imbalance posits two conflicting notions of social morality against each other. On one side are those that argue that justice should be fair regardless of the consequences for minority group members. According to this side, the essential quality of justice is that it is rational and clear. On the other side are those concerned with racial equality, and point to the enormous numbers of African-Americans arrested and convicted annually. For them, justice practices, rational or not, contribute to the concentration of African-Americans in urban ghettos and their isolation from participation in the mainstream economy.

For a "deterministic" social scientist, the social and economic inequities faced African-Americans is painfully evident. That African-American minority members are victimized, commit more crime, are more frequently arrested, and are incarcerated at numbers sharply disproportionate to other groups is clear, beyond dispute (Miller, 1996; Cole, 1999; Leadership Conference on Civil Rights, 2000; Building Blocks for Youth, 2000; Bureau of Justice Statistics, 1999; 1993). A black male born in the United States in 1991 faces a one-in-three lifetime chance that he will serve a sentence in an adult prison (Leadership Conference on Civil Rights, 2000). More than 25 percent of all black men aged 25 to 29 are currently in prison, on probation or on parole (Langan, 1991).[3]

Those carrying deterministic views worry about the "bridge effect." The bridge effect is the worn adage that *it is against the law for rich and poor alike to sleep under a bridge.* It is unlikely that we will find many rich people sleeping under bridges, yet the homeless will seek shelter where they can. A police officer, concerned that "bridge people" or the homeless will prey on passersby, will focus his or her discretionary attention on the homeless. The focused attention in and of itself will account for the perception of higher crime and fuel a self-fulfilling prophecy that the homeless are more criminogenic, thereby worthy of heightened scrutiny.

Determinists look at the background, environment, and predispositions of justice system actors, and note how moral and ethical predispositions lead to a heightened focus on African-Americans. Unchecked police and prosecutorial discretion and biased justice practices, from a deterministic perspective, contribute substantially to the widespread incarceration of African-Americans in the justice system.

Justice is also grounded in the idea of rational law. And one of the cornerstones of rational law is that it applies to all citizens impartially and equally. For legal practitioners, law serves democratic purposes when it is straightforwardly understandable and fairly applied. A law is unjust when it is unevenly applied, or if it is not clear. Consequently, the law, to be fair, cannot make distinctions based on race. Whether the blame lies somewhere in American life, or with intentional or unintentional racism, or by the unfortunate circumstances in which many African-Americans find themselves is of secondary importance: the criminal law requires that individuals are held responsible for their actions.

The law presumes personal responsibility. When the law is clearly stated, citizens carry the responsibility to obey it. Advocates of legal process may sometimes cringe at the impact of enforcement or correctional policy on minority communities. They nevertheless bring to the table a belief that, regardless of its consequences for defendants, the law must be fairly and rigorously applied. Put simply, when someone does the crime, they do the time. Skin color and origin are irrelevant.

In the tension between determinism and personal responsibility, how can we decide where to take a position? Is it better to choose the ethics of personal responsibility, arguing that the best long-term vision for all citizens, African-American and Anglo alike, is unambiguous equality? Alternatively, is there a way within the law to acknowledge the effects of the United States' slavery-tainted heritage and resultant systemic disadvantage for African-Americans? Which is more just? The conflict, in this case, is a controversy at the core of our ideas of democratic equality. We will return to this question in the section on ethnicity, where we consider Walzer's (1994) two rival notions of democracy.

Research on Race, Justice, and Injustice

The History of Race-Based Research on Crime. "All roads in American criminology lead to issues of race" (LaFree & Russell, 1993:274). However, the way in which race is studied has changed over the history of American criminology. Four historical periods identify the criminological study of race in the United States. These periods, described by LaFree and Russell, are presented below:

1. *The Birth of American Criminology, 1890-1919*. Explanations for crime often focused on genetic or physiological deficiencies. A survey by Breardley (1932:111-116), for example, noted that the high rate of homicide among African-Americans was due to their "peculiar genetically determined temperament" as well as "excessive emotionality." However, this view did not go unchallenged. Writers such as W.E.B. DuBois used empirical analyses to assess the impact of social and historical conditions on African-American criminality.

2. *Mainstream Academic Criminology, 1920-1950*. This period focused on the etiology of crime. The early part of this period witnessed the emergence of the Chicago School and the development of perspectives such as social disorganization theory (Shaw & McKay, 1942). Differences between the experiences of African-Americans and other minorities undermined the reach of social disorganization explanations. Uniform Crime Reports also emerged as the principal measure of crime during this era. The UCR findings concerning race effects in the production of arrests continue to be controversial today.

3. *Sociology of Law Perspectives, 1960-1974*. This period was marked by a transition in criminological study. Instead of focusing on the etiology of crime, researchers examined creation and application of the law. There was a dramatic increase in the quantity of research on the differential application of the law to African-Americans. Self-report data suggested that black-white differences in crime were not as extreme as suggested by official (UCR) data, and implied that police arrest decisions were strongly affected by racial considerations.

4. *Toward a Theoretical Synthesis, 1975 to the present*. This period is eclectic: both sociology of law and etiological explanations of crime have generated a great deal of research. Etiology explanations of crime have been furthered by the availability of national survey data on victimization. Research suggested that victimization and UCR data were in fact compatible, suggesting that UCR data was not as misleading regarding levels of true crime as previously thought. Research on police arrest practices began to focus on factors other than racial bias.

In the current era, the topic of race and criminal justice is as controversial as it has ever been. Some researchers argue that no racially biasing effects exist in the criminal justice system (Wilbanks, 1987). Many researchers have found racial disparities, and those disparities were specific to location or stage of adjudication process. In this case, racial differences are contextualized. According to the notion that race disparity is context-dependent, the criminal justice system is not racist, even though some of the contexts may be very widespread. Another view is that racist disparities are systemic. According to this idea, the cumulative effects of race-based decisions result in systemic racist practices. These decisions are made under the umbrella of discretionary practices, and are difficult to identify methodologically. The notions of race as a contextual problem versus race as a systemic problem are discussed below.

Race Injustice as a Contextualized Problem. Sampson and Lauritsen's (1997) review of research on race and justice provides an overview of linkages between race, victimization, crime, and the criminal justice system. The authors assessed racial differences in each step of the criminal justice process. Their paper is summarized below.

1. *Race and criminal victimization.* For violent victimizations, both rate and trend differences by race are substantial. Blacks suffer much higher rates of personal violence and homicide victimization than do whites. The leading cause of death among black males and females age 15 to 24 is homicide (National Center for Health Statistics, 1995).

2. *Criminal offending.* African-Americans are overrepresented in arrests reported in the UCR. Blacks are about six times more likely to be arrested for violent crimes than whites. The "drug wars" overfocused on African-American suspects:

    > Following the federal government's initiation of the "war on drugs," African-American arrest rates skyrocketed, while white arrest rates increased only slightly. By the end of the 1980s, African-Americans were more than five times more likely than whites to be arrested for drug related offenses. It is highly unlikely that these race differences represent general substance abuse patterns since drug arrests grew at a time when national self-report data showed that drug use was declining among both African- and Anglo-Americans. Rather, these differences reflect the government's targeting and enforcement of specific types of drug use and trafficking . . ." (Sampson & Lauritsen, 1997:327).

    > Reports by victims indicate that racial differences in arrest rates are explained by the greater involvement in personal crimes, particularly robbery.

3. *The community structure of race and crime.* African-American communities differ with each other with regard to crime and social organization. Variations in black violence are associated with characteristics of urban structure, hence, there is no unique "black" subculture. The concentration of urban poverty is associated with increases in both black and non-black violence, suggesting that the ecological context, rather than race, accounts for crime. The sharp concentration of poverty that began in the mid 1970s in urban areas seems to account for increases in African-American crime.

4. Criminal justice processing.

    A. *Juvenile justice.* Pope and Feyerherm's (1990) research showed that two-thirds of studies they reviewed showed evidence of either direct or indirect discrimination against minorities, or a mixed pattern of bias. Discrimination was widespread.

    B. *Police-citizen encounters and arrest.* Racial differences in arrests for street crimes are explained by black involvement in crime. Black suspects in minority neighborhoods are more likely to be treated harshly than black suspects in white neighborhoods, while white suspects are treated uniformly regardless of neighborhood (Smith, 1986). In a study in Memphis, blacks were found to be more likely to be shot by police while retreating (Fyfe, 1982).

    C. *Bail.* Race is related to bail in complex ways (Albonetti et al., 1989). Prior record had a stronger negative effect on pretrial release decisions among blacks than whites. Dangerousness and offense severity had stronger effects for white defendants.

    D. *Conviction.* Race does not affect case dispositions.

    E. *Sentencing.* From an exhaustive review of research, Wilbanks (1987) concluded that race and sentencing were unrelated once prior record was accounted for. Others have found evidence of "some discrimination, some of the time, in some places. Sampson and Lauritsen (1997:351) observe that ,"if the effects of race (on sentencing) are so contingent, interactive, and indirect in a way that has to date not proved replicable, how can one allege that the system is discriminatory?"

    F. *Imprisonment.* Generally, differences in black-white imprisonment are explained by differential offending. However, when individual states are examined, the impact of racial differences of offending on imprisonment varies considerably. States with extreme racial differences in arrests compared to imprisonment include Massachusetts (40 percent), Idaho (53 percent), Colorado (62 percent), Alabama (54 percent), and Maine (58 percent). (353).

    G. *Death penalty.* Research shows that the race of the victim interacts with the race of the offender, significantly influencing prosecutor's willingness to seek the death penalty and judges and juries willingness to impose a sentence of death. Black offenders found guilty of murdering white victims are at the highest risk for the death penalty (354-355) Offenders of either race found guilty of murdering black victims are the least likely to receive the death penalty.

Sampson and Lauritsen called for an examination of the cumulative effects of disadvantage. The juvenile justice system, they observed, shows the greatest overall levels of racial disparity. Juvenile processing, they note is highly implicated in the construction of a criminal record. Consequently, racial disparities in early justice experiences can accumulate, producing a "legal" record of prior convictions that appear to negate race as a factor. This issue is increasingly important as many states refer juveniles to adult courts for trial and sentencing.

In the 1980s Joan Petersilia undertook the Racial Disparities in the Criminal Justice System study for the National Institute of Corrections. Study data came from two sources: California Offender-Based Transaction Statistics (OBTS) and the Rand Inmate Survey. This survey focused exclusively on case processing, and looked for evidence of differential processing at each stage of the justice process.

1. Are minority group members over-arrested relative to the number of crimes they actually commit? Petersilia found that racial differences do not account for differences in the proportions of arrests to crime. Nor do minority group members have a higher probability of being arrested for crimes. However, the probability of being arrested is extremely low, regardless of race.

2. Are there racial differences in the processing of cases? Whites were more likely than minorities to be arrested on a warrant and less likely to be released without charges. Blacks and Hispanics are less likely to have initial felony charges subsequently dropped to misdemeanors. After a misdemeanor conviction, whites were more likely to get probation than jail. After a felony conviction, minorities were somewhat more likely to get prison instead of jail.

3. How about charges following arrest? White arrestees were more likely to be officially charged than minorities following arrest. Black arrestees were more likely to have their charges dropped by a prosecutor. After charges were filed, conviction rates were similar across groups.

4. Are here variations in the actual length of sentences served by Whites and minority members? Petersilia found that, controlling for defendant's age, conviction crime, and prior record, race made a difference. Blacks and Hispanics were likely to serve longer sentences.

5. Are there differences in sentencing and parole? In deciding on probation, prison, or jail, judges frequently use presentence investigation reports (PSR). PSR's are concerned with analyzing a person and his or her situation, and they contain a sentence recommendation. Hence, they take into account a person's socioeconomic and familial condition. However, problems associated with socioeconomic and familial conditions are concentrated in minority communities. Thus, they score high on recidivism measures. Yet research shows that recidivism occurs at the same rate across racial-ethnic categories. The use of background and income characteristics consequently results in a greater likelihood that minorities will be identi-

fied as potential recidivists, serve longer sentences, and will more likely serve prison rather than jail terms.

Petersilia found many instances of racial bias, some of it quite strong. But the instances were localized: bias tended to vary by place and conditions. She suggested that bias was not systematic but contextual. By "contextual" was meant that patterns of discrimination in one place may not be revealed in another, because the context in which it occurs is different.

Other research has identified contextual effects. Chiricos and Crawford's (1995) review of 37 papers identified several contextual elements affecting the race-sentencing relationship. After controlling for crime seriousness and prior record, they found that the incarceration of black defendants was significantly more likely 53 percent of the time when the South is compared to the non-South. Similarly, they found little evidence for lenient treatment of blacks, an idea that had been suggested by Wilbanks (1987). Also, where unemployment is high, the rate of incarceration of African-Americans is greater, controlling for crime seriousness and prior record. The authors conclude by emphasizing the importance of structural contexts—broad, somewhat stable features of the social and economic environments inhabited by justice agencies—for understanding the relationship between crime and sentencing practices.

The research described above has shown both substantive effects and no effects, depending on what element of the justice system is examined and what level of aggregation is used (individual-level, municipality, state, or nation). In order to identify racial disparities in the delivery of justice, we need to identify the correct contexts. A review of these two papers provides compelling evidence for differences in patterns of justice for African- and Anglo-Americans. But can we conclude from this research that the criminal justice system is racist? Put differently, can we conclude that there is a consistent, overall systemic pattern of racist intent in the way criminal justice is practiced in the United States?

Walker, Spohn, and DeLone (2000) described the justice-minority nexus in terms of its location on a discrimination continuum. At one end of the continuum was pure justice, which meant that there was no discrimination in justice practices. At the other end was systemic discrimination, which meant that discrimination prevailed at all times and at all levels of the criminal justice system. Neither correctly described the American system of criminal justice. A consideration of the evidence lead to an intermediate model of justice system discrimination, characterized by contextual discrimination.

We suggest that the U.S. criminal justice system falls between the two ends of the continuum. More specifically, we suggest that the system is characterized by contextual discrimination. Racial minorities are treated more harshly than whites at some stages of the criminal justice process (e.g., the decision to seek or impose the death penalty) and no differently than whites at other stages of the process (e.g., the selection of the jury pool). The treatment accorded racial minorities is more punitive than that accorded whites in some regions or jurisdictions, but no different than that accorded whites in other regions or jurisdictions. For example, some police departments tolerate excessive force directed at racial minorities, whereas others do not (Walker, Spohn & DeLone, 2000:288).

Whether discriminatory justice practices are contextual or systemic is partly semantic. The United States is characterized by several tens of thousands of justice agencies. Their inter-relationships are determined as much by the independence of political boundaries as by the conjoining of mutually binding legal obligations. In this sense, all justice practices are by definition contextual—there is no system of American justice.

Racial Injustice as a Systemic Problem. The research considered above suggests that discriminatory practices are contextual—they are identifiable in some jurisdictions and in some decision-points in the justice process. Another perspective, put forward by the Leadership Conference on Civil Rights (LCCR) (2000), is that discriminatory practices at each decisional point in the justice process lead to cumulative disadvantage. When the entire process is observed, the effects of cumulative disadvantage are highly discriminatory and pervasive. They observe, for example, that police anti-crime tactics:

> involve the exercise of a substantial amount of discretion—the police decide who they consider suspicious, which cars to tail, what conduct warrants further investigation and which neighborhoods are ripe for further investigation (LCCR, 2000:1).

Prosecutors make similarly discretionary decisions. A prosecutor can, for example, make a decision whether to prosecute a drug case in a federal or state court. The decision is momentous, because federal courts in 1990 sentenced drug traffickers to an average of 84 months in prison, without possibility of parole, while state courts sentenced the same offenders to an average maximum of 66 months, with average time served of 20 months. The LCCR observed that:

> From 1988-1994, hundreds of blacks and Hispanics—but no whites—are prosecuted by the United State Attorney's office with jurisdiction over Los Angeles County and six surrounding counties. The absence of white crack defendants cannot be ascribed to a lack of whites engaged in such conduct: during the 1986-1994 period, several hundred whites were prosecuted in California state court for crack offenses (LCCR, 2000:13).

Similarly disparate results can be noted with regard to the plea-bargaining process, the use of "two-strikes" and "three-strikes" standards requiring mandatory prison for some repeat offenders, bail, juvenile prosecution, sentencing, and the use of the Death penalty. Consider Georgia's "two-strikes" law, which can impose a life sentence for a second felony conviction:

> Under the Georgia scheme, the State's district attorneys have unfettered discretion to seek this penalty. As of 1995, life imprisonment under the "two strikes" law had been imposed on 16 percent of the eligible black defendants, while the same sentence had been imposed on only 1 percent of the eligible white defendants. Consequently, 98.4 percent of those serving life sentences under Georgia's "two strikes, you're out" regime are black (LCCR, 2000:15).

Significantly, the authors of the LCCR observe that disproportionate minority involvement in the justice system is unexplainable in terms of a greater number of crimes committed by minority group members. In some instances, higher minority group member involvement occurs in spite of data showing that minority group members are involved in proportionately lower crime than whites. Consider the following example:

> One of the most through studies of sentencing disparities was undertaken by the New York Division of Criminal Justice Services, which studied felony sentencing outcomes in New York courts between 1990 and 1992. The State concluded that one-third of minorities sentenced to prison would have received a shorter or non-incarcerative sentence if they had been treated like similarly situated white defendants (LCCR, 2000:24).

Similar disparities between offending behavior and justice system involvement were noted in all discretionary decisional points and their outcomes in the justice process. This results in the practice of widespread and pervasive discrimination, whether intended or not.

How can the two views—that racist practices are contextual versus the idea that pervasive discriminatory practices lead to cumulative disadvantage—be reconciled? First, consider the examples cited above by LCCR. Viewed separately, each view is consistent with a "context" theory. However, the LCCR argues, one should observe the overall pattern, not the isolated effects. When one does this, the picture is not one of isolated incidents of contextual discrimination but of a general pattern of widespread pervasive discrimination.

If an outside observer were to examine the likely disadvantage at each decisional process in the abstract, they would find a hodgepodge of disadvantages accruing to minority identity, some small, some large, and some nonexistent. However, when the entire justice process is examined, the overall process results in cumulative disadvantage what has enormous consequences for minority group members. The theory of cumulative disadvantage hence provides a perspective for linking together the disparate findings that constitute the basis of the "context" theory of discrimination.

A second linkage between the "context" theory and the notion of systemic cumulative disadvantage can be noted. It is this: That contemporary policies aimed at increasing system hardening through sentence enhancements and increases in discretion among prosecutors and the police have led to a systemic shift: from discriminatory practices that are contextual based to practices that are today systemic. Research conducted in the 1980s and early 1990s could reasonably conclude that discrimination was contextual. However, practices in the justice system from the mid 1980s through the current period, particularly the "war on drugs" and associated increases in prosecutorial and police discretion, have transformed these contextual factors into general, systemic patterns.

The discretionary nature of criminal justice system practices has been noted extensively in criminal justice literature. The presence of discretion is not a new event; it has always been central to system processes. Kleinig (1996:1) observed:

> In an American Bar Foundation (ABF) survey of 1956, it was discovered that at each stage of an individual's encounter with the criminal justice system the outcome was determined by a decision that was essentially "discretionary" in nature.

This quote is full of meaning. It recognizes that discretion is and has been accepted practice in system processes. Equally importantly is the perception that discretionary decisions—not rationally based decision-making—affected future involvement in decisional processes.

How can discretionary decisionmaking be racially biased even if not intended? Subtle cultural processes account for the discriminatory bent of criminal justice decisionmakers. These processes have been labeled the "tautology of common sense" (Crank, 1998:171) within the culture of justice organizations that accounts for the widespread discriminatory practices. According to this idea, common sense is a particular way of looking at work, arising from experiences and events shared with other professionals. In the form of anecdotes and stories, it tells professionals what kind of people they are probably dealing with, what kind of behavior to anticipate, and how to treat them.

Common sense exists in a reciprocal relationship with action (McNulty, 1994). On the one hand, common sense can be seen as causal to action: common sense provides a sensibilities to think about likely behavior. However, police behavior is intended also to produce a response, one that makes a situation manageable for an officer. The tautology is that common sense is both used to guide the action to a certain outcome, and once the outcome occurs, used to verify the appropriateness of the behavior. Common sense is consequently a self-fulfilling prophecy.

Members of justice cultures, acting on common sense ideas of the anticipated behavior of suspects and reconstructing the encounters using their common-sense way of looking at things, sharply limits their ability to see how their behavior predisposes the outcome of encounters with suspects and citizens. Common sense, central to police culture, consequently permits and indeed can encourage racial stereotyping, even among African-American police, and even when the officers themselves are certain of their lack of racist tendencies. It is a very difficult tautology to break.

When criminal justice actors are permitted wide discretion, they will inevitably fall back on their common sense ways of thinking through problems. And part of that common sense lore is the belief that minority group members are committing more crime than Anglos. Consequently, as the LCCR observes,

> There is a self-perpetuating, cyclical quality to the treatment of black and Hispanic Americans in the criminal justice system. Much of the unfairness visited on these groups stems from the perceptions of criminal justice decisionmakers that (1) most crimes are committed by minorities, and (2) most minorities commit crimes. Although empirically false, these perceptions cause a disproportionate share of law enforcement attention to be directed at minorities, which in turn leads to more arrests of blacks and Hispanics. Disproportionate arrests fuel prosecutorial and judicial decisions that disproportionately affect minorities and result in disproportionate incarceration rates and prison lengths for those minorities. The accumulated effect is to create a prison population in which blacks and Hispanics increasingly predominate, which in turn lends credence to the misperceptions that justify racial profiling and "tough on crime" policies (LCCR, 2000:43).

DWB and the Problem of Context. The difficulty in determining whether criminal justice practices are contextual or systemic is revealed in the "DWB" controversy. Consider the case of DWB, an acronym for "driving while black." The charge DWB has been made by defendants who charge that police routinely pull over African-American motorists. In recent years, DWB has become of interest to the courts. Consider the following four cases, cited by Roberg, Crank and Kuykendall (2000) and Cole (1999).[4]

> Eleven black motorists have filed a lawsuit in federal court, charging the Maryland State Police with using race as a factor in automobile stops and searches. The lawsuit charges that the police, in their zest to find illegal drugs and weapons, are selectively stopping automobiles because they believe that African-Americans are more likely to be involved in crime. A federal judge had ruled in the previous April (1998) that a police barrack in northeast Maryland targeted African-American motorists along I-95 in a "pattern and practice of discrimination" (Roberg, Crank & Kuykendall, 2000:281).

Racial profiling emerges as a problem in New Jersey. A 1996 state court finding observed that, although nearly all drivers exceed the 55 miles per hour speed limit, troopers pull over a disproportionate numbers of minorities. Maryland statistics indicated that 73 percent of motorists stopped and searched along I-95 were African-American, although they made up only 14 percent of al motorists. In an incident on April 23, 1999. New Jersey state police are accused of using racial profiles in a routine stop of a van with minority occupants. African-American and Hispanic men were shot in this incident. The police and the vehicle's occupants gave sharply different accounts of events. The incident is under investigation (Roberg, Crank & Kuykendall, 2000:282).

Volusa County, Florida, 1992: Nearly 70 percent of those stopped on an interstate highway in Florida were Latino or African-American, and were 80 percent of the cars searched after being stopped. Only five percent of the drivers were Latino or African-American (Cole, 1999:41).

Louisiana: A training film encouraged the State Police to carry out pre-textual stops against "males of Foreign nationalities, mainly Cubans, Colombians, Puerto Ricans, and other swarthy outlanders (Cole, 1999:41).

Federal judges often refer to sentencing standards when imposing sentences. However, in a case in December 1998, a judge departed from sentencing standards regarding criminal history because she thought that a Black defendant's criminal history reflected a pattern of discriminatory treatment.

In the case of *United States v. Leviner*, the judge had before her a defendant who had pleaded guilty to illegally possessing a firearm. He had been out joyriding, and had fired the weapon. The sentencing guidelines would have put Leviner in prison for 46 to 57 months. However, the judge noted that Leviner's criminal history was mostly comprised of driving-related charges. Regarding the traffic charges, the judge asked "What drew the officer's attention to Leviner in the first place?" This case falls into a category of police behavior widely believed to be discriminatory, called "DWB" or driving while black (Bumner, 1999).

Some states, in order to find out if their police officers are practicing DWB, are requiring departments to collect data on the race and ethnicity of all citizens stopped. North Carolina and Connecticut currently require such information. At the time of this writing, California is considering Senate Bill 78, which mandates the collection of annual figures on the "race, age, and gender of motorists stopped by the California Highway Patrol, and whether a search and arrest was made as a result of the stop" (Hutchinson, 1999). Departments in San Jose, San Francisco, Oakland, and San Diego have begun collecting such data.

Is the practice of DWB indicative of contextual or systemic discrimination? One can argue from the examples that it is contextual. This does not mean that its importance is lessened: The United States is a big country and some contexts are quite large. However, the examples cited above may represent only those places where covert police behavior has been uncovered. In the early 1990s, the relatively few instances of DWB reasonably led to the conclusion that it was a contextualized practice. As additional cases were discovered, it became increasingly reasonable to conclude that DWB was a systemic practice. Facilitated by the relaxation of discretionary and legal controls on police stop and search procedures under the current anti-drug campaigns, it stands out as an example of how a practice first becomes contextualized and later expands to systemic proportions.

It has been suggested that profiles are legitimate if race is one of many factors, because the overall profile is indicative of criminality and race is not the only factor. Yet, a review of such profiles reveals that race is the only profile elements that is trait based—the remainder are based on behavior (Kennedy, 1999). Moreover, research is beginning to emerge that the core reason for profiles that include race—that particular minority group members are indeed more likely to be involved in the vehicular transport of drugs—is fallacious. In New York City, for example, a study of stop-and-frisk practices found that although "police disproportionately stopped young black men, the hit rates were actually higher for whites than for blacks or Latinos. Similarly, for custom service searches in 1998, 43 percent of those searched were black or Latino, while "illegal materials were found on 6.7 percent of whites, 6.3 percent of blacks, and 2.8 percent of Latinos (Cole & Lamberth, 2001:1). Cole and Lamberth observed that drug use and dealing were evenly distributed among the population. Where agencies took remedial steps to abandon the use of racial identifiers, the proportion of stops that became hits improved sharply. Racial profiling, in other words, is ineffective and results in an increased liability for African-Americans.

Conclusion: The Pervasiveness of Race. Racial categorization and stereotyping permeates criminal justice practices. In the discussion of DWB above, we can see two distinct yet intertwined aspects of it. Police organizations are suspected of using race as a basis for routine traffic stops. Police reformers, on the other hand, want race data collected in order to assess the behavior of those organizations. Hence, for both groups, the concept of "race" and collection of data about it are integral to their political concerns and organizational behavior. This example shows how deeply infused the conception of race is in U.S. society.

Race has been and will continue to be central to our most fundamental issues of justice. And difficulties in eradicating its effects will undoubtedly endure. The presence of contextual effects should be considered in relation to our highly fragmented political system. With tens of thousands of criminal justice agencies existing at all governmental levels—municipal, county, state, and federal—it is doubtful that discrimination biases can be combated simply. Discrimination in criminal justice agencies flows from the views and practices of its employees, which in turn are a consequence of local and regional attitudes and perspectives about the meanings of race. Change, to occur, must consequently be carried out by local actors, in local agencies, one agency at a time.

A great deal of change is needed to remove the pernicious effects of race from justice practices. Consider the following observation from a Fourth District Judge in Ada County, Idaho in 2000:

> The 4th District judge . . . told voters in Idaho Falls over the weekend that analysis of the specific circumstances of each capitol crime shows there is no statistical difference in the imposition of the death penalty across income or racial lines.
>
> When blacks kill whites, [the judge] said, it is often during the commission of a crime. But when whites kill blacks, he said, they often know each other and the murder is committed in a heated moment, a circumstance that carries a lesser sentence than murder committed during a crime like theft. "Whites killing blacks tended to be people who had a relationship with each other," said [the judge] (Idaho Statesman, 4b May 9, 2000).

Does this judge truly think that, when whites befriend African-Americans, they are taking their lives into their hands? Does he understand how he advocates racial segregation? We elect our judges, and their "common-sense" attitudes reflect our sentiments. If we as a people are to become free of the harm caused by racial predispositions on discretionary decisions made by police, prosecutors, and judges, we as a people are going to have to do better than we have done thus far. We still have a very long way to go.

Part II: Ethnicity

What Is Ethnicity? If race is difficult to define, ethnicity is an equally fractured concept, capturing such disparate notions as historical predisposition, group culture, administrative labels, identity formation, body features, and individual behaviors. When people apply for jobs, they fill out forms that request that they mark a box identifying their ethnicity or race. When we read crime reports, newspapers routinely report the ethnicity of the suspect or the victim. In the social sciences, researchers routinely look for distinguishing ethnic attitudes, behaviors, or patterns of treatment from other groups. In all of these cases, ethnicity is used as a symbolic, economic, and cultural marker. It distinguishes "us" from "them," provides the basis for social and justice policy, determines marketing strategies, and affects employment opportunities and salary levels.

American life is dense with ethnic (and racial) distinctions in all areas of its social and cultural life. We common-sensically tend to use the term "ethnic" when visible traits, like skin color or hair tone, are not sufficiently different for us to think differences are "racial." Many Anglos refer to African-Americans as a "race" and to Latinos as an "ethnicity." And what are "Anglos?" A race? Several races? Several ethnic groups? A punch-hole in an administrator's record-keeping system?

Ethnicity is often used as a gloss to identify groups that are threateningly different, without clarity concerning what that difference is. The term ethnicity is freighted with occulted meaning—to be a member of an ethnic group carries baggage of minority status, disenfranchisement, perhaps a claim to historical repression and identity. Ethnicity can be a marker of inequality and political powerlessness, carrying hints of something that is "less." How often do we see the words *ethnic* and *minority* together, for example?

For some, the justice task is to enfranchise those who, because of ethnic identity, are excluded from participation in U.S. economic and/or social life. For others, ethnicity carries concerns about group conflict, violence, terrorism, and resistance to assimilation. And there are those who deny the relevance of ethnicity, arguing that equality under the law is more important that legal recognition of difference. As with race, ethnicity is an illusive and complex concept, one in which we as a democratic peoples are all implicated by virtue of our social arrangements, demographic relations, cultural practices, and immigration policies.

It is easier to frame ethnicity by first discussing what it is not. Ethnicity is not about biological difference, though some ethnic groups may lay claim to biological or trait distinctiveness. We sometimes use ethnicity as a way to think about fundamental underlying, biologically determined trait differences between ourselves and other kinds of people. But ethnicity is not bounded by genetic distinctiveness, at least not in the sense that different ethnic groups are somehow biologically distinct in a trait-based way. Indeed, ethnic identity may arise as a way for groups to distinguish themselves and to give their actions purpose in spite of cultural and historical similarity with neighboring groups.

Nor should ethnicity be viewed only as an administratively created label, although it is widely used for that purpose. We may encounter such terms as "Asian-American," for example, in employment applications. This term serves broader governmental purposes, and assists in the carrying out of governmental policy. But Asian-Americans are not an ethnicity—the organizing term "Asian-American" is so diffuse it encompasses groups that do not even share a common language or cultural traditions.

Ethnicity cannot be understood only in common-sense ideas of a group's history or emergence from some primitive state. Sometimes, groups will seek identity in the following form; *We are (ethnicity) because we all came from (historical source)*. However, these views are often as not the product of mythic identity formation, and emerge as a product of immigration or forced relocation in order to create group identity in troubled times.

Ethnicity becomes sensible against the backdrop of modern social and demographic processes. European and Soviet decolonization, nation-state attempts to impose inclusive identities, international media that threaten local moralities, contemporary stratification processes and migration and resettlement all contribute to the modern-day formation of ethnic groups. Indeed, rather than reflecting historical continuity, ethnicity may is often a response to the breakup of the old order and the subsequent formation of disadvantaged groups around mythical historical identities (Bell, 1975). Hence, though ethnic groups may have strong ties to the past, their formation may be precipitated by quite modern processes.

Ethnicity *is* about symbols, distinctiveness, and identity. The following discussion, adapted from Eller (1999), provides an overview of the concept of ethnicity.

Eller and the Idea of Ethnicity. The idea of ethnicity is multifaceted. One of those facets is culture, and ideas of cultural uniqueness are central to ethnic identity. A component of this identity is a set of values or ideology of cultural origin, continuity and difference from other groups. The idea or memory of common origin is subjective: the objective demonstration of kinship and blood linkage is an incidental consideration. This means that groups may not in fact have real historical traditions. Ethnic identity can suddenly spring forth where no identity previously existed.

Ethnicity organizes group beliefs and ideologies, even if the belief is unrelated to an objective characteristic of the group (Eriksen, 1993). Ethnicity exists where ethnic differences are perceived by members of a group, and requires no objective measure to clarify what those differences are. Ethnicity can be defined in the following way:

> . . . I am talking about a social and psychological process whereby individuals come to identify and affiliate with a group and some aspect(s) of its culture; ethnicity is then what emerges when a person, as affiliated, completes the statement: "I am a _____ because I share _____ with my group. Ethnicity is consciousness of difference and the subjective salience of that difference. It is also mobilization around difference—a camaraderie with or preference for socially similar others (Eller, 1999:8-9).

Ethnicity also invokes historical identity, though in a subjective way. Weber (1968:389), defined ethnicity as "those human groups that entertain a subjective belief in their common descent because of similarities of physical type or customs or both, or because of memories of colonization or and migration; conversely it does not matter whether or not an objective blood relationship exists." The central characteristic of this definition is the presence of a culture: cultural traditions provide an image or memory of the original or true condition of the group.

Ethnicity is very much about a group's perception of their past. The concept of the ethnic past is multi-vocal—it carries several meanings.

1. *Past as tradition or cultural past.* The past is a strong presence for people in many parts of the world. It is difficult for Anglo-Americans to understand the pull of the past, Eller observes, because their national memory is short. An ethnic group without a memory of and ties to its cultural past is unthinkable, even though the past may be a contemporary creation rather than measurable historical artifact.

2. *Past as history.* This is the record of actual (or believed to be actual) events that happened. For many ethnic groups, history can be broken down into three stages, ancient history, colonial past, and recent past. Groups with a limited store of or access to ancient history will sometimes actively seek to reconstruct it. Many ethnic groups were brought together during colonial periods. One of the effects of European colonialism was to bring diffuse groups into contact by the imposition of "nation-state" systems in Africa, thus increasing group identity and conflict. Europe does not stand alone—this phenomenon is also true for periods of Russian and Ottoman imperialism. Recent history has been marked by efforts toward self-determination in many parts of the world.

3. *Past as myth.* Myth carries its anthropological meaning of remote and unprovable history. Myths can, and frequently do, include ideas concerning origin, migration, liberation, descent, of an heroic age, decline, conquest, exile, of rebirth, and of a summons to action (Gurr & Harff, 1994:12-13). Myth is consequently not about objective truth, but about how the development of group cohesiveness and identity. The power of myth does not lie in its historical accuracy, but in its important contributions to group identity.

4. *Past as resource.* The past in this sense refers to the "useable" past. It provides cultural and historical symbols to identify with and rally around. Eller referred to this as its "charter" function. This part of the past also provides groups with backdrop against which to understand the present, and particularly importantly, a claim on the future. The past, in this sense, becomes a resource in political, economic, and cultural struggles (Roosens, 1989). In other words, the past, practically applied to group struggles, is a powerful tool in efforts for a group to achieve political recognition and strength.

These diverse ideas of "past" reveal the complexity of meanings that comprise ethnicity. The ethnic past is more textured with meaning than some objective description of common heritage. In the study of ethnicity we become aware of the rich and multivocal ways peoples look at their history. In the language of the methods chapter, the past is *intentional*—its meaning lies in relation to the current groups sense of identity and uniqueness, needs, and world-view. Its objective relationship to some historically objective *out there* is a secondary consideration.

Gurr: Ethnicity and Accommodation. One of the central issues addressed in this chapter is how different groups come to terms with their nation-states, and how dominant groups adapt to ethnic diversity. This is an issue of considerable importance to the field of justice studies, whose graduates are often responsible for policing the boundaries between different groups. Gurr (1993) presented an analysis of the world wide status of minorities and the way in which dominant regimes accommodated or resisted their interests. Gurr (see also Gurr & Harff, 1994) used the term "communal groups" to describe those groups for whom "the shared perception of the defining traits, whatever they are, set the group apart." [3] He identified six kinds of communal groups.

1. *Ethnonationalists.* These are groups who historically were autonomous, and have pursued nationalist objectives over the past 50 years. The Croats and the East Timorese, both of whom have pursued separatist agendas in the 1990s, represent such groups.

2. *Indigenous peoples.* These include native aborigines in Australia and native American Indians. All have lived a preindustrial existence until quite recently. Their political actions have typically been reactive, seeking to regain control of that which was lost.

3. *Ethnoclasses.* These are ethnically or culturally distinct minorities, often descended from slaves, who specialize in distinct, typically low status economies. Afro-Americans in many places in Latin America represent such groups.

4. *Militant sects.* These are politicized minority groups who are defined wholly or substantially by their religious beliefs. Islamic minorities in countries dominated by other religious traditions represent such groups, as do Jews in Argentina.

5. *Communal contenders.* These are found primarily in Africa, with a few in Asia and the Middle East. These exist where political power is based on intergroup coalitions. Disadvantaged communal contenders are subjected to economic or political discrimination. Advantaged communal contenders are dominant minorities with economic advantages. Some of the most devastating wars are in countries where no groups has dominance and communal contenders are unable to reach power-sharing agreements (Gurr, 1993:15-23).

Gurr considered the economic relationships between communal groups, their access to the political apparatus in their countries, their relative poverty, and patterns of conflict and accommodation in their resident nation-states. In the United States, Gurr observed that there were three communal groups who constituted "minorities at risk." By risk, he meant that these groups have collectively experienced systematic discrimination from dominant nation-state groups. African-Americans and Latinos were identified as "ethnoclasses," and were distinguished from

Native Americans whom he located in the category called native peoples. These three groups have been able to achieve a limited measure of political power in the United States, which has a history of pluralistic sharing of power. However, their power is limited: political backlashes have offset some of the political gains made by these groups. Of the three, Latinos may be emerging in the United States as a genuine communal contender, both because of dramatic population increases among this population and because of a powerful political and economic ally in Mexico. In many regions in the United States today, Latinos are increasingly political active, and are growing in their economic power as well. Migration policies, a high birth rate, and economic gains facilitated by NAFTA insure the continued political expansion of Latino influence into the twenty-first century.

Political power, Gurr noted, did not always translate into increased economic well-being. An example is the Civil Rights movement in the 1960s. Efforts at political mobilization of African-American citizens, though achieving political gains in the late 1960s and early 1970s, faced a backlash against equal rights laws, particularly in hiring and promotion policies in the 1980s and the 1990s. This backlash, Gurr suggested, prevented African-Americans from translating political gains into economic well-being. They were, Gurr observed, "culturally differentiated and materially deprived but are politically empowered." [144]. The continued de facto specter of discrimination has led many African-Americans to resist ideological assimilation and to pursue a path toward ethnic separatism. Gurr described the contemporary status of Latino and African-American "ethno-class" in the United States as follows:

> Historically, dominant groups defined the ethnoclasses as inferior peoples, which helped justify the discriminatory practices that kept them at the bottom of the status ladder. Such attitudes are still widespread among Europeans and North Americans and provide support for xenophobic and racist political movements. The liberal alternative, integration, coupled with policies designed to overcome disadvantage, has had mixed success: some ethnoclass members have chosen assimilation. . . , others have not. Preferences seem to be shifting toward multiculturalism, in which ethnoclasses (and indigenous peoples) maintain distinct identities in plural societies that guarantee all peoples equality of status and treatment (Gurr, 1993:171).

We can see from Gurr's exposition of ethnoclass formation that the development of ethnic identity is not a simple consequence of historical identity. In a causative sense, it stems from patterns of systematic disadvantage in its current economic setting. The past provided a model for the formation of identity after, not before, struggles against economically dominant groups.

Indigenous peoples—American Indians in the United States—are in a different position than the ethnoclasses vis-à-vis political remedies for historical grievances. Often having substantial local autonomy, they are more likely to obtain a local remedy to their demands. They also tend to have some resources in their regional areas. Their political successes, however, tend to be locally based and do not contribute into more national influence

Indigenous rights movements in the United States are accommodated within a framework of democratic pluralism. Political empowerment, however, has not led to a narrowing of social and economic differences with the political mainstream. Indigenous peoples have often lacked the public funding and private capitol to build their economic base. They are frequently located in marginal areas. When they have natural resources in those areas may have to contend with powerful economic interests, such as oil and lumber industry, for control of their resources. Thus, equality of rights and accommodation has not lead to an escape from economic disadvantage, and has made them vulnerable to exploitation. Hence, both ethnoclasses and indigenous peoples are well situated in the United States to obtain a full panoply of legal rights, and generally have done so in most circumstances, but have not been able to convert political influence into economic gain.[5]

Ethnicity and the Multicultural Debate

Gurr's formulation is international in scope, focusing on world-wide relations among diverse groups. For many people in the United States, ethnicity is a personal concern experienced by the in-migration of new and different peoples into their communities. They may welcome difference or fear it, recognizing that migration will bring unknown changes. How are contacts between locals and immigrants resolved? Will contacts between "locals" and "immigrants" lead to accommodation and blending of differences? Or will it further the perceptions of differences between the two groups and contribute to identity formation in each group and intergroup conflict (Coser, 1956). In this section, we consider issues related to the way the distinct but overlapping categories of immigrants and minorities are accommodated in the United States.

Multiculturalism Part 1: Melting Pot or Distinctiveness? One of the controversial issues in modern times lies in how locals—by locals I mean residents who perceive themselves to be established in a particular area—think immigrants should adapt to local ways of life. Do immigrants have a responsibility to merge into a common American identity, the "melting pot" perspective? Or should they be encouraged to go their own way, maintaining their ethnic and cultural identities?

The assimilation/multi-ethnic debate is rancorous. In a class at Harvard, Glazer (1997:96) noted the negative reaction of the students at the use of the word "assimilation." To the students, the word assimilation and its metaphor "melting pot" connoted a "forced conformity and reminds people today not of the welcome in American society but of the demands it makes on those it allows to enter." Why had assimilation, a once-proud conception of American identity, taken such a beating in recent years? Glazer captured the mystique and attraction of assimilation in the following quote:

> What was assimilation? It was the expectation that a new man would be born, was being born, in the United States. We can go back to that much quoted comment on what was the American, in Crèvecoeur's *Letters From an American Farmer* of 1782. "What then is the American, this new man? He is either a European or a descendant of a European, hence that strange mixture of blood, which you will find in no other country. I could point out to you a family whose grandfather was an Englishman, whose wife was Dutch, whose son married a French woman, whose present four sons have four wives of four different nations. *He* is an American, who, leaving behind him all his ancient prejudices and manners, receives new ones from the new mode of life he has embraced, the new government he obeys, and the new rank he holds."[6]

This passage, Glazer observed, has been widely cited to commemorate American diversity. Glazer continued:

> In 1996 we look at it (the passage above) with more critical eyes, and note what it does not include as well as what it does; There is no references to Negroes or blacks, who then made up a one-fifth of the American population, or to American Indians, who were then still a vivid and meaningful, on occasion menacing, presence in the colonies. In the course of an examination of the idea of assimilation in American history, we will find many other passages which to our contemporary eyes will express a similarly surprising unconsciousness, or hypocrisy, or unawareness. Today, we would cry out "There are others you are not talking about! What about them, and what place will they have in the making of the new American?" (Glazer, 1997:97-98).

The two indented quotes above show that the way we think about ethnicity is mutable. The latter view shows how ideas of assimilation have changed over time, as immigration has fostered an increasingly non-European multi-ethnic society. Certainly, ethnicity in the United States at the end of the twentieth century is marked by dramatic change. Figure 6.1 below provides a sense of current and anticipated levels of the major groupings in the United States.

Figure 6.1
U.S. Population by Race and Ethnicity, 2000, 2025, and 2050

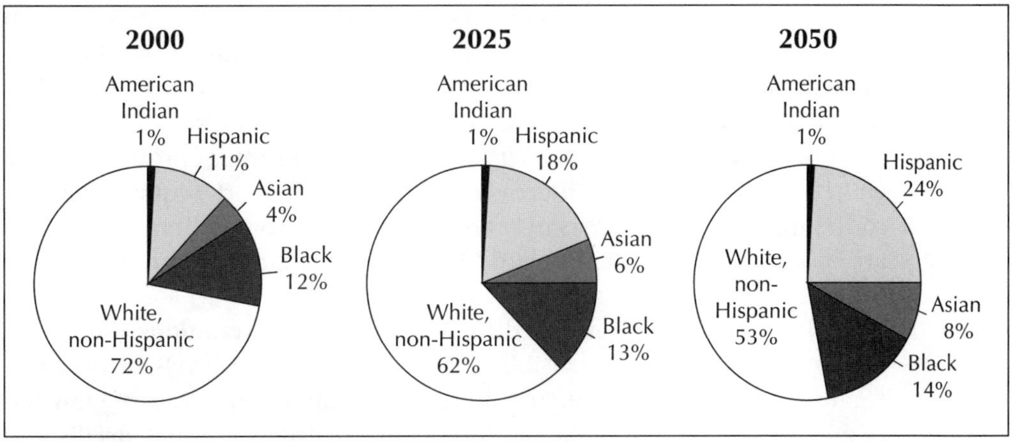

Source: Martin, P. and E. Midgley (1999). "Immigration to the United States." *Population Bulletin*, p. 23 Washington, DC: Population Reference Bureau 54-2.

Multiculturalism Part II: Democracy and the Nature of Rights

Justice is a goods that is provided to citizens as part of governance. In a multicultural setting, the nature of justice becomes extraordinarily complex. This complexity is discussed in this section.

To frame the issue of multicultural rights, we need to begin with a consideration of the rights government provides for all U.S. citizens. A large body of due process law creates a legal entity—an individual—and endows the individual with a basic set of rights. It is a conception of democracy that carries the idea of "individual rights and individual legal persons as the bearer of rights" (Habermas, 1994). The bill of rights surrounds the individual with a swath of protections against state intrusion that further expand the legal definition of individuals. But what is it that the government should protect?

At the center of the multicultural debate is a dialogue about what it means to be a democracy. To most people, democracy is about citizens' rights to life, liberty, and the pursuit of happiness. But what does the "pursuit of happiness" mean? Consider religion. Does democracy mean that one have an unabridged right to worship as one pleases, with the government taking a rigidly neutral stand? Or is one's pursuit of happiness provided when the government in some way protects the circumstances of worship, for example, by giving a particular religion or group of religions a property tax deduction?

If democracy is viewed as rigidly neutral, the government is concerned only with providing individuals with what is considered a primary good, the right to worship as one pleases. If the government believes that particular faiths carry core cultural values, the government might act to protect them. In that case the government is no longer neutral—it is identifying a particular cultural tradition as a primary goods. Hence, culture itself becomes one of the primary goods that government protects. As the United States becomes increasingly multicultural, the questions surrounding such laws increasingly are (1) are there core cultural values that are essential for U.S. identity, and (2) if so, whose cultural traditions are to be protected?

Within a society dominated by Anglo-American traditions, issues like the one above were less visible. However, increasing levels of multiculturalism and the accompanying diversity of values and points of view has begun to highlight hidden or unrecognized Anglo cultural predispositions. From English-only language conflicts to hate crimes legislation, the debate over whether mainstream, minority, ethnic, or gendered groups have certain rights that pertain to them as a culture is intense.

The multicultural issue can be stated as follows: Is the right to a *secure cultural context* among the primary goods provided by democratic society? Are African-Americans, for example, to be protected *as a group* from the destructive effects of economic discrimination? Should Christians be permitted to place a lighted cross on a hillside plainly visible to all citizens, including non-Christians? If the land on which the cross is public, can it be sold to a private religious organization for the purpose of creating a publicly visible religious display? Should pagans be similarly permitted to publicly celebrate Yule, for example, by burning an oak log to celebrate the return of the oak king on December 22? Should Spanish be taught in schools in California? Conversely, should the English language be legally mandated as a general cultural goods, or should we permit Spanish or French, the two other officially recognized languages on the North American continent, to also be required in a bilingual or multilingual format? The argument extends to the academic world: Should the canon of required reading in the University setting be defined by great works of American, European, and Greek authors, or should we leave the issue of canon open and undefined, permitting and even encouraging the teaching of works from groups historically unrecognized in academe?

When we consider the above questions, it is important to recognize that democracy is not being compared to non-democracy. Different notions of democracy are being compared to each other. Consider the example of the lighted cross. A democratic argument against the lighted cross is that society should be committed in the strongest possible way to neutrality in the pursuit of religion, which means that the government remains wholly outside the realm of religion. However, another view can be stated as well—the will of the public is favorable to the location of the cross in a visible setting. This will can be advanced as long as other faiths are provided with a general right to worship. A democratic argument for the lighted cross is that a society can be committed to the flourishing of a particular groups values as long as they do not disdain the values of other groups. From this, we have two notions of democracy, one in which the government is neutral to religious activities, and one views its responsibility as nurturing and protecting a particular idea of faith while protecting a basic core of rights for all faiths.

Walzer: Liberalism 1 and Liberalism 2. Walzer (1994:99) described these two notions of democracy as liberalism 1 and liberalism 2. Liberalism 1 "is committed in the strongest possible way to individual rights . . . and to a rigorously neutral state, that is, a state without cultural or religious projects . . . " Liberalism 2 "allows for a state committed to the survival and flourishing of a particular nation, culture, or religion . . . so long as the basic rights of citizens who have different commitments or no such commitments at all are protected." Liberalism 1, in the above example, is the democratic argument against the lighted cross. Liberalism 2 is an argument for the lighted cross.

For the most part, the United States is a liberalism 1 type country. The United States has been called a procedural republic (Sandel, 1984). This means that government is neutral with regard to what goals (their idea of the "good life") individuals or groups pursue. Government does not place particular group goods ahead of another groups. Its power as a democracy is that it takes no position about the pursuit of "primary goods," (those things that enable the "good life") only positions about procedures that enable citizens to seek those goods.

The idea of "primary goods" covers both physical well-being such as health care and basic rights such as the right to free association. Guttman (1994) describes proceduralism and primary goods as follows:

> It is the neutrality of the public sphere, which includes not only government agencies but also institutions like Princeton and other liberal universities, that protects our freedom and equality as citizens. On this view, our freedom and equality as citizens refer only to our common characteristics—our universal needs, regardless of our particular cultural identities, for "primary goods" such as income, health care, education, religious freedom, freedom of conscience, speech, press and association, due process, the right to vote, and the right to hold public office. These are interests shared by almost all people regardless of our particular race, religion, ethnicity, or gender. And therefore public institutions need not—indeed should not—strive to recognize our particular cultural identities in treating us as free and equal citizens (Guttman, 1994:4).

It carries liberalism not only as procedural issue, but as moral belief, what Taylor (1994) called a "fighting creed." Consider the following description of liberalism.

> For liberals like Dewey, the good life is a process, a way of interacting with the world, and of solving problems, that leads to ongoing individual growth and social transformation. One realizes the end of life, the good life, each and every day by living with the liberal spirit, showing equal respect to all citizens, preserving an open mind, practicing tolerance, cultivating a sympathetic interest in the needs and struggles of others, imagining new possibilities, protecting basic human rights and freedoms, solving problems with a method of intelligence in a nonviolent atmosphere pervaded by a spirit of cooperation.
>
> Liberal democratic politics are strong and healthy only when a whole society is pervaded by the spirit of democracy—in the family, in the school, in business and industry, and in religious institutions as well as political institutions. The moral meaning of democracy is found in reconstructing all institutions so that they become instruments of human growth and liberation (Rockefeller, 1994:91).

In other words, the neutrality of Liberalism 1 is not an abandonment of values, but itself carries powerful ideas of the good life guaranteed by government neutrality. It is a morality that refuses to accept as final any particular group's answers regarding stubborn questions of religion or politics. It finds personal growth in an open mind, in thinking through problems, in an unformulaic outlook on the world.

Liberalism 2 is not rigidly neutral. It allows government the legal "space" to protect preferred cultural values, as long as a basic body of rights protects all groups. It can be called a value-based liberalism. The central argument of Liberalism 2 is that culture itself is one of the primary goods protected by society.

Why should culture be considered a primary good? Taylor (1994) presented the following argument for making culture one of the primary goods that government can justifiably protect. He observed that people are fundamentally social, what he called "dialogical." By dialogical, he stated that we only become fully human through our rich and diverse ways of communicating and interacting with our significant others. Our minds are dialogical: they are not independent, truly individual entities, but in constant internal and external dialogue with others. Even when we reflect on problems and develop attitudes and opinions about things, we do so in internal dialogue with others, even if it is dialogue against their point of view.

Our dialogues continue throughout our lives. Even after we have developed mature and self-responsible identities, those around us continue to affirm or deny our various outlooks. Through our interactions with others we continue to grow. We also seek relationships with others to fulfill our outlooks and our values. Hence, our identity, in the most core sense of the term, is dialogical through and through. We become fully human through the development and use of language in the broadest sense, in all our expressions of art, love, sharing, communicating.

Our values and the culture that creates and sustains them are critically important to who we are. Then why shouldn't some cultural elements—those of central importance to individual identity—be recognized as a primary good guaranteed by society, recognized by government to be as important to us as health care or the right to assembly? Why should a citizen not be able to place a cross on the hill as long as he or she insures that other groups efforts to practice their religion are protected by a basic core of constitutional protections?

The notion of a dialogical self is consistent with Liberalism 2. From the perspective of Liberalism 1, however, Liberalism 2 appears to be a betrayal of principle (Taylor, 1994:40). Liberalism 2, when used to rectify historical mistreatment of minority or disadvantaged groups, is seen by its opponents as hypocracy and a failure of egalitarian democratic principles. When used to support affirmative action practices, for example, proponents of Liberalism 1 contend that Liberalism 2 is reverse discrimination. Affirmative action is an effort to protect a particular population from a history of mistreatment, to "level the playing field" by providing a jobs-based remedy. It is, however, often resisted as a practice that promotes favoritism of particular individuals over an objective, neutral skills, and qualifications-based evaluation.

Advocates of Liberalism 2 argue that the opposite is also true—when a de facto history of discrimination or mistreatment exists, Liberalism 1 does not provide a mechanism for its resolution. If particular groups have suffered a history of discrimination, then minimal changes in the law that fail to redress economic or social inequality may be unacceptable under a Liberalism 2 standard. Resistance to affirmative action, in the above example, is itself seen as proof that discrimination is embedded in informal cultural practices that the dominant groups resists abandoning.

Both Liberalism 1 and Liberalism 2 are present in the behavior of the criminal justice system. Liberalism 1 is carried in the idea that all individuals are equal before the law. The law is supposed to be rigorously neutral in its treatment of defendants in all of its proceedings. Justice is blind. Process rules are rigorously applied, and guilt or innocense is adjudicated regardless of who a person is or where he or she lives. However, Liberalism 2 is also present in the justice system. It is displayed in hate crimes legislation, which creates or enhances penalties for criminal acts against members of minority groups. Liberalism 2 is also revealed in victim rights legislation, which permits victims a special voice in determining penalties adjudicated by the courts or in deciding whether to provide a convict with early release from prison.

Liberalism 2 is not new to the criminal justice system. Historically, the United States has created a special dispensation for juveniles, treating them less severely than adults. In recent years, a trend has emerged toward treating juvenile offenders under the jurisdiction of adult courts if their offences are serious enough, a trend that is toward Liberalism 1. All of these examples are situations in which the law makes a decision about how to weigh the rights of groups (African-Americans, victims, juveniles) against a wholly neutral impartiality in which all are treated in the same way.

The conflict between Liberalism 1 and Liberalism 2 is profoundly ethical. Liberalism 1 is a fighting creed, a powerful corrective to central state authority, an idea that locates the purpose of the criminal justice system in the protection of its citizens from crime. Its ideological strength is in its neutrality; its refusal to take sides in disputes between different groups. Yet, as Warnke (1993) persuasively reminds us, all democratic systems carry powerful implicit meanings about what constitutes the good life, whether or not they officially proclaim neutrality. Habermas (1994) further cautioned that a set of constitutional rights always coexists with some notion of the common good We carry all sorts of beliefs and meanings that are reflected in the actual practice of democracy. Some of these may be very undemocratic. It should not be forgotten that the United States was founded not only as a republic but as a slaver society in which only propertied white males had the right to vote. Citizens today look back and recognize how contradictory slavery was with constitutional notions of Liberalism 1 equality. How will citizens look back 100 years from now at contemporary justice system practices?

Liberalism 2 provides a means to correct problems such as slavery or suffrage encountered in the way democracy is practiced. To use a more contemporary justice example, Liberalism 2 is displayed in hate crimes legislation aimed at adding an additional layer of legal protection for historically disadvantaged minority groups. Liberalism 2 will consequently always be controversial, because it uses seemingly inequitable ideas to reinforce democracy.

Liberalism 1 and Liberalism 2 are both products of liberalism and exist in fractious harmony with each other. The strength of Liberalism 1 is its location of the citizen as the primary outcome of governance, and its ability to fortify a philosophy of individual growth. Liberalism 1 tells us we are arriving at the promised land of democracy. Liberalism 2 reminds us that we're not there yet. The strength of Liberalism 2 is its ability to remedy the blind spots in the practice of democracy among fallible human populations. Together, they provide growth and perspective, energy and wisdom for Americans to think about their role in the changing world.

The Problem of Public Order in a Multicultural Society

The United States, Kaplan (1998) suggested, is becoming the first truly international civilization:

> . . . a vibrant America in the twenty-first century may become an America of "rooted cosmopolitans," reinventing itself in a larger world by

becoming history's first international nation (and the home of a value-driven international constabulary hunting down war criminals, plutonium terrorists, and so on), where the best and the brightest of Mexico and the other continents come to live and pay taxes . . ." (Kaplan, 1998:18).

For Kaplan, the internationalization of American society had profound implications for traditional notions such as the "melting pot" and the "common good." His observations of Kansas City, Missouri, are reminiscent of Glazer.

Kansas City, Missouri, like other American metropolises, is slowly separating out into economic and racial enclaves that have little in common with one another even as some of these enclaves become increasingly like those in Asia and Europe (Kaplan, 1998:16).

The world today is characterized by heightened interaction among peoples from trade, investment, tourism, media, and electronic media generally. Yet, increases in trade and communication, particularly since the end of the cold war, has not produced peace or security (Huntington, 1996). Increases in multiculturalism, as Eller (1999) suggested, can lead to an intensification of intra-ethnic identity.

Our history books have described the pattern of ethnic assimilation in the United States in terms of a melting pot idea. This means that groups are assimilated after immigrating to the United States, their distinctiveness and cultural uniqueness gradually disappearing. Over time, immigrants share common values and beliefs. Yet, the opposite may in fact occur. Huntington (1996) observed that cultural identities become more important with increased interactions between groups. He described this as distinctiveness theory (McGuire and McGuire, 1988) which means that people define themselves by what makes them different from others. Ethnic self-consciousness is intensified as diverse ethnic and cultural groups become more interdependent, a phenomenon Huntington called globalization theory (Robertson, 1987).

Both globalization and distinctiveness theory describe a very unmelting pot notion—that groups become more different as they interact with each other. Core cultural identities are based in religious beliefs, and increase contact has resulted, Huntington argues, in the rise of fundamentalism in and conflict between many of the worlds major religions. A global religious revival marks the onset of a "return to the sacred," in response to people's perception of the world as a single place (Huntington, 1996:68). If this is the case, there is a possibility that ethnic, religious, and cultural diversification will similarly result in internal conflicts in the United States (Crank & Caldero, 1999).

Kaplan also noted this phenomenon:

> An interconnected, globalized world seems to be encouraging the spread of Orthodox Judaism, as well as more extreme forms of Christianity, Islam, and other religions" (Kaplan, 1998:36).

The internationalization of the United States has implication for justice. If ethic groups are striving to maintain their uniqueness and cultural identity, then the justice task is enormously complicated. If a group has a clear cultural identity, then specific notions of morality and justice may be an important part its pre-existing cultural values. What if groups are thrown together with conflicting values? On what ethical basis do we conclude that one set of cultural values are correct and the others are wrong? How do we accept a common basis for the practice of justice? In the previous section, Liberalism 1 and 2 were presented as conflicting notions of democracy. This section takes a look at the issue that focuses specifically on the problem of public order in a multicultural society. When conflicts emerge among ethnic groups, how is public order to be kept?

Public order issues are among the most important problems that the criminal justice system has to deal with. Yet, the solution to problems of public order are unclear and complex. One popular strain of thought is the idea that police can act to assert informal ideas of order in troubled communities (see, e.g., Wilson & Kelling, 1982). However, the very absence of a shared notion of order makes this idea problematic. Problems of shared order emerge in communities without an informal standard of order, thus begging the question—from where do police gain a knowledge of some sort of order that supposedly exists in that community? (Mastrofski, 1991) Rieder (1985) discussed problems of shared order in Canarsie, where Jewish and Italian residents mobilized to resist African-American in-migration. Taft (1991) cited problems confronted by officers trying to police Cuban neighborhoods. Even where there appears to be common agreement on definitions of disorder, the police may be limited in their ability to do anything about it (Skogan, 1990). In the absence of shared order, the police are most likely to take the sides of the "haves" in a neighborhood, further contributing to the disenfranchisement of the "have-nots' (Bohm, 1984) or to assert their own particular morality (Crank & Caldero, 2000).

The justice system, with the police taking a leadership role, can negotiate order. By negotiate order is meant that:

> . . . they can provide a constructive environment and practical people-solving skills to negotiate solutions to commonly recurring people-problems—relations between landlords and tenants, between youth and oldsters, different ethnic and religious groups, the homeless and business, and traditional locals and recent arrivals (Crank & Caldero, 2000:210).

Negotiation applies to issues having to do with public order and how the state should comport itself in situations when public order becomes a problematic rather than a given. Different groups sometimes differing perceptions of justice and fair play. In order to peacefully coexist, some accounting of these differences needs to occur.

Justice professionals, whether they are police, the courts, or probation and parole personnel, should be prepared for work in a multi-ethnic country that contains contending and competing value systems. All the sorts of things that provide practical knowledge about different ethnic groups—language acquisition, communication skills, cultural practices, and the like—will contribute to order in the United States and should hold an important place in justice education.

Ethnicity, Crime, and the Criminal Justice System

The practice of criminal justice in a multicultural society is almost always controversial. Two contemporary issues central to multicultural-ism and criminal justice are (1) are immigrants more likely to commit crimes, and (2) is the criminal justice system biased against any or all minority groups? These two questions are discussed below.

Immigration and criminality. When criminality among immigrants are examined, no clear pattern of behavior emerges. Criminal behavior, when identified, appears to be contextualized by the process of immigra-tion and resettlement. This section begins with an overview of immigrants and criminality. Tonry (1997) provided several observations on crime among immigrant populations, listed below.

First, migrants from many Asian countries have lower rates of criminal activity than the resident population in the first and subsequent genera-tions. They have often been victims of bias in their new homelands, but they adapted differently to it, developing communities within ethnic enclaves.

Secondly, all else being equal, a country's policy for aiding the assimi-lation of immigrants can reduce crime rates not only for the arriving pop-ulation, but into the second and third generation of immigrants as well.

Third, reasons for migration powerfully shape the likelihood of suc-cessful adaption. Refugees, for example, may have suffered traumatic and negative psychological experiences such as apathy, lack of trust in per-sonal relationships, reduced self control, and social isolation. These prob-lems may lessen their ability to assimilate, increase their distrust of gov-ernmental authority, and increase problems of criminality.

Fourth, many immigrants fall into no predictable criminality pattern. For example, expatriate Hong Kong Chinese who relocated in Canada and the Pacific Northwest are "likely to be affluent and well educated, char-acteristics seldom associated with high crime rates" (Tonry, 1997:25).

Similarly, Americans who expatriated to Canada in protest to the Vietnam war were generally well-educated and middle-class, low-crime groups.

Sometimes immigration and crime are linked generationally, in that children of immigrants are widely believed to be more likely to commit crime. This is called the "second-generation" phenomenon. According to this idea, the children of immigrants tend to commit higher levels of crime than their parents. Waters (1999), in a meta-analysis of crime and immigrant youth, found that immigrant levels of crime were group specific—general conclusions could not be made about immigrants and crime. However, under particular conditions immigrant groups experienced crime increases among the second generation. These high levels of youthful crime generally disappears by the third generation. The emergence and desistance of crime was associated with three factors.

1. *The age structure* showed a high proportion of youth to immigrant elders, thus increasing the rate at which youth "unbecame" their immigrant traditions and were socialized into their local settings. Hence, youth could be predisposed to crime even while undergoing rapid socialization.

2. *The loss of traditional authority* undermined efforts of parents to maintain control. Traditional authority was lost in inverse proportion to the speed with which immigrant children adopted Western norms of behavior and language skills.

3. *The degree of social cohesion* provided an important community resource that forestalled the rapidity of the "unbecoming" process. Without cohesive resources within the immigrant community, a liminal state emerged in which second generation youth experience two legal normative states—one representing the traditional culture, and the other representing the new culture. Immigrant youth moved back and forth between the two states, depending on circumstances and personal advantage, and used local justice resources to protect themselves from more stringent traditional controls.

Waters recommended that the criminal justice system develop policy to reinforce local community controls. Rapid assimilation, rather than assisting immigrants, backfired. A policy aimed at reinforcing local immigrant parental controls over their youth would be more effective in reducing crime than practices that focused only on arrest and detention. By reinforcing cultural traditions, the police provided a measured pace of youthful assimilation into U.S. culture.

The various findings above reveal the inappropriateness in making general statements about the criminal behavior of immigrants. Can we state that immigrants reveal distinct patterns of criminality? Sometimes. Can we state that immigrants carry a criminal liability? Sometimes. Can we suggest that some immigrants assimilate rapidly and out-compete locals? Sometimes. How immigrants adapt to their new homeland depends on individual characteristics, the group's cultural characteristics, the crime studied, the assimilation policies of the new homeland, and the circumstances under which the group immigrated.

Bankston's (1998) research on southeast Asian gangs in the U.S. provides an overview of the complex processes involved in the immigration adaptation. Bankston identified three processes that linked immigration and gang formation:

Opportunity structure processes. central to this idea is that adolescents and young adults who are concentrated in cities are unable to find work due to a sharp decline in employment opportunities, and are disposed to joining gangs. Youth gangs are thus an alternative to economic organizations.

One source of economic opportunity for such groups is the sale and distribution of drugs. However, gang members may be heavy users of drugs, and not particularly disposed to their sales (Du Phuoc Long, 1996). Drug sales may provide extra cash to buy more drugs, but is an insufficient economic enterprise to provide a source of economic mobility. Another source is through robbery, extortion, and theft. Extortion may provide a predominant activity for Chinese gangs (Chin, Fagan & Kelley, 1992). House robbery is a preferred target for some Vietnamese gangs (Willoughby, 1993).

Bankston suggested that economic benefits are only a part of gang life, and that the seeking of social opportunities and prestige is more important. Many of the newer gang members are from groups who lack status and prestige among pre-1965 immigrant groups. Gang activity provides an expressive and social outlet for the formation of identity for these youth. however, social and economic structures cannot account for the ways peoples understand their experiences. Their histories and values affect their adaptation, and require a cultural approach.

Cultural processes. According to this approach, violent gangs represent a cultural response to the way they have adapted to low-income life. The particular behaviors they manifest reflect their life histories and cultural values—"norms interact with situational exigencies to produce varying outcomes" (Bankston, 1998:39).

Some observers of gangs, however, have observed a "cultural pidginization" effect—youth culture is marked by culturally diverse elements rather than reflecting the values of some particular ethnicity (Dannen, 1992). Gangs may be drawn from a broader youth culture, in the following way. The large-scale immigration fostered by the 1965 Immigration act brought members of diverse ethnic groups into conflict with each other and into conflict with previous ethnic groups. Communication between different groups fostered both exchange of cultural values as well as inter-group conflict. This youth culture is shared between already disadvantaged minorities and new immigrant groups (Bankston & Caldas, 1996). The intergroup competition between these groups in turn contributes to higher levels of violence.

Social Disorganization processes. According to this perspective, gangs are the product of the breakdown of social institutions brought about by rapid change. Social disorganization may stem from local communities' inabilities to express their residents' shared values (see also Bursik, 1988). One way in which shared values are undermined is through rapid immigration. Put simply, new and old groups may have little in common. School, an institution associated with socialization into the traditions of a community, can become a source of frustration because of language difficulties and conflicts with other ethnic groups. For Vietnamese children, the absence of extended family ties in the United States leads to a loss of parental authority (Du Phuoc Long, 1996).

If one pursues the idea of social disorganization to its logical conclusion, one is left, as Bankston (1998:42) observes, with a Hobbesian war of all against all. And, indeed, many gangs display attributes of "competitiveness, mistrust, self-reliance, social isolation, a survival instinct, and a Social Darwinist point of view" certainly Hobbesian traits. However, gang members form cohesive groups and are held together by loyalty. The gangs that result from social disorganization may reflect the emergence of a new social order, not simply the collapse of order.

Bankston's research allows us to understand how the immigration experience contributes to gang formation. His work has policy implications for criminal justice agencies. If the justice system seeks solutions to gang activities, it will likely be unsuccessful if it only focuses on suppressive strategies, which are likely to further mobilize cultural identities and increase gang formation. What it must do is recognize the way in which the immigration experience itself has contributed to maladaptive processes, and work with relocation, refugee, or immigration offices to contribute in a positive way to adaptation.

Ethnicity and justice practices. Tonry's (1997) assessment of justice practices in Western societies are considered here. International assessments of crime and ethnicity has found that racial and ethnic disparities in U.S. criminal justice processes are frequently paralleled in other countries. Below are, in summary form, are Tonry's findings with regard to these justice system processes.

1. Crime and incarceration rates for members of some minority groups greatly exceed those for the majority population. Disparities exist for both racial and ethnic minorities and for national origin minorities who are not visible racial minorities. These numbers, however, do not tell us about the kinds of crime they commit, and may in fact reveal demographic factors such as a large proportion of youth compared with the dominant population.

2. Minority groups with high levels of crime and imprisonment also display social and economic disadvantage.

3. In countries where the causes of crime and ethnic disparities in imprisonment have been studied, the explanation for differential crime appears to be group differences in offending rather than justice system bias. However, the bulk of this research has been done in the United States.

4. Seemingly neutral case processing practices, especially concerning pretrial confinement decisions and sentence reductions for guilty pleas, operate to the systematic disadvantage of members of minority groups. There are two aspects to this disadvantage.

    First, pretrial confinement is typically aimed at those least likely to appear for trial. Those least likely to appear are those who lead unsettled lives, lack permanent residents and stable jobs. This falls disproportionately on disadvantaged minority groups. The issue of unfairness is intensified by the finding that those detained prior to trial are more likely to be convicted and receive longer sentences. Hence, disadvantage in justice proceedings is cumulative.

    Second, minority members are less likely to receive favorable sentence reductions for guilty pleas. Tonry suggested that this may stem from the distrust minorities have of a country's justice system and a belief that they are treated unfairly. This distrust translates into a resistance to plead guilty at each hearing stage, they suffer a "progressive loss of mitigation." This means that defendants who plead guilty earlier in justice proceedings receive shorter sentences.

5. Subculture behaviors and stereotypes sometimes associated with minority group members often work to their disadvantage in contacts with the justice system.

These findings provide insight into crime and ethnicity in the United States. The first is that the United States is not alone in its trenchant problems of crime and justice for minorities. Its disproportionate processing of minority group members in the justice system is mirrored to a degree in all other Western countries studied by Tonry (1997). The relationship between ethnicity and justice practices is one of cumulative disadvantage for ethnic minorities. In Part 1 of this chapter on race, a cumulative disadvantage explanation was described as the propelling mechanism for the systemic perspective of a racist justice system. Tonry's findings described here suggest that the same perspective can be used to model justice practices as they affect other kinds of minority and ethnic groups as well.

Second, Tonry's research shows that problems of minority disadvantage in judicial systems are endemic to Western and European countries. This is similar to Gurr's findings discussed earlier that minorities in the Europe and the United States confronted traditions of xenophobia and systematic economic discrimination, creating historical traditions of disadvantage. Gurr found that increases in political power did not necessarily translate into economic gain. Tonry's findings suggest that legal parity also are not acquired. In the United States, for example, a felony conviction results in the loss of voting privileges. This "neutral" principle weighs heavily on minority group members, by removing minority voters from the political process. In some states, up to 25 percent of the adult African-American population has been excluded for this reason. Thus, political power seemingly gained by minority groups since the 1960s is offset by systemic disadvantage in justice system processes.

As Figure 6.1 showed, the growth and distribution of minority populations in the United States is in a period of substantial change. The percentages of minority populations in the United States were stable until the 1960s, at about 15 percent of the population. Because of proportionally low fertility rates among non-Hispanic whites and increasing immigration from Latin America and Asia, the proportion of minorities in the United States began increase (DeVita, 1996). From 1990 to 1995, the minority population grew by 15 percent, compared to three percent for the non-Hispanic white population. The most rapid rates of growth are among Asians and Latinos. The terms "Asian-American" and "Latino" are probably better understood as umbrella terms or meta-ethnic identities, since they encompass a variety of often dissimilar ethnic groups. The umbrella term "Latino" is discussed below, to provide a sense of the particular issues it faces in the United States and to provide a sense of the hidden complexity carried by immigrant identity and immigration policies.

Latinos in the United States

Latinos in the United States are a diverse population unified by the force of a common language, Spanish.[7] Many people, thinking of Latinos, tend to think of our border country to the South, Mexico. It is correct that Mexicans are the largest Latino population in the United States. However, this view does not accurately reflect either the political or cultural diversity of the Latino population in the United States today. Figure 6.2 below provides a graphic of the demographic diversity of Latinos in the United States.

Figure 6.2 shows that Mexicans make up 61.2 percent of the Latino population in the United States. However, only about 33 percent of Mexicans are foreign born—most are resident United States citizens. Central Americans make up the highest percentage of foreign-born Latinos, at 81 percent (Table 6-2). This diversity is reflected in different residential patterns in the United States. Latinos make up 40 percent of the Los Angeles population, nearly 80 percent of whom have Mexican roots. Miami, on the other hand, is dominated by Caribbean influences, particularly Cuba and Puerto Rico. Washington, D.C. is distinctive for its Central and South American populations (del Pinal & Singer, 1997).

Figure 6.2
Selected Characteristics of Hispanic Ethnic Groups, 1990

Hispanic group	1990 Population (thousands)	Percent of Hispanics	Foreign-born (percent)	Entered U.S. 1980-1990 (percent)
Hispanics	21,900	100.0	36	18
Mexicans	13,393	61.2	33	17
Puerto Ricans	2,652	12.1	na	na
Cubans	1,053	4.8	72	19
Central Americans	1,324	6.0	79	55
Salvadorans	565	2.6	81	61
Guatemalans	269	1.2	80	55
Nicaraguans	203	0.9	81	60
Hondurans	131	0.6	77	52
Panamanians	92	0.4	67	28
Costa Ricans	57	0.3	69	29
Other	7	—	71	41
South Americans	1,036	4.7	75	38
Colombians	379	1.7	74	38
Ecuadorians	191	0.9	74	32
Peruvians	175	0.8	77	48
Argentinians	101	0.5	77	31
Chileans	69	0.3	73	31
Venezuelans	48	0.2	73	50
Bolivians	38	0.2	76	47
Uruguayans	22	0.1	83	38
Paraguayans	7	—	72	42
Other	6	—	58	27
Other Hispanic origin	2,442	11.2	32	16
Dominicans	520	2.4	71	38
Spaniard	519	2.4	17	6
Spanish	445	2.0	16	7
Spanish American	93	0.4	1	1
All other	865	3.9	28	15

na—Not applicable.
—Less than 0.05 percent.
Populations for specific groups may not add to ethnic group totals because of rounding.

Source: del Pinal, George and Audrey Singer (1997). "Generations of Diversity: Latinos in the United States." *Population Bulletin*, pp. 10.

Latinos and Immigration. Immigration from Mexico has historically been driven by economic factors. From the 1880s to the 1940s, immigration was characterized by the importation of unskilled migrants into the seasonal labor market, particularly in the Southwest.

Farms, railroads, and mines became dependent on immigrants who were willing to accept intermittent employment for low wages—helping to explain why U.S. employers have persistently resisted restrictions on Mexican immigration. Farm employers often talked of obtaining Mexican workers in the same way that they obtain water—open the tap when they are needed, and close it when they are not . . . (Martin & Midgley, 1999:19).

In the 1940s, the Bracero program was implemented to permit Mexican workers to enter the United States to provide unskilled labor for the war effort. Mexican workers, typically recruited from the farming states in Central Mexico, were sometimes given parades when they entered the United States. However, the Bracero program had several unintended effects. It permitted agricultural labor to expand while wages stagnated. Many Mexican farm workers became dependent on the U.S. labor market. Employment networks were created that allowed illegal workers to find employment in the United States after the Bracero program was terminated in 1964. And electoral politics suggested that Anglos increasingly perceived Mexican labor as a competitive problem for unskilled U.S. workers, creating downward pressures on wages.

By the late 1980s, about 30 percent of the estimated 3.4 million resident illegal aliens in the United States were Mexican. In 1986, the Immigration Reform and Control Act (IRCA) attempted to close out unauthorized aliens. Penalties were assessed on U.S. employers who knowingly hired illegal aliens. At the same time, legal immigrant status was provided to illegal aliens who had established roots in the United States. Under the IRCA, 1.7 million undocumented aliens were granted legal status. In part facilitated by a growth in the fraudulent document industry, the flow of illegal aliens to the United Sates was not dampened (Martin & Midgley, 1999).

Studies carried out in conjunction with the IRCA provided a great deal of information on characteristics of undocumented workers. Sixty-nine percent were Mexican, and six percent were from El Salvador. About two percent were from Guatemala. Fifty-three percent of the applicants were already in residence in California at the time of their application for resident status, and 15 percent were in Texas. Most, about 75 percent, entered the United States without documents. The rest, about one in four, entered with legal documents but overstayed their legal limits (del Pinal & Singer, 1997).

Of all general meta-ethnic groups, the Latino population has experienced the most dramatic growth in the United States. As of 1996, about 7.3 million Mexican-Americans lived in the United States. Of these, about 4.9 million were legal residents and 2.4 were unauthorized.[8] Of these, In the mid 1990s, the numbers of legal and unauthorized Mexican-Americans in the United States By 2020, the Hispanic population will show the largest overall growth in population, and is expected to exceed 50 million (Martin & Midgley, 1999).

Latinos and Language. Spanish-speaking is at the center of Hispanic-American politics and a source of political controversy. Table 6.2 shows that the most common language other than English spoken at home is Spanish, accounting for more than one-third of foreign-speaking languages. Speaking Spanish is more controversial in the public domain. Many states have instituted "English-only" laws, requiring that English be recognized as the official language in public settings. These laws conflict with some treaty agreements. According to the treaty of Guadalupe Hidalgo, signed between the United States and Mexico in 1848 after the Mexican-American war, the United States formally provided the right of all Mexican citizens in the new territories to speak Spanish as their primary language. The provisions of this treaty have provided the stimulus for legal bilingual education in the United States (Cockcroft, 1996).

The shift from language-speaking to fluent English is a generational process that often occurs over three generations. Immigrants commonly do not speak English well. Their children are typically bilingual, and their grandchildren frequently speak only English. This transition reflects a natural process of acculturation. A survey of residents of Mexican, Cuban, and Puerto Rican origins found that more than 90 percent agreed that "all U.S. citizens and residents should learn English" (de la Garza, DeSipio, Garcia, Garcia & Falcon, 1992).[9]

Trends in Attitudes Toward Latinos. Attitudes toward minorities are complex. The 1994 general social survey conducted by the National Opinion research Center found that about 38 percent of the United States population supported assimilation, promoting the idea that minority groups should change so that they blend in with larger society. On the other hand, 31 percent supported pluralism, or the idea that groups should retain their ethnic distinctiveness, and 29 percent were neutral. However, when citizens were asked how they felt about assimilation or pluralism on political issues, 66 percent of the respondents agreed with "political organizations based on race or ethnicity promote separatism and make it hard for us all to live together" (Population Reference Bureau, 1999:7).

California reflects the largest percentage of Latinos, and is undergoing dramatic demographic change as the growing Latino population threatens to displace Anglos majority status. From 1990 to 1996, the California population grew by 2.6 million, and 9 of 10 of these were either Latino or Asian. In 1996, 29 percent of the population was Latino, 14 percent was African American, and 11 percent was Asian. Non-Latino whites account for 53 percent of the population, and will be a minority population in California by the beginning of the twenty-first century (Crawford, 1997).

California in the 1990s experienced anti-immigrant backlash. In 1994, Californians passed Proposition 187, which would have established a screening system to prevent unauthorized individuals, from state services, including public education. A court later ruled that the proposition was unlawful because it was inconsistent with federal immigration policy

(Martin & Midgley, 1999). On June 2, 1998, California voters passed Proposition 227, requiring English-only instruction.

Latinos, Crime, and Criminal Justice. Research on crime committed by and on Latinos is sparse. That a recent (1995) edited volume of papers on Latinos in crime or in the criminal justice community included several papers published in the 1970s reveals the scant research literature on Latino's in the U.S. criminal justice system (Lopez, 1995). In view of the dramatic growth in Latino population and culture in the United States, there is a clear and immediate need to expand research on this topic.

When research is conducted on Latinos in the criminal justice system, it has typically focused on tri-ethnic analyses of crime etiology among African-Americans, Latinos, and Anglo Americans (Crutchfield, 1995; Lockwood, Potteiger & Inciardi, 1995). For example, Spohn, Gruhl & Welch (1987) assessed the effects of ethnicity and gender on the decision to prosecute. The authors found that Anglos were also much more likely to have charges rejected. Latinos were prosecuted more frequently than African-Americans, who are prosecuted more frequently than Anglos. Within each ethnic group, males are more likely to be prosecuted than females. The authors noted that:

> The low rate for prosecution for Anglo females is particularly striking: at 19 percent, the rate is less than one-half the rate for Black males (39 percent) or Hispanic males (42 percent). In fact, both Anglo men and women are prosecuted at a lower rate than any other group (Spohn, Gruhl & Welch, 1987:184).

The authors noted that empirical research has generally failed to find discriminatory treatment, and recommended that researchers take into consideration the pretrial stage when conducting research on discriminatory justice practices.

Quantitative research has found inconsistent evidence of treatment differences between Latino and Anglo defendants. In a study of two jurisdictions in the Southwest—El Paso, Texas, and Tucson, Arizona, LaFree (1985) identified significant case-processing differences. But effects were influenced by various contextual factors, such as geography. In El Paso, Latinos received less favorable pretrial release outcomes than other defendants, were more likely to be convicted in jury trials, and received more severe sentences when found guilty by trial. However, Latino defendants with more serious criminal records received less severe sentences than Anglos. In Tucson, Latinos received more favorable pretrial release outcomes. No effects were observed for adjudication type, sentence severity, or verdict. LaFree concluded that the results presented a complex picture. Some effects suggested disparity in sentencing, while others were consistent with equal treatment. Factors such as proximity to the border and proportion of Latinos in the respective communities were suggested as possible contextualizing factors affecting the outcomes.

The limitations of comparative data are amply demonstrated by the research on Latin and Anglo misdemeanents conducted by Munoz, Munoz and Stewart (2001). Assessing sentencing practices in Nebraska, the authors found substantial evidence of misdemeanor sentence variation by ethnicity. Noting strong geographic effects, the authors concluded that Latinos were at a cumulative legal disadvantage from initial contact with police through sentencing. They recognized two interpretations to their data. It might have been that Latinos were charged more frequently because they were in fact committing more misdemeanor crimes. On the other hand, they might have been more highly represented because of the disproportionate mobilization of justice system resources against them.

A very limited research has focused solely on Latinos in the U.S. criminal justice system. The report carried out by Huspek, Martinez, and Jiminez (2001) on Latinos and the Immigration and Nationalization Service (INS) documented the use of excessive force against Latinos on the U.S.-Mexico border. Their investigation was initiated in response to concerns over patterns of civil-rights abuses along the border. Recent data had shown a decline in the mid 1990s, a surprising finding because of increases in INS activity along the area. Human rights workers in the area had suggested that reports were declining, not because actual incidents were declining, but because victims of violence were being deported before they could file reports of abuse.

Huspek, Martinez, and Jiminez carried out interviews at key entry-ports into the United States and interviewed known victims of INS violence in order to assess the actual extent and nature of abuses. Violations of human rights, the authors found, were routine, patterned, or as the authors described them, amounted to "a routinized infliction of terror upon persons who were targeted . . . " (Huspek, Martinez & Jiminez 2001:185). The authors called for the impanelment of a citizen review board to track and review complaints against the INS. Their report is not definitive, and can be compared in research style to a qualitative analysis, providing a detailed perspective in one place and time. The findings are sufficiently compelling to merit further investigation.

Carter (1983) explored the role of culture in understanding interactions between Latinos and the police. Culturally specific meanings created misunderstandings among participants police-citizen interactions. Carter also compared a random sample of Latinos in Texas to national fear of crime data produced by the NCS.[10] Latino levels of crime fear were significantly higher than those of Anglos. Fear of crime, he found, was also gendered: Males indicated fear of crime at nearly twice the rate (66.3%) than females. In a related (1985) paper, Carter found substantial Latino dissatisfaction with police service delivery. For many of his respondents, initially high expectations of police service were not met. Over time, perceptions of the police declined. Poor police service delivery, he concluded, was a crucial explanatory variable in understanding troubled police-Latino relationships.

When Latino-Americans are studied, it is typically in the form of "add minorities and stir" form—look at patterns of criminal justice activity and then compare Anglos, Latinos, and African-Americans. This literature is informative and important, but tends to present all findings in terms of deviations from Anglo patterns of justice. The literature does not provide a sense of the unique problems encountered by Latino-Americans in the U.S. criminal justice system, nor does it provide a sense of the issues and peoples encompassed by the umbrella term "Latino." If we are to explore the meanings that the term "justice" encompasses, it is important that we expand our research endeavors on this loosely-knit population.

On Teaching Race and Ethnicity

The task in this concluding section is to explore what race and ethnicity mean for justice education. The way in which we think about ethnicity and race—and for gender, to be discussed in the following chapter, is translated into an issue of canon. A canon is a body of literature recognized as constituting the essential identity of the field. Canon addresses the question: What is the essential literature we should teach in the field of justice studies? But the canon question masks a deeper issue. What intellectual framework do we bring to bear on decisions to select books?

The issue of canon at first blush appears to be different from considerations of ethnicity, race, and justice. However, the linkage becomes clear when we, attempting to define justice, ask "justice according to whom?" Traditional ideas of criminal justice as a normative or behavioral science will lead us to select particular kinds of books. If qualitative research is important to us, we will include other kinds of readings in the canon. And if we believe that understanding justice requires that we know the point of view of the "other," our readings will have multicultural breadth. Suppose we agree to all of these. Where, then, do we draw the line? How do we decide canon, and who decides?

In the first volume of the *Journal of Criminal Justice Education*, Thornberry (1990) suggested a canon for the field of criminology. The canon was presented with the idea that students needed a core intellectual exposure in order to be culturally literate, or the "basic information needed to thrive in the modern world." (Hirsch, 1987:xiii). Cultural literacy was not a "formulaic" concept, but "permeable and malleable." Knowledge about core ideas, concepts, and perspectives was "essential for a full understanding of contemporary topics, for effective communication about these topics, and for successful efforts to advance our understanding of them" (Thornberry, 1990:46).

Thornberry identified three criteria that determined the inclusion of particular works into criminology's "core ideas." First, works should be known by first-year graduate students and form the basis for advanced research. Second, They should have survived the test of time—they established their viability to the field. Third, materials should be included whose ideas are new, but will become important to the field in the future. Because the long-term contribution of new books is unclear in the long term, there should be a bias toward older books.

Cultural literacy within a field presupposes some notion of field identity. In Thornberry's (1990) article, the proposed canon focused specifically for the field of criminology. The issue of cultural literacy was extended to the field of criminal justice by Siegel and Zalman (1991). These authors recognized the critical question of identity: identifying the books that comprise a canon is integrally tied to one's definition of the field. They provided a definition of criminal justice that was both interdisciplinary and normative:

> In our view, criminal justice is not a science, a discipline, or a profession, although it is the subject of investigation, is multidisciplinary, and is comprised of numerous professional groups. Criminal justice, as an academic field, focuses on the primary formal agencies of social control which are assigned in our society to deal with the problems of crime and delinquency; it draws on the work of every relevant behavioral science and academic discipline (Siegel & Zalman, 1991:17).

Their inclusion criteria were similar to those developed by Thornberry, stated previously. They presented works in seven categories—Criminal justice history; concepts and policy; commission reports, standards and goals, and the work of sponsoring organizations; police and law enforcement; the adjudicatory process; punishment and sentencing; and corrections. The proposed canon also is strongly normative. The seven subdivisions all reflect areas of criminal justice practice.

At the current time, there is no agreed-on canon. Part of the reason for this is that the field is not quite as normative as it would need to be to use Siegel and Zalman's canon, and no one else has offered an alternative. Another reason is that field identity is itself fragmented around several theoretical and methodological foci. If justice studies continues on the path taken by the other social sciences, it will probably never cohere around a single field focus. Is canon even a reasonable goal? It may not be.

We may decide to reject the idea of canon, believing that it leaves us with a list of books that, for reasons of inadequacy or bias, fail to embody the multicultural dimensions of contemporary life. The criticism of canon is that it is typically described by the works of "dead white males," and does not reflect the contributions of other cultures, races, or gender groupings. The notion of canon was sharply challenged by Lynch et al. in 1992. The authors argued against canon, and identified several reasons for their view.

1.   A canon has a homogenizing effect that promotes unity and same-ness. In this process, it excludes the values of "excluded races, class-es, and cultures."

2.   The search for a general theory of cultural literacy fails to recognize problems encountered by real people in the cultural and historical context in which they live.

3.   Cultural literature's quest to seek out historically dominant themes place men in a superordinate position and subordinate women to minor or nonexistent roles.

4.   In the field of criminology, by focusing on lower-class and minority lawbreaking, minorities and women are objects for examination rather than communicative subjects to be engaged in dialogue.

5.   Because cultural literacy focuses on established literature, women tend to be excluded because they have only recently begun to achieve parity in the field and their work lacks adequate vintage.

Even if we were to decide to select a canon, how would we go about deciding what books were good? Canon carries a judgment of quality, that is, works are identified that are good enough to express the core ideas of a field. But how do we determine how good a work is? Taylor (1994:42) described the problem of quality with a frequently quoted statement: "When the Zulu's produce a Tolstoy we will read him." This statement is arrogant, and its intent is clear. Good works are good works, and a work should not be recognized simply because of some need for cultural diver-sity. By implication, we are asking if the ideas we derive from other cul-tures, whether in the form of reading materials or instructors to teach those classes, all have equal worth in the development of the field of jus-tice studies. Once we identify a canon, whatever that canon is, we are explicitly stating that some cultural goods have worth and others do not.

The hypothetical quote above also suggests that there are ways to select books that are rigorously neutral, uncommitted to the enhancement of any cultural, ethnic, or religious group. The problem with this view lies in our inability to expand beyond what we don't know. We are limited by our existing ideas, and we are out of touch with contemporary changes in both the academic marketplace of ideas and in the demographic diversity in American society. Taylor describes the problem this way:

> For a culture sufficiently different from our own, we have only the fog-giest idea ex ante of in what its valuable contribution might consist. Because, for a sufficiently different culture, the very understanding of what it is to be of worth will be strange and unfamiliar to us. To approach, for example, a raga with the presumptions of value implicit in the well-tempered clavier would be forever to miss the point (Taylor, 1994:67).

Taylor suggested that we adopt a perspective he calls a "fusion of horizons."[11] According to this idea, we situate that which we take for granted alongside that which is unfamiliar, without judgment. This will allow us to develop new "vocabularies of comparison," so that we can describe the contrasts. Over time, our increased vocabulary of understanding will permit comparisons of which we were originally incapable. If we then make judgments about relative worth, "we have reached the judgment partly through transforming our standards." (67). Taylor recommended that we begin the quest for knowledge with a *presumption* of equal worth.

> We only need a sense of our own limited part in the whole human story to accept the presumption. It is only arrogance, or some analogous moral failing, that can deprive us of this. But what the presumption requires of us is not peremptory or inauthentic judgments of equal value, but a willingness to be open to comparative cultural study of the kind that must displace our horizons in the resulting fusions. What it requires above all is an admission that we are very far away from that ultimate horizon from which the relative worth of different cultures might be evident (Taylor, 1994:7).

The student of justice may ask *Why is this information important to me?* If the student is going to practice in a criminal justice agency, she or he may not see the relevance of an abstract discussion about canon, race, culture, or ethnicity to their working life. My justification is ethical, and it is this: when we assume the responsibility for someone's life—as we do any time we arrest, incarcerate, or kill someone in the line of duty—we have a fundamental obligation to know who that person is and why he or she did what they did. This does not mean that we have to agree with their reasons for their behavior.

In order to adapt to American society in the twenty-first century, justice education must foster in students an awareness of social and cultural diversity. This can be difficult in justice studies, a field in which a person's personal values mobilizes their involvement and interest in justice work. Yet these students will someday practice justice, and will make discretionary judgments in the practice of their work. Decisionmaking that is grounded in a we-them morality or cultural racism can easily be masked by discretion. The task of education is to locate traditional values in the matrix of the world's ethnicity, and to foster in students an awareness of other perspectives of justice. A traditional canon grounded in normative ideas of criminal justice processes will not get us there.

The task of justice—the field's uniting theme—is to seek a better world than the one we inherit. The task of justice education is to provide students with a practical, ethical, and intellectual understanding of the possibilities justice can achieve. Consider the police: A police officer on the street may make an arrest, but may also decide to take a different course of action. In today's problem-solving world, the police task has changed, and officers are required to identify and address the problems that underlay patterns of criminal activity. The capacity of the police to deal with the problems faced by ordinary people comes from their understanding of people—what values motivate their behavior, how they think, how they react, their celebrations, and their misfortunes.

As a democracy, the United States is a work in progress. Increasingly multicultural, our diverse groups jostle and chafe each other, even as they learn how to co-exist in a democratic setting. A fusion of horizons places a burden on us—to withhold judgment, to learn before we act. In the field of justice studies, a fusion of horizons means that, to be just, we must measure our ideas of justice, without prejudice, against the view of the other. And this is the perspective we should pass on to our students—to withhold judgment, to acquire knowledge, and to participate wisely in a complex democracy.

Notes

[1]   This is of course an over-simplification. For example, the British in the 1700s referred to Indians as "blacks." And Eskimos are light-skinned.

[2]   This did not happen only in Africa. In the former Soviet union, Stalin drew state boundaries in many Soviet regions that contained internal ethnic conflicts. It has been suggested that Stalin acted strategically, so that interior conflict could prevent the mobilization of forces that would threaten the Soviet empire.

[3]   In LaFree and Russell, 1993:280. Even this number may be an underestimate. Bauer and Huling (1995) estimate that this number is one in three.

[4]   Cited in Leadership Conference for Civil Rights, 2000.

[5]   Legal rights can be abrogated by other minority-related problems. For example, the disenfranchisement of felons from voting rights falls heavily on African-American populations. In some states, up to 25 percent of the adult African-American population is unable to vote for this reason.

[6]   Crèvecoeur, 1980. "Letters from an American Farmer," Pp. 30 in Philip Gleason, "American Identity and Americanization." In *Harvard Encyclopedia of American Ethnic Groups*. Cambridge, MA: Harvard University Press.

[7]   Latino immigrants almost universally are Spanish speakers. The same does not apply to U.S.-born Latinos, who often speak no Spanish.

[8]   By unauthorized is meant those who came to the United States legally and overstayed their visa, and those who entered the United States illegally.

[9]   Cited in Martin and Midgley, 1999:37.

[10]   The National Crime Survey, now called the National Crime Victimization Survey.

[11]   The term is taken from Gadamer, Wahrheit, and Methode (Tübingen: Mohr).

Chapter 7

Gender and the Emergence of Feminist Perspective

If race and ethnicity compel us to come to terms with our country's historical conflicts, gender requires that we reconsider justice's breadth. Women have made substantial gains in many areas since the banner of economic inequality was raised in the early twentieth century. Moreover, unlike other disenfranchised groups, women's political and economic power continues to increase at the beginning of the twenty-first century. Women present the justice field with new ways of thinking about justice, ways that locate gender and sex as central issues in how we think about justice.

In many ways, gender issues represent a profound challenge to justice. Gender issues are relentlessly compelling: carried by an increasingly powerful constituency, they continue to reveal how justice practices and the field of justice studies are embedded in social traditions. By asking such seemingly straightforward questions as "what is a woman" we are forced to confront many ideas that have been traditionally treated as a part of the natural order of things, the violations of which we sometimes have punished harshly.

Feminism in justice studies is controversial. There is widespread resistance to the idea of a "feminist" perspective. Critics argue that feminism "balkanizes" justice studies, by which is meant that feminism breaks justice studies into hostile, conflicting camps concerned more about political recognition than the quest for truth. Proponents contend that women have been historically misrepresented and that issues of scholarship, crime, and criminal justice have inadequately dealt with women. And many of the issues that motivated the politization of a feminist perspective continue to be salient today. Criminal justice instructors routinely encounter male students who question whether, for reasons of emotional temperament and physical size, women are fit to be police officers.

What I hope to accomplish in this chapter is to provide an introductory sensibility about issues of gender, feminism, and masculinities. These topics are too often overlooked in justice curricula, and when they are encountered it is in the form of "specialty" courses. Further, ideas con-

277

cerning feminism tend to disappear from a student's intellectual horizons once he or she becomes a member of a justice agency, except for the occasional lawsuit against criminal justice agencies whose members are found to be practicing sexual or gender bias. Many students will be exposed to core gender ideas only infrequently. Accordingly, the purpose of this chapter is to familiarize justice students with feminist perspectives generally, applications of feminist perspective to the field of criminal justice, and important justice issues involving gender.

Feminist Perspective

Feminism is a term that covers a variety of perspectives. Most generally, feminism is an umbrella term whose domain of interest is gender inequality. Historically, feminism is embodied in a social movement whose goal is raising the status of women (Lorber, 1998:1). Feminism is multivocal, an umbrella term. It is more accurate to suggest that there are many different feminisms, each with a different idea of inequality and how to address issues of gender and sex inequality. In the opening section, I will identify and briefly sketch some of these different perspectives. I will use Lorber's (1998) characterizations to describe different feminisms—gender reform feminism, gender resistance feminism, and gender rebellion feminism—and to discuss their contribution to our understandings of gender inequality.

Gender Reform Feminism. Gender reform feminism has focused on overt and covert discriminatory practices against women. This feminism was prevalent in the 1960s and 1970s and focused on conventional ideas of sexual differences. According to Lorber, this feminism focused on equality of human potential—that women were restricted by prevailing social and economic mores from access to economic and employment opportunities. A goal of gender reform feminism was the equal participation of women and men in all aspects of their lives.

Gender reform feminism includes liberal, Marxist/social, and development perspectives. It can be traced to the early reform efforts in the 1960s. Betty Friedan's *The Feminist Mystique (1963),* an example of liberal gender reform feminism, was a seminal work that exposed the extent to which women's and men's roles were intensely gendered. By gendered is meant that women and men were socialized into roles that defined particular male and female traits. Of concern to gender reform feminists was that these roles were economically stratified, with roles corresponding to males provided greater access to social and economic rewards in American society. Women who wanted careers were suspect unless they were good mothers and wives first. Even as late as the 1960s, women were regarded by men as not too bright, oriented to clothes, and overly emotional (Lorber, 1998:20). Many of the liberal goals have been achieved today, though in the field of justice studies there continues to be resistance to these early goals of feminism.

Another variety of gender reform, development perspective, used colonial theories of economic development to assess the state of women's conditions in the United States as well as in other countries. This perspective particularly focused on the conditions of women in developing, third-world countries. This perspective was based in economic equality and focused on the global economy and how it disadvantaged female workers:

> The global economy links countries whose economic focus on service, information, and finances with manufacturing sites and the sources of raw materials in other countries. Men and women workers all over the world supply the labor for the commodities that end up in the stores in your neighborhood. They are not paid according to their skills but according to the going wage, which varies enormously from country to country because it is dependent on the local standard of living. Women workers tend to be paid less than men workers throughout the world whatever the wage scale, whatever the wage scale, because they are supposedly supporting only themselves (Lorber, 1998:46).

The systemic disadvantage of women caused by the international economy occurs as follows. First-world countries such as the United States invest in the global marketplace. The market is highly internationalized, and survival pressures to maximize profits lead companies to seek manufacturing locations where wages are the lowest. These are typically third-world countries with depressed economies. Yet it is often in third-world countries where gender inequality is the greatest, and where women confront exploitation. Because countries seek profit maximization, they see little incentive in raising the status of women. The international market economy consequently is a central factor in wage suppression and the exploitation of working women.

Development feminism seeks redress by altering traditional patriarchal patterns and male-dominated kinship systems. Strategies aimed at gaining economic equality for women in first and third-world economies differ. In first-world countries, women have tended to create micro-enterprises: they entered the labor force, notably in the service industry, and take over the tasks of childcare and eldercare. In third-world countries such as those in Latin America and the Caribbean Islands, women tend to collectivize rather than privatize their survival problems. They "organize at a neighborhood level around a broad list of issues that they redefine as women's concerns, such as running water or transportation or squatters communities" (Acosta-Belen & Bose, 1998:40).

Gender Resistance Feminism

Gender resistance feminism refocuses the debate away from the equality of the sexes and toward the development of a woman-oriented culture. The male-oriented culture, according to this perspective, is too politically and socially pervasive. Efforts to become equal simply result in women becoming like men. Patriarchy is present in every aspect of our culture and embedded in most U.S. religious practices. There is not a way to become equal without succumbing to patriarchal traditions. Some who hold this perspective argue for a separation of women's and men's culture, while others hold that women's groups should maintain political engagement with society.

One kind of gender resistance feminism is called standpoint feminism. According to this perspective, how we look at the world is determined by our standpoint, which is a blend of factual information and unrecognized values. Standpoints have been powerfully affected by male values and paternal authority. Even in so-called objective sciences, men have subtly shaped how we see the world and have predisposed the way in which knowledge is organized. Both scientific and social science knowledge have been produced by men, and they represent a man's perspective of the world. This is particularly apparent with social science knowledge where a great deal of knowledge presented as gender or sexual "facts" actually reflects existing values and beliefs about gender differences.

Standpoint feminism argues that perspectives on human behavior, however well intentioned, may conceal important aspects of people's relationships (Hartsock, 1998). The standpoint of dominant groups in society easily and naturally becomes the accepted way of perceiving human relations. To gain a perspective with adequate breadth of social phenomena, feminists argue for an "engaged" perspective, one which includes many different points of view. Both the views of the privileged as well as subalterns are necessary for an engaged point of view. Only an engaged perspective can provide an adequate breadth of what is actually going on in the marketplace and social world of human relations. Readers might note that this idea of an "engaged" perspective is similar to the discussion of method variety in Chapter 4.

Lorber (1998:117) provides the following example of how a male "standpoint" can distort seemingly objective science. Research on sex and gender differences compares genetically identified males and females, though data typically come from social behavior, which is a measure of gender differences. Since 1959, researchers in the field of biology have explained sex differences by three perspectives: first by XX and XY chromosomes, then by testosterone versus estrogen, and currently by prenatal hardwiring in the brain through genetic or hormonal input. Factors such as socialization, family, and peer pressures are relegated to a secondary role. In other words, research has focused on the trait and behavioral outcomes of biological *differences* between men and women.

There is evidence that an interpretation of gender that focuses only on differences misstates the nature of the sexes themselves. Research on sexual differences has tended to locate men as aggressors and as physically superior, thereby carrying an implicit presumption of dominance of the man over the woman. In this way, seemingly objective science has been interpreted in a way that maintains male superiority. Experimental evidence since the 1930s, however, shows that both male and female hormones are equally important in determining sex. Moreover, people with XY chromosome can have either male or female anatomy. An increasing body of research examines on the biological, chemical, and genetic *similarity* of the sexes. The standpoint—biological differences in gender—has overlooked perhaps a greater and more inclusive standpoint—biological similarity between the sexes.

Gender Rebellion Feminism

A third kind of feminism is called gender rebellion. The term *rebellion* carries a more aggressive connotation than the other two forms. However, to take the term "aggressive" in terms of violence or disagreement would miss its central meanings. Gender rebellion feminism challenges the underlying validity of the fundamental constructs of gender identity— what might be called the "out there" of gender. Gender rebellion advocates an examination of the social identity of males as well as females, and challenges the fundamental dualities of male and female, masculine and feminine. Male feminism, a form of gender rebellion, considers the existing pattern of social roles and asks whether men are as trapped by the existing institutional arrangements as are women. Some social values, for example, encourage male physical and sexual violence.

Multiracial studies in gender rebellion feminism focus on how gender, race, ethnicity, and social class all come together to construct social identity. To gain adequate understanding of a person's relative advantage or disadvantage, we need to assess all of these in conjunction with gender. For example, if we are describing someone who is dark of skin and male, we need to know if we are referring to a Latino black male, for example, or a Caribbean black male, an Indian (family history from India) in Trinidad or Tobago, or an African-American male born in the United States. All of these kinds of dark-toned people carry different status implications and place them in different positions vis-à-vis economic advantage and minority-majority status in their perspective societies. Their gender identity exists at the intersection of their various statuses.

Social construction feminism is based in the idea that humans are not simply "blind adherents" to pre-existing social roles, but are actively involved in creating the roles that they occupy. According to this perspective, humans are active participants in the creation of culture, even while they follow in traditional cultural roles. Culture in this sense is not an historic artifact, but a living social entity that changes and adapts to the people who participate in it. By recognizing the emergent vitality of culture, we gain the knowledge that we cannot hold traditions themselves accountable for our circumstances—we are actively involved in the ongoing creation of the inequalities that bind us.

Gender rebellion feminism is not represented by a single idea. It is a grouping of perspectives around several core ideas. These ideas have been summarized as follows (Daly & Chesney-Lind, 1988):

1. Gender is not a natural fact but a complex social, historical, and cultural product; it is related to, but not simply derived from, biological sex differences and reproductive capacities.

2. Gender and gender relations order social life and social institutions in fundamental ways.

3. Gender relations and constructs of masculinity and femininity are not symmetrical but are based on an organizing principle of men's superiority and social and political-economic dominance over women.

4. systems of knowledge reflect men's views of the natural and social world; the production of knowledge is gendered.

5. Women should be at the center of intellectual inquiry, not peripheral, invisible, or appendages to men (Daly & Chesney-Lind, 1988:504).

The following discussion, adapted from West and Zimmerman (1998) describes how we do gender, and provides the reader with an introduction to social construction feminism.

West and Zimmerman: Doing Gender. Many feminist perspectives parallel currents in sociological and psychological theory. Among these, the idea that gender is a social construction derives from the sociological tradition sometimes called the "social construction of reality" (see Berger & Luckmann, 1966). By saying that gender is a social construction, this perspective means that it is a phenomena that humans produce as a result of their ongoing social interactions. Gender is embedded in all major forms of social endeavor. Highly institutionalized, gender is a defining element of the roles played by participants in other social institutions. Marriage and family, for example, are based on the way in which we socially construct gender differences. Emphases in justice on physical strength and the widespread views that women are emotionally unstable typify traditional crime control values and practices as well.

We do gender. This means that we constantly act in ways that create and reinforce gender differences. Our daily activities produce gender inequality. Because gender differences are so widespread in our social order, we "do" gender all the time. Even when aware of it, we cannot stop doing it. We sustain and reinforce gender differences in our everyday life.

West and Zimmerman's (1998) article "Doing Gender" describes the way in which we construct gender differences in our daily activities. The article is discussed and cited at length below, in part for its contribution to the field of feminist study, and in part because it is an excellent corrective to our natural tendency to take gender differences as a part of the natural order of things.

West and Zimmerman begin by noting that gender differences are not inherent to the psychology of particular individuals, but a socially constructed product of individual interactions.

> When we view gender as an accomplishment, an achieved property of situated conduct, our attention shifts from matters internal to the individual and focuses on interactional and, ultimately, institutional arenas. In one sense, of course, it is individuals who "do" gender. But it is a situated doing, carried out in the virtual or real presence of others who are presumed to be oriented to its production. Rather than as a property of individuals, we conceive of gender as an emergent feature of social institutions: both as an outcome of and a rationale for various social arrangements and as a means of legitimating one of the most fundamental divisions in society (West & Zimmerman, 1998:161-162).

When we do gender, we are carrying on more than a role-enacted activity. Participants actively organize their activities organize their activities so that they can express gender, and they are disposed to receive gendered differences as well. The authors make several definitional distinctions.

> *Sex* is a determination made through the application of socially agreed upon biological criteria for classifying persons as females or males. The criteria for classification can be genitalia at birth or chromosomal typing before birth, and they do not necessarily agree with one another. Placement in a *sex category* is achieved through the application of the sex criteria, but in everyday life, categorization is established and sustained by the socially required identificatory displays that proclaim one's membership on one or the other category. In this sense, one's sex category presumes one's sex and stands as a proxy for it in many situations, but sex and sex category can vary independently, that is, it is possible to claim membership in a sex category even when the sex criteria are lacking. Gender, in contrast, is the activity of managing situated conduct in light of normative conceptions of attitudes and activities appropriate for one's sex category. Gender activities emerge from and bolster claims to membership in a sex category (West & Zimmerman, 1998:162).

Doing gender, the authors argue, is embedded in our everyday social arrangements.

> Doing gender means creating differences between boys and girls and women and men, differences that are not natural, essential, or biological. Once the differences have been constructed, they are used to reinforce the "essentialness" of gender. In a delightful account of the "arrangement between the sexes," Goffman (1977) observes the creation of a variety of institutionalized frameworks through which our "natural, normal sexedness" can be enacted. The physical features of social setting provide one obvious resource for the expression of our "essential" differences. For example, the sex segregation of North American public bathrooms distinguishes "ladies" from "gentlemen" in matters held to be fundamentally biological, even though both "are somewhat similar in the question of waste products and their elimination (Goffman, 1977:315). These settings are furnished with dimorphic equipment such as urinals for men or elaborate grooming facilities for women), even though both sexes may achieve the same ends through the same means (and apparently do so in the privacy of their own homes) . . . (West & Zimmerman, 1998:163).

Our social arrangements appear to us as normal. By interpreting our particular social arrangements as the inevitable consequence of historical progression, we perceive that gender differences are a consequence of the natural order of things:

> But doing gender also renders the social arrangements based on sex category accountable as normal and natural, that is, legitimate ways of organizing social life. Differences between men and women that are created by this process can then be portrayed as fundamental and enduring dispositions. In this light, the institutional arrangements of a society can be seen as responsive to the differences—the social order being merely an accommodation to the natural order. Thus, if in doing gender, men are also doing dominance and women are doing deference . . . the resulting social order, which supposedly reflects "natural differences," is a powerful reinforcer and legitimator of hierarchical arrangements (West & Zimmerman, 1998:164).

By doing gender, we legitimate the existing arrangement of things. If we fail to do gender right, it is we, not the existing order, who are brought into question. Our character, our motives, and our predispositions are questioned. We are labeled *strange* and morally flawed. Consequently, efforts to change the way we do gender—and establish more equitable relationships between the sexes—require actions broader than what can be accomplished by individuals acting alone. Groups with sufficient membership and clout, capable of resisting the powerful stigmatizing effects of moral labels, will have to carry the resistance to traditional gendering processes.

Social movements such as feminism can provide the ideology and impetus to question existing arrangements, and the social support for individuals to explore alternatives to them. Legislative changes, such as that proposed by the Equal Rights Amendment, can also weaken the accountability of conduct to sex category, thereby affording the possibility of more widespread loosening of accountability in general (West & Zimmerman, 1998:164).

Gender is so fundamental and pervasive that efforts to re-gender our social relationships inevitably mobilize resistance. Gender is intertwined with other unequal statuses (wife-husband, for example), and is seen as the "natural" element that justifies the unequal relations among other statuses. It is as prevalent in the white-collar boardroom as the blue-collar kitchen. Re-gendering for equality may be the most difficult of social rearrangements to put into place or to sustain (Lorber, 1998).

Coontz: The Confusions of Personal and Public Values. The social construction of gender is closely tied to the related notion of family. Gender identities, as Lorber (1998) observed, are integral to the organization and behaviors of families. In the current age of "family values" with its emphasis on U.S. patriarchal traditions, feminism represents a heretical view, a way of thinking that challenges our ideas about family. But does the view offered by feminism provide a more accurate representation of our history? Put differently, are traditional views of family life grounded in history or in myths of a past we never knew?

Coontz (1992) argues that the mainstream American culture has reconstructed our near-term history of family life around ideas that are more mythic than historically accurate. In *The Way We Never Were,* Coontz suggests that we have constructed notions of the "ideal" family life around a 1950s conception of TV families. Shows such as "Ozzie and Harriet" and "Leave it to Beaver" provided an image of family life and virtue that are often held up as a model for family values today. This image is a fakery of history.

The 1950s, Coontz observes, did not represent a morally righteous time in U.S. history. Consider teen sex and pregnancy:

[In the 1950s] teen birth rates soared, reaching highs that have not been equaled since. In 1957, 97 out of every 1,000 girls aged 15 to 19 gave birth, compared to only 52 of 1,000 in 1983. A surprising number of these births were illegitimate, although 1950s census codes made it impossible to identify an unmarried mother if she lived at home with her parents . . . there was an 80% increase in the number of out-of-wedlock babies placed for adoption between 1944 and 1955 (Coontz, 1992:39).

Illegitimate behavior did not always result in more babies born out of wedlock. Young people, Coontz noted, were sometimes "handed Wedding rings" and forced into marriage. Contemporary out-of-wedlock motherhood among teenaged women is not an indication of some collapse in morality or disintegration of the family, but simply a continuation of 1950s patterns. The patina of legitimacy provided by forced weddings masked behavior that was, well, very much like behavior today.

The image of husband and wife had a dark side that is poorly understood by advocates of 1950s family life. In the 1950s, technological advances and ideological shifts freed men from traditional responsibilities, allowing them to adopt the ideological platitudes of self-reliance and independence. One of the powerful myths of American life in the 1950s was that of the individual economic entrepreneur, commonly called the breadwinner. This was a particularly male myth. This myth could only occur if women were subjugated to the family and carried the responsibilities for family maintenance. The liberal theory of human nature and political citizenship, Coontz noted, did not simply leave women out, it intentionally harnessed them to a workload that allowed men to think that they were somehow different and special.

> It worked precisely because it was applied exclusively to half the population. Emotion and compassion could be disregarded in the political and economic realms only if women were assigned these traits in the personal realm. Thus the use of the term individualistic to describe men's nature became acceptable only in the same time periods, social classes, and geographic areas that established the cult of domesticity for women. The cult of the self-made man required the cult of the true woman (Coontz, 1992:53).

Thus, the 1950s marked the emergence of an idealized "husband," individual, self-reliant, working all day to bring his paycheck home. In real life, women became slaves to domestic life. The doing of gender emphasized sexual differences and female servitude. And if the gendered male role was one emphasizing self-reliance, what was the female role? Think of the 1950s television classic "I Love Lucy"—a show about a harebrained, emotional woman. Lucy was always trying to do the right thing, yet she hopelessly confused everything. She inevitably attempted to hide her inappropriate behavior from her husband. The show typically concluded with him uncovering her incompetent behavior, scolding her, and fixing the problems. At the end of the show they "hugged and made up," the droll tensions created by her lame attempts at independent action exposed and resolved, and the pattern of dominance/subservience reasserted. Lucy was a popular comedy figure, and her show was widely enjoyed. But it represented a dependency myth of marriage and womanhood that, vis-à-vis the power of the media of TV to reinforce values, helped trapped women in familial subservience.

Coontz argued that the contemporary "family values" movement confused social and personal values. The family is expected to display quite public ideas of morality, while public values of civic morality have been replaced by individualistic economic enterprise and cutthroat competition. We encourage public values in the private sphere and private values in the public sphere.

In the United States, public values and civic responsibility have historically been the pillars of societal relations. Family life was not concerned with public displays of virtue, and a family's business was theirs. And public life was about involvement with civic groups and secondary associations, the honoring of contracts and obligations. Central to public life was mutual obligation and reciprocity or sharing. Granges—co-ops where farmers shared common concerns and interests about their goods, for example, acted in concert to protect individual farmers. We certainly did not expect farmers to act independently, without caring for each other. The relations of family members to each other were considered private activity, of nobody's business. Self-reliance was about how people interacted to protect themselves and deal with common problems, not how individuals interacted with regard to each other.

The "family values" movement has reversed public/family patterns of moral obligation. Today, in the public realm, participants are expected to be calculating, rational, and individualistic. Civic traditions of mutual dependency and obligation have been replaced with myths of the lonesome cowboy, beholden to no one but himself. The family, an institution poorly equipped to handle such an obligation, has become the showplace of public morality, acted out in filial displays of emotional commitment and warmth. Today, family values are everyone's business.

We end up with the "virtuous family" as a model for public life, judging public figures not by their capacity for civic contribution but by the quality for their private lives. In the current era, Coontz noted, political candidates sell themselves to the public, not for their capacity to govern or position on issues, but on the quality of their private, family life. Coontz was prophetic in her vision of the fundamental contradictions of personal and family life. Though she wrote this book several years before the impeachment of democratic President Bill Clinton and contemporaneous resignation of Newt Gingrich from the Republican Speakership for "family values" reasons, she could not have better captured the dilemmas that characterized the impeachment of a president who had displayed a respectable record as a statesman but a poor example of the idealized, virtuous 1950s husband.

> Periodically, of course, we are disillusioned by the authenticity or the private lives of public figures, but seldom do we question the very nature of our expectations. Instead, in an almost total reversal of logic, we blame the public person for betraying our expectations of love, just as we blame the family for failing to create justice and equality. The anger against bad mothers in the private sphere has a corollary in our disappointment with bad father figures in the public (Coontz, 1992:115).

Into Criminology: Trends in Criminological Feminism

The history of crime causation is thick with the misrepresentation of women (Naffine, 1987; Mann, 1984). This history, to be discussed later in this chapter, carries many hidden assumptions: that individual female characteristics accounted for their criminal behavior, that these characteristics were biologically based, that offending women were more masculine than non-offenders (Belknap, 1996).

In 1975, the publication of Freda Adler's *Sisters in Crime* and Rita Simon's *Women and Crime* marked a change in the way women were represented in justice research (Belknap, 1996). These two books presented an image of women and crime that has been characterized as liberation theory. *Liberation theory* held that the women's liberation movement was associated with a rise in female crime (Belknap, 1996). The ideas presented in liberation theory are summarized below (in Belknap, 1996:38; from Naffine, 1987):

1. Feminism brings out women's competitiveness.

2. The women's movement has created opportunities to increase places were women can offend.

3. Women have won the battle of equality.

4. Feminism makes women want to behave like men.

5. Crime itself is inherently masculine.

The critical difference between liberation theory and traditional justice views of women was the location of criminality in learned behavior and in the structure of social opportunities, rather than in some innate differences between men and women. These perspectives initiated research into the gendered bases of crime and how social trends differentially affected men and women.

Through the latter 1970s and early 1980s, feminist theorists focused on the intersection of gender, crime, and social structure. Yet by the mid 1980s, feminist literature had scant impact on criminology. As Daly and Chesney-Lind (1988:498) observed, "With the exception of feminists treatments of rape and intimate violence, the field remains essentially untouched." Feminism was marginalized as a sub-discipline of criminology. In the mid and late 1980s, a variety of papers began the work of bringing feminism to bear on central issues in criminology and criminal justice. In a series of papers, Chesney-Lind (1986, 1987) provided feminist perspective for understanding the dilemmas of female offenders. Daly (1987a, b) assessed issues of gender and treatment in criminal courts. Eaton (1986) questioned the meaning of equal treatment in a legal environment where equality might mean accepting existing inequities.[1] This body of research represented a break from previous research in an important way: It considered not only differences in the roles occupied by men and women but also examined the way in which workplace power was gendered.

Women's Studies in the Criminal Justice Classroom. On another front, efforts were made to locate gender issues in mainstream criminal justice instruction, largely through the publication of books on women in justice with textbook-oriented presses. Weisheit and Mahan (1988), for example, presented an overview of issues of women and criminal justice. Their work located women in generally traditional perspectives of crime and justice. The primary focus of their work was on the etiology of female offending, though sections also emphasized issues in victimization, prisonization, and in female employment in the justice system. Their work also recognized the importance of power in issues of gender inequality, and as such was theoretically reasoned and in some ways advanced beyond feminist perspectives grounded primarily in the then-popular liberal debate over gender equality. Their work thus served as a bridge, linking the first and second wave of gender research to the third, and provided a pedagogy of the changes occurring in the 1980s. In the intellectually stifling textbook marketplace, Weisheit and Mahan's book contributed to the dramatic expansion of concerns over gender issues and pedagogy that would mark the 1990s.

Even with the expansion that occurred in the mid and late 1980s, justice students had thin exposure to feminist issues. Women's studies were typically relegated to secondary interest topics (Gelsthorpe & Morris 1988). Studies that identified no gender were treated as "general knowledge," while studies that focused on women were viewed as special interest and tended to be marginalized. The difficulties and frustrations encountered in bringing feminist justice issues into the criminal justice classroom were summarized by Wilson (1991):

> I think we will all agree that ours is an exceedingly masculine discipline. some will agree that far too often, it is also a "macho" discipline, riddled with Rambo approaches to crime. Where does a criminology of women belong in our discipline? Does it require that women working in criminology become men (i.e., accept a masculinist view of the world), or, alternatively, encapsulate themselves in a narrowly conceived women's studies that shrinks rather than expands their vision? For male students does it mean that women's studies and the woman's viewpoint is foreign, aline, "for women only"—something to fear, trivialize, and ultimately ignore? doesn't gender color their world too? (Wilson, 1991:87).

Wilson identified a central problem in criminal justice instruction. The central problem with feminist scholarship and pedagogy is not whether it has a place in justice issues—it inheres in justice issues, intertwined, inseparable. The problem is that gendered distinctions continue to characterize the field of criminal justice. It is the written and acted embodiment of patriarchal interests. This biasing tradition needed to be stated clearly and forcefully—and repeatedly.

And so Renzetti (1993) did. "They still don't get it, do they!" The title of Renzetti's paper was clear and unequivocal—gender is important, figure it out, deal with it. She recognized the core problems in getting gender issues into the "malestream." Many students tend toward patriarchy don't like to discuss female equality. Faculty don't want to mainstream gender issues because the issues upset comfortable teaching routines—and sometimes threatens departmental status hierarchies. Criminal justice agencies continue even today to struggle with gender biases against women. And it is at the practical level that pedagogical issues concerning gender need to be addressed. If students don't want to hear about gender issues, tough. They must learn anyway, because it's a great big chunk of what the real world is about.

How are women's issues associated with general ideas of education? Wilson (1991) envisions an integrated curriculum, embedded in classic principles of liberal arts education.

> Is it enough to house our programs in liberal arts colleges, where our students will be exposed to general education courses with a liberal cast? Is it enough to send our students to history to learn history, to political science to learn politics, to philosophy to learn ethics—and then to teach them in our curriculum a Western, white, male, Twentieth-century criminal justice? No, no, and no (Wilson, 1991:87).

Feminist issues could be introduced in pedagogy by providing material that showed how women have worked for women and as women. This could take many forms, such as the historical role of female advocacy for justice issues, the publication of gender-oriented research, and how women re-construct traditional criminal justice roles. In a liberal arts/social science environment, the role of feminist pedagogy was to integrate with other important areas, and to bring to these areas the capacity for female students to "find themselves as positive"—that is, to identify justice roles that are female and personally meaningful.

At the beginning of the twenty-first century, women's studies are increasingly found in criminal justice curricula. In a national study of undergraduate criminal justice curricula in 1997, Smith (1999) observed that 41 percent (119 of 287) offered a course on women in criminal justice. Substantial curricular variability was noted by region: only 30 percept of the programs in the South offered a course on women's studies, and more than twice as many, 65 percent, did so in the West. Variability was also associated with size: of the programs that did not offer a course on women in criminal justice, 48 percent responded that "Their program was too small to venture beyond traditional courses in criminal justice"

(Smith, 1999:11). Thirty-one percent stated that they did not have such a course because the department lacked a qualified instructor, a factor that also might be associated with the size of the department. Although these might appear to be reasonable responses for the absence of a course on women's studies, they nevertheless underscore the point that courses about women are not yet considered to be among mainstream offerings in many places.

Criminal justice classes on women also tend to be elective. Of the programs that responded to Smith's questionnaire, 80 percent offered women in criminal justice as an elective, and 10 of the 14 programs that required the course offered it as a component of a course on a broader topic, such as "Public Safety in a Diverse Society." In sum, curricular offerings on women in criminal justice are absent for more than one-half of the undergraduate criminal justice programs in the United States, and where it is offered, it is marginalized as an elective offering.

How should women's courses be integrated into a criminal justice curriculum? It has been suggested that special courses on women marginalize gender-related issues by defining them as "women's work," and delay the integration of gender into criminal justice (Wonders & Caufield, 1993). Special courses delay integration for several reasons.

First, special courses "ghettoize" gender issues. By this, Wonders and Caulfield (1993) mean that women's issues are segregated from other issues, removing pressure for integration in other courses and justifying faculty reluctance to familiarize themselves with gender issues. Second, by treating women's issues as special topics, they are labeled negatively by many students and faculty as "a semester-long exercise in male-bashing."

Third, instructors often meet resistance when they employ feminist pedagogy in the classroom. Fourth, that women in criminal justice courses are taught by women reinforces the perception that such courses are "women's work" and reinforces existing gender stereotypes. And fifth, the social distance is increased between male and female faculty members when women identify themselves as concerned with gender issues.

Gender issues should be integrated into regular instruction. Yet, such integration will require a transformation in criminal justice instruction. Observing that "you can't just add women and stir" (see Tamark Minnich, 1990:30), Wonders and Caufield (1993) observed that feminist pedagogy was not achieved simply by adding women to the faculty. Feminist pedagogy and theory required a revision of how we conduct this business called criminal justice.

The field of criminal justice is densely gendered. Its history, theory of crime and justice, pedagogy, practice—in short, its essence—is profoundly biased by gender predispositions. For advocates of feminist pedagogy and feminism in justice issues, the field must take its next step toward degendering. This step is more profound than simply adding more information about gender. It involves a reconceptualization of every aspect of the justice studies field. Tamark Minnich (1990) drew a flat-earth metaphor: we cannot add the discovery that the world is round to an existing theory of the earth as flat. It doesn't work. Feminist work is about a transformation of justice, not an expansion of it.

Gender problems extend to textbooks. Reviews of the literature suggest that textbook authors are themselves guilty of "doing" gender and perpetuating stereotypes. Wright (1992) undertook an investigation into textbook depictions of women, surveying 44 introductory textbooks. He compared two time intervals—1956-1965 and 1981-1990. He found that the average number of pages devoted to texts in 1981-1990 was 19.7 pages, a 5.6 page increase over the earlier period.[2] He identified four sexist themes in the first period: (1) support for rape myths that exonerate offenders and blame victims, (2) the depiction of female offenders as more deceitful and cunning than male offenders, (3) the image of women as intellectually and physiologically inferior to and less rational than men, and (4) an implicit condemnation of the "increased promiscuity" of "modern" women (Wright, 1992). Among the more recent period, he found that only (3) above, that women are less rational and psychologically and physiologically inferior, had disappeared from textbooks in criminal justice. The other three themes continued to be present, though their depiction is much less "strident and blatant."

Examining textbooks for corrections, Mahan and Anthony (1992) found that writing on women paralleled real increases in female crime, with dramatic increases in the late 1970s and early 1980s, then leveling in the 1990s. They also noted a change from "women's studies" to a broader focus on "gender studies" (see also Evans, 1990). Conducting a case-study of one popular textbook, they identified a contradiction, mentioned here because it reflects a common way of thinking about women in justice studies. On the one hand, the book stated that women's crime has become increasingly like men's crime. On the other, the book argued for differential treatment of women and emphasized the differences between male and female offenders.

A Feminist Pedagogy. The introduction of feminist issues in a criminal justice classroom is always difficult—the justice studies classroom continues to be gendered, and male students tend to bring pre-existing stereotypes about women into the classroom. Women continue to be marginalized in textbooks, preempting a challenge to gender stereotypes.

One of the purposes of education is to challenge stereotypical predispositions. A feminist pedagogy has emerged that can provide a positive learning environment, and also challenge stereotypes about men and women. Smith (1999) identified four components of a feminist pedagogy (see also Bright, 1993; Travis, 1992).

1. *Mastery.* This refers to how information is constructed in the classroom. Under a feminist pedagogy, students are encouraged to take a more active role in their education. Student's discussion is allowed to

set its own course, and students are encouraged to learn from each other. Students may be permitted to grade their own assignments.

2. *Voice.* Students are encouraged to use their own voices and express their intuitive perceptions and ideas. The purpose of this more intuitive approach is to allow for the recognition of predispositive sentiments and stereotypes by students. Criminal justice students sometimes carry conflicts about the role of women in the justice system. It is important that these conflicts are recognized if students are to be promoters of gender equality rather than perpetuators of difference.

3. *Authority.* Direction by instructors in minimized. Students are accustomed to a traditional pedagogy, where the instructor has all the authority. This challenges that tradition, leaning on students, motivations in learning.

4. *Positionality.* Students carry particular views of crime and criminal justice. Positionality refers to the location of their views from particular ideological or political vantage-points. Hence, on controversial issues they often have already fixed views, and faculty may be hesitant to challenge these views. Under a feminist pedagogy, students learn about the relativity of their views develop an understanding of other points of view.

Feminist pedagogy differs from a traditional pedagogy, which tends to be instructor-centered. In criminal justice classrooms (and indeed in classes across the curricula), teachers often use an authoritarian style, in which they state clear ground rules, use a syllabus as a "contractual" device, and place in it a clause that provides instructors the right to change the syllabus at any time.

In the advocacy of feminist pedagogy, we begin to understand why feminism is more than "adding women and stirring." If feminist pedagogy were to be taken seriously, instructors would have to think about what they are trying to accomplish in the classroom, what they wanted students to think about, and how they wanted students to think about it. We would have to recognize that students were active learners, not passive recipients of "truth." Students would learn that relations among humans work better in a positive, reinforcing learning environment than in an authoritarian setting. Such a notion is far-reaching. It suggests that giving orders and stating rules does not convey information very effectively. It suggests that substantive means shape ends. In other words, the goal of feminist pedagogy is no less than a re-shaping of the meaning of justice itself.

There is no articulable pedagogical style in criminal justice. Indeed, the distinctive feature of instruction in many classrooms is an absence of pedagogical style. Teaching pedagogy has been little more than "sink or swim," with many faculty sinking under the weight of negative student evaluations. In this context, feminist pedagogy represents an improvement, if for no other reason that it inserts a pedagogical style where none currently exists except in the most informal sense—educators' recollections of their instructor's style.

In some other academic fields, pedagogy is a highly developed instructional art, and classes on pedagogical technique and learning theory are integral to advanced education. Feminist pedagogy, rather than replacing an authoritarian teaching, may in fact be inserting pedagogy into a vacuum, a much needed corrective on currently inadequate training. In most Ph.D. programs, future educators are mentored in scholarship. They learn the ins and outs of survival in a "publish or perish" profession. Rarely do they learn much about how to teach. Yet teaching represents the center of the justice occupations to a greater degree than either scholarship or service. At a minimum, feminist pedagogy should engage us in a debate about the meanings and goals of teaching, about how teaching style carries in it values and predispositions about justice itself.

Women as Scholars. Women are active in the professional organizations of criminal justice. As measured by participation at the two major criminal justice associations (the American Society of Criminology and the Academy of Criminal Justice Sciences), women account for 21.9 percent of the membership in both organizations. They also author 28.4 percent of the papers that are presented (Eigenberg & Baro, 1992). However, when published scholarship is examined, women author only 16.5 percent of the papers published by four major journals.[3] In other words, women are overrepresented in the presentation of papers at major conferences, but underrepresented in the publication of refereed journals.

What accounts for this difference? One possible explanation is that women are underrepresented as reviewers of articles, and hence issues pertaining to women do not receive a fair editorial review. There is some support for this idea. Eigenberg and Baro (1992) found that women were less likely to be published in journals where women were also underrepresented on the journal's editorial board. Only in the journal *Crime & Delinquency* did women have representative proportion of editors, and it was in this journal that articles by women were most likely to be published. Similarly, *The Journal of Criminal Justice* had the smallest representation and also was the least likely to publish works by women. This pattern of representation-publication suggests a gatekeeping function: representation on a journal's editorial board is a necessary precondition for publication equality. Yet, as the authors note, one cannot infer editorial philosophy from the make-up of the editorial board. And we would need to study the actual editorial processes in order to understand the dynamics that lead to an informal tendency to select papers by men over women.

Gender Issues in Crime and Justice

Broadly, speaking, we can describe two general types of gender issues affecting justice. The first is gender in the justice workplace. The second concerns gender in criminological research. These are discussed below.

Martin and Jurik: The Gendered Criminal Justice Workplace. Women have made occupational inroads into many organizational fields. Yet, occupational successes in the field of criminal justice have been limited, and women continue to face obstacles and encounter resistance. Criminal justice organizations are highly gendered, which means that patterns of control, advantage and disadvantage, actions, emotions, meanings and identities are structured and enacted around gender differences (Acker, 1990). Martin and Jurik (1996) provide insight on the extent to which criminal justice organizations are gendered, and how women encounter systemic resistance when they seek employment and participation in justice organizations. Their research is reviewed below.

Police training and organizations. Ideas of "appropriate behavior" in the police profession reveal an idealized sense of maleness, what some call "macho" (a Spanish word that translates as "male animal"). When casual observers of policing think about its physical dimensions, they associate aggressive and physical police practices with the rough demands of the street, catching "bad guys," getting in fights with drunk or stoned felons, and the like.

Aggressiveness is encouraged throughout the training and promotional process. Training can emphasize a macho orientation by encouraging the development of physical skills and using them in aggressive encounters. Some counter that aggressive physical training is needed in police work, where unpredictable encounters with citizens can turn violent. Martin and Jurik, however, observe that even the most minimal physical conditioning requirements are absent in most organizations after the first year. On the other hand, stories, an important part of the informal socialization process in training, are oriented toward men, and often describe aggressive encounters. Male recruits learn local cultural precepts about safety and toughness; that personal safety is enhanced by physical prowess, even though data show that the primary cause of death is improper police actions (Martin & Jurik, 1996:77). The emphasis on physical prowess, they assert, is more symbol than substance, and may in fact conflict with good police work.

After training, recruits are assigned to training officers (TOs). When women are placed with a TO, they sometimes face overprotective paternalism. They are not invited to participate in many of the activities that will help them learn critically needed patrol skills. Consequently, when assigned to a permanent position, women are over-assigned to administration and underrepresented in patrol, a pattern that undercuts opportunities for promotion (Martin, 1990).

Performance evaluations perpetuate gender differences in police organizations. Evaluations are an important component in the promotional process, but tend to be subjectively rated by superior officers. For a variety of gender-based reasons, women are consistently rated below men. Performance ratings emphasize patrol activity, and women who are not on patrol—perhaps because TOs pushed them into administrative positions—do not fare well. And evaluators often grade women poorly on aggressiveness and on their ability to get along with other patrol officers—good scores are associated with male notions of aggression and social skills. Consequently, for many women, police work is a revolving door on the first floor—they are able to enter, but unable to gain promotion.

Martin (1980) observed that the occupation of policing was gendered to such an extent that work roles simply did not exist for women. Women had limited choices—they either could openly resist efforts of males to place them in traditional feminized roles and risk being labeled in derogative terms, or they could accept their place as women and accept their limitations as police officers. Some women chose to emulate their male counterparts by being tough, productive, emotionally detached, and professional. Women that follow this path tended to be labeled "bitches" or "dykes" and treated with hostility. Because they elected to emphasize their role as a police officers, Martin referred to these women as POLICE-women. Alternatively, if women wanted to get along with their male counterparts, they could give in to male paternalism and adopt traditional, feminized roles. They accepted the less dangerous assignments, abandoned interest in crime-fighting elements of police work, and were sexually active with men on the force. These, Martin states, were policeWOMEN.

Central to Martin's analysis was the recognition that there was not a "normal" role for women to occupy in many police organizations. Police departments were sometimes so gendered that all female roles were maladaptive. Organizations did not have a way for women to be both professionally active and retain a gendered identity—be a woman.

Some women, Martin and Jurik (1996) observed, are beginning to successfully adapt to these conflicting role expectations. They represent a "new policewoman." They balance the conflicting expectations of women and police by "projecting a professional image, demonstrating unique skills, emphasizing a team approach, using humor to develop camaraderie and thwart unwelcome advances, and gaining sponsorship to enhance positive visibility" (Jurik, 1988; in Martin & Jurik, 1996:98). They are rule-oriented, display a willingness to use physical force, and seek patrol activity. They also work very hard.

The Legal Profession. The legal profession, like the police, has a history of female exclusions, though women have made significant gains in recent years. In 1960, women were only 3.5 percent of enrollees at ABA-approved U.S. law schools; by 1986 they accounted for 40.2 percent (Abel, 1989; in Martin & Jurik, 1996:109). Currently, nearly a quarter of the legal profession and nearly half of law students are women. However, these numbers disguise "overt and subtle barriers" that continue to deny to women full integration in the law professions.

The training and practice of law tends to be gender-scripted. Consider the language of the law. Women must spend an extended period learning the "reasonable man's" perspective (Angel, 1988). Textbooks isolate issues that concern women to topics of domestic relations and sex discrimination, perpetuating the myth that women's concerns are with the house or are personal, while men take care of the rest of the world (Frug, 1992).

Once they gain employment, women often encounter explanations for their success and failure that are sexual rather than professional:

> . . . the characteristics generally associated with masculine dominance are used to explain men's successes; their failures are explained as "bad luck." Thus, men's success is regarded as a function of innate analytic and rhetorical abilities that presumably make them more suitable for practicing law. But women's success is attributed to luck, chance, or inappropriate use of their sexuality; their failures are explained as inability to "think like a lawyer" (Rhode, 1988; Martin & Jurik, 1996:124).

Women face role conflicts that are similar to those they confront in the police profession. Women who are tough face disapproval from their colleagues and are seen as masculine. If they adapt to the gender expectations of femininity, they are accused of behaving in ways that are unlawyerly. This process is reflected in informal socialization processes as well. Female law students have difficulty finding mentors in school, a problem that undercuts their ability to learn the informal norms of the world of law and places them at systematic disadvantage in the highly connected world of legal practice.

These problems limit womens' abilities to achieve success in the legal professions. A woman's chances of becoming a law partner in the United States and Canada is 39 percent less than are a comparable man's, and women who have "made it" required about 20 percent more time (Hagan, 1990; in Martin & Jurik, 1996:133). In other words, women face a cumulative disadvantage that limits their ability to participate in the lives of their professions, even though the legal barriers do not prohibit their participation. Ultimately these factors have a long-term affect on their salary: for each year of experience that women gain on the job, the gender income gap increases between them and men (Hagan, 1990).

Both policing and law are gendered professions, though they do gender differently. Among the police, maleness is associated with cultural images of working-class masculinity. Traits of physical aggressiveness, emotional reserve, and trustworthiness are emphasized. Women were challenged for being physically or emotionally weak. Even police professionalism, associated with rationality and emotionless affect ("just the facts, ma'am") is not gender neutral but is an idealized view of white masculinity in a professional setting.

The legal profession also does gender by focusing on women's toughness, though toughness is in terms of legal aggressiveness and courtroom demeanor. In spite of its more genteel appearance, the legal profession is fully as gendered as the policing workplace. Martin and Jurik conclude that:

> Because of their supposedly emotional natures and "lower" level of moral reasoning, women are considered insufficiently rational and objective for legal work. Resistance tactics in the legal profession have focused on withholding sponsorship on important cases, tracking to less prestigious specialties, excluding women from key referral networks, and engaging in verbal and nonverbal displays of disrespect that discourage potential clients and threaten the livelihood of women attorneys (Martin & Jurik, 1996:215-216).

How can an instructor prepare the women in her or his classes for the gender hostility, barriers, and role confusions they would like to deny but that they are likely to face when they take a position in a criminal justice organization? This concern is practical. On the one hand, educators in the field of justice studies want their students to obtain employment. They also want to provide students with a realistic expectation of what their working environment will be. Of concern is that female students do not fully understand what lies ahead for them in the "professional" world of the justice occupations. Should they be warned of the perils of the gendered workplace? Should they be prepared for litigation and occupational self-preservation? Or should the problems they will encounter be downplayed, even though it is likely that their problems will involve the same males with whom they exchange casual, sexualized banter in the classroom? Research has shown that males receive criminal justice educations and still depart from the academic experience with sharply sexist attitudes (Austin & Hummer, 1994).

The fundamental purpose of education is to inform, for all the frustrations and fears that such knowledge might bring. Students may not want to hear it, but hear it they must. Perhaps, if they are adequately prepared for the inevitable dangers and frustrations that will assault them in the highly sexualized world of American criminal justice, they can "make their mark" and having done so, help transform the criminal justice workplace into a workplace characterized by human justice.

Crime and Women

Women have held a star-crossed place in the research on crime. It is widely believed that women are favored, that they commit "less important" crimes and that they are treated more leniently than men. On the other hand, women have sometimes been treated harshly, and occasionally their treatment has been brutal. Gendered differences and the way they have been neglected are the central themes uniting the various areas of research in the following section.

Women and Criminology. An increasingly large body of criminological research is examining the way in which women have been misrepresented. A number of authors have observed the way in which male and female stereotypes have influenced the seemingly objective development of the field. Belknap's (1996) literature review provided a much-needed sensibility for thinking about criminological history. Her research demonstrated how many foundational perspectives on the etiology of crime carry in them gender biases or take for granted gender stereotypes. Early criminological theory was characterized by four assumptions regarding female criminality (Belknap, 1996:23):

1. Individual (female) characteristics, not society, are responsible for criminal behavior.

2. There is an identifiable biological nature inherent in all women.

3. Offending women are "masculine," which makes them incompetent as women and thus prone to break the law.

4. The differences in male and female criminality are due to sex.

In short, women turned to crime because of their perversion to or rebellion from natural feminine roles. Consider the work of Lombroso, considered by many to be the "father" of criminology:

> Lombroso and (his son-in-law) Ferrero's (1895) now-discredited book *The Female Offender* explains female criminality through atavism. Atavism is a concept that defines all deviant behavior as a "throwback" to an earlier evolutionary stage in human development . . . Lombroso and Ferrero concluded that women offenders showed less degeneration than men simply because women had not evolved as much as men.
>
> Lombroso and Ferrero also assumed that criminal behavior was a sex, not a gender, trait. This lead to the erroneous assumption that a woman exhibiting criminal tendencies "is not only an abnormal woman, she is biologically like a man" (Smart, 1976:33; Belknap, 1996:23).

What does it mean, to be "biologically like a man?" If we are applying biological theory of that day, we consider women to be biologically inferior. Women display arrested physical development; they stopped growing too soon. They are forever trapped in puberty (Walklate, 1995). They are consequently arrested emotionally as well, lacking the rigorous rationality of men.

Strain theory brought about a welcome departure from biological theories of crime predominant in the nineteenth century. Strain theory, simply put, is that individuals share similar goal aspirations, but opportunities to achieve those aspirations are unequal. Strain is the disjunction between the (desired) goal and the presence of legitimate opportunities to achieve it. Strain theory, however, also carried predispositive ideas of female criminality. Albert Cohen, for example, adapted Robert Merton's development of strain theory to delinquent gangs. However, Cohen's ideas of goals were male goals—the competitive goals of the "American dream." Women only sought narrow ambitions around males, such as dating, dancing, attractiveness, and acquiring a boyfriend or husband. Similarly, Cloward and Ohlin (1960) observed that women were neither expected to achieve the major success goals of society nor offered delinquent outlets. Their offending was of a sexual nature, and focused on personal considerations (Naffine, 1987).

Labeling theory suffered similar gender biases. Labeling theorists tended to view criminal men as having exciting, interesting lives. Women, on the other hand, were without direction, boring and lifeless. Consider Becker's (1963) work on jazz and dance musicians:

> When women are examined in Becker's work, it is most frequently as the wives of the male musicians, and in these instances they are portrayed as boring, laughable, and "square." They are depicted as nags who threaten the livelihood of the band by trying to convince their husbands to get "real" jobs (Belknap, 1996:31).

Biological, strain, and labeling theory are only three of the perspectives discussed in Belknap's work. In these, Belknap shows how predispositions among criminological theorists, both historically and currently, have contributed to a poor understanding of the influence of sex and gender on crime. In a great deal of research on the etiology of crime, a close examination shows that male crime (or decidedly male explanations of crime) have been in high relief against a backdrop of all crime. Female crime has been obscured, as if it were a shadow of male crime. In Belknap's work, we begin to understand the shadow.

Prison Reform. In an edited series of papers, Miller (1998) argues that contemporary crime control interventions have had unexpected and disproportionate effects on women. Fears over crime, have lead to blind political expediency in the development of crime control policy. Lawmakers have ignored the effects of these policies on women, minorities, and the poor.

Gender effects can be seen in the growth of prisons and in get-tough legislation. The criminal justice system has undergone dramatic expansion in recent years. The United States incarcerates more than 1.5 million people in federal and state prisons. These prisoners increasingly are women: in the 1980s, the rate of women's incarceration was twice as fast as that of men. The expansion of the criminal justice system is embodied in "get-tough" legislation. Consider the "three-strikes and you're out" legislation, currently popular among crime control advocates. By early 1995, 15 jurisdictions had passed "three-strikes" legislation, and it had become part of the California Constitution. Danner (1998) argues that women pay a hidden cost for this legislation, in three ways.

1. State money away is channeled away from social services and into crime control. Social services programs are targeted primarily to poor women and children. Justifications for rechanneling monies into crime control and away from social services are that people on social services are lazy and unwilling to work for their keep. Social service reforms promise a savings dividend that lawmakers can channel into anticipated crime control policies. Many states are investing in expensive crime control measures in the hope that costs can be offset by other reductions. Whether or not these anticipated savings will offset costs remains to be seen.

2. A second hidden effect is in the loss of jobs for women who are employed by social service agencies as social workers, case workers, counselors, and support staff. Sixty-none percent of social workers are women, and their participation as front line and case workers in social services is even higher. Critics, Danner states, will counter that new positions are created for women in criminal justice. Yet, the vast majority of positions in the criminal justice occupations are male— only 9 percent of police jobs belong to women, as are only 18 percent of correctional guards (Maguire & Pastore, 1995). Hence, crime control will benefit male applicants for positions far more than females.

3. Responsibility for taking care of children of incarcerated parents falls disproportionately to women. Most people imprisoned are men. Care for their children falls to their wives, mothers, or girlfriends. Because imprisoned men cannot contribute to the livelihood of their children, the impact on their children and their sponsors is financially severe. And when women are imprisoned, their mothers often take responsibility for the well-being of children. This hidden cost is large: there are today about 1.5 million children of prisoners (Johnson, 1995).

The real costs of incarceration of women are substantial. When a woman is imprisoned, her children participate in that experience. Forcible separation of the mother from the child and lack of close contact create psychological and behavioral problems for the children, aggression, poor school performance, attention deficit, poor social skills, depression, and sleep disruptions (Snyder-Joy & Carlo, 1998). This contributes to further expansion of the justice system: children of inmates are five to six times more likely to become incarcerated (Bloom, 1993).

The state bears a responsibility to assist mothers in their efforts to continue parenting during incarceration. As Snyder-Joy and Carlo (1998:134) note, mothers will someday be released, and when this happens there is a high likelihood that they will re-unite with their children. Unless the state provides a way to keep mother and child united, "there is likely to be repetition of the behaviors that brought the women into the criminal justice system in the first place. Contemporary [punitive] uses of incarceration alone are not designed to address these problems." As Renzetti (1998:185) further stated, there is a contradiction between the rhetoric of 'saving the family' and punitive prison policies that tear families apart and exacerbate preexisting family problems.

The impact of prison life on families is immediate and destructive. Efforts of women to maintain any semblance of family life are overwhelmed by the prison experience (Mahan, 1984). Using ethnographic methods to women's adaptive processes, Mahan found that the state's control over time and space was so overwhelming that alienation was the dominant feature of women's lives. Those held in prison manifested its destructive cultural consequences, and the long-term post prison impact was criminogenic—to increase the likelihood of criminal activity in the future.

Boot Camps. One of the other new reforms is boot camp, an increasingly popular correctional reform. Morash and Rucker's (1998) assessment of boot camps is a troubling insight into how criminal justice programs can manifest hostile and destructive elements of male dominance, and how it may consequently encourage criminal activity. Boot camps, Morash and Rucker note, are modeled after military-style training. The offenders are usually first time and nonviolent. The regimen at boot camps tends to be severe, including the use of strict discipline, rigorous physical training, harsh punishments, and authoritarian decisionmaking.

Boot camp practices, however, reveal a distorted image of socialization processes in terms of a highly gendered and authoritarian idea of male-female relations. Boot camps convey the idea that forceful control is to be valued. Prosocial attitudes encouraging empathy are not encouraged. What is particularly ironic, Morash and Rucker observe, is that correctional settings emphasize this aggressive model of masculinity when these very characteristics are used to explain criminality. Boot camps, by borrowing the military model of discipline, carry with them the male-oriented culture of the military environment. In such an environment, to fail is to be weak, perhaps to be called some derogatory term for "female" (Eisenhart, 1975). Boot camp, rather than providing a cure, sustains and reinforces some of the more troubling elements of our gendered culture: aggressiveness, dominance, and authoritarianism. Female prosocial attitudes, which might help them in a post-release environment, are discouraged. Ironically, those skills that will help readjustment may become a casualty in the aggressive, proto-military boot-camp "war on crime." As the authors concluded, how can an institution—boot camp—designed to prepare its participants for war assist them in becoming peaceful?

Lutz and Murphy (1999) followed with boot-camp research on men. What, they asked, was the impact of subjecting men to an ultramasculine environment that typified correctional boot camps? Their research found that the environment of these programs was associated with helplessness, a low sense of safety, little support, and highly coercive. These, the authors noted, are factors associated with the production of criminality. Potential problems were greatest for those who successfully adapted to the boot camp environment:

> Inmates who internalize repeated examples of confrontation and assertive interaction as acceptable behavior for gaining control of others may experience problems after release by overasserting their position and refusing to compromise (Lutz & Murphy, 1999:727).

Morash and Rucker's (1990) research showed how women's failure to adapt to boot camp settings interfered with their ability to reintegrate into society. Lutz and Murphy's (1999) research revealed that men's successful adaptation was counterproductive to reintegration. This research suggests that the penological effects of boot-camp programs are poorly understood. Research on boot camps described above suggests that, at least for boot camps and perhaps to a much broader variety of prison-based programs, the internal logic that drives the institutions of punishment is as likely to invigorate the attitudes that produce crime than to protect individuals from it.

The Amnesty International Report on Women in Prison. In 1999, Amnesty International reported on a study of the condition of women prisoners in the United States (Amnesty International, 1999). Their findings fell into two general categories. The first category of concerns were those cases where women were treated illegally in prison. Cases of sexual abuse of prisoners figured prominently among Amnesty's concerns. Consider the following examples:

> Arizona: A U.S. Department of Justice investigation into women's prisons found that authorities failed to protect women from sexual misconduct, specifically rape, sexual relations, sexual touching and fondling, and prolonged and close-up viewing during showering, dressing, and urinating. Since the report, more than 60 people working with female inmates have been dismissed, resigned, or been reprimanded.

> Michigan: A U.S. Department of Justice investigation of women's prisons in 1994-1995 reported evidence of widespread sexual abuse, including rape. Additionally, the Justice Department reported that officers abused

women during pat-down searches by touching all parts of the woman's body, fondling and squeezing their breasts, and genital areas. Officers also stood outside prisoner's cells and watched them undress, shower, and use toilet facilities.

It is difficult for a prisoner to protect herself from brutalization. A woman can only use prison or jail complaint procedures when facing a sexually aggressive or brutal guard. Opportunities for retaliation are easily available. In the Michigan case mentioned above, Amnesty International published a follow-up report on retaliatory measures against female complainants. Retaliations included sexual and physical assault, confiscation of legal mail, unnecessarily intrusive body searches, verbal threats and harassment, and false accusations of misconduct (Human Rights Watch, 1998).

Violations of human rights take other forms as well. The use of physical restraints during pregnancy and birth were particularly troubling.

On 18 November 1998, Amnesty International delegates visited Madera County Hospital in California. Prison officials took them through a ward where women are held when they are seriously ill or in labor and for a short period after giving birth. The ward is locked. Inside the ward are four armed guards. Yet every women is chained by her leg to a bed. A woman showed the Amnesty International Delegates her shackle. She could lie on her side but she could not roll over. Prison officials explained to the delegates that the shackle is removed only if a doctor informs them that it is interfering with medical treatment or is injurious to a woman's health. Shortly before Amnesty International's visit, the organization received a report from a lawyer that at the same hospital in 1998 she had seen a woman who was shackled having a seizure and that guards refused the request of nursing staff to remove the restraint (Amnesty International, 1999:28-29).

Women also face difficulties acquiring equal prison opportunities to educational and service programs. In Washington, D.C., female prisoners brought legal action to gain equal access to vocational and educational programs. This case was still under consideration when Amnesty International published their report. This case illuminates a dilemma associated with the relatively small size of resident female populations in prisons: Fewer programs may be offered because there aren't enough women to use them. It should be noted that the U.S. Bureau of Prisons requires that any new or revised federal prison policy address gender.

These cases show how aggressive control strategies used on men are adapted to women. Prisons have demonstrated a blind spot when it comes to dealing with the particular problems that women face in a prison environment. So-called "rational" or gender neutral justice policies can have a disproportionately negative impact on women.

The prison process permitted in the United States also conflict with international standards of justice. The standard of justice used by Amnesty International to consider the treatment of prisoners in the United States is an internationally accepted standard. Unfortunately, it frequently conflicts with prison administrative protocols in the United States. Amnesty International's concern over female prisoner mistreatment stems in part from U.S. reluctance, and at times outright refusal to recognize international standards. For example, the *Standard Minimum Rules for the Treatment of Prisoners*, Rules 53(2) and 53(3) of the International Covenant on Civil and Political Rights state that:

1. female prisoners should be attended and supervised only by female officers.

2. male staff such as doctors and teachers may provide professional services in female facilities, but should always be accompanied by female officers.

The mixing of male guards and female inmates is common in U.S. prisons. Forty-one percent of correctional officers working with female inmates are men. This is a clear violation of International standards—or would be, if we participated.

That the United States lags the rest of the world in prison reform for women is characteristic of its international stance toward gender. The United States has refused to sign the convention on the *Elimination of All forms of Discrimination of Women.* The Convention was initially signed by the United States in 1980 after being adopted by the United Nations. At the present time the United States has not formally ratified the treaty, though 165 countries have (Amnesty International, 1999).

How should we think about the conflicts between the United States and the international community regarding women? Clearly, two different formal standards of justice are positioned against each other. The position of the U.S. government has been clear: international standards are supported only insofar as they are in agreement with the U.S. Constitution. Or should the government affirm the standards brought by Amnesty International, even knowing that such a stance would alienate prison officials in the United States and conflict with popular sentiment? The question here is not simply what is right, but more fundamentally, what criteria are used to arrive at a "right" decision?

Certainly, citizens want our prison guards to act legally. But the legal questions provide detail—they do not frame the issue. What standard of justice is appropriate? The justice responsibility is to take the debate seriously without taking sides, to provide students and professionals with the full scope of argumentation, to comprehend both the position of the United States and of Amnesty International, and to encourage research.

In the debate about prisoner treatment lies the way we think about justice and crime, what we believe we should be achieving. Then bring on the debate! Amnesty International's findings should be a wake-up call for anyone complacent about women in prisons. Yet their findings are only a beginning in the effort to find justice for women in prison. Justice requires that we engage ourselves in the effort.

The Other Gender: Masculinities and Crime

There are not many facts about crime. One of the few that we can state with confidence is that males commit the vast majority of criminal acts. Why? Research on gender and the etiology of crime has tended to focus on females. The question most frequently asked is "Why do women commit so much less crime than men?" This may be the wrong question. What needs explaining may not be the relative scarcity of crime committed by women but the substantial volume committed by men. Increasingly, researchers are asking "Why is the rate of offending of men so much greater than women?"

The word "masculinities" has entered our vocabulary on crime. Newburn and Stanko (1994:2) suggest that we should use the word "masculinities" to discuss male gender and crime, because it is plural and allows us to think about the "power and variety of masculine values, the processes by which they become internalized, the processes of identification, the ways in which certain core values become associated with specific social groups, together with a historical analysis of masculinities and masculine practices." Hence, patterns of patriarchy may vary by race and by social class.

Research on masculinities distinguishes between hegemonic and subordinated masculinities (Connell, 1987).[4] *Hegemonic masculinities* refer to the way men acquire and hold power, and how they legitimate and reproduce the social relations that maintain their power. For example, American men, until only recently, held virtually all the executive authority in major American businesses. *Subordinated masculinities*, on the other hand, refer to gender statuses that are discredited or oppressed. Homosexual masculinity is an example of subordinated masculinity: behavior associated with homosexual relations is criminalized in many states.

Stanko: Men and Violence. In the field of criminal justice, we have a common-sense way we think about violence. However, our ideas of violence come from men, are about men, and reflect the way men look at violence. This image is gender-distorted: It does not take into consideration how violence is a predominantly male phenomenon. Uninformed by the way violence affects women or family life, we have developed a uniquely individualistic, socially aberrant, idea of violence. These ideas of violence may be wrong. As Stanko (1994) observes, they certainly are gender based and inconsistent with what goes on among men and women. She provides the following observations:

1. Violence is commonly treated as an aberrant, phenomenon, atypical of and violating social life. Yet in many cases it is patterned and continuing. Stanko notes that we tend to think of violence as an "aberrant event, piercing the harmony of normality" [34]. Women's studies have been criticized for blaming all men for violence. Yet, as Stanko notes, women live in the threat of potential danger from all men as an ordinary part of their lives, and organize their lives in response to this threat. Violence, in some cases, is the norm and peace is aberrant.

2. We tend to view violence as an individual phenomenon. When the police measure violent crime, for example, they group together like unrelated events for reporting purposes, like burglary and arson. Crime control policy—deterrence, for example—consequently focuses on the prevention of individual acts. What is missing is a discussion of state-sanctioned and institutional violence. For example, the way in which family violence is institutionalized and sanctioned is shown in research that shows that stranger rape is much more likely to be coded by the police as a crime than intimate violence, such as espousal rape. Yet they are both the same act.

3. When we focus on fear of crime, we inevitably focus on fears outside the home. This perspective is pervasive to community policing today. We focus on street crime, and support policies such as "put more police on the streets." We have wholly neglected the most important fears for women—fear of personal victimization inside the home. That we can't put police inside the home suggests for a fundamental rethinking of justice policy to deal common patterns of victimization.

4. Men are commonly the targets of institutionalized violence from the state, especially the police, the military, and the prison system. Yet, because of the way masculine identity is formed, they are highly unlikely to report it, thus permitting its perpetuation.

5. Is gender-specific behavior the result of socialization or of biology? The nature-nurture debate is the source of a great deal of contention in the field of justice studies. There is a popular perception, exaggerated in the media, that men are fueled by testosterone and unable to control their aggression. Hormonal explanations legitimate male violence as natural, and thus perpetuate the social structural bases of hegemonic masculinity. In a peculiar about-face, many theorists who believe in "natural" sex differences castigate feminists who blame violence on maleness.

6. Violence—instrumental or expressive? Criminal justice students are commonly taught to think of violence in terms of its instrumental or expressive nature. How then do we think about spousal violence? Do men simply "fly into a blind rage" when feeling jealousy or loss of control? Or is it more instrumental? The early work of Dobash and Dobash (1979) suggests that men's violent behavior against their spouses may appear expressive and intensely emotional, but it is in fact instrumental, and is used as a means of control.

7. Finally, male violence is implicated in the way in which men relate to each other. Violence serves to save face or to establish status. This is particularly the case among the poor and disenfranchised. Social competition and violence are greatest among poor males precisely because they have so few resources from which to establish social status. Hence, violence is not aberrant, but is at the core of social relations among men.

Violence and Schools. Of all statuses associated with crime, those most criminogenic are youth and maleness. Simply, young men commit an astonishingly high percentage of overall crime (Chesney-Lind & Shelden, 1992). Why?

It may be that young men are socialized into traditions of violence, and that the principal institutions of socialization socialize males into violence as well. Consider schools. Among white, middle-class youth, schools provide specific socialization tracks for the development of masculine identity. Sports provide an "environment for the construction of a masculinity that celebrates toughness and endurance, incessantly advocates competitiveness and shame of losing . . . " (Messerschmidt, 1994:87).

Schools also connect maleness with a taste for violence and confrontation. These masculinities are associated with other more civic qualities such as a sensibility toward academic success, familial emphases on appropriate qualifications and credentialing, and desires for respectable careers.

> For the white middle class, then, manliness is about having a secure income from a "respectable" professional occupation. Thus, there is an important link between school and family in middle-class life, and both transmit class-specific notions of hegemonic masculinity to white, middle-class boys—a particular type of work in the paid-labor market, competitiveness, personal ambition and achievement and responsibility (Messerschmidt, 1994:880).

Adaptation to the school environment requires that students submit to the "rock-hard" authority of the school system. Students tend to be penalized for creativity and independence. White, middle-class boys conform to this hierarchy in order to achieve success (Messerschmidt, 1993). This is an "accommodation" masculinity: students, in order to achieve expected success, develop accommodation strategies to the authoritarian school environment.

School is both authoritarian and emasculating, and when students are away they seek to reestablish their masculine identity. Pranks, minor crime, drinking, and nuisance behavior are ways that school-age males construct their masculine identities around their peers. This behavior focuses on masculine elements of independence, dominance, daring, and control, all elements often learned at home but suppressed in the school environment.

White working-class males develop their masculine identity in ways different from middle-class youth. Whereas white, middle-class males are conforming inside the school and oppositional outside the school, white, working-class boys are oppositional both inside and outside the school. Their masculine identity is formed in opposition to the authoritarian nature of the school setting. This is an *oppositional masculinity*, because it is formed in opposition to the general values associated with participation in the life of the schools. Criminal behavior provides a basis around which some white, working-class boys develop masculine identity in opposition to school-based values. Masculine identity is also constructed through hostility to anything considered effeminent or non-white. Masculinity is constructed around a specific racial gender—white and heterosexual—and other combinations are subject to violence. What we today call "hate crimes" are sometimes the outcomes of oppositional socialization among working-class youth:

> . . . for some white, working class youth, homosexuality is simply unnatural and effeminate sex, and many turn this ideology into physical violence. As one white, working class youth put it, "My friends and I go 'fag-hunting' around the neighborhood. They should all be killed (Weissman, 1992:173).

Young men can fortify their masculine identities through attacks on racial minorities. Violence, particularly when it is acted out in groups against other groups or lone individuals, was an important part of the way in which young males developed identity and perpetuated racist and anti-gay views.

Intermittent theft characterized this group as well, which provided extra pocket money. School did not provide socialization experiences for adult life for working-class youth. Important experiences leading to the development of adult roles occurred in jobs these young men held out of school. They tended to take part-time jobs, and looked down on middle-class, school involved youth. Their opposition was expressed in terms of a work ethic around the physical labor involved in their part-time jobs. They saw themselves as becoming more adult and getting financially ahead while middle-class youth were school-bound. However, this way of thinking backfired, and led them to take dead-end jobs. A cycle was thus perpetuated in which the schooled children of blue-collar workers were trapped into demeaning, dead-end jobs.

Lethal Violence. Maleness is strongly implicated in lethal violence. Male-on-male homicides represent a distinctively male crime, violent and lethal. It also represents the most common form of homicide (Polk, 1994). What accounts for it?

To be sure, situational factors contribute to lethal violence. Situational factors provide the immediate context for the construction of male-male contests. Homicidal confrontations often begin as "contests of honor" in which the maintenance of face cannot be ignored (Polk, 1994). They also are about masculine matters. They involve perceived slights to a man's manhood, the virtue of his wife, sister, or mother, and the like. They are not premeditated but invariably emerge from a spontaneous series of events and affronts, imagined or real. They happen in public settings, from which males cannot easily withdraw and save face. And alcohol is heavily implicated. All of these factors provide structure and meaning for contests of honor to take place and become lethal.

However, the immediate context of these events is not enough to explain them. A broader social and cultural context makes the precipitating incidents—a perceived slight, an insult to a woman—meaningful. Daly and Wilson (1988) note that the most common male-on-male killings have to do with issues of honor and reputation. They tend to emerge from seemingly trivial events. To an outside observer, they might appear to be a minor concern; yet to the participants they are taken (and sometimes rightly) as a deliberate provocation. The audience, typically composed of like-minded young aggressive males, reinforces broad social expectations that one assert one' masculinity. To consider only the immediate context overlooks an central feature of masculinity: assertiveness, aggressiveness, and violence are acceptable cultural responses to particular kinds of perceived insults. Hence, to understand lethal violence, one has to consider it in the context of its social and cultural milieu. A man's reputation in many social circles depends on his ability to maintain a credible treat of violence.[5]

Conclusion: A Personal Reflection. When I reflect on the research on male violence, I sense an uncomfortable possibility. I think about violence as deviance from the norm, as sociologists and criminal justicians do. But is violence truly deviant? It is when criminals use it to further their ends. But what if I use it to deal with criminals? Is my sense of violence somehow part and parcel of the same violence used by criminals to further their ends? My discomfort is clear—are the ideological and moral tools I use to combat violence precisely those that in fact encourage it? Can it be that the socialization processes that I and men such as myself go through make us singularly unequipped to deal with justice?

I imagine being interviewed by a social scientist. Was I violent as a youth? Yes. Am I still aggressive? Sometimes, when I think I need to be. Do I draw pleasure from the idea of hurting someone that has wronged me? Depends. Do I imagine committing violence against bad people? Not as much as I used to. Would I kill someone that threatened my wife? Unhesitatingly. Do I think this way because I am a man? Ah, there's the rub. And an important rub it is, because it may be that I cannot conceive of a truly nonviolent world—a world where justice prevails over revenge, where we are more interested in doing good than in getting even.

Who, then, am I to think that I have a clue as to what justice is? I can't even separate the ideas of justice and violence. How can I arrive at a concept of justice that is *not* grounded in violence? How can I say that my way of thinking about justice is not gendered in some toxic way when my solution to violence is—violence? And, reader, how about you? Can you think in language and emotions that I cannot? Can you comprehend something that might be truly just?

Even as I conclude this chapter, my wife prepares dinner in the kitchen. I thank her, and she, a talented actor, smiles and says that it's nothing. We play this game, knowing its intrinsic unfairness but justifying it easily—I in terms of book-writing and she in terms of nutrition. I am imprisoned in the habitus—that strange space where personal identity, corporeality, and social reality intersect. My behavior is intentional, but I perceive and act on our gendered relationship as if it were natural, a simple statement of the way things are. Personal habits and social reality intertwine, invigorating one another. The habitus is insistent. Yet I know better.

From this, I grasp an important point: knowledge about gender and justice is in itself not enough. The achievement of gender equality will require a forceful and strong-willed intentionality; that political action, litigation, and federal intervention are the only ways to effect the kinds of fundamental changes needed to breach the rituals of inequality. If we do gender badly, then we can re-do it. If we in justice studies are uncomfortable in the marketplace of feminist ideas, then we must expand our comfort zone. There is much in feminist study and the knowledge it produces that can widen our ideas about who we are and how we create meaning in the worlds that we inhabit. And such knowledge is a necessary precondition of justice.

Notes

[1]   See Daly and Chesney-Lind (1988) for a review of this literature.

[2]   Wright (1992) observed that this difference in textbook length was not statistically significant; however, his collection of textbooks may have been a population rather than a sample, rendering measures of significance meaningless. He noted that he had measured "all known" textbooks in the two periods.

[3]   Five journals were surveyed: *The Journal of Criminal Justice, Crime & Delinquency, Criminology, Federal Probation*, and *The Journal of Police Science and Administration*.

[4]   In Newburn and Stanko, 1994: 3.

[5]   In Polk, 1994:184.

Chapter 8

Ethics and Morality:
The Power to Do Good;
The Power to Bind and Divide

> We learn to be just by doing things that are just.
> *Aristotle, Nicomachean Ethics*

Overview: Is This All There Is?

I sleep. I awake and eat. I decide when to fix dinner and when to do the dishes. I take vacations in the summer, when work is not so intense. I pay taxes, and one day I will die. Is this all there is?

All of us have asked this question at one time or another. It takes other forms, such as *What is the meaning of life?* It is a profound question, imbued with existential pathos, carrying the intimation that we are somehow not engaged in that which is really important, that our lives are vacuous and meaningless.

The question carries into our work. If we can find no meaning in life, then work has no meaning either. It is empty of purpose, a task only to be accomplished to pay the bills, to keep the wolves from the door.

This chapter is about the meanings that guide our behavior. Ethics and morality are about more than following a formal organizational policy posted in the cafeteria, to be read while waiting in line. The nature of meaning itself, the reasons we do what we do, is central to issues of ethics and morality. We may have reasons only to justify our behavior so that we don't get into trouble. We may have reasons for doing something that in fact get us into a great deal of trouble, but to which we feel honor-bound to follow. We may have conflicting obligations, each with their own justifications. Or we may be committed to a true vision of what we should do, and a single ethic guides our behavior. In all of these situations, our reasonings and the ethics that guide them constitute what is meaningful to us. By recognizing how ethics are situated in our reasoning, we begin to see how ethical issues are not something that we need to use on specific occasions, but are integral to our every action.

313

Part I: Thinking About Ethics

This chapter is not about teaching students what morality they should have or what ethical principles they should bring to their work environment. This inquiry begins with a discussion of what morality, ethics, and justice are. Nor shall I start at the usual starting point, a comparison of liberal and conservative traditions. A comparison of conservative and liberal standpoints are insufficient because they derive from the same ethical tradition of western L-liberalism.[1] There are ethical traditions fundamentally different from and outside of the western L-liberal tradition, and we might be surprised how important they are to us.

This chapter is written in the spirit of the sociological imagination, according to which we are encouraged to think beyond people's day-to-day problems and comprehend the larger issues from which their problems emerge. One of these issues is that the nature of justice and morality are up for grabs in the current age. What is needed is an understanding of the different ethical traditions that bear on ethical decisionmaking.

Ethical issues are particularly trenchant with regard to juvenile offenders, where we find ourselves caught between conflicting ethical traditions of personal and family responsibility, care, and the culpability of youth. Community leaders are considering how they can contribute to problems faced by juveniles, and may look to academicians and religious leaders alike for answers. Parents look to their schools and to local government for resources for their children's activities. Some justicians try to sort out who is more responsible—the child or the parent—and seek a way to allocate punishment accordingly. Others argue that the punishment and imprisonization of youth contributes to their future criminality, and that given time, most will simply age out of crime. All of these questions might be assisted with data and empirical analysis. But in the end, all are ethical questions, answerable in the court of ethics and morality, not scientific investigation.

The ordinary justice problems people face carry powerful currents of morality. Most commonly, we view justice issues through the lense of "personal responsibility." The idea of personal responsibility is itself a moral position that does not make sense from other standpoints of justice and morality. It is a highly relativistic concept, located in a notion of L-liberal justice.

In this chapter, I argue that four distinct traditions of justice and morality reside in the United States. In the give-and-take of social life, we can see the interplay of these moral-historical traditions. There are those around us who justify their behavior on traditions, located in ideas of small-town America. Others are committed to a life devoted to religious ideals. Still others believe that moral behavior is learned in and inseparable from the communities in which they grow up, and it is these communities that provide the basis for moral judgment. And there are those who are committed to a vision of equality, according to which no moral standard should hold greater sway than simple fairness.

We tend to borrow from one or the other tradition in different settings, infrequently recognizing that they are different or that different ways of thinking—what MacIntyre (1988) called rationalities—guide them. Yet, their differences are profound and have substantial implications for how we practice justice. What is important, and is the purpose of Part I of this chapter, is to identify these traditions and examine how they infuse our thinking about right and wrong. By assessing and comparing these traditions, we can see how the problems experienced by families, community leaders, and justice professionals are framed in broad and often contradictory moral traditions. And we can begin to acquire some insight into the reasons that guide our own efforts to be just.

Each tradition considered in this chapter provides both a rationality—a way of thinking that links one's actions to one's thoughts and considerations—and a morality—a basis for determining what constitutes good behavior. Hence, the answer to the question *what is the meaning of life* depends on which rational tradition is used to guide our moral behavior. Once we recognize these moral traditions, we can think in an informed way about the practice of justice around us.

Whose Justice? Which Rationality?

In the practice of justice, we tend to adopt a perspective based on responsibility, which means that we use a notion of rational decisionmaking based on free will. Free will is itself the product of a rational tradition—that the interests and needs of individuals determine the nature of the kind of justice and ethical positions appropriate for seeking justice. In some moral systems, behavior is a product of principled sources such as the church, historical traditions, or community, whose morality provides the standard against which ours is judged. A notion of ethics so principled by forces exterior to individuals is important to many criminal justice audiences, and derives from ethical traditions that predate the enlightenment.

In an historical analysis of moral traditions, MacIntyre (1988) asked the following question: when we seek moral justification for our behavior, how do we select among rival and incompatible accounts of justice? The discussion below borrows heavily from MacIntyre's discussion, and frequently quotes and paraphrases his work.

The way in which we conceive of right behavior is embedded in traditions, and each tradition exists and finds meaning within its particular historical and social times. Rationality itself is a tradition that occurs within social space and historical time, so there are rationalities rather than rationality, and there are justices rather than justice.

MacIntyre traces four traditions that have produced different rationalities and justices. The first three each find a basis for behavior in principles external to the individual. These are the Aristotelian, which finds its rationality in the polis and morality in the idea of practical justice and virtue; the Augustinian, which locates rationality in natural law and morality in Christian traditions; and the Scottish enlightenment, which finds morality in Scottish traditions and rationality in self-evident truths. Each is considered below.

The Aristotelian Polis. We learn to be just by doing things that are just. With this profound statement, Aristotle develops a widely studied notion of justice that continues to be meaningful today. The statement makes clear that justice and behavior are interrelated ideas. One cannot be just unless one acts justly.

The begged question is "How can we know which acts are just?" It is useful to have some idea of what constitutes justice before we act, otherwise there is no way to know if we are doing just acts. The answer to this question required practical education, and this education could only occur in a just community. This conception of justice locates community—in Aristotle's language, polis—as the source of just ideas. One's community is the source of one's just temperament and one's highest purpose will be to participate in its life. Rationality—the reasoning that connects thought to action—is thus wholly determined by the constitution of the good for which we strive, and the good is determined by participation in the life of the polis.

> The courage and skill required in military actions, the temperateness required in respect of pleasures, the liberality of munificence which deserves will of the polis because of the provisions of resources for public use, the intellectual and aesthetic excellence which makes this dramatist or lyric poet deserve the prize rather than that, all these may at different times have to be judged rightly if a just judgment is to be made. [106]

Citizens who have not been educated into the virtues lack the full capacity for justice. They may figure out on their own some ways of acting that are virtuous, but they will never fully understand the interplay of the virtues, virtuous education, and how such education results in a sense of justice. A just polis provides the education for its citizens to learn how to be just. Education in justice is essential for citizens to become virtuous and to contribute to a just polis.

Education into justice is practical, and proceeds from the specific to the general. In a just community, we become just by performing just acts. Over time and with practice, we learn how to expand our sense of the virtues and justice from immediately concrete situations to more general ones. Justice is thus a practical skill: it is the capacity to reason from the particular to the general.

When our sense of justice is fully developed, we have a full and defensible concept of what is good. Hence, practical justice is a precondition for rationality. The way we think through what is best for us, and what constitutes virtue from which we act, is determined by our knowledge of justice practically learned. A citizen consequently cannot be rational, that is, have an understanding of what is good and how he or she should act to achieve that good, without prior knowledge of justice. Once a citizen has learned the practical skill of justice, she or he can begin the work of learning other virtues. These will enable the citizen to participate in the life of the Polis, seeking the goods distributed justly by the polis.

> In both the earlier stages, the young person needs to receive education into both the virtues of character and those of intelligence. As a young man the citizen owes the polis his service as a soldier. Later he owes it his service in public office . . . As he moves from role to role, both as one who is ruled and one who rules he will need, if he is to merit honor, to learn how to exercise a whole range of virtues [106].

These virtues are learned within the polis and the polis is the basis of a citizen's behavior. A citizen acquires what he or she deserves according to their contribution to the polis. This is a desert notion of justice, according to which what one receives depends on what one contributes. Hence, the standards to which individuals measure the extent to which their behavior is just are wholly determined by the polis. There exists no other standard:

> So there is no standard external to the polis by which the polis can be rationally evaluated in respect to justice or any other good. To apprehend what a polis is, what the good is which is its function to achieve, and to what extent one's own polis has successfully achieved that good, all require membership in a polis. Without such membership, one is bound to lack essential elements of the education into the virtues and of the experience of life of the virtues which is necessary for such apprehension. But more than this, one is bound to lack also the capacity to reason rationally. [122-123]

The interests and passions of citizens are always secondary to the polis. The polis provides a set of criteria for just behavior exterior to the individual's needs and wants. Interests and passions, separated from the practical education into a just polis, are full of errors of education or of learning. To act only on the basis of untempered interests and passions is a sign that a person is not apprenticed in a just polis.

It has been suggested that Aristotle developed his conception of justice during times of great change and injustice, and the purpose of his writings were to provide a guide to correct behavior in a stable social setting. According to this idea, his musings about the nature of the polis were unrepresentative of actual events. Whether this is true or not, his ideas have had a powerful effect on European thought throughout the middle ages and into current times.

The Augustinian Tradition. The Augustinian tradition emerged as a religious challenge to the Aristotelian tradition. Of concern to practitioners of this tradition was not the behavior of individuals in relation to their polis, but their place in the cosmos itself. The central precepts of the law were the Ten Commandments and were exceptionless and applied to all people. Justice in practice was exercised within a community characterized by a hierarchy of offices, and office-holders determined who owed what to who according to religious standards. Desert—the distribution of rewards—was based on religious status.

In this tradition, a new element of human nature was added that changed the nature of ethical and religious thought. This is the idea that knowledge of good is not itself enough to produce good or just behavior. Knowledge is linked to behavior through the self-directed will.

Human will, existing prior to reason, was the ultimate determinate of action [157], and right willing led to good behavior. But what directed the will? In its natural state, the will was directed by love of God. Adam, however, committed the sin of self-love[2] and lost sight of God. Because the other virtues depended on the will and Adam directed his will away from God, he lost the ability to apprehend and love God. Because of Adam's sin, only divine grace could restore the opportunity to choose good, and divine grace could only occur with humility. The most fundamental human virtue, in the Augustinian tradition, was the virtue of humility, which redirected the will toward love of God.

This was a new conception of rationality. Right action could only come from right willing. The faith that moved the will was prior to understanding, and could only come from the practice of humility and acceptance of God. The standard of behavior was determined by God, and humility was a precondition for God's will to direct one's behavior. Justice existed only in the city of God, which was everywhere in the physical world, but only existed among the humble who placed God's will before their own.

Augustine elaborated a new account of human action. Morally right action is based on right willing, which required the virtue of humility. Faith informed and moved the will. Augustine differed from Aristotle in four ways:

1. Aristotle found justice to be a property of the polis, and Augustus located it in all mankind.

2. Virtues, for Augustus, included humility and charity, preconditions for justice. These elements were not present for Aristotle.

3. Aristotle had no conception of the will. For Augustus, the will, when enslaved to the self, kept humans from acquiring good. The will had to be redirected toward humility and the love of God in order to acquire good.

4. The key to Augustine morality and justice was the relationship of a biblical understanding of the relationship of the soul to God. Aristotle had no place for a divine creator.

The Scottish Enlightenment. The Scottish enlightenment provided the third tradition of rationality and justice. In this tradition, justice was to be found in the traditions and beliefs of Anglicizing communities, ordered in terms of mutual goals and passions, and whose traditions were understood as self-evident truths. It was a theological tradition, in which knowledge of the will of God was the key to all inquiry. Evident truths provided the touchstone to all other moral claims. These evident truths were the principles of natural law.

> The principles of law are such that are known without arguing, and to which the judgment upon apprehension of, will give it ready and fully assent; such as, God is to be adored and obeyed, children are to be loved and entertained [227].

The foremost human obligation was obedience to God and to his law. In this, the Scottish enlightenment was similar to the Augustinians. Similarly, both carried a conception of the natural law. However, for the Scottish enlightenment knowledge of natural law did not come from correct willing, but from knowledge of local custom and traditions, described by MacIntyre as anglicizing traditions.

How were mortal humans to know God's law? Certainly, natural law provided a guide for behavior. But how did citizens apply the natural law? The guide for right behavior—the application of the natural law—was located in the traditions of Scottish society. These traditions provided a body of precedents and rules, and were to be followed. Hence, natural law and local traditions were seamlessly fused.[3] Individual passions and interests served principles of natural law and were guided by tradition.

How could a person know which traditions were right or proper or what behavior was appropriately traditional? The answer to this question lay in the cultivation of the "moral sense." The moral sense provided the sensibility through which a person could perceive right behavior. The moral sense carries within it three elements. First, within it were the properties of the conscience itself, through which a citizen would know what is good. The second element was the facility to discriminate between the good and the other claims on behavior. Third, the moral sense could order the perceptions it received, so that citizens could pursue a way of life that best ensured their happiness. The moral sense ensured that natural law would guide human passions and interests, and that just behavior would be located in community "anglicizing" traditions. Reason, guided by the moral sense, based in natural law, and observable in local traditions, was the master of the passions.

Western Liberalism. Western (large-L) Liberalism, the tradition of economic interests and governance inherited from the enlightenment, represented a fundamental break from the three traditions described above. The first three presented right behavior in terms of external standards or first principles, to which individual interest and passions were sublimated. The L-liberal standpoint was that of a tradition-independent society, one which emphasized individual interests, and in which one's standpoint was a matter of individual preference.

One of the central political goals of the enlightenment was a notion of shared citizenship and enacted governance to act as a bulwark against "what was felt to be the tyranny of tradition" [335]. But how could individuals of sharply different moral persuasions coexist within a common political framework? The answer to this question lay in the construction of a political system in which one's standards of justice and morality did not provide economic or legal advantage over another's—justice was based on interests and needs, in which all had equal access to goods.

A political, legal, and economic framework was developed that would enable those who held different and sometimes incompatible conceptions of the good life to live together peaceably within the same society, enjoying the same access to social and economic goods. This goal was achieved vis-à-vis a notion of individualistic "expression of preferences." Expression of preferences means that the basis for determining what is good is a decision a citizen makes according to her or his needs and desires, not because of some standard based on religion, tradition, or community well-being. It is the citizen's will, and the citizen's preference.

A citizen's behavior stems from his or her perceptions of needs and desires. Each individual, in comptemplating prospective action, first asks "What are my wants? And how are they ordered" [338]. The values of goods, and the reasons for action, did not lie outside the individual in terms of some standard of polis (Aristotle), God (Augustus), and common-sense traditions embodied in anglicizing communities and known through the moral sense (Scottish enlightenment).

> What was new was the transformation of first person expressions of desire themselves, without further qualification, into statements of reason for action, into premises for practical reasoning. In the market and in politics, the ultimate data are preferences. How they are arrived at is irrelevant to the weight assigned to them. "I want" becomes a premise, not a conclusion. [338]

In the L-liberal conception there is no overriding good external to preferences of individuals. Each person, within their political, economic, familial, artistic, athletic, and scientific spheres, pursues their own goods. The rules of justice in L-liberal society consequently were rules of distributive justice: law set the constraints on the bargaining process and ensured access to it by the otherwise disadvantaged. Individual liberty was also protected: individuals were provided the freedom to express their preferences.

L-liberal rationality was grounded on two premises, which together defined individuals qua individuals. The first premise was "I want," in which individual interests and passions identify the basis for action. The second premise is "Doing so will help me achieve such and such." These two premises construct the following three-part rationality:

1. Each individual personally orders her or his preferences.

2. The soundness of a person's arguments depends on how well they can translate their preferences into action.

3. Individuals seek to maximize the satisfaction of the preferences in accordance with their ordering.

In 3 above, we see that the rational structure of L-liberalism creates the conditions for utilitarian ways of thinking. That is, once "I want" becomes the basis for action, the purpose of action is to satisfy that desire. When we face alternative courses of action, we select the one that brings us the greatest reward. Utilitarianism is central for modern public discourse and political and moral philosophy; it is part and parcel of L-liberalism. And it is central to deterrent notions of justice. Utilitarianism, however, cannot exist where behavior is gauged independently of "I want" and where the ordering of goods or the means to achieve goods are determined by external or first principles.

The purpose of justice in a L-liberal society is the regulation of cooperation in the pursuit of preferences. Justice ensures that no particular group, including the church and the state, defines the overall good of citizens. Justice operates at four levels.

1. Different groups and individuals express their views and attitudes in their own terms. Each group has their own standpoint that supplies it with a set of premises from which its adherents argue to conclusions. These standpoints often bring them into conflict with other groups. However, because there is no external theory of moral good, groups can do no more than make claims. Standpoints are often construed as attitudes and feelings (and, MacIntyre observes, often come to no more than that).

   For example, a recent controversy emerged around the "Kenniwick Man," a skeleton of a man, about 4,000 years old, found in the Pacific Northwest of the United States. Indigenous peoples in the state of Washington contended that the skeleton should be treated with appropriate respect for the dead per indigenous practices. Anthropologists, on the other hand, countered that by studying the skeleton, they could learn more about the history of habitation of the Pacific Northwest. These two standpoints represented alternative conceptions of the good, the first scaled in terms of religious practices, and the second in terms of scientific knowledge. Because there exists no standpoint-free idea of the good to guide decision-making, groups at this level can do no more than make their claims.

2.   At the second level, participants in the debate find their point of view included in the tallying and weighting of expressions of preference which the institutions of L-liberalism always involve—counting votes, responding to consumer choice, and surveying public opinion. This presupposes that the rules of tallying and weighing are themselves the outcome of rational debate. The decision is made politically, and is likely to be made in one of the two forms of L-liberal justice—egalitarianism (equality of access to goods) or utilitarianism (satisfaction of personal wants).

The decision of what to do with the Kenniwick man decision was made in the political arena. A decision to return the skeleton to the indigenous people was made by then-Secretary of Interior Bruce Babbitt. The outcome was made after deliberation of all facts, and according to Babbitt, was a "close call." This decision located the just decision in terms of the equality of groups to access the political process and acquire political goods (the Kenniwick skeleton, in this case) rather than allowing science to establish a standard of "legitimacy" independent of political process. Importantly, we observe in this that science has no more claim to "right" or "moral good" than any other standpoint.

3.   At the third level is the debate about debate. L-liberalism, MacIntyre ryely observed, required perpetually inclusive debates over the rules of political practice. Justice is about tallying and weighing preferences. Any inequality of individuals qua individuals requires justification.

Here, the debate is over the legitimacy of the rival claims to the Kenniwick man. The debate provided endless talk-show fodder. The secretary of state was accused of playing politics in an election year. Additionally, the appellate courts might receive an appeal from the scientists, questioning the Secretary of State's decision. Because L-liberal societies are in a constant state of change (Wallerstein, 1997), debate is endless.

4.   Appeals to justice are heard at the fourth level. These appeals are about "The goods about which it is egalitarian in this way are those which, it is presumed, everyone values: freedom to express and to implement preferences and a share in the means to make that implementation effective [344]. These appeals are structured into the political process. In the executive branch, Governors and the President make decision from appeals to fairness; the highest appellate courts take appeals based on observance of due process.[4]

At each of the four levels in the L-liberal conception of rational justice, we witness a higher appeal to the evaluation of the relative merits of personal preferences. At no point beyond the originating or "lowest" level do external "first principle" standards provide the basis for rational decision-making.

The notion of different rationalities and justice has several implications, summarized below.

1. Justice and rationality are historically bounded notions. Consequently, there is not a "justice" but there are "justices." Each kind of justice is a standpoint.

2. Ideas of rationality, justice, and morality cannot be meaningfully challenged from other standpoints, except insofar as those other standpoints define meaning. There exists no exterior, "neutral" standpoint from which to challenge them.

3. Rationality—the way in which we move from ideas to action—is inseparable from justice. The rationality that we bring to bear on a problem determines what constitutes justice.

4. The way in which we value goods—those things that we seek that provide us with meaning and well-being—is itself a product of our rationality. Goods don't find meaning as goods independently of how we create value.

5. L-liberalism is itself one of the traditions that define what constitutes rationality and justice. It aims at the provision of a setting in which all claims to a persons allegiance have equal standing. It, however, imposes its own notion of the goods, which are the expression of individual preferences.

Interests and Passions Versus First Principles. A central incongruity emerges when we compare all previous traditions to the L-liberal standpoint. The first three traditions discussed above located rationality in sources external to the individual, and described justice as to the extent to which behavior matched those external sources.

The foundations of self-interest are located in an expanding capitalist economy in the sixteenth and seventeenth century, the French revolution, and the scientific revolution. These cataclysmic historical forces stimulated a way of thinking that was harshly anti-traditional. Enlightenment philosophes rejected the notion that the moral basis of behavior should depend on principles external to the nature of individuals. Indeed, the organizing rationality of the enlightenment could be described as a rejection of all traditions. They called for a rationality which in governance prized the rights of individuals to seek their passions and interests unfettered by the past obligations of church and state. In the social sciences, they demanded that we focus on empirical reality to construct our sciences, not from a metaphysic that sought explanation for the world around us in terms of the first, divine principles. Methods were provided wholly by what people saw, guided by rules of observation.

A similar rationality characterized political governance—citizens were not to be governed through an appeal to first principles, often in a religious form bolstered by the authority of the state and appeals to natural law. Governance was to be based on appeals to constituent passions and needs, the most fundamental of which were life, liberty, and the pursuit of happiness. Laws involved equity issues including personal opportunity to seek those things individually wanted and needed.

The United States is a L-liberal state based on the rationality of self-interest. Within an overarching political structure that locates self-interest as a fundamental constitutional right. Utilitarianism provides a logic for the selection of goods, goodness defined in terms of personal needs and wants. Utilitarianism asks *How can I maximize the satisfaction of my preferences?* Justice is about the guarantee of one's opportunity to pursue what one wants under conditions of complex equality (Walzer, 1988). The goods thus become ends of one's own choosing, whatever one chooses them to be. Utilitarianism and free will are related notions, in that one's ability to satisfy one's needs stems from the presumption that one has the free will to make one's own choices.

The United States also is the recipient of the other three traditions. And they carry powerful prescriptions for justice for large segments of the American population. First principle notions of justice carried by the other three traditions is widely practiced by many communities of interest. Communities of interest—churches, volunteer organizations, and some municipalities, certainly many members of the criminal justice professions—are committed to first principles. These first principles may be religious, and scale individual behavior against Christian traditions and beliefs about right behavior. They may also be based in ideas of community and in local traditions, or believe in the importance of behavior guided by natural rights and moral sensibility. In the community policing and restorative justice movements we witness the increasing legitimation of community as the source of justice and standard for citizen behavior.

A consideration of politics can only confirm the presence of powerful currents of first-principle morality in American governance. Under President George W. Bush, Attorney General Robert Ashcroft was widely noted for accepting an honorary degree at Bob Jones University, where interracial dating was prohibited at the time of his appearance in 1999. In his acceptance speech, he stated that:

> Unique among the nations, America recognized the source of our character as being godly and eternal, not being civic and temporal. And because we have understood that our source is eternal, America has been different . . . We have no king but Jesus (Idaho Statesman, 4A, Jan 13, 2001).

There could be no stronger statement than this—that the responsibility of the highest elected criminal justice official in the United States was to a higher power, to rationality, and sense of justice based on first principles.

This chapter is written in the spirit that there are a diversity of versions of justice and ethics, that a variety of ethical positions affect how we think about and react to the world around us. To provide examples of these different ethical positions, I will discuss and compare two books, one that locates ethics within the L-liberal tradition, and another that situates justice and ethics within the traditions of first principles.

Ethics as Equality Under the Law. Muraskin (2001) develops an image of justice that is squarely within the L-liberal tradition. Central to her discussion is that the interests of justice are served by fairness, which is distinguished from law. "Fairness" means that the law does not intentionally or unintentionally operate to the disadvantage of particular individuals or groups. This also applies to practices of the criminal justice system. She noted that "The players in the criminal justice system have the obligation of promoting the fair administration of justice." [2], and "our system is based on fairness" [3]. The purpose of justice is to protect individuals access to social and economic goods. Justice is about good means—that all elements of the criminal justice system act in accordance with fair play, and that due process is provided at every juncture by the courts, by the police and prosecutors, and by corrections officers.

This image of ethics locates justice squarely within personal interests and needs. The standard of justice is not something external to individuals—it lies in the relationships individuals have with each other. It is a conception of justice based on equity in accessibility to goods. In this conception, the criminal justice system is not simply about punishing wrongdoers, but operates to insure equity in the government's treatment of citizens. Five themes can be identified that are associated with "justice as fairness."

1. Law that fails to recognize unequal access to goods itself is suspect. Law serves broader interest in the preservation of equality.

2. Rationality—the logic that guides the behavior of criminal justice officials—is based on considerations of fairness, formally defined as due process.

3. Justice is achieved by the application of due process procedures, which secure rights for individuals.

4. An overfocus on the ends of the system—arrest, prosecution, finding guilt—can displace due process.

5. Ethical training for justice system professionals can overcome an overfocus on system "efficiency" and contribute to due process.

We can see in Muraskin's discussion that due process, which recognizes the rights of the individual qua individual, is a central element to be considered in assessing the just behavior of the criminal justice system.

Ethics as a Moral Sense. Wilson (1993) suggested that moral sensibility might be innate, a human trait, that exists prior to reasoning. With this notion, he describes a standpoint that falls outside the L-liberal tradition. It is a conception of morality that stems, not from interests and needs, but in a biological or genetic predisposition toward particular virtues. He refers to this predisposition as a "moral sense" and suggests that it, not self-interest, provides the social glue that enable people to get along.

Wilson presents the moral sense to counter what he perceives as the moral relativism of the current age. He challenges the enlightenment idea of tradition-independent society, suggesting that the moral relativism of a tradition independent society contributes to both crime and the shameless pursuit of selfish interest. As a prescriptive ethic, relativism gives way to cold utilitarianism, by which we justify our behavior on the basis of self-interest alone. Wilson rejects the idea that humans can be described only in utilitarian terms. Lost in Enlightenment "amorality" is a recognition of the moral rootedness of citizens in their civic and social life. In the ordinary give-and-take of daily activities, people naturally tend to take a moral outlook on what they do. Whether or not accepted by social scientists, a moral sense is widely recognized and employed in the daily lives of citizens. If we want to understand the moral sense, we need to look at the behavior of ordinary citizens, not what social scientists say.

Wilson locates the moral sense in a biologically based sensibility about what's right, nurtured in a familial setting and encouraged by processes of evolutionary selection: "the moral sense must have had adaptive value; if it did not, natural selection would have worked against people who had such useless traits as sympathy, self-control, and a desire for fairness and in favor of those with the opposite tendencies" [23]. It has four characteristics, or what one might call virtues: sympathy, fairness, self-control, and duty.

The moral sense is not a hard, fixed rule-like predisposition. It is a predisposition whose strength requires nurturing from the right kinds of familial and social settings. This is reminiscent of the Scottish enlightenment, which located moral sensibility in anglicizing traditions. The moral sense manifests itself in two ways: (1) everyone makes moral judgments that distinguish between right and wrong actions, and (2) virtually everyone acquires social habits that we find satisfying when we practice them.

The moral sense exists prior to reason, and is in this sense a standard external to individual needs and wants. We act out of the moral sense instinctually without reasoning. When we employ moral reasoning it is to justify our behavior, not to create it. The moral sense is irrational, preceding reason. This means that, when we think about right behavior, we invoke a pre-existing moral sense, strong in some people and weak in others depending on their social and familial circumstance.

If we have a biologically based moral sense, how can so much wrong-doing happen? Wilson recognizes this problem. Clearly, the moral sense is neither dominant nor particularly powerful. A great deal happens that is very bad and seems to argue against general moral predispositions for human behavior. This leads to the question—under what circumstances does the moral sense exert its influence? He frequently describes the role of traditional, two-parent families as a source of moral growth. The values he describes are traditional notions of morality. Like the Scottish enlightenment, property holds an important place in the moral community.

The moral sense is a predisposition. But it is only one of several senses, and it can easily be overwhelmed by other impulses.

> Mankind's moral sense is not a strong beacon light, radiating outward to illuminate in sharp outline all that it touches. It is, rather, a small candle flame, casting vague and multiple shadows, flickering and sputtering in he strong winds of power and passion, greed and ideology. But brought close to the heart and cupped in one's hands, it dispels the darkness and warms the soul. 251.

The moral sense represents a standard against which one can gauge behavior. It is not Aristotelian, for it locates the sense of rightness within all people rather than the polis. Nor is it Augustinian, because it does not base one's behavior on a moral sense whose purpose is to illuminate divine intent. Moreover the Augustinian tradition held humility to be the highest virtue, and humility is not discussed by Wilson. The moral sense is similar to what MacIntyre (1988) described as an evident substantive truth. Wilson repeatedly describes the moral sense as what people do naturally, without first thinking about it.

Wilson also finds his work preceded by Hume, and much of Hume is reflected in his moral philosophy. Hume, for example, also viewed moral judgments as occurring prior to reasoning. And like Hume, Wilson described humans as facing contradictory passions, particularly the self-interested seeking of needs (a utilitarian focus) and the desire to live together peacefully. Hence, Wilson's work is located within the Humean tradition.

Wilson also owes much to Aristotle, whom he acknowledges. His conception of virtue, for example, is as something that arises through the practice of virtue [1993:244]. It arises in youth, and is developed through practice, and becomes habituated. Other work carried out by Wilson, such as "Broken Windows" (Wilson & Kelling, 1983), located moral value in local communities, and described an Aristotelian standpoint according to which the character of the polis contributed to the virtuous development of its citizens. Indeed, throughout *The Moral Sense*, Wilson makes clear that the strength of the moral sense cannot arise under any conditions, but rather require particular familial and community circumstances if they are to affect behavior.[5] The right kind of community can provide an informal moral standard to which its residents can be held accountable.

Traditions of family and community provide an ameliorative for the morally disruptive effects of L-liberal relativism. Wilson provided a moral sense that exists outside L-liberal conceptions of equity or utilitarianism, and located rationality and justice in external standards of family and tradition. Like the Scottish enlightenment, it is sympathetic to religious interpretation.

I have not described Muraskin's and Wilson's work in order to challenge them. Both, in their original form, contain challengeable inconsistencies. Yet, both, if challenged, could shore up their reasoning and resolve those inconsistencies. The wrongness or rightness of either view depends on one's standpoint, and the standpoints are inconsistent with each other. There is no ethical prescription independent of place and time that provides a neutral standpoint from which Wilson's and Muraskin's perspectives may be weighed against each other.

So how can we, given the L-liberal smorgasbord of moral-ethical alternatives, choose which is right for ourselves? Where do we, as individuals and as an academic field of justice studies, locate ourselves in the chapter-opening question *What is the meaning of life?* Which morality is right for you, dear reader, depends on *who you are and how you understand yourself* (MacIntyre, 1988:393). This may seem like an unsatisfactory answer, but it is not. It contains two compelling elements. First is this—whatever one selects as an ethical touchstone to provide a sense of right and wrong undoubtedly contains much that is good. From all standpoints discussed, this is an inevitable conclusion. Secondly, there are not an infinite number of moral standpoints. A finite number of moral systems have motivated human behavior, and they are located in historical time and place. Each has provided or currently provides an idea of morality and justice for its moral audience. This means that the recognition of moral diversity in the study of justice is different from abandoning all to moral relativity. If we view our responsibility as a field of academic study concerned with developing knowledge about justice, we are compelled to consider the diversity of perspectives available to us, and to try to understand what they mean to different people.

Pollock: Thinking About Ethics and Morality

The organization and discussion of ethical systems presented by Pollock (1998) is consistent with a L-liberal discussion of ethical goods. That is, a variety of alternative ethical systems are presented and students are encouraged to examine and apply them to their circumstances, according to their particular interests and needs. This does not mean that Pollock only discusses ethics consistent with L-liberalism—she devotes a balanced measure to first-principle ethics, though she does not make the needs and interests versus first-principle distinction central to this chapter. Her descriptions of ethical systems provides a perspective on contemporary images of ethics, and also permits us the opportunity to discuss and compare L-liberal, interest-based ethics to first-principle ethics.

Two ethical systems that fall within a L-liberal conception of justice are ethical formalism and utilitarianism, each discussed below.

Ethical formalism. This ethical perspective is concerned only with the inherent nature of our actions, not their consequences. An act in itself is good or bad, regardless of its effects. This perspective is sometimes called a deontologcal ethical system. Deontology is the idea that our behavior is justified in terms of rational principles, not pregiven ends (Warnke, 1993).

Ethical formalism is associated with the writings of Immanuel Kant (1724-1804). Moral worth comes from doing one's duty (Pollock, 1998:28-29) describes this perspective as follows: "People, as flesh and spirit combined, are in constant dynamic conflict over base desires and morality; only by appealing to higher reason can they do what is right." A person is consequently expected to act in "a manner one would hope all would follow." The intent of a person's act is what is important, regardless of the result. It is the intent that demonstrates a person's morality. Morality is consequently about good will. "If someone does an action from a good will, then even if it results in bad consequences, it can be considered a moral action" (29). On the other hand, if an action is morally wrong, then it is wrong regardless of the good ends that it might achieve. One cannot judge an immoral act on the basis of good consequences.

Utilitarianism. Utilitarianism is the philosophy associated with the greatest good that is provided by our actions. Actions are perceived to be good if they produce more good than harm. If an action "contributes significantly to the general good, then it is good" (Pollock, 1998:32). To provide a simplistic example, if one has to choose between an individual and society, one should choose society.

There are two kinds of utilitarianism. According to act utilitarianism, we look at the consequences of an action for everyone involved. Under rule utilitarianism, on the other hand, we consider the precedent set by the act. This means that we judge an act not only by its immediate consequences, but by what would happen if others carried out the act in the future.

Both these ethical systems fit within a L-liberal conception of justice. Both focus on interests and needs of individuals, and neither contains within it a justification for action based on principles exterior to individuals. The calculus of individual behavior, however, differs across the two ethical systems. In the Kantian tradition of ethical formalism, a just society can only emerge where individuals are free to pursue their interests and needs. Such a just system is provided by a system of law that includes substantive law, proscribing behaviors that interfere with interests and needs, and due process, that prohibit a government from interfering with individual interests and needs.

In the utilitarian tradition, justice is an appeal to the general good. Utilitarianism, like ethical formalism, constitutes individual identity from personal preferences and needs, not from standards external to individuals. Moral goods are determined, however, not simply by the right to seek one's preferences, but to do so with an eye toward the consequences of one's behavior, so that what constitutes goods is the greatest benefit for the most people. Put differently, ethical formalism is about egalitarianism in the pursuit of goods—the social contract exists with the provision of opportunity, and is not concerned for what actual outcomes are. Utilitarianism is about what those outcomes are and how they contribute to the general good. Both perspectives agree that the pursuit of an individual's goods is the highest ethic for a free society. They simply disagree on the appropriate ethical calculus to constitute a society of individuals free to pursue their interests.

In the practice of criminal justice, utilitarianism and ethical formalism are opposing perspectives related by what can be called a means-ends conflict. Pollock identifies two additional ethical systems—the ethics of care and situational ethics—whose sensibility is grounded in L-liberal notions of individual needs and desires.

> *The ethics of care.* The ethics of care emphasizes the relationships that exist between people. The ethics of care is a feminist response to an overemphasis on masculine notions of ethics, grounded in notions of universalism, rights, and laws. The ethics of care instead is about meeting needs. Abortion issues, for example, are framed in terms of the rights of the mother versus the rights of the child. In the ethics of care, the questions become "What would happen to the mother if she chooses the abortion, and what would happen if she did not? Would the child receive the care if born?" [46]. Taoism, according to which individuals are encouraged to follow a path of caring, is a moral system consistent with the ethics of care.

> *Situational ethics.* Situational ethics is the idea that different situations are best resolved by using different ethical standards. It represents ethical flexibility, not the abandonment of ethics. Pollock introduces this conception of ethics as a way to resolve the problems in both the absolutist and relativist approaches to ethics. She identifies its following principles [51-52]:
>
> 1.   There are basic norms or principles of human behavior.
>
> 2.   These can be applied to ethical dilemmas and moral issues.
>
> 3.   The norms might call for different results in different situations, depending on the needs, concerns, relationships, resources, weaknesses, and strengths of the individual actors.

The native habitat of justice studies is the social sciences, and is dominated by L-liberal conceptions of justice and ethics. First-principle moralities rarely intrude into this habitat. However, in the local territories of justice professionals, we often find a different conception of justice, one in which first principles are central to the construction of personal ethics. Pollock identifies three such ethics below.

Religion. Religion is defined as "that body of beliefs that addresses fundamental issues such as "What is life?" and "What is good and evil?" [37]. All religions provide a basis for ethical decisionmaking. Religions that have a god figure, such as Christianity and Islam, consider the will of that figure to be the source of principles of ethics and morality. Religions such as Pantheism and Wicca promote the belief that there is a living spirit in all things.

Religious systems are based on God's will. But how can Gods will be known? Aquinas sought to link Aristotelian ideas of virtue and rationality by deriving reason from God's nature. A virtuous person is one who thinks rationally—indeed, one cannot be rational without being virtuous. Virtues are the enactment of Gods will. Rationality allows us to order the goods of the earth in a way that comports with divine will.

Natural law. Natural law is similar to religion in that it is grounded in a universal set of rights and wrongs. However, no supernatural figure wills what is right and wrong. What is good is natural. Morality conforms to the natural world, and ones basic inclinations form the basis of natural law. A basic principal of morality, for example, is self preservation. Also, sociability is a natural human inclination that provides the morality of altruism and generosity.

The ethics of virtue. The ethics of virtue asks the question "what is a good action?" It is a teleological system that focuses on actions that bring about good ends. However, happiness in this case refers to a good life, achievement, and moral excellence. This is very different from the utilitarian idea of "pleasure," which provides its basis for action. Habits that are virtuous are learned from moral "exemplars," individuals who have a balanced set of virtues. Moral virtue also follows the principle of the "golden mean." This means that virtue is always the median between two extremes of character. In the area of fear, for example, courage is the mean between cowardice (too much fear) and recklessness (not enough fear). Virtue-based ethical systems, Pollock observed, are traced to Aristotle. The ends of virtuous behavior are happiness and emerge in a virtuous setting—in Aristotle's example, in the best kind of polis.

The final three ethical systems roughly correspond to the first principle systems described by MacIntyre (1988), discussed previously. Religion is the general phenomenon of the Augustinian tradition. Natural law resonates with the tradition of the Scottish enlightenment. And the ethics of virtue contain elements similar to the Aristotelian tradition. The diversity of ethical systems advanced by Pollock, when considered in light of Mac-Intyre's analysis of justice traditions, suggest that the United States is constituted by a variety of ethical systems, many with deep historical roots.

Ethical systems also may relate to each other in highly variable ways. For example, it has been suggested that religious conservatives are more oriented to crime-control, suggesting an affinity between utilitarianism and a religious ethic (see Grasmick et al., 1992). However, Applegate and his colleagues (2000) found that religious fundamentalists' views of crime and offenders were complex, and contains elements that favor forgiveness and rehabilitation as well as punishment. This suggests that no "one-size-fits-all" ethical description will adequately describe criminal justice professionals, or any other justice group (such as academicians) for that matter.

Part II: The Practice of Justice in a L-Liberal Society

The characteristic feature of justice in a L-liberal society, MacIntyre observed, is its focus on interests and needs. Two moral philosophies—ethical formalism and utilitarianism—have emerged that are consistent with a justice focus on individual preferences. Ethical formalism finds its expression in actions, and locates government in its actions, independent of the ends achieved. Citizens are entities more fundamental than the state and have an identity, in terms of rights, that the state is not permitted to usurp. The state emerges as an entity only after citizen freedom is guaranteed. Due process guarantees this identity, and L-liberal society cannot exist without such a primordial concept of citizen. Utilitarianism locates the role of the state in the production of citizen security. The state cannot exist without some means to guarantee the security of its citizens, which in our system of justice justifies its actions against the few in terms of the interests of the many. In the provision of security, citizens' interests are secondary to the state's interest. These two moral philosophies differ in that one focuses on the means of justice, formalized as due process and its ends, and the other emphasizes the efficient and effective production of citizen security by the state.

The practice of criminal justice in a democracy is a marriage of irreducible conflicts. On the one hand, the practice is embodied in the enforcement of criminal law by the state. Its values are conceived in terms of crime control. Its primary function is the suppression of crime (Packer, 1968). The criminal law is a L-liberal product and embodies the Beccarian principle that the law guarantees citizen security vis-à-vis a utilitarian logic of deterrent penalties. It seeks efficiency, which refers to the system's capacity to apprehend, try, convict, and dispose of a high number of criminal offenders whose offenses become known. It carries a presumption of guilt for suspects.

Opposed to this is the concept of citizenry as participants in democratic process. This concept is embodied in the notion that citizens have an identity that is in part *independent* of the state, and that the state has a limited and formal authority to intervene in citizen's affairs. This concept carries what Packer (1968) called due process values. It recognizes and places a priority on the presumption of innocence—the state is obligated at each step that it has a right to intercede into the affairs of a citizen. As an enlightenment product, the idea of justice in which citizens are equal required equality of access to all goods, that access was not in some way mitigated because of whom a citizen was. In Figure 8.1 below is a diagram of Packer's two models of the criminal justice system.

Figure 8.1
Herbert Packers Two Models of the Criminal Justice Process

Crime Control Model	*Due Process Model*
1. Repression of criminal conduct is the most important function performed by the criminal justice process.	1. The reliability of the criminal justice process is closely examined. The model focuses on the possibility of error. It is particularly concerned with the third degree and coercive tactics.
2. A failure of law enforcement means a breakdown of order, necessary for freedom.	2. The outcome is in question as long as there is a factual challenge. Finality is not a priority.
3. Criminal process is the positive guarantor of social freedom.	3. There is an insistence on prevention and elimination of mistakes in factual assessments of culpability.
4. *Efficiency* is the top priority of the model. By efficiency is meant the ability to apprehend, try, and convict high numbers of criminals whose offenses become known.	4. If efficiency demands shortcuts around reliability, then efficiency is to be rejected as a system goal. The aim of the process is as much the protection of innocents as punishment of the guilty.
5. There is an emphasis on speed and finality. Facts can be provided more quickly through interrogation than through courtroom examination and cross-examination.	5. The combination of stigma and deprivation that government inflicts is the end goal.
6. The conveyor belt is the model for the system. This is a steady stream of cases from arrest through conviction.	6. The coercive power of the state is always subject to abuse. Maximum efficiency means maximum tyranny.
7. A presumption of guilt makes it possible for the system to deal efficiently with large numbers of felons.	7. A person is to be found guilty if and only if a factual finding of guilt is accompanied with procedural rigor in the criminal justice process.

Packer's model (Figure 8.1) is a model of conflicting values. Many readers are undoubtedly familiar with this model. Let's consider each side of the model.

The crime control perspective is on the left side of the figure above. As a perspective, it incorporates many interrelated values. These values, briefly stated, are a belief in the importance of criminal process, efficiency in justice proceedings, an emphasis on speed and finality, and a presumption of guilt. The state provides security vis-à-vis Beccarian ideas of deterrent punishments. The state monitors individual behavior and sanctions individuals who do not act in legally acceptable ways. Implicit in the crime control perspective is the notion that the state can act responsibly in the distribution of the law. The state's responsibility in the protection of individual interests lies in the provision of security, which is best carried out by an efficient and effective justice apparatus.

The due process perspective is on the right side. The due process perspective emphasizes the idea that citizens have rights that supersede the authority of the state. The perspective carries values that reveal a profound distrust of central state authority. To control the arbitrary use of central state authority, state processes are transparent, and focus on evidence and on procedural formality.

From a consideration of Packer's model we witness the unresolved tension between free will and determinism in the practice of justice today. The practice of justice does not resolve the conflicts. It would be better to say that the conflict between free will and determinism is institutionalized in the structure and ideology of contemporary criminal justice process. In our efforts to simultaneously provide a utilitarian notion of state security and protect individuals from arbitrary state power, we act out the essential conflicts that characterize the emergence of the enlightenment. The values that marked Europe's movement out of the so-called dark ages are embedded in justice practice today, inseparable from a notion of justice and morality based on needs and desires. It may be that, for democracy to work, these conflicts must be engaged in eternal battle.

The ethics of due process and crime control are inexorably linked in time and place. They live and fall together. They embody many values integral to democratic governance, though those values are separated by arbitrary political divisions and legal structures that play due process and crime control against each other. When we as scholars write about justice, or when we as professionals seek justice in the courts or on the streets, we are acting out values represented in one or the other of these two ethics. In profound ways, we as a peoples are their living embodiment. The values they represent are at the core of our social thought and central to justice processes. These ethics, central in tandem to L-liberal society, are greater than we individually are, and they carry core elements of the enlightenment in them. They are mighty ideological waves and they roll through and past us, carrying us into an unknown and unknowable future.

Fairness and Utilitarianism: Alderson and High Police. Justice systems in democracies carry responsibilities to both their governments and to citizen constituencies. However, the marriage of justice systems and states is not isomorphic—that is, states and justice systems don't exist in a perfect symmetry. Justice systems, staffed by capable and committed leadership, can contribute to the stability of democracy even when a state faces destabilizing processes, or in not-well-ordered states (Alderson, 1998).

The opposite is also true: justice systems can contribute to the destabilization of democracies. As Alderson observed, in Germany prior to the Second World War, the police contributed to totalitarian tendencies within the state. The Secret State Police, also called the Gestapo, emerged from the ranks of the ordinary professional police in Germany.

Alderson described the progressive reorientation of the police by Hitler toward order control and eventual reorganization under Himmler in terms of the outlooks and philosophies of leaders of the German police.[6] There were many whose orientation was motivated by raw ambition. There were also those whose commitments were to provide the most professional police available to the regime. The problem, Alderson suggested, lie in the nature of a professional police ethos:

> It is said that the professional police ethos 'is an amoral one, as proven by the constantly observed phenomenon that professional policemen make the transition from one regime to another without difficulty,' and that 'their professional ethic discounts the ideological nature of the regime they are serving.'

What is there about professional police that contributes to an amoral posture with regard to their political regimes? One such problem is that police tend to take a utilitarian view of their work. Utilitarianism, it will be recalled, is a sort of economic calculus of these actions that will provide the greatest happiness for the greatest number. The police do not produce happiness; however, they can decrease fear of crime and of terrorism. Utilitarianism, for the police, is practical and straight-forward. It is of the form—"If I remove one bad guy from the streets, then the world is a safer place to live" (Crank, 1998).

However, an over-concern for utilitarian motives justifies quite undemocratic behavior in the name of state security. Again describing the Nazi history in Germany, Alderson observed that the burning of the Reichstag building in 1933, after a "purported discovery of plans for a communist revolution" provided a basis for the government to sharply increase their efforts to provide internal security. For the protection of the people and the state, and as a defensive measure against communist activities, the guarantees of individual liberty under the Weimar Constitution were suspended. Using a utilitarian logic, the government played on citizen's fears and sharply restricted liberties. Alderson concluded that:

> This is not to suggest that utilitarianism intends such behavior, but that the central place of human rights in modern politics may not be compatible with the doctrine. Protective security still has to grapple with the conundrum of maximizing freedoms and at the same time controlling disorder, and this calls for great skill and determination (Alderson, 1998:24).

Utilitarianism, providing a basis for police behavior that aims at the maximization of public good by reducing fear of crime, easily becomes seen by its advocates as the maximization of police authority in the preservation of order, in which a benefit for public good is an assumed outcome. In some cases, even the execution of an innocent person can be justified in terms of a justice system, operating efficiently, that provides the greatest protection of the greatest number (see also Rawls, 1971).

The ethics of its leaders are central to the behavior of a police organization, whom Alderson calls "high police." Alderson (36) defines high police as "those with power to make and to implement policies affecting the organization as a whole." The high police are those who carry the highest responsibility for the ethics of their particular organizations. They are responsible for their organization's relationship with their government, implement security concerns, and oversee their organization's behavior regarding the rights of citizens. If high police, even at the will of their legislators, pursue policies whose outcomes are unethical, then the organization will be unethical even if its behavior is narrowly legal. Here, Alderson breaks from the notion that ethics and legality are equivalent terms. Alderson recognizes that democratic governments can veer harshly in the direction of totalitarianism, as did Germany under Hitler. It is the responsibility of the high police to resist such governmental turns.

What is essential is that police recognize that they must balance utilitarian concerns with humanitarian concerns. High police must also be principled police. Alderson develops a concept of justice as fairness, as defined by international standards of human rights. *The Universal Declaration of Human Rights* (1948), and *The European Convention on Human Rights and Fundamental Freedoms* (1950), drawn up to provide an initial mechanism for the enforcement for the Universal Declaration of Human Rights, locate egalitarian concerns at the center of the ethical behavior of high police. Police in free countries exist "the point of balance, on the one hand securing Human Rights whilst, on the other, exercising their lawful powers given to them by governments in the name of the people—to protect the people and their institutions" [73].

Alderson's concept of ethics locates the preservation of human rights as a central concern of the high police. Sometimes, even in democratic regimes broad sections of the public identify with police practices that may preserve law or protect order. The role of ethical high police are particularly important to insure that human rights are not violated. This is, he acknowledges, a large moral burden on police, yet it is essential for the preservation of democracies, in order to insure that "the system created for their protection does not become the instrument of their bondage" [74]. By relying on international standards of human rights, Alderson develops a notion of justice grounded in ideas characteristic of L-liberal society.

Noble Cause Ethics and the Ends/Means Dilemma. Moral systems are not equally relevant to the practice of justice. In a L-liberal society, the idea of justice is embodied in a legal system that provides security while at the same time limits government influence into citizen's rights to pursue happiness.

The conflicts between the means and ends of justice are routinely faced by professionals. As creatures of the law, they are obligated to the means of justice, as embodied in due process. Yet they are also obligated to the ends of justice—the provision of security. I have described these two systems as twin offspring of democratic notions of justice, both expressing the interests of individuals, yet in perpetual conflict with each other. Justice workers, in the conduct of their work, must somehow balance these two ethics. In the practice of their work they enact the conflicts inherent in contemporary L-liberalism.

The means-ends conflict has been characterized in terms of the "noble cause" (Crank & Caldero, 2000; see also Delattre, 1996; Klockars, 1983). The noble cause—a commitment to do something good for society, to get the bad guys off the streets—is a central element in the values regimen of many professionals in the criminal justice system. Noble cause problems are an occupationally based variant of the means-ends conflict, and are eloquently described by Klockars (1983) and expanded in the work of Crank and Caldero (2000). In the sections below, I will look at noble cause ethics across the occupational settings of police, prosecution, and parole and probation. We can see its relevance in each of these fields and assess how internal dynamics in each field resist the tendency towards the corruption of the noble cause—violation of the law in order to do something about crime.

The Means-Ends Conflict and Noble Cause. The means-ends conflict, most simply put, is this: should a person's behavior be determined by principles of correct behavior (means), or should it be guided by the consequences of her or his actions (ends)? The conflict represents an opposition of democratic ethical systems. As discussed previously, means-based decisionmaking is associated with deontological or "rational rule" ethical systems, and is most similar to ethical formalism. Ends-based decision-making is teleological, and is typically described in terms of utilitarianism motives.

The conflict between ends and means is particularly acute in criminal justice. Police professionals sometimes weigh the legality of their behavior against the "good end" of arresting and prosecuting an suspect. In the courts, a prosecutor weighs the advantages of an aggressive prosecution against the responsibilities to act as a member of the court, whose primary responsibility is justice under due process. Their "good end" is the conviction of a factually guilty person. Their "good means" is the scrupulous commitment to court procedures and their right, as one justice put it, to "strike hard blows, but not foul ones." Defense counsel serve both as advocates for their clients and as court officers responsible for the full disclosure of the truth. Their "good end" is the prevention of conviction of a factually innocent person. Their "good means" is to do all within their power to demonstrate that a prosecutor did not establish the evidentiary standard needed for a conviction.

The means-ends conflict has been discussed primarily in research on the police. Klockars (1983) coined the phrase *the Dirty Harry problem* to describe the means ends conflict for the police. In the movie titled *Dirty Harry*, an incident occurs in which the protagonist, "dirty" Harry Calahan, violates due process law in order to achieve what he believes is an incontestably good end. The good end he seeks is to locate the victim of kidnaping, a young girl who is buried and has a limited air supply. He believes that he has to extort a confession from the victimizer, and uses graphically violent third degree tactics—a bad means—to find the information about the location of a young girl. There is also the connection between the end and the means—as Klockars notes, a means that can be justified if what must be known, and, importantly, known before the act is committed, is that it will result in the achievement of the good end.

Klockars presented a compelling argument that the "Dirty Harry" problem is at the core of the police role. Police officers, according to Klockars, tend to think that they are dealing with people that are factually guilty, even if they can't prove it in the current instance. Police think that they must use tricky means to find the guilt that suspects have but are hiding. Bad guys know the ins and outs of the law, and must be tricked or forced into telling the truth. For officers who think in this way, "due process" legal restrictions on police behavior have a backfiring effect, intensifying the need to use dirty means to uncover wrongdoing.

> . . . Dirty Harry problems can arise wherever restrictions are placed on police methods and are particularly likely to do so when police themselves perceive that those restrictions are undesirable, unreasonable, or unfair (Klockars, 1983:141).

If a police officer faces a dirty Harry problem, how should it be resolved? Are there circumstances under which it is acceptable for police officers to set aside legal means for "good ends?" An observer whose morals or job-related ethics are means-oriented could justifiably claim that any solution that placed ends ahead of means is unethical. Behavior inconsistent with the criminal law, Federal civil rights law, or of administrative process is ethically wrong. However, an observer with an ends orientation could conclude that the rightness of incontestably good ends justified a certain degree of behavioral latitude.

Herein lies the central quandary of the dirty Harry problem. Dirty Harry is not unethical. He in fact may be very ethical. He is committed to victims, and desperately wants to insure that some "bad guy" doesn't do any more harm. Harry is not simply ethical. He's moral to a fault. He's a warrior for good, and he *believes.*

Crank and Caldero (2000) suggested that the dirty Harry conflict was an example of "noble cause corruption." The term "noble cause" was coined by Delattre (1996). Delattre wrote that the way we as humans think about our own worth is in terms of the "causes" that we take on. We are frequently judged and often judge ourselves, he observed, by whether our goals are admirable or despicable. Commitment to a noble cause can lead us to believe that some ends are so important that any means to achieve them is acceptable.

The actual conduct of police work, they argued, could not be understood in terms of the ministerial application of the law. Nor was it about how to refine officer's use of discretion through formal ethical training. Values, they contended, were at the heart of police work.

> The values carried by police officers determine their decisions to intervene in the lives of citizens, what they do when they intervene, and the way in which they bring interventions to a conclusion. And the most important values that mobilize officers are embodied in the noble cause. The noble cause is, for most officers, the touchstone from which value-based decisionmaking occurs. Indeed, values are the cornerstone of the work police do—they dispense justice by controlling people. [34]

Police officers, Crank and Caldero stated, engaged in value-based decisionmaking. At the center of their values was the noble cause, described as follows.

> . . . a profound moral commitment to make the world a safer place to live. Put simply, it is getting bad guys off the "street." Police believe that they're on the side of angels and their purpose in life is getting rid of bad guys. They are trained and armed to protect the innocent and think about that goal in terms of "keeping the scum off the streets."
>
> The noble cause is practical and immediate. It's about an officers' conduct in day-to-day police work. It motivates officer's behavior with citizens and mobilizes a great deal of police solidarity.[35]

Value-based decisionmaking meant that police officers made judgments about the likely predispositions, behaviors, and social worth of citizens, suspects, citizens, street people, and troublemakers they interacted with, and their behavior followed from those judgments. Those judgments are always value-informed. And central to police values were a commitment to the noble cause and the departmental loyalties that reinforced that commitment.

Many aspects of the police environment, from the hiring process, training and related police cultural processes to prosecutorial and public pressures for arrests and convictions reinforced the noble cause. Belief in the noble cause was so strong that some officers were corrupted by it. Noble cause corruption referred to the violation of the criminal law or administrative process in order to achieve good ends. Noble cause corruption consequently was a special case of ends-oriented ethics with particular relevance to police organizations.

Noble cause corruption was particularly hard to deal with because it sometimes represented the actions of a department's best officers. The acts that constituted noble cause often were produced by values that all officers held highly—doing something about criminals. Traditional corruption prevention strategies, Crank and Caldero observed, often focused on "rotten apples," bad cops whose ethical inadequacies and corrupt behavior tainted other officers, especially recruits. Noble cause corruption on the other hand, was sometimes committed by a department's "golden apples," its best officers.

In the ethical systems described above, noble cause corruption is an ethical problem if a person has a means-oriented perspective, since the idea of corruption carries in it the violation of the criminal law or administrative protocols. It is also inconsistent with the virtue perspective, because corruption represents an "excess" of the values carried in the noble cause. Yet, noble cause corruption can also reveal a commitment to an ethical perspective—a commitment to good ends. Noble cause corruption is entirely consistent from the perspective of "good ends" or utilitarianism—but only if the good ends are in fact achieved.

Means-Ends Ethics and Justice System Processes

Utilitarian concerns about good ends are not unique to the police. The noble cause—a commitment to the noble end of protecting citizens from dangerous offenders—is present for other actors in the criminal justice system. In this section, I will explore how this way of thinking is facilitated by informal organizational processes and concerns over efficiency.

Courts and Plea Arraignments. The plea arrangement, commonly called a "plea bargain," is a guilt-obtaining process that is carried out during arraignment and that substitutes for formal trial proceedings. The plea arrangement process enables the principal actors in a courtroom—the judge, prosecutor, and defense counsel—to achieve findings of guilt without having to engage in formal adversarial proceedings. The actions of this group, sometimes called the courtroom work-group—represent organizational processes aimed at a particular end—acquiescence of guilt by a defendant.

For many citizens, a negotiated plea appears to be a "plea bargain" with emphasis on the word bargain, and in which the defendant receives a reduced penalty in return for pleading guilty. Yet, research on pleas of guilt at arraignment has consistently shown that those who plea do not receive shorter sentences than those in similar legal circumstances who go through formal trials. It is more accurate (and simpler) to view the negotiated plea as a state-sponsored guilt-finding process.

Plea-arraignment is an informal process. Organizational theorists sometimes distinguish between formal and informal organizational processes. The formal organization is represented by the organizational chart, administrative process and bureaucratic decisionmaking. The informal organization is represented by more informal processes, horizontal and vertical unofficial lines of communications, and informal procedures that process cumbersome work processes.

Finally, pleas are an ends-oriented process aimed at justice system efficiency. Consider pleas in the context of Packer's model. Packer noted that efficiency was a characteristic of the crime control model and was measured by the ability to convict high numbers of criminals whose offenses become known. Plea bargaining satisfies this concern. Note that "not guilty" is not a possible plea outcome. When we look at plea arraignment in this way, it clearly represents the interests of state efficiency. Indeed, there is little about plea arraignment that is consistent with "due process" ideas of justice system processes. Research suggests that about 90 percent of all cases are decided by plea bargaining. This means that, in general, a crime control model dominates case-processing in the courtroom.

Policing. Similar processes can be seen in policing, where informal processes are tied with an ends-oriented crime control efficiency. The police and ends-oriented ethics have already been discussed. Here I will only review the linkage to informal organizational processes. Manning (1997) recognized that informal processes contribute to noble cause corruption. Formal organizational processes conflicted with the uncertainties of police work. Officers formed informal vertical and horizontal "cliques" that provide control over information about what they did. Vertical cliques—informal relations across the chain of command—provided routine solutions to problems that, if addressed formally, would be time consuming and potentially embarrassing. Horizontal cliques—across officers at the same rank—enabled line officers to act in "the public interest" while protecting their actions from administrative inspection. Manning (1997:167) concluded that " informal control substitutes for formal controls, and cliques become an active force in procedural matters."

The development of cliques furthers officers' abilities to act on their particular moral precepts instead of having to follow formal rules:

> Police regulations, in the officer's eyes, are soon stripped of moral coat-
> ing . . . Humans are seen as translucent Machiavellis, easily uncovered by
> insightful probing or police action (Manning, 1997:166).

In Manning's work, we can see the that the conflict between ethical
systems is present in the formal-informal agency dynamic, and that the
ends-oriented ethics of the informal system become central for understanding organizational activity.

Prosecutorial Misconduct. Like the police, prosecutors represent
the state in state-citizen conflicts. Individuals holding positions as prosecutors, like police officers, represent the state in the affairs of citizens.
Also like police, they are committed to the noble cause. A belief in the
rightness of the state's case, and the importance of imprisoning dangerous people, characterizes the passion that they bring to their work. The
protection of the innocent, and the vengeance of helpless victims, mobilize prosecutor's passions. For some prosecutors, it also breeds noble
cause corruption.

In 1999, the *Chicago Tribune* presented a series of articles on prosecutorial misconduct (Armstrong & Possley, 1999a). The articles focused
specifically on misconduct in 381 cases since 1963 in which a homicide
conviction was thrown out because prosecutors concealed evidence
suggesting innocence or presented evidence they know to be false. The
cases examined by the *Chicago Tribune* had two elements in common.
They were all homicide cases, and all were overturned on review by
appellate court for prosecutorial misconduct. Of the 381 defendants, 67
had been sentenced to death. Almost all of the death row inmates spent
at least five years in prison.

Prosecutorial misconduct occurred in several ways. In one case, red
blood was portrayed as human, and in another, hog blood was similarly
used. An African-American defendant was found guilty after a prosecutor
kept secret an eyewitness account that the murderer was white. A Colorado prosecutor hid a victim's gun and then argued that there was no
gun. An Illinois prosecutor hid a piece of pipe and then argued that there
was no pipe. A Florida man, convicted in the poisoning deaths of his children, was set free after evidence was found in the prosecutors office
undermining the state's case. The Florida man had served 21 years before
being freed.

The authors of the *Chicago Tribune* article attributed misconduct to
several factors. First, the threshold for reversing a case was high. Under
Brady v. Maryland (1963), courts reversed a conviction only if there
existed a reasonable probability of a different verdict. A prosecutor's use
of reprehensible actions, the authors noted, was not enough to reverse an
outcome. Second, winning cases was important to prosecutors. The
drive to win, the *Chicago Tribune* observed, was intensified by the satisfaction of putting away a dangerous criminal, providing public satisfac-

tion that a wrong has been addressed, colleague and professional esteem, delivering "justice" (i.e., a conviction) for the victim and/or their survivors. Finally, prosecutors were unlikely to be punished, even in cases of egregious misconduct. The factors noted by the *Chicago Tribune* authors are strikingly similar to pressures observed by Manning and Redlinger (1978) that contributed to corruption of police officers.

A review of many of the comments in the *Chicago Tribune* series reveal elements comparable to noble cause corruption among police officers. Consider the comments of one of the prosecutors interviewed in the series.

> Owens prayed before closing arguments. "I said, 'Lord, if this guy didn't do it, don't give me the strength to do this.' I was like crusader and the Lord was on my side. "All I cared about was making sure the defendant would not hit the street," he says." "There ain't no appeal if I lose." (Possley & Armstrong, 1999).

These comments reveal a commitment to the good end—"getting the bad guy off the streets." The unwavering belief that a defendant was guilty, in spite of evidence to the contrary, is characteristic of noble cause corruption. Such an example can be seen in the following quote, which is from a civil case in which a former prosecutor is being sued by a cleared defendant.

> "Sitting here today, Mr. Arthur (the former prosecutor), do you believe that any of the Ford Heights 4—Willie Rainge, Keny Adams, Verneal Jimerson and Dennis Williams—had any involvement in the murders of Larry Lionberg and Carol Schmal?" asked one of Jimerson's attorneys.

> "Yes," Arthur said. "I think they did."

> Arthur clings to his belief (that the defendants are guilty of homicide) even though other men have confessed, even though DNA tests implicated one of those who confessed and eliminated Williams and his friends as suspects; even though prosecution witnesses have either recanted or been discredited and the scientific evidence at the trial exposed as bunk; even though Williams and his friends have received pardons from the governor and apologies from the state attorney's office (Armstrong & Possley, 1999b).

In this example, the former prosecutor displayed a sentiment similar to what Klockars (1983) described as an "operative assumption of guilt." This is a presumption of a person's guilt regardless of evidence. Guilt is believed to be factual, and failure to prove it simply reflects on the skills of the prosecutor or on the ability of the defendant to obscure or mislead. A finding of "not guilty" is not proof of innocence, but instead that a guilty defendant got away with a crime.

Parole/Probation. A review of literature suggests that noble cause corruption does not appear as prevalent as in other areas of the criminal justice system. This may stem from value conflicts experienced by many parole and probation officers, though it should be acknowledged that this may simply be a shortcoming of the literature as well.

Agencies of parole and probation carry a unique and conflicting responsibility with regard to offenders. Their daily work embodies correctional philosophies of rehabilitation and control, and they are expected to both help and surveill clients. Their rehabilitation responsibilities are consistent with the ethics of care, focusing on offender's needs and the relationship of the offender to the community (Pollock, 1998). Their efforts to reintegrate clients are also consistent with the idea of restorative justice, according to which the offender is expected to contribute to the healing of the victim and the community. Agents provide critically needed assistance so that clients can undergo the transition from criminal activity to constructive social behavior. They are concerned with the well-being of offenders, and try to provide them opportunities to better their lives (Sluder & Reddington, 1993).

Agents also serve a social control function. They exert control over the behavior of their clients, acting in the interests of community protection. They keep track of offenders, and carry the formal responsibility to report any lawbreaking or violation of contract in which clients engage. In some departments, agents are sworn officers and view their work in terms of enforcement rather than rehabilitation.

These dual responsibilities carry conflicting values. On the one hand, social-work responsibilities commit an officer to values associated with rehabilitation. On the other hand, officers are engaged in tracking and surveilling clients and view their work in terms of controlling offender populations. That these responsibilities contribute to role conflict has been noted (Tomaino, 1975).[7] Value conflict is straightforwardly comparable to the means-ends conflict, in which a social-work orientation matches a means ethic and surveillance is understandable as crime control.

The value conflict between social work/control-surveillance is exacerbated by the large case loads often carried by parole and probation officers. Large caseloads have always been characteristic of parole and probation, fostering an adaptive response of managerial control and focus on problem cases (McCorkle & Crank, 1996). Rehabilitation, however, requires individualized treatment and an attention to the needs of particular offenders, and such individualized treatment can be lost in efforts to control burgeoning caseloads.

Historically situated as the rehabilitative component of corrections, parole and probation departments have moved toward crime control through the final three decades of the twentieth century (Cohen, 1985). Organizational demands for surveillance and contemporary hiring practices drive a crime-control mentality (Harris, Clear & Baird, 1989). A "new penology" has emerged with managerial objectives, to separate felons according to dangerousness and to deploy control strategies rationally (Feeley & Simon, 1992:452). This "new" managerial penology focuses on the management and control of risk populations. This represents a profound transformation from the "old penology," which emphasized individualized treatment. Community corrections displays a tough crime control mission characterized by broad, diverse and punitive community based sanctions, elaborate testing for drugs, and technologically sophisticated surveillance (Byrne, 1990).

The conflict between rehabilitation and control, represents a conflict in value systems. For individual officers, the ethical issue is summarized by Pollock as follows:

> The formal ethics of the profession is summarized by the ideal of service—to the community and to the offender—and herein lies the crux of most of the ethical issues that present themselves. Whether to favor meeting offender's needs over community needs or vice versa is at the heart of a number of different ethical dilemmas for the parole and probation officer (Pollock, 1998:310).

Problems between these value systems are experienced practically in the day-to-day working environment and infuse probation and parole culture with meaning. Parole and probation officers develop common-sense ways of dealing with problems and thinking about their work. These common-sense ways of problem-solving, shared with other officers, provide the substance of officer culture. Elements of the culture of probation and parole officers has been described as an emphasis on individualism and personal responsibility, concerns over how to balance bureaucracy against offenders needs, cynicism toward offenders, and a crime-control orientation (Crank, 1996; Pollock, 1998; Souryal, 1992).[8] These elements of parole and probation focus on control ends, and might seem to encourage noble cause corruption.

Other aspects of parole and probation work seem to mitigate against noble cause corruption. The "blue code of secrecy" seen in police organizations does not appear to be as intense in parole and probation, though there are norms against informing on fellow officers for unethical or illegal behavior (Pollock, 1998). And due process issues, central to studies of police resistance to formal oversight, do not appear to preoccupy parole and probation officers with the same intensity (Crank, 1996).

Other aspects of parole and probation further distinguish it from the isolation associated with police work. Parole and probation officers have normal working hours, consequently, their work does not of its nature separate officers from the normal working routines of mainstream society. They do not wear uniforms, which in other justice organizations clearly separate their employees from most citizens. Moreover, they provide a social service to their clients, for all the value conflict that caring ethic may cause. They are often more educated then police. Many states require parole and probation officers to have a Baccalaureate degree in the helping professions. Finally, parole and probation officers are required to contact their line commanders, usually a Sergeant prior to taking formal actions against a client. They are also required to keep detailed paperwork about their actions. Hence, their decisions are held to a high level of organizational accountability. For these reasons, the institutional and organizational dynamics that foster the formation of secretive informal organization processes in police organizations do not seem to be as pervasive in parole and probation departments as in police organizations.

Role conflict has been presented consistently in the literature as a negative outcome. Yet it may be that role conflict can also have positive outcomes as well. An officer facing conflicting value systems of rehabilitation and control must become personally involved in their reconciliation. In the face of value dissonance, officers must think through the central issues and decide on a course of action. The control-rehabilitation conflict in parole and probation practice may carry with it an uncomfortable sense of moral conflict, a feeling that an officer is psychologically entangled in opposing ethical worlds. Yet that conflict also might be liberating, encouraging officers to think and reason through alternative ethical commitments. The outcome of value conflict may be a certain degree of ideological freedom and the capacity to think creatively.

Informal Organization and Crime Control

Each of the kinds of agencies discussed above earlier carry different ethical dilemmas. These dilemmas emerge as practical problems involving citizens, suspects, parolees and probationers, and defendants, and are played out in terms of the tension between due process and crime control. All the different groups we have examined carry a mission that includes crime control, and in them we can see the ethical drama created by the tension between crime control ends and due process means.

In the justice organizations and processes discussed here, ethical conflict between due process and crime control is highlighted in the distinction between the formal and informal organization. Formal organization processes are means-oriented, in that justice system personnel are expected to obey fundamental principles of procedure, policy, and law in the accomplishment of broad goals. The informal organization, on the other hand, carries an ends-oriented ethic, aimed at solving problems made clumsy or unattainable by formal processes. Informal organization bypasses procedural controls, allowing crime-control predispositions of justice system actors to carry out a de facto ends-oriented agency policy.

The crime control mission occurs within and is contextualized by its occupational and organizational setting. Among police officers, informal organizational elements and the relative insularity of line officers limit oversight, creating opportunities for the corruption of noble cause. Among prosecutors, organizational checks on crime control are generally weak. Like the police, prosecutorial commitments to the noble cause energize and give meaning to work but also carry the seeds of corruption. In the current era, minimum sentencing laws have prohibited judicial discretion. Prosecutors on the other hand, can informally negotiate with a defendant in exchange for the most highly valued goods of all—physical freedom or life. These powers have made the position of the prosecutor so strong relative to defense counsel, both formally and informally, that a prosecutor can engage in noble cause corruption with relative impunity.

Among parole and probation agents, rehabilitation considerations bolstered by an ethic of caring provide a balance to crime control in this field increasingly constrained to a managerial, controlling function. An ends-orientation concerned with community protection is balanced against a means-orientation of care. Organizational and occupational dynamics work against line-level insularity, a predisposing condition of noble-cause corruption among the police. Yet, as the field of parole and probation has become enforcement oriented, informal crime control dynamics may become more powerful.

Ethics in Justice Studies: Preparing for Practice

Ethics is undergoing an efflorescence across the study and practice of justice. Both in academics and in criminal justice practice, we have witnessed an increased role for ethics instruction and training. Ethics training among justice professionals takes forms such as specialized "train the trainer" programs that provide local agency professionals with ethical training, information and training through the Southwestern Law Enforcement Institute, and in-service and pre-service routine training. Research at the federal level funds efforts to assess and improve on the ethics of professionals as well. And ethics instruction is mainstreaming in academic curricula. Textbooks increasingly have sections on ethics, and specialized ethics books and courses are on the increase. The growth of interest in ethics has not been balanced by clarity of purpose. Precisely what ethics training should provide is unclear. Cederblom and Spohn (1991) describe this problem:

> When the public calls for "more teaching of ethics," probably it really
> wants people to act more ethically. They want police, lawyers, judges,
> and other professionals to quit taking bribes, quit lying, quit involving
> themselves in conflicts of interest. They probably want them also to

become less selfish, less materialistic, and more concerned about the public good. Apparently the presumption is that some procedure for teaching ethics, which can affect the way people are, can be carried out in the schools and colleges and that as a result they will act more ethically (Cederblom & Spohn, 1991:201).

But what should the content of instruction be? Is the content, as some have suggested, little more than a repeating of youthful 'feel-good" maxims, such as "don't lie?" Should schools engage in ethical indoctrination, presenting as morally "right" only one ethical vision of the complex world inhabited by justice professionals? The authors continue:

> It is doubtful that many of those who call for the teaching of ethics have considered in detail what this teaching would or should involve. In fact, many are probably unclear about what they want, aside from the result that people act more ethically. We propose that our task should not be to determine how the public wants us to carry out the teaching of ethics—that's our job as educators, and we can claim it as such. We should take this opportunity to do something that we can defend as worthwhile . . . we must determine how to engage our students in a serious dialogue about how they should conduct their lives as they embark on their careers (Cederblom & Spohn, 1991:202).

In other words, the proper subject matter of ethical instruction is unknown. Indeed, in the field of justice, the central ethical issues may themselves be controversial (Crank & Caldero, 2000). Instructors of ethics sometimes resort to "surface teaching," covering a little bit of all kinds of ethics, in order to make sure that students know something about the study of ethics. It is not clear that such instruction provides students with any substantive ethical utility except the knowledge that ethical systems are relative to each other, and anything can be justified from some ethical vantage-point.

What should instruction in ethics focus on? Ethical dilemmas can take a wide variety of forms. A person might concentrate on issues of discretion, contrasting formal justice system processes to discretionary decisionmaking (see, for example, Kennedy, 1977; Kleinig, 1996). Students can study deviant behavior and learn about corrupt practices (Kappeler, Sluder & Alpert, 1994). Or different ethical systems can be compared for their relevance to specific and recurring circumstances encountered by justice professionals (Cederblom & Spohn, 1991). Students can be provided with overviews of ethics, in order to comprehend the breadth of the topic and its diverse applications to justice (Pollock, 1998; Braswell, McCarthy & McCarthy, 1998). Students can study different scenarios, trying to determine correct or ethical outcomes (Miller & Braswell, 1997). All of these are different strategies for teaching ethics, and none has demonstrable advantages over another. This stems, in part, from the nature of ethical instruction in a L-liberal society: the content of ethics instruction is a goods, like other goods. Its value depends on marketplace considerations of personal interest, not on external principles.

Ethics Instruction as a Goods. The books we use to teach about ethics tend to locate ethics within the L-liberal tradition. Ethics books can be described as of three types, each of which represent a different aspect of the L-liberal tradition. Some books present a grab-bag of ethical positions and faculty teach how to distinguish among them. We are then asked to take such and such a case and state how we would act based on this or that ethical position. The second way is to provide students with different sides on controversial views. These sorts of books inevitably present their work in terms of crime-control versus due process notions of L-liberal justice, and rarely look at other kinds of moralities or justice. Both of the first two are wonderfully egalitarian approach to ethics and consistent with the way in which we distribute goods in post-enlightenment society.

The third is the type that presents students with various situations and discusses the ethical implications of each. This is a normative approach to ethics, aimed at increasing the extent to which students become aware of legal organizational pitfalls of various alternative courses of action. Any prescription departing from L-liberal ethical prescriptions is unlikely to be presented in such material—its aim is not the expansion of ethical perspective, but how existing ethical sensibility can be applied to new situations.

All three ways to teach ethics are L-liberal, in that ethics itself is treated as a goods, available for dissection and selection according to one's needs and desires. In a society based on personal needs and desires, ethics is like other goods. It is ordered by one's preference and utility. There exists no independent, external standard to determine what constitutes an ethical position. This is not to say that such material has no value—to the contrary it can be very useful in preparing students for occupational hazards and for thinking within the L-liberal tradition.

The value of ethical standpoints in an academic environment is determined by marketplace issues. Were an ethics perspective to be offensive to its readers, regardless of its internal consistency, logic, or appeal to practical or divine reason, it would be quickly abandoned by textbook publishers. How often is the ethical cosmology of the Wicca tradition or the I-Ching presented in criminal justice textbooks? When we consider the instruction of ethics, consequently, we receive issues of justice and morality as we do other goods—as a tallying and weighing of preferences, in which primary consideration goes to the egalitarianism of access of all participants to these views.

Ethics-as-a-goods is often unsatisfying for teacher and student alike, because it leaves a pall of relativity in its instructional wake. For faculty and students seeking hard answers to difficult questions, ethics-as-a-goods provides few answers. A review of the literature shows that ethics writers in justice studies have sought non-relativistic solutions to ethics instruction. Two such bases for instruction are presented below. The first fully accepts the principles of L-liberal ethics, and provides students with a general way to think about the relationship between due process and crime control. The second reveals the powerful pull that "first principle" ethics has on criminal justice practice.

Spader: Teaching in the Breach. How should due process and crime control be taught? Spader (1994) captures an important part of this debate in his discussion of the conflicts between court efficiency and due process. The means-ends debate, Spader observes, is central to due process concerns. Means-ends in a court are represented by procedural and substantive law where procedure is about lawful means and the substance of the law is about the ends the law seeks.

Due process can be thought of as a set of procedures that provide for formal information gathering. He describes due process as a common sense concern:

> Due process has a number of purposes, but one is paramount. Students and practitioners must understand this central purpose. Without this understanding and a deeply embedded emotional belief in the purpose, students and practitioners can become, I believe, case-hardened cynics who perceive all due process requirements as obstacles rather than opportunities.
>
> I insist that students continue until we reach the obvious: the purpose of due process is to uncover facts and obtain more truth. Due process aids the fact-finder's search for accurate evidence (Spader, 1994:85).

Spader (1994) identifies three aspects of due process. Due process is first and foremost a search for truth. It is secondly a means to protect citizens against the invasion of privacy vis-à-vis exclusionary rules (See also Spader, 1984). Third, due process protects against the natural tendency to judge too rapidly "that which is not yet fully known." It is an ethical counter-weight to the tendency to cut corners in order to obtain administrative efficiency. In sum, due process is a set of conditions that allow for knowledge to inform justice.

Spader provides a two-step consideration of due process. First, one has to determine if due process applies to the current case. Due process is about cases involving life, liberty, and property and is intended to limit the state's power to act. It protects individuals from the state. Due process does not apply to circumstances where the state fails to protect an individual from private violence.

Second, we ask *how much due process is necessary?* Generally, the more due process, the greater the quantity of information that can be acquired in any particular case. Due process is important, he observes, in cases involving life, liberty, and property.[9] However, not every situation demands the full panoply of due process protections, and that the criminal justice system cannot simply ignore concerns over "dollars, time, and efficiency" (98). Maximum due process is associated with the potential loss—the greater the loss to an individual, the more due process the courts are likely to provide. Not every incident is sufficiently serious to require maximum due process. Spader's perspective is one of balance:

> If the Court pursues either goal too strenuously—maximum due process or maximum cost savings—and takes one or the other to its logical extreme, that goal will clash with its other (Spader, 1994:98).

Issues of due process and crime control mobilize students' sentiments. One side will bother and even alarm students, and the other will be welcomed as friendly and *right*. But this is how ethical issues are. The only place students may receive an introduction to ethics that examines the interplay of due process and crime control is in an academic classroom. By providing a balanced approach to ethics, in which the relationships between the citizen and the state are fully explored, students can be provided the kinds of ethical introduction needed in the practice of criminal justice today.

Braswell: Toward a Principled Basis for Ethics Instruction

In several papers, Michael Braswell has sketched a first principle notion of justice. Braswell and Whitehead (1999) noted that the "left" versus "right" ideologies in criminal justice, represented by crime control versus due process values, polarized debate on crime policy and obscures efforts to obtain valid and accurate information useful for the development of criminal justice policy. Advocates for either position, they observed, tend to describe justice processes and interpret data from their particular ideological positions, denigrate other points of view, and fail to see the weaknesses in their own positions.

They suggested that researchers should engage in a search for truth based on a principle they called "whole sight" (Palmer, 1983). Whole sight requires using the heart as well as the head:

> The search for truth requires not only intelligence and personal responsibility but also compassion and humility. One can possess knowledge, but the search for truth requires a humility of service. Put another way, knowing the facts is not as liberating as loving the truth. (Braswell & Whitehead, 1999:54).

Whole sight is a balance between the heart and the head. "The heart gives the head a sense of humility and humanity while the head provides the heart with a focus and a course of action in resolving problems." [54]. The purpose of while sight is not simply to seek a middle ground between conservatism and L-liberalism, but to develop a larger perspective that incorporates the strengths of both into a larger, more truthful vision of crime and justice practices. Put differently, the search for justice involves not only an objective assessment of the facts, but a subjective recognition of how other people think about the facts—for example, researchers should try to understand how professionals think through what they are doing, and liberals should try to empathize with conservative viewpoints.

The paper by Braswell and Whitehead is compelling, as much for what it doesn't state as for what it does. It doesn't seek a middle ground between crime control and due process, though it argues for a balanced approach. Like Wilson discussed previously, *it seeks a standpoint outside the due process-crime control debate* from which to assess the relative strengths and weaknesses of each. What is the standpoint from which due process and crime control are considered?

The standpoint is a "search for truth." Truth is acquired through whole sight. Whole sight is acquired from the heart and the head in combination, and the heart acquires its perspective, its fuller vision by trying to understand the views of others with whom one might intellectually disagree.

In order for the heart to acquire perspective, it has to cultivate particular virtues. These virtues are "compassion," "truth," and most importantly, "humility." These virtues, in combination, provide someone with "heart." Why cultivate these virtues? Braswell and Whitehead note that both crime control and due process advocates tend to use data to strengthen their arguments. But data becomes a slave to one or the other of these standpoints, and an independent search for truth is lost. By cultivating these passions, one can develop a deeper understanding of the implications provided by data. One's data analysis is transformed from an ideological interpretation of data to a genuine effort to expand knowledge. Hence, the passions are irrational—they exist prior to knowledge and provide a foundation from which to develop a sense of justice.

How are these virtues learned? This question is unanswered, and is begged off by Braswell and Whitehead at outset of their paper when they disclaim a search for epistemological truth. Elsewhere, Braswell speaks of caring communities (Braswell & Gold, 1998) and peacemaking and connectedness (Braswell, 1998). These notions carry the idea that citizens are connected to each other through the local communities in which we participate. There is in his considered works the elements of first principles as they are applied to a methodology of instruction. His ideas are in this sense are Aristotelian in that local communities are infused with values, and these values are learned through the practice of virtue.

Braswell consequently has provided a "first principle" standpoint, though not fully developed, for challenging the L-liberal dichotomy of due-process and crime control conceptions of justice. His work infuses what Wilson (1993) called the barrenness of utilitarian morality with meaning. That meaning comes prior to needs and interests, and exists in caring communities that can provide their citizens with the virtue to see beyond individualistic conservative and liberal ideologies.

The ethics put forth by Braswell and his colleagues in it are fundamentally different from ethics understood normatively in terms of the lawful negotiation of conflicting principles of crime control and due process, to an inquiry into the nature of justice itself. This inquiry, once initiated, requires us to broaden our study of ethics beyond normative confines and explore the range of meanings justice may have. Our inquiry, having been "how do we teach criminal justice professionals about practical ethics that will enhance their ability to operate in a complex L-liberal society," becomes "What is justice?" We embark on an intellectual voyage that locates our field in the humanities as much as the social sciences, and begin to incorporate into our teachings such works as Walzer (1983), Dworkin (1985), Rawls (1971), Warnke (1993) and Habermas (1993).

Conclusion: Ethics and Justice Studies. The developing academic identity of justice studies is tied to how we approach ethics, both as an area of instruction and as a source of scholarship. As an area of professional instruction, justice education should place its aim in the direction of a balance between due process and crime control—these, after all, are the central normative themes of our system of governance. Because it is in part a humanities, justice studies also has the responsibility to investigate and assess the breadth of possible justices and the moralities those justices are based on. Consistent with idiographic developments in the social sciences, we might follow MacIntyre's (1988; 1990) lead and study the time and place rootedness of our ideas of ethics. As an intellectual endeavor, the study of ethics requires breadth so that students understand not only the meanings underlying ethical positions but comprehend how these meanings intersect with the peoples they will have to work with.

As a social science in an age where many colleges and universities increasingly carry a community college component to their mission, we need to prepare our students for practical ethical problems they will confront. However, the goals of higher education in justice studies extend beyond preparation for practice. Our ethics instruction should be broad enough to broach this important question, whether the answer takes us to ideas of justice grounded in complex democracy or to first principles that find meaning in polis, religion, community traditions, or ethics yet unknown.

Notes

[1]   By Liberalism (large L) I refer to the kind of governance and rationality bequeathed by the enlightenment, and embodied in the Constitution of the United States. Wallerstein (1992:337) described "large L" Liberalism as a course of social amelioration, grounded in a capitalist logic, based on the rational assessment of existing problems by specialists. All forms of Liberalism are primarily concerned with the needs and preferences of individuals, though each addresses those needs in different ways depending on their view of the government's role in social amelioration. Socialism, small liberalism, and conservatism are all forms of large L Liberalism, each differing primarily on the extent to which they think that government should intercede in the social disruptions caused by capitalist change.

[2]   MacIntyre notes that "We have to learn, however, that the satisfaction of all our desires will not in itself achieve happiness. It is only the satisfaction of desire for that which is right to desire—here again Augustine is following Cicero—which is happiness. So our desires need to be directed toward objects other than those to which we first find them directed and ordered hierarchically" [154].

[3]   The doctrine of the law is this: that precedents and rules must be followed, unless flatly absurd or unjust: for though their reason not be obvious at first view, yet we owe such a deference to former times as not to suppose that they acted wholly without consideration. Edward Christian, Commentaries (1973-1975), introduction, section 3, in MacIntyre, 1988: 229.

[4]   Substantive issues are not in theory relevant here, though in practice Governors and the President may commute criminal penalties for substantive reasons or provide "litmus tests" of candidates for positions that assess their favorability of substantive political issues

[5]   Wilson (1993) explicitly recognizes and acknowledges the historical sources of his ideas.

[6]   Under Himmler, the police were reorganized into two sections. The criminal detection and Gestapo positions were reorganized into the Sicherheitspolizei [security police] and the urban uniformed police into a single Ordnungspolizei [literally, order-keeping police] (Padfield, 1991: 185).

[7]   This value conflict may be overstated. In a study of Alabama State and Federal Parole and Probation, Sigler (1988) found that a statewide change toward enforcement, marked by a change in policy mandating that officers carry weapons, did not produce conflict in state employees and only modest conflict in federal employees.

[8]   Although these elements have been reported in various research monographs, the body of research on parole and probation is inadequate to conclude that they are universal across agencies.

[9]   The idea that *more due process is better* is a reasonable though imperfect assumption. Spader (1994) notes that at times, due process can be manipulated to obscure the truth. Also, there may be threshold effects, and that beyond a certain quantity, more due process does not add new information to the body of information available to a court.

Conclusion: Toward Justice

At the 1984 meetings of the Academy of Criminal Justice Sciences, Lawrence Travis presented a paper on policing. The central theme of this presentation was that, in police research, investigators tended to construct a "catechism" of policing. By catechism, he meant that contemporary police problems were presented as if they emerged divinely, independent of their social, moral, and historical contexts. In this book, I have taken his theme to heart. Throughout this book I have sought to answer the question *Why is this topic important?* Each chapter has accordingly been introduced with an extended discussion of the broader contexts and controversies of the topic at hand. My purpose in discussing justice topics in this format was to ensure that, when students had completed the book, their knowledge would be broader than if only the criminal justice dynamics were studied. My intent has been to push out the bubble of comprehension, so that students are intellectually prepared for graduate work and will be ready to participate in the complex world around them.

Justice as a Problematic

The many themes used throughout this book cohere around a central, simple idea. By exploring the diversity of forms that justice can take, we elevate the study of justice from a legally defined normative endeavor into a larger inquiry into the nature of justice itself. Each chapter is about justice as a *problematic,* whose meaning is a cipher, undetermined and undeterminable. Justice education is about the enquiry into the nature of justice itself.

The characteristic feature of academic growth has been a shift of field identity from its community college origins, with their focus on police training, to social science affiliation in four-year and graduate-level institutions. However, as the field has matured, the social sciences have themselves undergone change. The have historically been nomothetic, grounded in scientific methodologies with their concern for the identification of underlying regularities in human behavior. Increasingly, there is a recognition that human behavior is mutable. Across the social sciences, there is an interest in the unique and particular. This change was associated with the increased realization of the limitations of Eurocentric thought and an expansion of intellectual horizons in multicultural directions. The language of change is expressed by the notion of the re-enchantment of the social sciences—we are embarked on a new quest, to find out what it is that constitutes the human variety.

Changes in the social sciences are closely tied to contemporary efforts to build justice programs. From the mid 1970s forward, the development of academic justice studies has been behavioral, though containing critical or conflict theoretical tendencies. This development mirrors similar traditions in the social sciences, particularly the fields of sociology, political science, and criminology. As justice studies programs moved into the university setting, they often aligned with academic sociology or political science, and mirrored a criminological or public administration focus. Others attempted to become interdisciplinary.

These models no longer are adequate to contain the many ideas that today characterize the justice fields. Further growth and intellectual development requires a consideration of justice programs as domains concerned with the notion of justice as a problematic. This view situates normative ideas of justice, crime, and criminality as a subfield of justice studies generally, and locates at the center of the field an inquiry into the nature of justice itself.

The methods chapter was organized and written around the idea that no particular method adequately assessed the practice of criminal justice. This chapter began with an inquiry into the nature of reality itself. This discussion, though abstract, was intended to make a simple point—that researchers should take none of their findings for granted, and that even seemingly obvious elements of research design should be challenged. The discussions of metaphor emphasized the notion that the language we use is itself full of hidden assumptions and meanings. The discussion of intentionality was presented to emphasize that the moral meanings that we impart to justice work, so important in the structure and practice of criminal justice, have no objective *out there*. This is not meant to undermine the importance of morality, which is a special gift to humans regardless of its origins. Rather, it is that our morality should not be taken as definitive or conclusive, but only as a starting point for a broader inquiry into justice. If justice is indeed a problematic, then justice workers carry a responsibility to understand the morality of those with whom they work, teach, study, or over whom they enforce the law.

The field of justice studies tends to emphasize a model of knowledge development based on quantitative methods and analysis. This is consistent with its behavioral history and of the history of the social sciences generally, outside the field of history. In the present era, the social sciences are undergoing a rethinking of fundamental premises, precipitated by an awakening from a Eurocentric view, the increasing political and intellectual clout of minority groups, and the expanded study of other cultures. The notion that the social sciences could identify regularities in human behavior has undergone a sea change, with both theory and study emphasizing the way events and processes are fixed in space and time. Human reality today appears to be more malleable and unpredictable than the social sciences had thought 40 years ago. Today we are nearly as occupied with comprehending the uniquenesses of our different objects of analysis as in finding regularities among them.

The field of justice studies is undergoing a similar transition. Justice is not rule-like, but a malleable product of human efforts to get along under changing circumstances. When justice is treated as a problematic, our focus is on its variety, what Mills (1959) eloquently called "the human variety." The hidden trap of determinism was to lock the human variety into predictable behaviors. Today, the field of justice studies, like the other social sciences, is waking to the variety that marks human action and meaning.

The limits of traditional ideas of justice are particularly evident when we broach multicultural issues. Multicultural issues are among the most trenchant hot-button topics in academe as well as in political and social life in the United States. Anyone who has taught a class in criminal justice can cite chapter and verse about multicultural controversies in the classroom. Yet, for all the opinions that emerge in the classroom, faculty and students alike are often surprisingly uninformed about multicultural issues underlying justice problems. Accordingly, the multicultural debate was decomposed into three kinds of identity—race, ethnicity, and gender—and central issues were addressed in each. Learning about the full meanings of ethnicity, race, and gender, emerge from a recognition that many different standpoints have a legitimate claim to authenticity. This is called a "fusion of horizons," and provides a way to prepare ourselves to accept, at least initially, that which we do not yet know.

The inquiry into race and criminal justice began with a fundamental question—what is race? Much of the justice research is based on uncritically accepted administrative racial categories, and students are untrained to think other than superficially about deeper issues concerning race. Yet, the notion of race is fundamental to how we think about justice itself. The United States is today becoming the first fully international society; yet we continue to struggle with fundamental problems of racial identity and equality. Issues of race pervade the justice system, from covert arrest practices by police officers to inmate conflicts in the nation's prisons. In a troubling variety of justice practices, race is a determinative factor, used as if it contained meaning about individuals or their behaviors. It is not enough to simply inquire as to the effects of race-based differences, though this has stimulated very good research. Focused qualitative research is needed to investigate the meanings race has across the practice of criminal justice.

Ethnicity is a different notion from race, even though it is commonly treated similarly. Ethnicity is also treated as a problematic—we need to ask what it is before we look at its causes or consequences. We commonly use meta-ethnic categories such as Asian-American as if they held some sort of meaning. But what are those meanings? Who holds them? And is there a useful way to think about ethnicity? By approaching ethnicity in this way, we open the door to thinking about how people find meaning in the world around them. Hence, treated in this way, by studying ethnicity we uncover a bit of what it means to be human.

Gender carries the most occulted meanings of all. Gender is pervasive to the way U.S. citizens think about each other, and we are only beginning to comprehend the way gendered identity pervade society. Even the seemingly liberal environment of academia is sharply gendered. As scholars focus on gender, they increasingly find that taken-for-granted ideas of crime and justice behavior contain significant biases. What had appeared to be good criminology is increasingly recognized as gendered standpoints that work well for some kinds of people—usually heterosexual males—but are not useful for understanding other standpoints. As we begin to explore the role of gendered standpoints, we are again pulled in a nomothetic direction, and today we are trying to comprehend the ways our seemingly deterministic ideas of the world are complicated by gender. Justice becomes a problematic again, as we try to sort out the way in which we construct meanings by assigning male and female roles to humans.

The final chapter deals with ethics. Conceptually, this chapter may have been the most difficult of all—ethical issues are the native habitat of philosophers, and their language is concise and intricate. The goal in this chapter has been to take everyday ideas of right and wrong and show how they represent only one possible of many points of views. Again, the language of standpoint is important here—a broad consideration of ethics requires that we see our morality as only one standpoint, and that others may have equal claim to legitimacy.

The ethics chapter particularly focused on the distinction between an ethical standpoint grounded in L-liberal traditions and a standpoint based on first principles. Politically and legally, the United States is heavily invested in a L-liberal standpoint, which means that personal needs and interests, captured by the phrase "pursuit of happiness" are central to human endeavors. Yet, powerful themes involving first principles—the idea that the "right" and the "good" exists external to individuals—are pervasive to American culture, and are identifiable in the works we use to teach criminal justice ethics. These standpoints are both integral to everyday life. However, that they conflict with each other shows how ethics was itself also a problematic, and that different peoples have very different notions of what constitutes the good life and how we go about achieving it. As justicians, our ethical responsibility is only accomplished in part by acting in an ethical way. It is also accomplished by taking the ethical standpoint of the other. Growth as a person, and as a field, lies in our willingness to take a look at breadth of ethical perspectives.

All chapters have carried the theme that justice is a problematic. Amidst the many conflicts and debates surrounding the idea of justice emerges a central theme—that which we call "human" is not comprised of fixed and determinative behavior, attitudes, or predispositions, but is capable of change and growth. Justice cannot be captured by normative ideas of criminal justice practice. It is something more. We may educate and train our students for positions in the professional fields of criminal justice, and we should also prepare them for a "further territory," beyond criminal justice practice, where justice work is carried out. This book concludes with a discussion of further territory

The Further Territory: From Criminal Justice to Justice

> No single instrument, not even the law, is sufficient to make a just society. As a result, the passion for justice that brings us to the study of the law must be sustained by other tools as well. (Stones, 2000)

The passage above was delivered by Christopher Stones to the graduating class of Wake Forest University's Law School. The address was titled "the territory between law and justice." In it, he stated that law and justice are different commitments, and the skilled practice of law is in itself inadequate to bring about just outcomes. Justice, he argued, was found in a "further territory." What was this territory? And if the skilled use of the law is inadequate to reach this territory, how then is it achieved?

This territory, Stones stated, was something all lawyers shared when they began their academic training in law. Stones reflected on his commitment to justice, and how this commitment mobilized his desire to be skilled in the practice of law. However, school taught him that law was not necessarily about justice. He recalled one professor stating to him "Stop! You are arguing justice. Argue law." Law and justice were different kinds of notions, and his ability to be successful at law was not measured by his just purposes, but by his ability to apply legal skills.

Stones recognized that the application of legal skills did not provide justice. For him, however, this did not mean that justice was inconsequential. The desire for justice, that bright force that inspired his entry in to legal education, also provided a foundation for his commitment to a life in the pursuit of justice. His recommendation to those at the commencement address was to recognize that the law could be a tool—a means—in the service of the ends of justice. He reminded the graduating class that this too should guide their professional development:

> I urge now to recall those arguments about justice, and to build professional lives for yourselves that begin with your legal skills but take you into that farther territory between law and justice (Stones, 2000:1).

The territory between law and justice was a human domain occupied by the poor, the disadvantaged, and those in need but ill-equipped or unable to marshal the resources to use the law on their behalf. They were the people who fell through the cracks of the legal and criminal justice systems. He spoke of foster children who, in part due to the administrative structure of the criminal justice system, were detained at rate substantially higher than non-foster children. He described battered women who could find no safety from the storms of rage that sometimes overwhelmed their lovers and spouses. For these people, a lawyer's skills and savvy provided no remedy. Other kinds of skills were needed, to organize and investigate, to work with colleagues or collaborate with professionals in other fields, to commit one's time and energy to fair treatment unobtainable under the existing law. The mastery of the law was only the beginning. The quest for justice was the end.

Stones described the justice work of Molly Armstrong, who developed Project Confirm (a Vera Project) to address problems faced by foster children:

> The tools that Molly Armstrong is using to even the scales of justice for these children make a good starting kit for any lawyers who would explore this territory between law and justice. She new the law as well, or better, than anyone in the system, but she also watched the money. She invented a new role in government for people who could use a crisis as a moment for focused, effective intervention. She manipulated the bureaucratic incentives within government; she found a set of public officials who cared enough to take the risk of innovating; and she worked with social scientists to measure the results (Stones, 2000:3).

Molly had become more than a lawyer: she was a justice worker, and she lived and worked in the territory between law and justice. The territory was filled with those for whom life was not just, and they were her concern. The territory contains justice workers like her, those among us who commit their lives to justice; for whom their education or training provides a beginning not an end.

This book has been about the further territory for students in the field of justice studies. Like the law, justice studies education is frequently about employment and practice in the criminal justice system. Students necessarily think about what they will do when they graduate. And, like the law, occupational activity can overwhelm youthful idealism. The practice of criminal justice is not itself enough to provide justice. More is needed.

This book carries a purpose parallel to that expressed by Stones, to identify and discuss the spirit of justice that animates criminal justice education. Our capacity for justice is ultimately measured by our ability to comprehend and work through the problems that ordinary people face. It is in their troubles that our work finds meaning. To paraphrase Skolnick and Bayley (1986), we find our measure in our ability to provide help for the mean and overwhelming problems faced by ordinary people.

The practice of criminal justice is full of justice workers. Ted Bowers, a Lieutenant in the Ada County Sheriffs Office, is one of them. He serves on and informally carries out the work of the Sheriffs Youth Foundation (SYF), a board that funds youthful school drop-out and delinquency prevention programs. The SYF is not a criminal justice program, nor does it involve the intervention of the criminal justice system. The program is aimed at the identification of at-risk youth in elementary school programs and provides scholarships so that participants can participate in after-school and weekend activities of their choosing. His work is justice work, aimed at youth that otherwise might fall through the cracks in the educational system and become at-risk for juvenile justice system involvement.

The Sheriffs Youth Foundation is staffed by others similarly committed, from the police, academicians and school teachers, health and welfare representative, and private sector representatives all voluntarily committing their time, all engaged in justice work. Each justice worker brings ideological predispositions to the work, and their views range from stern conservatism to sharp liberalism. They work together to a common solution to problems they care about.

Make no mistake—justice work is hard. It demands two qualities of its workers. The first is the willingness and energy of spirit to work beyond one's simple occupational requirements. The commitment to justice is a calling, in Weber's clear meaning of the term. Once embarked on the justice path, we continue to wherever it takes us. We may travel the road of education, when we commit our energies to our students. We may travel the road to practice, where we learn how to work with others in our communities, cop and social worker, priest and teacher, and learn how to find within ourselves the meaningfulness of their views. Or we may travel the road to high professional involvement in the state or nation, where our obligation is to speak truth to power.

Our second responsibility is to continually expand our views, to push back the frontiers of our knowledge. Central to this book has been the notion that justice lies not in particular standpoints, but in the nexus of many, often conflicting, views. In each chapter I have poised fundamental ideas central to one standpoint against other, opposing ideas. It is in the tension between these oppositions that the capacity for intellectual and spiritual growth occurs. So it is in our individual justice paths. Often in our field, we encounter fundamental disagreements and opposed ways of thinking about crime and justice. Our obligation is to find in ourselves a capacity to suspend our beliefs so that we can consider others. In our collaborations, in our willingness to work with those with whom we disagree, we explore the diverse forms that justice can take.

Once embarked, we travel a worldly path, a path whose demands pull us continually beyond the confines of our beliefs and knowledge. We will change and we will grow. And with luck, we will find justice along the way.

Bibliography

Abel, Richard (1989). *American Lawyers.* New York, NY: Oxford.

Abu-Lughod, Janet (1989). *Before European Hegemony: The World System A.D. 1250-1350.* New York, NY: Oxford University Press.

Academy of Criminal Justice Sciences (1995). *Guide to Graduate Programs in Criminal Justice and Criminology 1994-1995.* Highland Heights, KY: Academy of Criminal Justice Sciences.

Acosta-Belen, Edna & Christine E. Bose (1998). "Gender and Development." In Lorber (ed.) *Gender Inequality: Feminist Theories and Politics*, pp. 48-54. Los Angeles, CA: Roxbury.

Acker, Joan (1990). "Hierarchies, Jobs, and Bodies: A Theory of Gendered Organizations." *Gender and Society*, 4:139-158.

Adler, Freda (1975). *Sisters in Crime: The Rise of the New Female Criminal.* New York, NY: McGraw-Hill.

Akers, Ronald (1994). *Criminological Theories: Introduction and Evaluation.* Los Angeles, CA: Roxbury.

Alderson, John (1998). *Principled Policing: Protecting the Public with Integrity.* Winchester: Waterside Press.

Albanese, Jay (1989). "A Proper Model for Criminal Justice Education?" *Northeastern Criminal Justice Reporter*, (Spring):4.

Albonetti, Celesta, Robert Hauser, John Hagan, and Ilene Nagel (1989). "Criminal Justice Decision Making as a Stratification Process: The Role of Race and Stratification Resources in Pretrial Release." *Journal of Qualitative Criminology*, 5:57-82.

Amnesty International (1999). *"Not Part of My Sentence." Violations of the Human Rights of Women in Custody.* United States of America. Report AMR 51/01/99. March.

Angel, Marina (1988). "Women in Legal Education: What It's Like to Be Part of a Perpetual First Wave or the Case of the Disappearing Women." *Temple Law Review*, 61:799-846.

Appadurai, A. (1988). "Patting Hierarchy in Its Place." *Cultural Anthropology*, 3-1.

Appleby, Joyce, Lynn Hunt and Margaret Jacob (1994). *Telling the Truth About History.* New York, NY: W.W. Norton & Company.

Applegate, Brandon, Francis Cullen, Bonnie Fischer, and Thomas Vander Ven (2000). "Forgiveness and Fundamentalism: Reconsidering the Relationship Between correctional Attitudes and Religion." *Criminology*, 38(3):719-754.

Austin, Thomas and Donald Hummer (1994). "Has a Decade Made a Difference? Attitudes of Male Criminal Justice Majors Toward Female Police Officers." *Journal of Criminal Justice Education*, 5(2):229-239.

Armstrong, Ken and Maurice Possley (1999a). "The Verdict: Dishonor." Chicagotribune.com, January 8.

Armstrong, Ken and Maurice Possley (1999b). "Reversal of Fortune." Chicagotribune.com. January 13, 1999.

Bankston, Carl (1998). "Youth Gangs and the New Second Generation: A Review Essay." *Aggression and Violent Behavior*, 3(1):35-45.

Bankston, C. and S. Caldas (1996). "Adolescents and Deviance in a Vietnamese American Community: A Theoretical Synthesis." *Deviant Behavior*, 17:159-181.

Barak, Gregg (1986). "Is America Really Ready or the Currie Challenge?" *Crime and Social Justice*, 25:200-203.

Barak, Gregg (1997). "Criminal Justice Research and International Paradigms: Neoliberal Institutionalism, Regimes, and emerging Structures." *International Criminal Justice Review*, 7:113-129.

Barak, Gregg (1998). *Integrating Criminologies*. Boston, MA: Allyn & Bacon.

Barak, Gregg and Stuart Henry (1999). "An Integrative-Constitutive Theory of Crime, Law, and Social Justice. In B. Arrigio (ed.) *Social Justice, Criminal Justice: The Maturation of Criminal Justice in Law, Crime, and Deviance*, pp. 152-175. Belmont, CA: West/Wadsworth.

Barlow, David, Melissa Barlow, and Ted Chiricos (1993). "Long Economic Cycles and the Criminal Justice System in the U.S." *Crime, Law and Social Change*, 19:143-69.

Barlow, David, Melissa Barlow, and W. Johnson (1996). "The Political Economy o Criminal Justice Policy: A Time-Series Analysis of Economic Conditions, Crime, and Federal Criminal Justice Legislation, 1948-1987." *Justice Quarterly*, 13(2):223-241.

Baumgartner, Frank and Bryan Jones (1993). *Agendas and Instability in American Politics*. Chicago, IL: University of Chicago Press.

Baudrillard, J. (1981). *For a Critique of the Political Economy of the Sign*. St. Louis, MO: Telas.

Baudrillard, J. (1983a). *In the Shadow of the Silent Majority*. New York, NY: Semiotext(e).

Baudrillard, J. (1983b). *Simulations*. New York, NY: Semiotext(e).

Bayens, Gerald, Michael Manske, and John Smykla (1998). "The Impact of the New Penology on ISP." *Criminal Justice Review*, 23(1):51-62.

Becker, Howard (1963). *Outsiders: Studies of the Sociology of Deviance*. New York, NY: The Free Press.

Belknap, Joanne (1996). *The Invisible Woman: Gender, Crime and Justice*. Belmont, CA: Wadsworth Publishing Company.

Bell, Daniel (1975). "Ethnicity and Social Change." In N. Glazer and P. Moynihan (eds.) *Ethnicity: Theory and Experience*, pp. 141-174. Cambridge, MA: Harvard University Press.

Bell, Katherine (1992). *Ritual Theory, Ritual Practice*. New York, NY: Oxford University Press.

Bellamy, J. (1998). *The Criminal Trial in Later Medieval England: Before the Courts from Edward I to the Sixteenth Century*. Toronto, CN: University of Toronto Books.

Berberet, J. and F. Wong (1995). "The New American College: A Model for Liberal Learning." *Liberal Education*, (Winter):48.

Berger, Peter and Thomas Luckmann (1966). *The Social Construction of Reality*. New York, NY: Doubleday.

Bernard, Thomas (1990). "Twenty Years of Testing Theories: What Have We Learned and Why?" *Journal of Research in Crime and Delinquency*, 27(4):325-347.

Bernard, Thomas and Robin Engel (2001). "Conceptualizing Criminal Justice Theory." *Justice Quarterly*, 18(1):1-30.

Bets, G. and R. Marsh (1974). "Problems in the Development of an Undergraduate Criminal Justice Curriculum." *Federal Probation*, 38:34-40.

Bierne, Piers and James Messerschmidt (2000). *Criminology*, Third Edition. Boulder, CO: Westview Press.

Binder, Arnold and Virginia Binder (2001). "The Relationship Between Research Results and Public Policy." In H. Pontell and D. Schichor (eds.) *Contemporary Issues in Crime and Criminal Justice*, pp. 33-44. Upper Saddle River, NJ: Prentice-Hall.

Black, Donald (1976). *The Behavior of Law*. London: Academic Press.

Bloom, B. (1993). "Incarcerated Mothers and Their Children: Maintaining Family Ties." In *Female Offenders: Meeting the Needs of a Neglected Population*. Laurel, MD: American Correctional Population.

Bohm, Robert (1984). "The Politics of Law and Order" (Book review). *Justice Quarterly*, 3-1:449-455.

Bottomore, Tom and Robert Nisbet (1975). "Sociological Thought in the Eighteenth Century." In T. Bottomore and R. Nisbet (eds.) *A History of Sociological Analysis*, pp. 3-38. United States Basic Books, Inc.

Box, S. and C. Hale (1982). "Economic Crisis and the Rising Prison Population in England and Wales." *Crime and Social Justice*, 17:20-35.

Boyer, Ernest (1990). *Scholarship Reconsidered: Priorities of the Professoriate*. Ewing, NJ: The Carnegie Foundation.

Boyer, Ernest and Fred Hechinger (1981). *Higher Learning in the Nation's Service*. Washington, DC: Carnegie Foundation for the Advancement of Teaching.

Braswell, Michael (1998). "Criminal Justice: An Ethic for the Future." In M. Braswell, B. McCarthy, and B. McCarthy (eds.) *Justice, Crime, and Ethics*, Third Edition, pp. 395-406. Cincinnati, OH: Anderson Publishing Co.

Braswell, Michael, Belinda McCarthy, and Bernard McCarthy (1998). *Justice, Crime, and Ethics*. Third Edition. Cincinnati, OH: Anderson Publishing Co.

Braswell, Michael and Jeffrey Gould (1998). "Peacemaking, Justice and Ethics." In M. Braswell, B. McCarthy, and B. McCarthy (eds.) *Justice, Crime, and Ethics*, Third Edition, pp. 25-42. Cincinnati, OH: Anderson Publishing Co.

Braswell, Michael and John Whitehead (1999). "Seeking the Truth: An Alternative to Conservative and Liberal Thinking in Criminology." *Criminal Justice Review*, 24-1:50-63.

Breardley, H. (1932). *Homicide in the United States*. Chapel Hill, NC: University of North Carolina Press.

Brewer, Garry D. (1974). "The Policy Sciences Emerge: To Nurture and Structure a Discipline." *Policy Sciences*, 5(3):239-244.

Bright, C. (1993). "Teaching Feminist Pedagogy: An Undergraduate Course." *Women's Studies Quarterly*, 3(4):129-133.

Brint, Steven and Jerome Karabel (1991). "Institutional Origins and Transformations: The Case of American Community Colleges." In W. Powell and P. DiMaggio (eds.) *The New Institutionalism in Organizational Analysis*, pp. 337-360. Chicago, IL: University of Chicago Press.

Brown, Michael (1981). *Working the Street: Police Discretion and the Dilemmas of Reform*. New York, NY: Russell Sage Foundation.

Building Blocks for Youth (2000). *And Justice for Some.* http://www.buildingblocksfor youth.org/justiceforsome/jfs.html.

Bumner, Robyn (1999). "The Spillover Effect of 'Driving While Black.'" The Record (Online), April 19.

Bureau of Justice Statistics (1999). *Criminal Victimization in the United States, 1997.* Washington, DC: U.S. Government Printing Office.

Bureau of Justice Statistics (1993). *Comparing State and Federal Inmates, 1991.* Washington, DC: U.S. Government Printing Office.

Burgess, E. W. (1925). "The Growth of the City." In R. Park, E. Burgess, and R. McKenzie (eds.) *The City*. Chicago, IL: University of Chicago Press.

Bursik, R. (1988). "Social Disorganization and Theories of Crime and Delinquency: Problems and Prospects." *Criminology*, 56:519-551.

Byrne, J. (1990). "The Future of Intensive Probation Supervision and the New Intermediate Sanctions." *Crime & Delinquency*, 36:6-41.

Carter, David (1985). "Hispanic Perception of Police Performance: An Empirical Assessment." *Journal of Criminal Justice*, 13:487-500.

Carter, David (1983). "Hispanic Interaction with the Criminal Justice System in Texas: Experiences, Attitudes, and Perceptions." *Journal of Criminal Justice*, 11:2130227.

Cavallli-Sforza, L. Luca, Paolo Menozzi, and Alberto Piazza (1994). *The History and Geography of Human Genes*. Princeton, NJ: Princeton University Press.

Cederblom, Jerry and Cassia Spohn (1991). "A Model for Teaching Criminal Justice Ethics." *Journal of Criminal Justice Education*, 2(2):217.

Chambliss, William and Robert Seidman (1971). *Law, Order, and Power*. Reading, MA: Addison-Wesley.

Chamlin, Mitchell (1989). "Conflict Theory and Police Killings." *Deviant Behavior,* 10:353-368.

Chesney-Lind, Meda (1986). "Women and Crime: The Female Offender." *Signs: Journal of Women in Culture and Society*, 12(1):78-96.

Chesney, Lind, Meda (1987). "Female Offenders: Paternalism Reexamined." In L. Crites and W. Hepperle (ed.) *Women, the Courts, and Equality*, pp. 114-138. Newbury Park, CA: Sage.

Chesney-Lind, Meda and Randall Shelden (1992). *Girls, Delinquency, and Juvenile Justice*. Pacific Grove, CA: Brooks/Cole.

Chin, K., J. Fagan, and R. Kelley (1992). "Patterns of Chinese Gang Extortion." *Justice Quarterly*, 9:625-643.

Chiricos, T. and W. Bales (1991). "Unemployment and Punishment: An Empirical Assessment." *Criminology* 29:701-724.

Chiricos, Theodore and Charles Crawford (1995). "Race and Imprisonment: A Contextual Assessment of the Evidence." In D. Hawkins (ed.) *Ethnicity, Race, and Crime: Perspectives Across Time and Place*, pp. 281-309. Albany, NY: State University of New York Press.

Christie, N. (1994). *Crime Control as Industry: Toward Gulags, Western Style*. New York, NY: Routledge.

Clear, Todd R. (1998). Societal Responses to the President's Crime Commission: A Thirty-Year Retrospective." In L. Robinson (ed.) *The Challenge of Crime in a Free Society: Looking Back, Looking Forward*, pp. 131-158. Washington, D.C: U.S. Department of Justice.

Clear, Todd (1993). "On the Core of the Criminal Justice Curriculum." *Journal of Criminal Justice Education*, 4(2):395-400.

Clifford, J. (1992). "Traveling Cultures." In L. Grossberg, C. Nelson and P. Triechler (eds.) *Cultural Studies*. London: Routledge.

Cloward, R. and L. Ohlin (1960). *Delinquency and Opportunity: A Theory of Delinquent Gangs*. New York, NY: The Free Press.

Cockcroft, James (1996). *Latin America: History, Politics, and U.S. Policy*, Second Edition. Chicago, IL: Nelson-Hall Publishers.

Cohen, S. (1985). *Visions of Social Control: Crime, Punishment and Classification*. Oxford: Polity Press.

Cohen, Stanley (1988). *Against Criminology*. New Brunswick NJ: Transaction Books.

Cohn, Bernard (1989). "Law and the Colonial State in India." In *Starr and Collier*.

Cole, David (1999). *No Equal Justice: Race and Class in the American Criminal Justice System*. New York, NY: The New Press.

Cole, David and John Lamberth (2001). "The Fallacy of Racial Profiling." *New York Times*, May 13.

Conley, John (1993). "Historical Perspective and Criminal Justice." *Journal of Criminal Justice Education*, 4(2):349-360.

Connell, R.W. (1987). *Gender and Power: Society, the Person and Sexual Politics*. Cambridge, MA: Polity Press.

Conrad, J. and R. Myren (1979). *Two Views of Criminology and Criminal Justice*. Chicago, IL: Joint Commission on Criminology and Criminal Justice.

Coontz, Stephanie (1992). *The Way We Never Were: American Families and the Nostalgia Trap*. New York, NY: Basic Books.

Cooper, R. and G. Burrell (1988). "Modernism, Postmodernism, and Organizational Analysis: An Introduction." *Organizational Studies*, 9(1):91-112.

Coser, Lewis (1956). *The Functions of Social Conflict*. New York, NY: The Free Press.

Coser, Lewis (1978). "American Trends." In T. Bottomore and R. Nisbet (eds.) *A History of Sociological Analysis*, pp. 287-320. New York, NY: Basic Books.

Crank, John (1998). *Understanding Police Culture*. Cincinnati, OH: Anderson Publishing Co.

Crank, John (1996). "The Construction of Meaning During Training for Probation and Parole." *Justice Quarterly*, 13(2):401-426.

Crank, John (1994). "Watchman and Community: A Study of Myth and Institutionalization in Policing." *Law and Society Review,* 28(2):325-351.

Crank, John and Michael Caldero (2000). *Police Ethics and the Corruption of Noble Cause*. Cincinnati, OH: Anderson Publishing Co.

Crank, John and Robert Langworthy (1996). "Fragmented Centralization and the Organization of the Police." *Policing and Society*, 6:213-229.

Crank, John and Robert Langworthy (1992). "An Institutional Perspective of Policing." The *Journal of Criminal Law and Criminology*, 83:338-363.

Crawford, James (1997). "California's Proposition 227: A Post Mortem." *Bilingual Research Journal*, 21(1):1-30.

Crime Commission (1967). See U.S. President's Commission on Law Enforcement and Administration of Justice (1967).

Crutchfield, Robert (1995). "Ethnicity, Labor Markets, and Crime." In D. Hawkins (ed.) *Ethnicity, Race, and Crime: Perspectives Across Time and Place*, pp. 194-211. Albany, NY: State University of New York Press.

Cullen, Francis and Robert Agnew (1999). *Criminological Theory: Past to Present*. Los Angeles, CA: Roxbury Press.

Cullen, Francis and Karen Gilbert (1982). *Reaffirming Rehabilitation*. Cincinnati, OH: Anderson Publishing Co.

Cullen, Francis, John Wright, and Mitchell Chamlin (1999). "Social Support and Social Reform: A Progressive Crime Control Agenda." *Crime and Delinquency* 45(2):188-207.

Currie, Elliott (1985). *Confronting Crime: An American Challenge*. New York, NY: Pantheon.

Daly, Kathleen (1994). *Gender, Crime, and Punishment*. New Haven, CT: Yale University Press.

Daly, Kathleen (1987a). "Structure and Practice of Familial-Based Justice in a Criminal Court." *Law and Society Review*, 21(2):267-290.

Daly, Kathleen (1987b). "Discrimination in the Criminal Courts: Family, Gender, and the Problem of Equal Treatment." *Social Forces*, 66(1):152-75.

Daly, Kathleen and Meda Chesney-Lind (1988). "Feminism and Criminology." *Justice Quarterly*, 5(4):497-538.

Daly, M. and M. Wilson (1988). *Homicide*. New York, NY: Aldine de Gruyter.

Dannen, F. (1992). "Revenge of the Green Dragons." *The New Yorker*, 68:76-82.

Danner, Mona (1998). "Three Strikes and It's Women Who Are Out: The Hidden Consequences for Women of Criminal Justice Policy Reforms." In S. Miller (ed.) *Crime Control and Women: Feminist Implications of Criminal Justice Policy*, pp. 1-14. Thousand Oaks, CA: Sage.

Dawe, Alan (1978). "Theories of Social Action." In T. Bottomore and R. Nisbet (eds.) *A History of Sociological Analysis*, pp. 362-417. New York, NY: Basic Books.

DeKeseredy, Walter and Martin Schwartz (1991). "British and U.S. Realism: A Critical Comparison." *International Journal of Offender Therapy and Comparative Criminology*, 35(3):248-262.

de la Garza, Rodolfo, Louis DeSipio, Chris Garcia, Jon Garcia, and Angelo Falcon (1992). *Latino Voices*. Boulder, CO: Westview Press.

Delattre, Edwin J. (1996). *Character and Cops: Ethics in Policing*, Third Edition. Washington, DC: American Enterprise Institute.

del Pinal, George and Audrey Singer (1997). "Generations of Diversity: Latinos in the United States." *Population Bulletin* 52(3). Washington, DC: Population Reference Bureau.

Denzin, N. and Y. Lincoln (1994). "Introduction: Entering the Field of Qualitative Research." In N. Denzin and Y. Lincoln (eds.) *Handbook of Qualitative Research*, pp. 1-17. Thousand Oaks, CA: Sage.

Derrida, J. (1982). *Margins of Philosophy*. London: Harvester.

Derrida, J. (1978). *Writing and Difference*. London: Routledge & Kegan Paul.

Derrida, J. (1973). *Speech and Phenomena*. Evanston, IL: Northwestern University Press.

DeVita, Carol (1996). "The United States at Mid-Decade." *Population Bulletin* 50 (4). Washington, DC: Population Reference Bureau.

DiCristina, Bruce (1997). "The Quantitative Emphasis in Criminal Justice Education." *Journal of Criminal Justice Education*, 8-2:181-200.

DiCristina, Bruce (1995). *Method in Criminology: A Philosophical Primer*. New York, NY: Harrow and Heston.

Dobash, R. and R. Dobash (1979). *Violence Against Wives: A Case Against Patriarchy*. New York, NY: Free Press.

Dostoevsky, Fyodor (1991). *The Brothers Karamazoff*. Trans. Richard Pevear and Larissa Volokhonsky. New York, NY: First Vintage Classics Edition.

Douglas, Mary (1986). *How Institutions Think*. New York, NY: Syracuse University Press.

Duffee, David (1990). *Explaining Criminal Justice: Community Theory and Criminal Justice Reform*. Prospect Heights, IL: Waveland.

Duffee, David (1989). "Introduction." *Journal of Research in Crime and Delinquency* 26(2):107-115.

Duffield, John (1999). "Political Culture and State Behavior: Why Germany Confounds Neorealism." *International Organization*, 53(4):765-803.

Du Phuoc Long (1996). *The Dream Shattered: Vietnamese Gangs in America*. Boston, MA: Northeastern University Press.

Durham, Alexis M. III (1992). "Observations on the Future of Criminal Justice Education." *Journal of Criminal Justice Education*, 3-1:35-52.

Dworkin, Ronald (1985). "How Law is Like Literature." In *A Matter of Principle*. R. Dworkin. Cambridge, MA: Harvard University Press.

Dye, Thomas (1981). *Understanding Public Policy*, Fourth Edition. Englewood Cliffs, NJ: Prentice Hall.

Eaton, Mary (1986). *Justice for Women? Family, Court, and Social Control*. Philadelphia, PA: Open University Press.

Eigenberg, Helen and Agnes Baro (1992). "Women and the Publication Process: A Contingent Analysis of Criminal Justice Journals." *Journal of Criminal Justice Education*, 3(2):293-314.

Eisenhart, R. (1975). "You Can't Hack It Little Girl. An Examination of the Covert Psychological Agenda of Modern Combat Training." *Journal of Social Issues*, 31:13-23.

Eller, Jack (1999). *From Culture to Ethnicity to Conflict: An Anthropological Perspective on International Ethnic Conflict*. Ann Arbor, MI: The University of Michigan Press.

Eriksen, Thomas (1993). *Ethnicity and Nationalism: Anthropological Perspectives*. London: Pluto Press.

Etzioni, A. (1960). "Two Approaches to Organizational Analysis: A Critique and a Suggestion." *Administrative Science Quarterly*, 5:257-278.

Evans, M. (1990). "The Problem of Gender for Women's Studies." *Women's Studies International Forum*, 13 (5):457-462.

Farnsworth, Margaret (1989). "Theoretical Integration Versus Model Building." In S. Messner, M. Krohn, and A. Liska (eds.) *Theoretical Integration in the Study of Deviance and Crime*. Albany, NY: State University of Albany Press.

Farrell, Ronald and Carole Case (1995). *The Black Book*.

Featherstone, Mike (1995). *Undoing Culture: Globalization, Postmodernism, and Identity*. Thousand Oaks, CA: Sage.

Feeley, Malcolm (1997). "Two Models of the Criminal Justice System: An Organizational Perspective." In B. Hancock and P. Sharp (eds.) *Public Policy: Crime and Criminal Justice*, pp. 119-132. Upper Saddle River, NJ: Prentice Hall.

Feeley, Malcolm and Austin Sarat (1980). The Policy Dilemma: Federal Crime Policy and the Law Enforcement Assistance Administration, 1968-1978.

Feeley, Malcolm and Jonathan Simon (1992). "The New Penology: Notes on the Emerging Strategy of Corrections and its Implications." *Criminology* 30:449-474.

Felson, Markus (1998). *Crime and Everyday Life*, Second Edition. Thousand Oaks, CA: Pine Forge Press.

Fields, Charles and O. Robertson (1988). "Statistics in Criminal Justice Curricula." *Journal of Criminal Justice*, 16:139-150.

Flanagan, Timothy (2000). "Liberal Education and the Criminal Justice Major." *Journal of Criminal Justice Education*, 11(1):1-13.

Flanagan, Timothy (1990). "Criminal Justice Doctoral Programs in the United States and Canada: Findings From a National Survey." *Journal of Criminal Justice Education*, 1-2:195-213.

Fogelson, Robert (1977). *Big-City Police*. Cambridge, MA: Harvard University Press.

Foster, J. (1974). "A Descriptive Analysis of Crime-Related Programs in Higher Education." Unpublished Doctoral Dissertation. Florida State University.

Foucault, M. (1991). *Discipline and Punish: The Birth of the Prison*. New York, NY: Vintage Books.

Frake, C. (1964). "A Structural Description of Subanun Religious Behavior." Pp. 111-129 in W. Goodenough (ed.) *Explorations in Cultural Anthropology*. New York, NY: McGraw-Hill.

Freedman, J. (1996). *Idealism and Liberal Education*. Ann Harbor, MI: University of Michigan Press.

Friedan, Betty (1963). *The Feminine Mystique*. New York, NY: W.W. Norton.

Frug, Mary (1992). *Postmodern Legal Feminism.* New York, NY: Routledge.

Fyfe, James (1982). "Blind Justice: Police Shootings in Memphis." *Journal of Criminal Law and Criminology*, 73:707-722.

Galtung, Johan (1967). *Theory and Methods of Social* Research. Oslo, Norway: Universitetsforlaget.

Garland, David (1990). *Punishment and Modern Society: A Study in Social Theory*. Chicago, IL: The University of Chicago Press.

Garland, David (1985). *Punishment and Welfare.* Brookfield, VT: Gower.

Garn, S. (1971). *Human Races*. 3. Springfield IL: Charles C Thomas.

Geertz, Clifford (1973a). "Thick Description: Towards an Interpretive Theory of Culture." In *The Interpretation of Cultures*, pp. 3-32. New York, NY: Basic Books.

Geertz, Clifford (1973b). "The Impact of the Concept of Culture on the Concept of Man." In C. Geertz *The Interpretation of Cultures*, pp. 33-54. New York, NY: Basic Books.

Geertz, Clifford (1973c). "Religion as a Cultural System." In *The Interpretation of Cultures*, pp. 87-125. New York, NY: Basic Books.

Gelsthorpe, Loraine and Allison Morris (1988). "Feminism and Criminology in Britain." *British Journal of Criminology*, 28(2):93-110.

Giddens, Anthony (1994). *Central Problems in Social Theory*. Berkeley, CA: University of California Press.

Giddens, Anthony (1976). *New Rules of Sociological Method*. London: Hutchinson.

Giddens, Anthony (1978). "Positivism and its Critics." In T. Bottomore and R. Nisbet (eds.) *A History of Sociological Analysis*, pp. 237-286. New York, NY: Basic Books.

Gilly, Adolfo (1997). *Chiapas: la razón Ardiente: Ensayo Sobre la Rebelión del Mundo Encantado*. Ediciones Era, D.F., Mèxico.

Gilsinan, James (1997). "Public Policy and Criminology: A Historical and Philosophical Reassessment." In B. Hancock and P. Sharp (eds.) *Public Policy: Crime and Criminal Justice*, pp. 22-34. Upper Saddle River, NJ: Prentice Hall.

Gilsinan, James (1988). "They is Clowning Tough: 911 and the Social Construction of Reality." *Criminology*, 27(2):329-344.

Glazer, Nathan (1997). *We Are All Multiculturalists Now*. Cambridge, MA: Harvard University Press.

Goffman, Irving (1977). "The Arrangement Between the Sexes." *Theory and Society*, 4:301-331.

Goldstein, Herman (1986). "Higher Education and the Police." In M. Pogrebin and R. Regoli (eds.) *Police Administrative Issues: Techniques and Functions*, pp. 243-256. Millwood, NY: Associated Faculty Press, Inc.

Gordon, Diane (1991). *The Justice Juggernaut: Fighting Street Crime, Controlling Citizens.* London: Rutgers University Press.

Gottfredson, Michael (1982). "The Social Scientist and Rehabilitative Crime Policy." *Criminology*, 20:29-4.

Gould, Stephen Jay (1989). *Wonderful Life: The Burgess Shale and the Nature of History*. New York, NY: W.W. Norton and Company.

Grasmick, Harold, Elizabeth Davenport, Mitchell Chamlin, and Robert Bursik, Jr. (1992). "Protestant Fundamentalism and the Retributive Doctrine of Punishment." *Criminology*, 30:21-25.

Greenburg, D. (1977). "The Dynamics of Oscillatory Punishment Process." *Journal of Criminal Law and Criminology*, 68:643-651.

Greenwood, Peter (1982). *Selective Incapacitation*. Santa Monica, CA: Rand Corporation.

Guttman, Amy (1994). "Introduction." In A. Guttman (ed.) *Multiculturalism: Examining the Politics of Recognition*, pp. 3-24. Princeton, NJ: Princeton University Press.

Gurr, Ted (1993). *Minorities at Risk: A Global View of Ethnopolitical Politics*. Washington, DC: United States Institute of Peace Press.

Gurr, Ted and Barbara Harff (1994). *Ethnic Conflict in World Politics*. Boulder, CO: Westview Press.

Habermas, Jurgen (1993). *Moral Consciousness and Communicative Action*. Cambridge, MA: The MIT Press.

Habermas, Jurgen (1994). "Struggles for Recognition in the Democratic Constitutional State." Pp. 107-148 in A. Gutmann (ed.) *Multiculturalism: Examining the Politics of Recognition*. Princeton, NJ: Princeton University Press.

Hagan, John (1990). "The Gender Stratification of Income Inequality Among Lawyers." *Social Forces*, 68:835-855.

Hagan, John (1989). "Why Is There So Little Criminal Justice Theory? Neglected Macro- and Micro-Level Links Between Organization and Power." *Journal of Research in Crime and Delinquency*, 26-2:116-135.

Hagan, Frank (1982). *Research Methods in Criminal Justice and Criminology*. New York, NY: Macmillan.

Hagan, John, Ilene Nagel, and Celeste Albonetti (1980). "The Differential Sentencing of White-Collar Offenders in Ten Federal District Courts." *American Sociological Review*, 45:802-820.

Haggard, S. and B. Simmons (1987). "Theories of International Regimes." *International Organization*, 41:491-517.

Hale, Donna (1998). "Criminal Justice Education: Traditions in Transition." Presidential Address Delivered at the 34th Annual Meeting of the Academy of Criminal Justice Sciences, Louisville, Kentucky, March 1997." *Justice Quarterly*, 15(3):385-394.

Halfpenny, Peter (1982). *Positivism and Sociology: Explaining Social Life*. London: Allen & Unwin.

Halstead, James B. (1985). "Criminal Justice Education and the Humanities: A New Era?" *Educational and Psychological Research*, 5-3:149-164.

Harriman, Sidney (1983). *Policing a Class Society: The Experience of American Cities, 1865-1915*. Piscataway, NJ: Rutgers University Press.

Harris, Marvin (1991). (first edition 1977) *Cannibals and Kings*. New York, NY: Vintage Books.

Harris, P., T. Clear and S. Baird (1989). "Have Community Supervision Officers Changed Their Attitudes Toward Their Work?" *Justice Quarterly*, 6:233-246.

Hartsock, Nancy (1998). "The Nature of A Standpoint." In Lorber (1998) *Gender Inequality: Feminist Theories and Politics,* pp. 118-122. Los Angeles, CA: Roxbury Publishing Company.

Hassard, John (1993). Postmodernism and Organizational Analysis: An Overview." In J. Hassard and M. Parker (eds.) *Postmodernism and Organizations*, pp. 1-24 London: Sage.

Hawkins, Keith (1986). "On Legal Decision-Making." *Washington and Lee Law Review* 43(4):1161-1242.

Henry, Jules (1963). *Culture Against Man*. New York, NY: Random House.

Hindus, M. (1979). "The History of Crime: Not Robbed of Its Potential, But Still on Probation." In S. Messinger and E. Bittner (eds.) *Criminology Review Yearbook,* pp. 217-21. Beverly Hills, CA: Sage.

Hirsch, E., Jr. (1987). *Cultural Literacy*. Boston, Houghton-Mifflin.

Hojnacki, William (1997). "The Public Policy Process in the United States." Pp. 5-21 in B. Hancock and P. Sharp (eds.) *Public Policy: Crime and Criminal Justice*. Upper Saddle River, NJ: Prentice Hall.

Holmes, Malcolm (2000). "Minority Threat and Police Brutality: Determinants of Civil Rights Criminal Complaints in U.S. Municipalities." *Criminology*, 38(2):343-366.

Holmes, M. and W. Taggart (1990). "A Comparative Analysis of Research in Criminology and Criminal Justice Journals." *Justice Quarterly*, 7:421-437.

Homer-Dixon, Thomas F. (1994). "Environmental Scarcities and Conflict: Evidence from Cases." *International Security*, 19(1):5-40.

Hughes, Gail (1992). "Misimpressions, Distortions, and Corrections." *Overcrowded Times*, 3(5):2-3.

Human Rights Watch (2000). "Punishment and Prejudice: Racial Disparities in the War on Drugs." Human Rights Watch: www.hrw.oprg/reports/2000/usa/Rcedrg00.htm.

Human Rights Watch (1998). *Nowhere to Hide: Retaliation Against Women Prisoners in Michigan State Prisons*. New York, NY: Human Rights Watch.

Hunt, Jennifer (1985). "Police Accounts of Normal Force." *Urban Life*, 13 (4):315-341.

Huntington, Samuel (1996). *The Clash of Civilizations and the Remaking of World Order*. New York, NY: Touchstone.

Huspek, Michael, Roberto Martinez, and Leticia Jiminez (2001). "Violations of Human Civil Rights on the U.S.—Mexico Border, 1995 to 1997: A Report." In D. Baker and R. Davin (eds.) *Notable Selections in Crime, Criminology, and Criminal Justice*, pp. 183-202. Guilford, CT: McGraw-Hill/Dushkin.

Hutchinson, Earl (1999). "Police Must Keep Statistics." *Idaho Statesman*, Oct 1:B6.

Inverarity, J. and R. Grattett (1989). "Institutional Responses to Unemployment: A Comparison of U.S. Trends, 1948-1985." *Contemporary Crisis*, 13:351-370.

Jenkins, Philip (1999). "Book Review: The Criminal Trial in Later Medieval England" (by J.G Bellamy). Toronto, CN: University of Toronto Press.

Johnson, J. (1995). *Conclusion*. In K. Gabel and D. Johnson (eds.) *Children of Incarcerated Parents*. New York, NY: Lexington Books.

Johnson, Herbert A. and Nancy Travis Wolfe (1996). *History of Criminal Justice*, Second Edition. Cincinnati, OH: Anderson Publishing Co.

Jurik, Nancy (1988). "Striking a Balance: Female Correctional Officers, Gender Role Stereotypes, and Male Prisons." *Social Problems*, 32:291-305.

Kaplan Robert D. (1998). "Travel's Into America's Future." *Atlantic Monthly*, 282:2 (August):37-61.

Kaplan, Robert D. (1998b). *An Empire Wilderness: Travels Into America's Future*. New York, NY: Random House.

Kappeler, Victor, Richard Sluder, and Geoffrey Alpert (1994). *Forces of Deviance: Understanding the Dark Side of Policing*. Prospect Heights, IL: Waveland Press.

Kraska, Peter (1996). "Enjoying Militarism: Political/Personal Dilemmas in Studying U.S. Police Military Units." *Justice Quarterly*, 13(3):405-429.

Kelling, G. and M. Moore (1988). "The Evolving Strategy of Policing." Washington, DC: National Institute of Justice.

Kennedy, Daniel (1977). *The Dysfunctional Alliance: Emotion and Reason in Justice Administration* Edited. Cincinnati, OH: Anderson Publishing Co.

Kennedy, Randall (1994). "Suspect Policy." *The New Republic*, Sept. 13-20:30-35.

Kerner Commission (1968). See National Advisory Commission on Civil Disorder (1968).

Kerr, Clark (1991). *The Great Transformation in Higher Education 1960-1980*. Albany, NY: State University of New York Press.

Kiser, Larry and Elinor Ostrom (1982). "The Three Worlds in Action: A Metatheoretical Synthesis of Institutional Approaches." In E. Ostrom (ed.) *Strategies of Political Inquiry*. Beverly Hills, CA: Sage.

Kleinig, John (1996). *Handled with Discretion: Ethical Issues in Police Decisionmaking*. Edited. New York, NY: Rowman and Littlefield Publishers, Inc.

Klockars, Carl (1983). "The Dirty Harry Problem." In C. Klockars (ed.) *Thinking About Police: Contemporary Readings,* pp. 428-438. New York, NY: McGraw-Hill.

Kohfeld, Carol and John Sprague (1990). "Demography, Police Behavior, and Deterrence." *Criminology*, 28(1):111-16.

Kraska, Peter (1996). "Enjoying Militarism: Political/Personal Dilemmas in Studying U.S. Police Paramilitary Units." *Justice Quarterly*, 13:405-429.

Krasner, S. (1983). Regimes and the Limits of Realism: Regimes as Autonomous Variables. In S.D. Krasner (ed.) *International Regimes*, pp. 355-368. Ithaca, NY: Cornell University Press.

Kratochwil, F. and J. Ruggie (1986). "International Organization: A State of the Art on the Art of the State." *International Organization*, 40:753-775.

Kuhn, Thomas (1962). *The Structure of Scientific Revolutions*. Chicago, IL: University of Chicago Press.

Kuykendall, Jack (1977). "Criminal Justice Programs in Higher Education: Courses and Curriculum Orientations." *Journal of Criminal Justice*, 5:149-164.

Lakoff, George and Mark Johnson (1980). *Metaphors We Live By*. Chicago, IL: University of Chicago Press.

Langworthy, Robert (1992). "Organizational Structure." In G. Cordner and D. Hale (eds.) *What Works in Policing*, p. 87.

Langworthy, Robert (1986). *The Structure of Police Organizations*. New York, NY: Praeger.

Langworthy, Robert and Edward Latessa (1989). "Criminal Justice Education: A National Assessment." *The Justice Professional* 4-2:172-188.

Langworthy, Robert and Lawrence Travis III (eds.) (1994). *Policing in America: A Balance of Forces*. New York, NY: Macmillan Publishing Company.

Lanier, Mark and Stuart Henry (1998). *Essential Criminology*. Boulder, CO: Westview Press.

LaFree, Gary (1985). "Official Reactions to Hispanic Defendants in the Southwest." *Journal of Research in Crime and Delinquency*, 22(3):213-237.

LaFree, G. and K. Russell (1993). "The Argument for Studying Race and Crime." *Journal of Criminal Justice Education*, 4(2):273-289.

Langan, P. (1991). "Race and Prisoners Admitted to State and Federal Institutions, 1926-1986." U.S. Department of Justice. Washington, DC: U.S. Government Printing Office.

Lasswell, Harold (1951). "The Policy Orientation." In D. Lerner and H. Lasswell (eds.) *The Policy Sciences.* Stanford, CA: Stanford University Press.

Lea, John and Jock Young (1986). "A Realist Approach to Law and Order." In B. MacLean (ed.) *The Political Economy of Crime: Readings for a Critical Criminology*, pp. 358-364. Englewood Cliffs, NJ: Prentice Hall.

Leadership Conference on Human Rights (2000). *Justice on Trial: Racial Disparities in the Criminal Justice System.*

Legro, Jeffrey (1996). "Culture and Preferences in the International Cooperation Two-Step." *American Political Science Review*, 90(1):118-137.

Lippman, Walter (1961). *Drift and Mastery: An Attempt to Diagnose the Current Unrest.* Englewood Cliffs, NJ: Prentice Hall.

Liska, Allen (1992). "Introduction to the Study of Social Control." In A. Liska (ed.) *Social Threat and Social Control.* Albany, NY: SUNY Press.

Litwak, Eugene and Lydia Hylton (1974). "Interorganizational Analysis: A Hypothesis on coordinating Agencies." In Y. Hasenfeld and R. English (eds.) *Human Service Organizations.* Ann Arbor, MI: University of Michigan Press.

Locke, Hubert (1996). "The Color of Law and the Issue of Color: Race and the Abuse of Police Power." In W. Geller and H. Toch (eds.) *Police Violence: Understanding and Controlling Police Abuse of Force.* New Haven, CT: Yale University Press.

Lockwood, Dorothy, Anne Pottieger, and James Inciardi (1995). "Crack Use, Crime by Crack Users, and Ethnicity." In D. Hawkins (ed.) *Ethnicity, Race, and Crime: Perspectives Across time and Place*, pp. 212-234. Albany, NY: State University of New York Press.

Lombroso, Cesare and William Ferrero (1895). *The Female Offender.* London: Fisher Unwin.

Lopez, Antionette (1995). *Criminal Justice and Latino Communities*, Edited Volume. New York, NY: Garland.

Lorber, Judith (1998). *Gender Inequality: Feminist Theories and Politics.* Los Angeles, CA: Roxbury.

Lowi, Theodore (1985). "Foreword." In T. Seidelman, *Disenchanted Realists: Political Science and the American Crisis, 1884-1984.* Albany, NY: SUNY Press.

Lutz, Faith and David Murphy (1999). "Ultramasculine Prison Environments and Inmates' Adjustment: It's Time to Move Beyond the 'Boys Will Be Boys' Paradigm." *Justice Quarterly*, 16(4):709-734.

Lynch, Michael, Jackie Huey, J. Nunez, Billy Close, and Carolyn Johnson (1992). "Cultural Literacy, Criminology and Female-Gender Issues: The Power to Exclude." *Journal of Criminal Justice Education*, 3(2):183-202.

Lynch, Michael and Paul Stretesky (1999). "Marxism and Social Justice: Thinking about Social Justice, Eclipsing Criminal Justice." In B. Arrigo (ed.) *Social Justice, Criminal Justice: The Maturation of Critical Theory in Law, Crime, and Deviance*, pp. 14-29. Belmont, CA: West/Wadsworth.

MacIntyre, Alasdair (1990). *Three Rival Versions of Moral Inquiry: Encyclopedia, Genealogy, and Tradition.* Notre Dame, IN: University of Notre Dame Press.

MacIntyre, Alasdair (1988). *Whose Justice? Which Rationality?* Notre Dame, IN: University of Notre Dame Press.

Maguire, K. and A. Pastore (eds.) (1995). *Sourcebook of Criminal Justice Statistics.* Washington, DC: Bureau of Justice Statistics.

Mahan, Sue (1984). "Imposition of Despair—An Ethnography of Women in Prison." *Justice Quarterly*, 1(3):357-384.

Mahan, Sue and Aimee Anthony (1992). "Including Women in Correctional Texts." *Journal of Criminal Justice Education*, 3(2):261-276.

Mann, Coramae Richey (1984). *Female Crime and Delinquency*. Montgomery, AL: University of Alabama Press.

Manning, Peter (1999). "Semiotics and Justice: 'Justice,' *Justice*, and JUSTICE." In B. Arrigo (ed.) *Social Justice, Criminal Justice: The Maturation of Critical Theory in Law, Crime, and Deviance*, pp. 131-149. Belmont, CA: West/Wadsworth.

Manning, Peter (1997). *Police Work: The Social Organization of Policing*, Second Edition. Prospect Heights, IL: Waveland Press, Inc.

Manning, Peter (1995). "The Challenges of Postmodernism." In J. VanMaanen (ed.) *Representation in Ethnography*, pp. 245-272. Thousand Oaks, CA: Sage.

Manning, Peter (1989). "Occupational Culture." In *Encyclopedia of Police Science*, pp. 360-363. New York, NY: Garfield Publishing.

Manning, Peter 1988). *Symbolic Communication: Signifying Calls and the Police Response*. Cambridge, MA: MIT Press.

Manning, Peter (1987). *Semiotics and Fieldwork*. Newbury Park, CA: Sage.

Manning, Peter and Lawrence Redlinger (1978). "Invitational edges of Corruption: Some Consequences of Narcotic Law Enforcement." In P. Manning and J. VanMaanen (eds.) *Policing: A View From the Street*, pp. 147-166. Santa Monica, CA: Goodyear Publishing Company, Inc.

Marquart, James, Madhava Bodapati, Steven Cuvelier, and Leo Carroll (1993). "Ceremonial Justice, Loose Coupling, and the War on Drugs in Texas, 1980-1989." *Crime and Delinquency*, 39(4):528-542.

Martin, Philip and Elizabeth Midgley (1999). "Immigration to the United States." *Population Bulletin*, 54(2). Washington, DC: Population Reference Bureau.

Martin, Susan (1990). *On the Move: The Status of Women in Policing*. Washington, DC: Police Foundation.

Martin, Susan (1980). *Breaking and Entering: Policewomen on Patrol*. Berkeley, CA: University of California Press.

Martin, Susan and Nancy Jurik (1996). *Doing Justice, Doing Gender: Women in Law and Criminal Justice Occupations*. Thousand Oaks, CA: Sage.

Martindale, Don (1960). *The Nature and Types of Sociological Theory*. Boston, MA: Houghton Mifflin Company.

Martinson, Robert et al. (1975). "What Works?—Questions and Answers About Prison Reform." *Rehabilitation, Recidivism, and Research*. Hackensack, NJ: National Council on Crime and Delinquency.

Marx, Karl and Friedrich Engels (1947). *The German Ideology*. New York, NY: International Publishers.

Massey, Douglas and Nancy Denton (1993). *American Apartheid: Segregation and the Making of the Underclass*. Cambridge, MA: Harvard University Press.

Mastrofski, Stephen (1991). "Community Policing as Reform: A Cautionary Tale." In C. Klockars and S. Mastrofski (eds.) *Thinking About Police: Contemporary Readings*, Second Edition, pp. 515-529. New York, NY: McGraw-Hill.

Matthews, Roger (1987). "Taking Realist Criminology Seriously." *Contemporary Crisis*, 10:81-94.

Maynard, Douglas (1982). "Defendant Attributes in Plea Bargaining: Notes on the Modeling of Sentencing Decisions." *Social Problems*, 49:347-360.

McCorkle, Richard and John Crank (1996). "Meet the New Boss: Institutional Change and Loose Coupling in Parole and Probation." *American Journal of Criminal Justice*, 21(1):1-25.

McGuire, William and Claire McGuire (1988). "Content and Process in the Experience of Self." *Advances in Experimental Social Psychology*, 21:102.

McNulty, Elizabeth (1994). "Common-Sense Making Among Police Officers: The Social Construction of Working Knowledge." *Symbolic Interaction*, 17:281-294.

Mertz, Elizabeth (1994). "A New Social Constructionism for Sociolegal studies." *Law and Society Review* 28(5):1243-1265.

Messerschmidt, James (1994). "Schooling, Masculinities and Youth Crime." In T. Newburn and E. Stanko (eds.) *Just Boys Doing Business? Men, Masculinities and Crime*, pp. 81-99. London: Routledge.

Messerschmidt, James (1993). *Masculinities and Crime: Critique and Reconceptualization of Theory*. Lanham, MD: Rowman and Littlefeld.

Messner, Stephen, Marvin Krohn, and Allen Liska (1989). *Theoretical Integration in the Study of Deviance and Crime*. Albany, NY: State University of Albany Press.

Meyer, John, John Boli, and George Thomas (1994). "Ontology and Rationalization in the Western Cultural Account." In W. Richard Scott and J. Meyer (eds.) *Institutional Environments and Organizations: Structural Complexity and Individualism*, pp. 9-27. Thousand Oaks, CA Sage.

Meyer, John and Brian Rowan (1977 [1992]). "Institutionalized Organizations: Formal Structure as Myth and Ceremony." In J. Meyer and W.R. Scott (eds.) *Organizational Environments: Ritual and Rationality*, pp. 45-67. Updated Version. Newbury Park, CA: Sage Publications.

Meyer, John and W. Richard Scott (1992). "Centralization and the Legitimacy Problems of Local Government." Pp. 199-216 in in J. Meyer and W. Scott (eds.) *Organizational Environments: Ritual and Rationality*. Updated Edition. Newbury Park, CA: Sage.

Meyer, John, W. Richard Scott, and Terrence Deal (1992). "Institutional and Technical Sources of Organizational Structure: Explaining the Structure of Educational Organizations." In J. Meyer and W. Scott (eds.) *Organizational Environments: Ritual and Rationality*, Updated Edition, pp. 45-70. Newbury Park, CA: Sage.

Michalowski, Raymond (1983). "Crime Control in the 1980s: A Progressive Agenda." *Crime and Social Justice*, 19:13-23.

Michalowski Raymond (1985). *Order, Law and Crime: An Introduction to Criminology.* New York, NY: Random House.

Milovanovic, Dragan (1994). *A Primer in the Sociology of Law*. Second Edition. Albany, NY: Harrow and Heston Publishers.

Milovanovic, Dragan (1988). "Autonomy of the Legal Order, Ideology and the Structure of Legal Thought." In M. Schwartz and D. Friedrichs (eds.) *Humanistic Perspectives on Crime and Justice*. Hebron, CT: Practitioner Press.

Miller, Jerome (1996). *Search and Destroy: African-American Males in the Criminal Justice System*. Cambridge, MA: Cambridge University Press.

Miller, Larry and Michael Braswell (1997). *Human Relations and Police Work*, Fourth Edition. Prospect Heights, IL: Waveland Press.

Miller, Susan (1998). *Crime Control and Women: Feminist Implications of Criminal Justice Policy*, Edited Volume. Thousand Oaks, CA: Sage.

Mills, C. Wright (1959). *The Sociological Imagination*. London: Oxford University Press.

Morash, Merry and Lila Rucker (1998). "A Critical Look at the Idea of Boot Camp as a Correctional Reform." In S. Miller (ed.) *Crime Control and Women: Feminist Implications in Criminal Justice Policy*, pp. 32-51. Thousand Oaks, CA: Sage.

Morn, Frank (1995). *Academic Politics and the History of Criminal Justice Education*. Westport, CT: Greenwood Press.

Munoz, Ed, David Munoz, and Eric Stewart (2001). "The Misdemeanor Sentencing Decision: The Cumulative Disadvantage Effect of 'Gringo Justice'." In D. Baker and R. Davin (eds.) *Notable Selections in Crime, Criminology, and Criminal Justice*, pp. 271-282. Guilford, CT: McGraw-Hill/Dushkin.

Muraskin, Rosalyn (2001). "Overview." In R. Muraskin and M. Muraskin (eds.) *Morality and the Law*, pp. 1-6. Upper Saddle River, NJ: Prentice-Hall.

Naffine, Ngaire (1987). *Female Crime: The Construction of Women in Criminology*. Sydney, Australia: Allen & Unwin.

National Advisory Commission on Civil Disorder (1968). *Report of the National Advisory Commission on Civil Disorder* ("Kerner Commission"). Washington: GPO.

National Center for Health Statistics (1995). "Advance Report of Final Mortality Statistics, 1992." *Monthly Vital Statistics Report*, Vol. 43 No. 6, suppl. Washington, DC: U.S. Department of Health and Human Services.

Newburn, Tim and Elizabeth Stanko (1994). *Just Boys Doing Business? Men, Masculinities and Crime*. London: Routledge.

Nemeth, C. (1991). *Anderson's Dictionary of Criminal Justice Education, 1991*. Cincinnati, OH: Anderson Publishing Co.

Newman, Oscar (1972). *Defensible Space*. New York, NY: MacMillan.

Nietzsche, F. (1982). *The Portable Nietzsche*. Trans. and Ed. W. Kaufmann. New York, NY: Viking Penguin.

Nisbet, Robert (1978). "Conservatism." In T. Bottomore and R. Nisbett (eds.) *A History of Sociological Analysis*, pp. 80-117. New York, NY: Basic Books.

Nisbet, Robert (1966). *The Sociological Tradition*. New York, NY: Basic Books.

Ogle, Robbin S. (1999). "Prison Privatization: An Environmental Catch-22." *Justice Quarterly*, 16(3):579-600.

Oliver, Melvin and Thomas Shapiro (eds.) (1995). *Black Wealth/White Wealth: A New Perspective on Racial Inequality*. New York, NY: Routledge.

Ortner, Sherry (1984). "Theory in Anthropology Since the 1960s." *Comparative Studies in Society and History*, 26:126-166.

Ostrom, Elinor (1999). "Institutional Rational Choice: An Assessment of the Institutional Analysis and Development Framework." Pp. 35-72 in P. Sabatier (ed.) *Theories of the Policy Process*. Boulder, CO: Westview Press.

Packer, Herbert (1968). *The Limits of the Criminal Sanction*. Palo Alto, CA: Stanford University Press.

Paine, Thomas (1981). "The Rights of Man," pp. 668 in M. Curtis (ed.) *The Great Political Theories*. Volume 2. New York, NY: Avon Books.

Padfield, P. (1991). *Himmler*. Papermac: London.

Palmer, P. (1983). *To Know As We Are Known*. San Francisco, CA: Harper and Row.

Paris, D. and J. Reynolds (1983). *The Logic of Policy Inquiry*. New York, NY: Longmans.

Park, Robert (1926). "The Urban Community as a Special Pattern and a Moral Order." In E.W. Burgess (ed.) *The Urban Community*. Chicago, IL: University of Chicago Press.

Park, Robert and E. Burgess (1920). *Introduction to the Science of Sociology*. Chicago, IL: University of Chicago Press.

Pelfrey, W. (1978). "Innovation in Criminal Justice Education: The Professional Approach." Paper presented at the annual meetings of the American Society of Criminology.

Pellicani, Luciano (1994). *The Genesis of Capitalism and the Origins of Modernity*. (Trans. James Colbert). New York, NY: Telos Press.

Pepinsky, Hal (1993). "What Is Crime? What Is Peace? A Commentary." *Journal of Criminal Justice Education*, 4(2):391-394.

Pisciotta, Alexander (1994). *Benevolent Repression: Social Control and the American Reformatory-Prison Movement*. New York, NY: New York University Press.

Polk, Kenneth (1994). "Masculinity, Honor, and Confrontational Homicide." Pp. 166-188 in T. Newburn and E. Stanko (eds.) *Just Boys Doing Business: Men, Masculinities and Crime*. London: Routledge.

Pollock, Joycelyn (1998). *Ethics and Crime in Criminal Justice: Dilemmas and Decisions*, Third Edition. Belmont, CA: West/Wadsworth.

Pollan, Michael (1999). *A Very Fine Line. New York Times Magazine*, Sept. 12:27.

Pope, Carl and William Feyerherm (1990). "Minority Status and Juvenile Justice Processing: An Assessment of the Research Literature" (pts 1 & 2), *Criminal Justice Abstracts* (June):327-335 and (September):527-542.

Population Reference Bureau (1999). "America's Diversity: On the Edge of Two Centuries." *Reports on America* 1 (2). Washington, DC: Population Reference Bureau.

Possley, Maurice and Ken Armstrong (1999). "The Flip Side of A Fair Trial." Chicagotribune.com, January 11.

Rabinow, Paul (1996). *Essays on the Anthropology of Reason*. Princeton, NJ: Princeton University Press.

Rawls, John (1971). *A Theory of Justice*. Cambridge, MA: Harvard University Press.

Regoli, R., E. Poole and A. Miracle (1982). "Assessing the Prestige of Journals in Criminal Justice: A Research Note." *Journal of Criminal Justice*, 10:57-67.

Reiman, Jeffrey (1998). *The Rich Get Richer and the Poor Get Prison: Ideology, Class, and Criminal Justice*. Fifth edition. Boston, MA: Allyn and Bacon.

Remington, Frank (1990). "Development of Criminal Justice as an Academic Field." *Journal of Criminal Justice Education*, 1-1:9-20.

Renzetti, Claire (1998). "Connecting the Dots: Women, Public Policy and Social Control." In S. Miller (ed.) *Crime Control and Women: Feminist Implications of Criminal Justice Policy*, pp. 181-189. Thousand Oaks, CA: Sage.

Renzetti, Claire (1993). "On the Margins of the Malestream (Or, They Still Don't Get It, Do they): Feminist Analyses in Criminal Justice Education." *Journal of Criminal Justice Education*, 4(2):219-234.

Rhode, Deborah (1988). "Perspectives on Professional Women." *Stanford Law Review*, 40:1164-1207.

Richardson, Laurel (1990). "Narrative and Sociology." *Journal of Contemporary Ethnography*, 19(1):116-135.

Rieder, J. (1985). *Canarsie: The Jews and Italians of Brooklyn Against Liberalism*. Cambridge, MA: Harvard University Press.

Roberg, Roy, John Crank and Jack Kuykendall (2000). *Police and Society*, Second Edition. Los Angeles, CA: Roxbury.

Robertson, Roland (1987). "Globalization Theory and Civilizational Analysis." *Comparative Civilizations Review*, 17:22.

Rockefeller, Steven (1994). "Comment." In A. Gutmann (ed.) *Multiculturalism: Examining the Politics of Recognition*, pp. 87-98. Princeton, NJ: Princeton University Press.

Roosens, Eugeen (1989). *Creating Ethnicity: The Process of Ethnogenesis*. Newbury Park: Sage.

Rorty, Richard (1989). *Contingency, Irony, and Solidarity*. Cambridge: Cambridge University Press.

Rothman, David (1971). *The Discovery of the Asylum: Social Order and Disorder in the New Republic*. Toronto: Little, Brown.

Rothman, David (1980). *Conscience and Convenience: The Asylum and its Alternatives in Progressive America*. Toronto: Little, Brown.

Rush, George (1994). *The Dictionary of Criminal Justice*, Fourth Edition. Guilford, CT: The Dushkin Publishing Group, Inc.

Rush, George (2000). *The Dictionary of Criminal Justice*, Fifth Edition. Guilford, CT: The Dushkin Publishing Group, Inc.

Russell, Gregory (1997). "Criminal Justice Research and International Paradigms: Neoliberal Institutionalism, Regimes, and Emerging Structures." *International Criminal Justice Review*, 7:113-129.

Sabatier, Paul (1999). "The Need for Better Theories." Pp. 3-18 in P. Sabatier (ed.) *Theories of the Policy Process*, pp. 3-18. Boulder, CO: Westview Press.

Sabatier, Paul and Hank Jenkins-Smith (1999). "The Advocacy-Coalition Network: An Assessment." In P. Sabatier (ed.) *Theories of the Policy Process*, pp. 117-166. Boulder, CO: Westview Press.

Sampson, Robert (1995). "The Community." In J. Wilson and J. Petersilia (eds.) *The Community*, pp. 193-215. San Francisco, CA: ICS Press.

Sampson, Robert and Janet Lauritsen (1997). "Racial and Ethnic Disparities in Crime and Criminal Justice in the United States." In M. Tonry (ed.) *Ethnicity, Crime, and Immigration: Comparative and Cross-National Perspectives*, pp. 311-374. Chicago, IL: University of Chicago Press.

Sandal, Michael (1984). "The Procedural Republic and the Unencumbered Self." *Political Theory*, 1281-1296.

Schlager, Edella (1999). "A Comparison of Frameworks, Theories, and Models of Policy Processes." In P. Sabatier (ed.) *Theory of the Policy Process*, pp. 233-260. Boulder, CO: Westview Press.

Schneider, D. (1965). "Kinship and Biology." In A.G. Coate et al. (eds.) *Aspects of Analysis of Family Structure*. Princeton, NJ: Princeton University Press.

Schwartz, Martin (1991). "The Future of Criminology." In B. MacLean and D. Milovanovic (eds.) *New Directions in Critical Criminology*. Vancouver, BC: The Collective Press.

Schwartz, Martin and Walter DeKeseredy (1991). "Left Realist Criminology: Strengths, Weaknesses, and Feminist Critique." *Crime, Law and Social Change*, 15:51-72.

Scott, Richard (1992). "Unpacking Institutional Arguments." In W. Powell and P. DiMaggio (eds.) *The New Institutionalism in Organizational Analysis*, pp. 164-183. Chicago, IL: University of Chicago Press.

Seidelman, Raymond (1985). *Disenchanted Realists: Political Science and the American Crisis, 1884-1984.* Albany, NY: SUNY Press.

Selznick, Philip (1957). *Leadership in Administration*. New York, NY: Harper and Row.

Selznick, Philip (1949). *TVA and the Grass Roots*. Berkeley, CA: University of California Press.

Shaw C. and H. McKay (1931). *Social Factors in Juvenile Delinquency: Report on the Causes of Crime. National Commission on Law Observance and Enforcement #13.* Washington, DC: U.S. Government Printing Office.

Shaw, C. and H. McKay (1942). *Juvenile Delinquency and Urban Areas*. Chicago, IL: University of Chicago Press.

Shearing, Clifford and Richard Ericson (1991). "Culture as Figurative Action." *British Journal of Sociology*, 42:481-506.

Shelden, Randall (2001). *Controlling the Dangerous Classes: A Critical Introduction to the History of Criminal Justice*. Boston, MA: Allyn and Bacon.

Sherman, Lawrence, Denise Gottfredson, Doris Mackenzie, John Eck, Peter Reuter, Shawn Bushway, and the Members of the Graduate Program, University of Maryland (1997). *Preventing Crime: What Works, What Doesn't, What's Promising*. Washington, DC: U.S. Department of Justice.

Sherman, Lawrence and the National Advisory Commission on Higher Education for Police Officers (1986). "Higher Education and Police Reform." In M. Pogrebin and R. Regoli (eds), *Police Administrative Issues: Techniques and Functions*, pp. 233-242. Millwood, NY: Associated Faculty Press.

Shernock, S. (1990). "Social Control and Criminal Justice Education." *Northeastern Criminal Justice Reporter*, (Fall):2-4.

Shively, W. Phillips (1997). *Power and Choice: An Introduction to Political Science*, Fifth Edition. New York, NY: McGraw-Hill.

Shoemaker, Donald (1996). *Theories of Delinquency: An Examination of Explanations of Delinquent Behavior*, Third Edition. New York, NY: Oxford University Press.

Shweder, Richard (1991). *Thinking Through Cultures: Expeditions in Cultural Psychology*. Cambridge, MA: Harvard University Press.

Silberman, Charles E. (1978). *Criminal Violence, Criminal Justice*. New York, NY: Vintage Books.

Siegel, Larry and Marvin Zalman (1991). "'Cultural Literacy' in Criminal Justice: A Preliminary Assessment." *Journal of Criminal Justice Education*, 2(1):15-44.

Simon, Jonathan (1993). *Poor Discipline: Parole and the Social Control of the Underclass, 1890-1990*. Chicago, IL: University of Chicago Press.

Simon, Rita (1975). *Women and Crime*. Lexington, MA: D.C. Heath.

Singer, Joseph (1984). "The Player and the Cards: Nihilism and Legal Theory." *Yale Law Journal*, 94:1.

Situ, Yirgyi and David Emmons (1996). "Academy of Criminal Justice Sciences: Teaching Environmental Crime in a Criminal Justice Curriculum." *Journal of Criminal Justice Education*, 7:147-154.

Sigler, Robert (1988). "Role Conflict in Adult Parole and Parole Services: Fact or Myth. *Journal of Criminal Justice*, 16(2):121-130.

Skogan, Wesley (1990). *Disorder and Decline: Crime and the Spiral of Decay in American Cities*. New York, NY: The Free Press.

Skolnick, Jerome (1966). *Justice Without Trial: Law Enforcement in a Democratic Society*. New York, NY: John Wiley.

Skolnick, Jerome and David Bayley (1986). *The New Blue Line: Police Innovation in Six American Cities*. New York, NY: The Free Press.

Schlager, Edella (1999). "A Comparison of Frameworks, Theories and Models of Policy Processes." In P. Sabatier (ed.) *Theories of the Policy Process*, pp. 233-260. Boulder, CO: Westview Press.

Sluder, R. and F. Reddington (1993). "An Empirical Examination of the Work Ideologies of Juvenile and Adult Probation Officers." *Journal of Offender Rehabilitation*, 20 (1):115-137.

Smart, Carol (1976). *Women, Crime and Criminology: A Feminist Critique*. London: Routledge and Kegan Paul.

Smith, Douglas (1986). "The Neighborhood Context of Police Behavior." In *Communities and Crime*, edt. A. Reiss, Jr. and M. Tonry (eds.), Vol, 8 of *Crime and Justice: A Review of Research*, M. Tonry and N. Morris (eds.). Chicago, IL: University of Chicago Press.

Smith, Sherri (1999). "The Status of Women and Criminal Justice Courses in Baccalaureate Criminal Justice Curriculum: A National Perspective." *Journal of Criminal Justice Education*, 10(1):1-20.

Snyder-Joy, Zoann and Teresa Carlo (1988). "Parenting Through Prison Walls: Incarcerated Mothers and Children's Visitation Programs." In S. Miller (ed.) *Crime Control and Women: Feminist Implications of Criminal Justice Policy*, pp. 130-150. Thousand Oaks, CA: Sage.

Sorensen, Jonathan, Alan Widmayer, and Frank Scarpitti (1994). "Examining the Criminal Justice and Criminological Paradigms: An Analysis of ACJS and ASC Members." *Journal of Criminal Justice Education*, 5-2:149-166.

Souryal, Sam (1992). *Ethics in Criminal Justice: In Search of the Truth*. Cincinnati, OH: Anderson Publishing Co.

Spader, Dean (1994). "Teaching Due Process: A Workable Method of Teaching the Ethical and Legal Aspects." *Journal of Criminal Justice Education*, 5(1):81-105.

Spader, Dean (1984). "Rule of Law v. Rule of Man: The Search for the Golden Zigzag Between Conflicting Fundamental Values." *Journal of Criminal Justice*, 12:379-394.

Spengler, Oswald (1926). *The Decline of the West*. Trans. C. Atkinson. New York, NY: Alfred A. Knoph.

Spradley, J. (1980). *Participant Observation*. New York, NY: Holt, Rinehart and Winston.

Spradley, J. (1979). *The Ethnographic Interview*. New York, NY: Holt, Rinehart and Winston.

Spohn, Cassia, John Gruhl, and Susan Welch (1987). "The Impact of Ethnicity and Gender of Defendants on the Decision to Reject or Dismiss Felony Charges." *Criminology*, 25(1):175-192.

Stanko, Elizabeth (1994). "Challenging the Problem of Men's Individual Violence." In T. Newburn and E. Stanko (eds.) *Just Boys Doing Business? Men, Masculinities and Crime*, pp. 32-45. London: Routledge.

Steinbeck, John (1994). *Of Mice and Men*. New York, NY: Penguin Books.

Stones, Christopher (2000). "The Territory Between Law and Justice." Commencement Speech at Wake Forest University's Law School.

Sullivan, Robert (1994). "The Tragedy of Academic Criminal Justice." *Journal of Criminal Justice*, 22(6):549-558.

Sun, Key (1995). "The Definition of Race." *American Psychologist*, January: 43-44.

Swidler, Ann (1986). "Culture in Action: Symbols and Strategies." *American Sociological Review*, 51:273-286.

Taft, Philip B. Jr. (1991). "Policing the New Urban Ghettos." In C. Klockars and S. Mastrofski (eds.) *Thinking About Policing: Contemporary Readings*, Second Edition, pp. 307-315. New York, NY: McGraw, Hill Inc.

Tamark, Minnich (1990). *Transforming Knowledge*. Philadelphia, PA: Temple University Press.

Taylor, Charles (1994). "The Politics of Recognition." In A. Gutmann (ed.) *Multiculturalism: Examining the Politics of Recognition*, pp. 25-74. Princeton, NJ: Princeton University Press.

Toch, Hans (1990). Falling in Love With a Book." *Journal of Criminal Justice Education*, 1(2):245-255.

Tomaino, Louis (1975). "The Five Faces of Probation." *Federal Probation*, 39(4).

Thomas, William and Florian Znaniecki (1920). *The Polish Peasant in Europe and America*. Boston, MA: Gorham.

Thompson, Richard (1989). *Theories of Ethnicity: A Critical Appraisal*. New York, NY: Greenwood Press.

Thornberry, Terence (1990). "Cultural Literacy in Criminology." *Journal of Criminal Justice Education*, (1)1:33-49.

Thrasher, Frederick (1927). *The Gang*. Chicago, IL: University of Chicago Press.

Tonry, Michael (1998). "Building Better Policies on Better Knowledge." In L. Robinson (ed.) *The Challenge of Crime in a Free Society: Looking Back, Looking Forward*, pp. 93-124. Washington, D.C: U.S. Department of Justice.

Tonry, Michael (1997). "Introduction: Ethnicity, Crime and Immigration" Pp. 1-29 in M. Tonry (ed.) *Ethnicity, Crime, and Immigration: Comparative and Cross-National Perspectives*. Chicago, IL: University of Chicago Press.

Tonry, Michael (1995). *Malign Neglect: Race, Crime, and Punishment in America*. New York, NY: Oxford University Press.

Toynbee, Arnold (1934-1954). *A Study of History*, 10 Volumes. New York, NY: Oxford University Press.

Travis, C. (1992). *The Mismeasurement of Women*. New York, NY: Simon & Schuster.

Travis, Lawrence (1989). "Criminal Justice Graduate Education: An Assessment of the Albany Model." *Northeastern Criminal Justice Reporter*, (Fall):2, 4.

Trice, Harrison and Janice Beyer (1984). "Studying Organizational Cultures Through Rites and Ceremonials." *Academy of Management Review*, 9-4:653-669.

Turner, Jonathan (1982). *The Structure of Sociological Theory*, Third Edition. Homewood, IL: The Dorsey Press.

Universal Declaration of Human Rights (1948), United Nations, resolution 217A (111):10 December.

U.S. Department of Justice (1991). *Attorney General's Summit on Law Enforcement Responses to Violent Crime: Public Safety in the 1990s: Conference Summary.* Washington, DC: U.S. Department of Justice.

U.S. President's Commission on Law Enforcement and the Administration of Justice (1967). The Challenge of Crime in a Free Society "Crime Commission"). Washington: GPO.

Van den Haag, Ernest (1975). *Punishing Criminals.* New York, NY: Basic Books.

VanMaanen, John (1995). "An End to Innocence: The Ethnography of Ethnography." In J. VanMaanen (ed.) *Representation in Ethnography*, pp. 1-35. Thousand Oaks, CA: Sage.

VanMaanen, John (1988). *Tales of the Field: On Writing Ethnography.* Chicago, IL: University of Chicago Press.

VanMaanen, John (1978). "Observations on the Making of Policemen." In P.K. Manning and J. VanMaanen (eds.) *Policing: A View From the Street*, pp. 292-308. Santa Monica, CA: Goodyear Publishing Co.

Vold, George and Thomas Bernard (1986). *Theoretical Criminology*, Third Edition. New York, NY: Oxford University Press.

Ward, R. and V. Webb (1984). *Quest for Quality.* New York, NY: University Publications.

Walker, Samuel (1998). *Sense and Nonsense about Crime and Drugs: A Policy Guide*, Fourth Edition. New York, NY: McGraw-Hill.

Walker, Samuel (1977). *A History of Police Reform.* Lexington, MA: Lexington Books.

Walker Samuel, Cassia Spohn and Miriam DeLone (2000). *The Color of Justice: Race, Ethnicity, and Crime in America*, Second Edition. Belmont, CA: Wadsworth.

Walklate, Sandra (1995). *Gender and Crime: An Introduction.* Hertfordshire, Britain: Prentice Hall/harvester Wheatsheaf.

Wallace, Donald (1991). "Social Science Research and Policy in Education: An Interdisciplinary Approach." *Journal of Criminal Justice Education*, 2(2):219-236.

Wallerstein, Immanuel (1992). "Liberalism and the Legitimation of Nation-States: An Historical Interpretation." *Social Justice*, 19(1):22-34.

Wallerstein, Immanuel and the Gulbenkian Commission (1996). *Open the Social Sciences: Report of the Gulbenkian Commission on the Restructuring of the Social Sciences.* Stanford, CA: Stanford University Press.

Walsh, Anthony (1995). *Biosociology: An Emerging Paradigm.* Westport, CT: Praeger.

Walzer, Michael (1983). *Spheres of Justice: A Defense of Pluralism and Equality.* New York, NY: Basic Books.

Walzer, Michael (1994). "Comment." In A. Gutmann (ed.) *Multiculturalism: Examining the Politics of Recognition*, pp. 99-103. Princeton, NJ: Princeton University Press.

Ward, Richard and Vincent Webb (1984). *Quest for Quality: A Publication of the Joint Commission on Criminology and Criminal Justice Education and Standards.* New York, New York: University Publications.

Warnke, Georgia (1993). *Justice and Interpretation.* Cambridge, MA: The MIT Press.

Warren, Roland (1978). *Community in America,* Third Edition. Chicago, IL: Rand-McNally.

Warren, Roland (1963). *Community in America.* Chicago, IL: Rand-McNally.

Waters, Tony (1999). *Crime and Immigrant Youth.* Thousand Oaks, CA: Sage Publications.

Weber, Max (1954). "Rational and Irrational Administration of Justice." In Max Rheinstein (ed.) *Max Weber on Law in Economy and Society.* Cambridge, MA: Harvard University Press.

Weisheit, Ralph and Sue Mahan (1988). *Women, Crime, and Criminal Justice.* Cincinnati, OH: Anderson Publishing.

Weissman, Eric (1992). "Kids Who Attack Gays." In G. Herek and K. Berrill (ed.) *Hate Crimes.* Newbury Park, CA: Sage.

West, Candace and Don Zimmerman (1998). "Doing Gender." In J. Lorber *Gender Inequality: Feminist Theories and Politics,* pp. 161-166. Los Angeles, CA: Roxbury.

White, Susan and Samuel Krislov (1977). *Understanding Crime: An Evaluation of the National Institute of Law Enforcement and Criminal Justice. A Report of the Committee on Law Enforcement and Criminal Justice.* Washington, DC: National Academy of Sciences.

Wilbanks, William (1987). *The Myth of the Racist Criminal Justice System.* Monterey, CA: Brooks/Cole.

Williams, Hubert and Patrick V. Murphy (1990). "The Evolving Strategy of the Police: A Minority View." Pp. 29-52 in V. Kappeler (ed.) *The Police and Society: Touchstone Readings.* Prospect Heights, IL: Waveland Press.

Williams, F., M. McShane, and C. Wagoner (1992). "The Relative Prestige and Utility of Journals: Developing a Rank System for Criminal Justice." Paper presented at the annual meetings of the American Society of Criminology, New Orleans.

Williams, Frank (1984). "The Demise of the Criminological Imagination: A Critique of Recent Criminology." *Justice Quarterly*, 1(1):91-106.

Willoughby, J. (1993). *Vietnamese Gangs and Other Criminals.* New Orleans, LA: New Orleans Police Department.

Wilson, Nancy (1991). "Feminist Pedagogy in Criminal Justice." *Journal of Criminal Justice Education*, 2(1):81-93.

Wilson, William J. (1987). *The Truly Disadvantaged: The Inner City, the Underclass, and Public Policy.* Chicago, IL: University of Chicago Press.

Wilson, J.Q. (1993). *The Moral Sense.* New York, NY: The Free Press.

Wilson, J.Q. and George Kelling (1982). "The Police and Neighborhood Safety: Broken Windows." *Atlantic Monthly*, 127 (March):29-38.

Wolcott, Harry (1995). "Making a Study 'More Ethnographic'." In J. VanMaanen (ed.) *Representation in Ethnography*, pp. 79-111. Thousand Oaks, CA: Sage.

Wolfgang, M. (1989). "Preface." In W. Laufer and F. Adler (eds.) *Advances in Criminological Theory.* Volume One. New Brunswick, NJ: Transaction Publishers.

Wolfgang, M.R. Figlio and T. Thornberry (1978). *Evaluating Criminology.* New York, NY: Elsevirer North Holland, Inc.

Wonders, Nancy and Susan Caulfield (1993). "Women's Work?: The Contradictory Implications of Courses on Women and the Criminal Justice System." *Journal of Criminal Justice Education*, 4(1):79-100.

Wright, Kevin (1990). "The Desirability of Goal Conflict Within the Criminal Justice System. Pp. 30-42 in S. Stojovic, J. Klofas and D. Kalinich (eds.) *The Administration and Management of Criminal Justice: A Book of Readings*. Prospect Heights, IL: Waveland Press, Inc.

Wright, Richard (1992). "From Vamps to Tramps to Teases and Flirts: Stereotypes of Women in Criminology Textbooks, 1956 to 1965 and 1981 to 1990." *Journal of Criminal Justice Education*,3(2):223-236.

Young, Jock (1986). "Confronting Crime. The Failure of Criminology: The Need for a Radical Realism." In R. Matthews and J. Young (eds.) *Confronting Crime*, pp. 4-30. Beverly Hills, CA: Sage.

Zahn, Margaret (1999). "Thoughts on the Future of Criminology—The American Society of Criminology 1998 Presidential Address." *Criminology*, 7(1):1-15.

Index